PURSUING JUSTICE

SUNY series in American Labor History
Robert Asher and Amy Kesselman, Editors

PURSUING JUSTICE

Lee Pressman, the New Deal, and the CIO

GILBERT J. GALL

STATE UNIVERSITY OF NEW YORK PRESS

Published by
State University of New York Press, Albany

For information, address State University of New York
Press, State University Plaza, Albany, N.Y., 12246

Production by E. Moore
Marketing by Nancy Farrell

Library of Congress Cataloging-in-Publication Data

Gall, Gilbert J.
    Pursuing justice : Lee Pressman, the New Deal, and the CIO /
Gilbert J. Gall.
        p.   cm. — (SUNY series in American labor history)
    Includes bibliographical references and index.
    ISBN 0-7914-4103-2 (hardcover : alk. paper). -- ISBN 0-7914-4104-0
(pbk. : alk. paper)
    1. Pressman, Lee, 1906–   . 2. Lawyers—United States—Biography.
3. Labor laws and legislation—United States—History. 4. Trade
-unions and communism—United States—History. 5. Congress of
Industrial Organizations (U.S.)—History. I. Title. II. Series.
KF373.P65G35 1999
340'.092—dc21
    [B]   98-20002
                                                                       CIP

10 9 8 7 6 5 4 3 2 1

CONTENTS

Preface   *vii*

Abbreviations   *xi*

Prologue: "For the same reasons, the same response."   *1*

1. World of Our Sons   *5*

2. Certainty in Human Form   *23*

3. Hammer and Steel   *46*

4. Mobilizing the Administrative State   *75*

5. Establishing the Commonwealth of Steel   *113*

6. General Counsel   *158*

7. The Road to Gideon's Army   *192*

8. The Miscalculation   *232*

9. Pursuing "Comrade Big"   *263*

Epilogue: "A quiet law practice . . ."   *299*

Notes   *313*

Bibliographical Note   *351*

Index   *353*

PREFACE

In the early 1970s, Nathan Witt, a left-wing labor lawyer, sat down to do an oral history interview for the Steel Workers Oral History Project at Penn State University. Witt, a Harvard Law School graduate, had represented left-wing unions in New York City for many years and had been a friend of former United Steel Workers of America and Congress (Committee) for Industrial Organization (CIO) general counsel Lee Pressman until their break during the McCarthy Era. In that conversation, Witt was asked about the role that lawyers played in the historical development of the labor movement of the 1930s and 1940s—were they essentially professional staff or policy makers? He answered that, like most other things in life, "it depends. It depends on the personality; it depends upon the leadership of the institution; it depends on personal relationships; it depends upon involvement. . . ." Since he himself hailed from a very poor working-class background, Witt maintained an emotional identification with his roots and believed that lawyers should not shape policy for union leaders—they were too much the pushers and big mouths, he judged. No matter what their politics, for the most part, he said, "They don't have that rank and file feel that people like . . . John [L.] Lewis, [and] Phil Murray . . . had." Witt admitted that for some years, though, it had become obvious that people like Pressman and his successor, Arthur J. Goldberg, had indeed exercised much influence during the rise of the labor movement during the middle decades of the twentieth century, when the New Deal state ruled supreme in American political life. But by the 1960s, all that had changed, Witt asserted. The "lawyer's role—the sort of role, whether for good or" bad "that a Pressman played, is really no longer possible. . . ." Labor's legal advisors were now technicians, mostly. "The labor movement has been engulfed by these other overwhelming streams of [adjustment to] American life, and" it is "conforming to them. So . . . the Pressmans can't do the job to the same extent that they did it, that they were able to do [it], even ten years ago."[1]

What follows is a biography of the man who in many ways wrote the book on the "labor lawyer as policy shaper," Lee Pressman, CIO and United Steel Workers of America general counsel from 1936 to 1948. It is mostly a study of Pressman's historical contributions to the founding and consolidation of a viable industrial union movement in the United States and of the factors that helped him make those contributions. To a lesser extent, the biography also examines his role as a New Deal administrator within the Agricultural Adjustment Agency in the early Roosevelt years, and his involvement in the Alger Hiss case and the communist witch-hunts of the late 1940s and early 1950s. Pressman's public life of nearly twenty years—when he was one of the most famous lawyers in the United States and certainly *the* most famous labor lawyer—thus neatly traverses the New Deal–Fair Deal eras. As such, I hope that in varied ways the biography has elements that will contribute to the discussion of a variety of significant themes in the history of this period—among them the role of ethnicity in political development and the personal political impact of the Great Depression; the nature of progressivism under the New Deal and its inherent limitations; the role of industrial unionism in establishing the predominance of the executive branch of the federal government; the personal consequences of the anticommunist hysteria and Cold War; and the contributions of Progressive labor lawyers to American social reform.

The research of this biography began nearly ten years ago with an initial review that implied a paucity of sources and a sincere question in my mind as to whether there was enough primary source material to write a meaningful biography of Pressman who, because of his communism, remained for all of his life closed to questions about his personal politics. Thanks to the help of a number of individuals, within a few short years I discovered not that I had too little, but that I was gathering too much. Early in the project, Harold Ruttenberg, a CIO colleague of Pressman's during the 1930s and 1940s, rendered for me an enlightening account of his association and was instrumental in making subsequent contacts with a variety of other former CIO officials and lawyers who knew and worked with Pressman—Eugene Cotton, Joseph Kovner, Tony Smith, John Abt, Harold Cammer, and Ernest Goodman all gave interviews. In addition, I eventually located Pressman's three daughters—Ann Pressman, Marcia Pressman, and Susan Sragow Pressman—and his brother Irving Pressman, and convinced them to share their memories with me. They and Alan Draper pointed me to still other friends of Pressman's— Jack Rabkin and Lynne and John Weiner—for information on various aspects of his life. Sadly, Tony Smith, John Abt, Ann Pressman, Ernest Goodman, and Irving Pressman have all since passed away. To them I render my thanks posthumously, and to those still with us, my gratitude goes out as well. Susan Pressman Sragow, Harold Ruttenberg, and Lynne Weiner also graciously made photographs available.

Since Pressman left no personal collection of papers, organizational records became quite important. I also thank former and current archivists—Peter Gottlieb, Diana Schenk, and Denise Conklin—at the Historical Collections and Labor Archives at Penn State University, where the United Steel Workers organizational records are housed. Archivists at the National Archives, Wayne State University's Walter P. Reuther Archives, Catholic University, and the Franklin D. Roosevelt Library also assisted in my research. In addition, I would like to express my appreciation for research travel grants from the Institute for Arts and Humanistic Studies at Penn State University and the Lubin–Winant Fellowship from the Franklin and Eleanor Roosevelt Institute. The journals *Labor History* and *Labor's Heritage* also granted me permission to use material that had previously been published in their pages, and Cornell University, Catholic University, and Harvard University granted permission to publish photographs. Harvard University also granted permission to quote from the Thomas Reed Powell papers. A word of thanks also goes, tongue in cheek, to the late J. Edgar Hoover, whose obsessiveness about domestic communism enabled the collection of much of the material on Pressman that I obtained from the FBI's files under a Freedom of Information Act request. Last, but certainly not least, I want to thank my family—my wife Beth and my sons Ryan and Kevin for having shared their father's time and attention with someone long dead, but who deserves to be remembered for his accomplishments that touch all of our lives still.

ABBREVIATIONS

AAA	Agricultural Adjustment Administration
ABA	American Bar Association
ACWA	Amalgamated Clothing Workers of America
AFL	American Federation of Labor
AFL-CIO	American Federation of Labor-Congress of Industrial Organizations
ALUCP	American Labor Union Constitutions and Proceedings
CIO	Congress (Committee) for Industrial Organization
CIOEB	CIO Executive Board Transcripts
CIOPROC	CIO Convention Proceedings
CLU	Civil Liberties Unit, U.S. Department of Labor
COHC	Columbia Oral History Collection
CP	Communist Party
CPA	Communist Political Association
CU	Catholic University, Washington, D.C.
DOJ	U.S. Department of Justice
DOL	U.S. Department of Labor
ERP	Employee Representation Plans
FBI	Federal Bureau of Investigation
FDR	Franklin D. Roosevelt
FDRL	Franklin D. Roosevelt Library, Hyde Park, New York
FERA	Federal Emergency Relief Agency
FLSA	Fair Labor Standards Act
FOIA	Freedom of Information Act

GM	General Motors
HCLA, PSU	Historical Collections and Labor Archives, Penn State University, University Park, Pennsylvania
HLS	Harvard Law School Library, Cambridge, Massachusetts
HSTL	Harry S. Truman Library, Independence, Missouri
HUAC	House Un-American Activities Committee
IJA	International Juridical Association
IJAB	International Juridical Association Bulletin
ILGWU	International Ladies Garment Workers Union
ILWU	International Longshoremen's and Warehousemen's Union
INS	Immigration and Nationalization Service
IUFLW	International Union of Fur and Leather Workers
IWO	International Workers Order
LC	Library of Congress, Washington, D.C.
LMDC	Labor-Management Documentation Center, Cornell University, Ithaca, New York
LNPL	Labor's Non-Partisan League
LPPC	Lee Pressman Personal Collection
MHC, UM	Michigan Historical Collections, University of Michigan, Ann Arbor, Michigan
MMSWU	Mine, Mill, and Smelter Workers Union
NA	National Archives, Washington, D.C.
NAM	National Association of Manufacturers
NDMB	National Defense Mediation Board
NIRA	National Industrial Recovery Act
NLG	National Lawyer's Guild
NLRA	National Labor Relations Act
NLRB	National Labor Relations Board
NMU	National Maritime Union
NMUPROC	National Maritime Union Convention Proceedings
NRA	National Recovery Administration
NWLB	National War Labor Board
OHI	Oral History Interview
OHI/GJG	Oral History Interview with Gilbert J. Gall
OPM	Office of Production Management
PAC	Political Action Committee
RA	Resettlement Administration
RG	Record Group
RWLA, NYU	Robert Wagner Labor Archives, New York University, New York, New York
SWOC	Steel Workers Organizing Committee
TUC	Trades Union Congress (Great Britain)

TWOC	Textile Workers Organizing Committee
TWU	Transport Workers Union
TWUPROC	Transport Workers Union Convention Proceedings
UAW	United Auto Workers
UFWA	United Federal Workers of America
UK	University of Kentucky at Louisville, Louisville, Kentucky
UMWA	United Mine Workers of America
USCC	United States Chamber of Commerce
USCS	United States Civil Service
USSCRB	U.S. Supreme Court Records and Briefs
USWA	United Steel Workers of America
USWAEB	United Steel Workers of America Executive Board Transcripts
USWAPROC	United Steel Workers of America Convention Proceedings
WFTU	World Federation of Trade Unions
WPA	Works Progress Administration
WPB	War Production Board
WPRL, WSU	Walter P. Reuther Library, Wayne State University, Detroit, Michigan
YUL	Yale University Library, New Haven, Connecticut

Prologue:
"For the same reasons,
the same response."

The Communist experience was, both in its glory and in its debasement, an awesome move toward humanness; an immense and tormented effort of the heart, will, and brain that cried out, "I must have justice or I will die."
—*Vivian Gornick,* The Romance of American Communism[1]

"I understand your testimony to be," declared second-term Congressman Richard M. Nixon (R-CA), "that the only three people besides yourself who were members of the Communist Party in the Government, to your knowledge, were Nathan Witt, John Abt, and Charles Kramer. Is that correct?"

Whatever the future U. S. president's understanding was, his wording was not the way the witness, labor attorney Lee Pressman, would have characterized it. "I said three members of my group . . . were the three persons who have been named who were in the Department of Agriculture when I was there. I am not trying to quibble," he told Nixon, who disagreed. "I prefer not to leave it in that unsettled state of affairs," the congressman responded. For his part, Pressman appealed to the House on Un-American Activities Committee's (HUAC) Chairman John S. Wood (D-GA), claiming the issue had been disposed of hours earlier in his testimony before the committee. "If Mr. Nixon would care to interrogate me on any other individual, I will be delighted to answer," he said.

This was not good enough for Nixon, who was, after all, the main political engine that drove the committee's investigation in the celebrated Hiss–Chambers case for the previous two years. Now, on this hot August Monday in 1950, about two years since HUAC had originally called Pressman before the committee as an unfriendly witness in the Hiss case, he once again crossed swords with a mutually aggressive adversary. "Mr. Chairman," a somewhat exasperated Nixon insisted, "I don't care to question him on any other matter until he has answered that question. He has issued a statement denouncing the Communist Party, and I think there is a moral issue here. . . . There are individuals who are involved, and individual feelings, and I can appreciate your individual feelings," he told Pressman, "but there is a greater moral issue involved, and that is the security of the country, and I think under the circumstances you should answer the question." Nixon therefore asked Wood for a ruling requiring a direct answer from the lawyer.

Pressman, a bit disingenuously claiming he "did not refuse" to answer the question, pleaded for fairness, while Nixon pointed out, correctly, that "he did not answer the questions he was asked." "I think since he has now stated there has been a complete ideological break from the Party, there should be a forthright answer to the question," Nixon contended. "I think, Mr. Pressman, you are aware of the fact there are a number of people in the country who are wondering whether your break was a complete break. I want to give you the benefit of the doubt," he asserted, perhaps with less-than-great enthusiasm. "But I will say you are not going to be able to convince a great majority of the people of the country that the break has been complete unless you come clean and answer the questions forthrightly, and place the security of the country above personal issues."[2] In the end, he did so, after a fashion, by tacitly "naming the names" of Abt, Witt, and Kramer for the committee. "He would stand henceforth," as journalist Murray Kempton summarized Pressman's testimony, "for America and the United Nations in Korea," and thus against communist aggression. The journalist noted, however, that Pressman "said it flatly and with all the passion of a school child reciting the flag oath. . . . He was drained. He had lost the great dream of his life, and he could bring no passion to the dreams of other men."[3]

Nixon's confrontation with Pressman made headline news for the aspiring politician. It was not the first time these two strong-willed, power-seeking individuals had collided. Twenty-four months earlier, on August 20, 1948, during a much more hopeful time in Lee Pressman's life, Nixon faced the lawyer before the same committee. During that engagement, however, Nixon showed a bit less confidence that he could press the labor attorney into divulging critical information.

On August 3 of that year, *Time* magazine editor and former underground communist operative Whittaker Chambers revealed to HUAC that the American Communist Party (CP) had infiltrated several New Deal agencies in the early 1930s. Chambers' claim created a public reaction of truly monumental proportions. One of the agencies involved had been the Agricultural Adjustment Administration (AAA). According to Chambers, young New Dealers Alger Hiss, Lee Pressman, John Abt, Nathan Witt, and Charles Kramer, among others, had formed a clandestine underground communist cell that aimed to influence government policy in directions favorable to the communist cause.

After leaving the AAA, Hiss went on to achieve high governmental positions in the State Department. At the peak of his public career, he served as a Roosevelt advisor at the Yalta Conference in early 1945 and helped organize the founding meeting of the United Nations. Pressman left full-time government service in 1935 and shortly thereafter became general counsel for labor leader John L. Lewis's Committee for Industrial Organizations (CIO). In that position, Pressman helped midwife the rebirth of the American labor movement during the tumultuous struggle to establish industrial unionism in the 1930s and 1940s. The other individuals moved into varied jobs, with Abt and Witt becoming Pressman's closest friends for the better part of the next two decades.[4]

Following Chambers' testimony, and Hiss's denials, HUAC subpoenaed Pressman, Abt, Witt, and Kramer to testify before the committee. Nixon, then a freshman congressman, had quickly become aware of the career-making possibilities inherent in the growing Cold War anticommunist hysteria. He was, however, wary of these witnesses, for he respected their sharp intelligence. Accompanying the four before the committee was Harold Cammer, Pressman and Witt's law partner, who served as their legal counsel. Nixon temporarily chaired the hearing in executive session and committee investigator Robert Stripling questioned.

The witnesses' strategy was to object on technical grounds to the legislative authority of the committee to conduct such an inquiry, and to exercise their rights against self-incrimination. As Abt, who testified first, later recalled, it "was clear that these were not regular, garden variety hearings. Implicit was the threat of great danger. We had engaged in no illegal activities," he protested, "but we were radicals, with unacceptable politics, and thereby suspected of high crimes against the stae."[5]

After confronting Pressman with the question of whether he had now or ever been a member of the Communist Party (which he refused to answer), Stripling presented the former CIO general counsel with a litany of questions regarding his personal associations. Some of thse individuals—such as Alger Hiss and his brother Donald Hiss (also alleged by Chambers to have been part of the Ware Group), were clearly under direct suspicion. Others were simply prominent individuals with or for whom Pressman had worked.[6]

"Do you know an individual by the name of Alger Hiss, Mr. Pressman?" asked Stripling. "Mr. Chairman," Pressman informed Nixon, "for the same reasons which I have given before, I decline to answer that question." "Donald Hiss?" asked the committee counsel. "For the same reasons I have given before, I decline to answer that question," Pressman responded again. "Do you know Victor Perlo?" "Mr. Chairman, for the same reasons—can I merely at this point say, in answer to that question and to the others of similar character, the same response for the same reasons? Would that be satisfactory?" Pressman asked. Nixon agreed that it would; subsequently every question Pressman did not wish to answer directly he dismissed with "for the same reasons, the same response." However, when Pressman refused to answer an apparently innocuous question, Nixon took him to task for being evasive.

"I want to state to the witness . . . that the Chair would appreciate it if the witness would be responsive to those questions which, obviosuly, do not involve constitutional rights. . . . The Chair is aware of the fact that the witness has probably as good a knowledge of his constitutional rights as any person could have," Nixon observed. He did not want the "hearing to become completely farcial [sic]," which he feared it would, if Pressman continued to refuse to answer questions that "do not raise consitutional grounds."

Indeed, the only notable—and intriguing—event in Pressman's entire testimony occurred as a result of Nixon's characterization of the HUAC investigations as being not only an investigation into communist infiltration in the U.S. government, but also into "alleged espionage activities conducted by those involved in the Communist apparatus. . . ." He briefly conferred with Cammer, then asked whether there had "been any charge made by any witness that has appeared before this committee that I have participated in any espionage activity, either while a member—or rather an employee—of the Federal Government[,] or thereafter?" Both Nixon and Stripling affirmed that there had been no such allegations, and Pressman inquired as to whether that fact could be shown on the record. They agreed to so indicate.[7]

When the sessions ended, according to Abt, "Nixon rushed out to the corridor—the original spin doctor—to challenge us before the press, which he seemed incapable of doing while facing us in the closed hearing room." Nevertheless, the eruption of the Hiss case had started the unraveling of Lee Pressman's public life. At that moment he was a Progressive Party official in the independent presidential campaign of former Democratic Vice-President Henry Wallace and an American Labor Party (ALP) candidate for a congressional seat from Brooklyn. Pressman, though, had not yet realized how the Cold War had entangled him. Over the next few years, the energy of Progressive politics of the New Deal era, and along with it the vitality of the American labor movement, would be sapped by the anticommunist fears of the American people. These fears would ultimately cast this brilliant attorney, whom Yale legal scholar and judge Jerome Frank once called "probably the best lawyer I've ever met," from the corridors of high power, a two-year journey that in reality encompassed a lifetime.[8]

ONE

❖

WORLD OF OUR SONS

"Forty thousand Jewish workers in one city, each living on his ten fingers!" an amazed Phillip Davis, a Russian–Jewish immigrant, wrote of his early days in turn-of-the-century New York City. Since the mass immigration from eastern Europe and Russia had begun in the 1880s, the city's garment industry had employed hundreds of thousands of fingers relentlessly, and, some would say, without pity. Brutish hours and working conditions in Lower East Side tenement sweatshops ground down human life into an existence of mindless survival, without much chance to experience any other aspects of life. Reflecting on how he had abandoned his former religious commitments under the assault, Davis noted that "[i]mmediately upon entering the sweatshop[,] I seemed to have plunged into a struggle so intense that it absorbed all my energy and simply incapacitated me from any other normal human activity." Life, or what made life human, was impossible "because my work consumed it all."[1]

On July 3, 1891, somewhere in the mass of Jewish immigrants from Russia who were headed for the sweatshops, stood Harry Pressman, twelve years old and a refugee from Minsk. His parents had not registered his birth in the old country in order to protect him, if possible, from forced military service. As he approached conscription age, however, he fled to the United States to ensure avoidance of the Russian military and, according to his son Irving, to "seek his fortune." In short order, he, as had Davis and so many others, found his way into the garment industry of New York City where "he became pretty handy with a sewing machine." Though entirely devoid of education other than religious training, over the next decade and a half he was

5

able, through hard work, perseverance, and perhaps good fortune, to accumulate sufficient capital to become a garment employer himself. Soon that economic prosperity enabled Harry to take a wife, Clara, a young woman he had known slightly in Minsk, the sister of a good friend. On July 1, 1906, their first child Leon (Lee) was born, followed by their second child Irving, seven years later.[2]

If Harry Pressman's life experience was part and parcel of the "world of our fathers," to use the title of Irving Howe's evocative study of that immigration era, Lee Pressman's life experience was to become centered in the "world of our sons." A good deal of *that* world involved cultural assimilation into the new country and intense pursuit of the promise of social mobility. Pressman's father climbed into the ranks of the *petty bourgeoisie* by becoming a manufacturer of silk ribbons for ladies' head wear. Even so, he remained, as did so many other immigrants, "caught in the grip of the old world, the old ways," wrote Howe. Having achieved some advancement in America, Harry Pressman's generation stayed "trapped in the limitations of their skills, in the skimpiness of their education, in the awkwardness of their speech, in the alienness of their manners." Not so for their sons and daughters! The culture of New York's Lower East Side thus "became a culture utterly devoted to its sons," Howe noted. "Onto their backs it lowered all its aspirations and delusions, expecting that the children of the New World would reach the goals their fathers could not reach themselves."[3]

BRIGHT AND CLEAN AND POLISHED

For many of the new generation, exalted aspirations could prove a psychological burden. "The Jewish child in America grows in a complex of social relationships," wrote social worker Pauline Young in *Social Forces*. The "child is placed at an early age in an environment which is characterized by detachment from the simpler primary group relations, and the high degree of mobility encourages his 'escape' from family and communal control." In America, Jewish children attended public schools, whose objective was not "to make better Jews" but "better American citizens." "The children learn a new and different moral code through their associations at public school," Young contended. "They begin to live simultaneously in two different worlds: their home, their religious and communal life represent one culture, and the public school and the larger community represent another."[4]

Indeed, it was in and through the process of public education that many immigrant parents hoped for their family's future. "My father and mother worked in a rage to put us above their level," wrote Alfred Kazin in his poignant memoir of his New York City youth, *A Walker in the City*. "We were

the only conceivable end to all their striving; we were their America." It was
no wonder, then, that to Jewish immigrant parents, the predominantly
Anglo–Saxon teachers of the New York City school system "were to be
respected like gods."

> They were the delegates of all visible and invisible power on earth—of
> the mothers who waited on the stoops every day after three for us to
> bring home tales of our daily triumphs; of the glacially remote Anglo-
> Saxon principal, whose very name was King; of the incalculably impor-
> tant Superintendent of Schools who would someday rubberstamp his
> name to the bottom of our diplomas in grim acknowledgment that we
> had, at last, given satisfaction to him, to the Board of Superintendents,
> and to our benefactor the City of New York—and so up and up, to the
> government of the United States and to the great Lord Jehovah Him-
> self.[5]

However, "[I]t was never learning I associated with that school," Kazin
reminisced, "only the necessity to succeed, to get ahead of others in the daily
struggle to 'make a good impression' on our teachers." Kazin perceived that
it was not only his performance that teachers evaluated, but his *character*, that
is, his ability to acculturate to "American" ways. The teachers' rule books
remorselessly recorded both academic results and behavioral appropriateness.
"We had to prove that we were really alert, ready for anything, always in the
race," he recalled. Proper deportment proved to be as important as intelligence. The refined use of the English language was prized by the teachers
above all, a language not naturally spoken by children born of immigrant parents who spoke little, if any, English at home. "This English was peculiarly
the ladder of advancement. Every future young lawyer was known by it,"
wrote Kazin. "It was bright and clean and polished. . . . When the teacher
sharply called a question out, then your name, you were expected to leap up,
face the class, and eject those new words fluently off the tongue." Consequently, Kazin "felt that the very atmosphere of learning that surrounded us
was fake—that every lesson, every book, every approving smile was only a
pretext for the constant probing and watching of me, that there was not a
secret in me that would not be decimally measured" and noted.[6]

The language factor was particularly important in separating the "world
of our fathers" from the "world of our sons." "The English language is a
strange vehicle of expression to the parents," observed Pauline Young. "To the
child, however, the English language is a native tongue, he learns it during his
childhood simultaneously imbibing American customs which become second
nature to him at an early age." The parents' difficulty with the language and
their accents "symbolize 'Europe' to the child's mind," sometimes even gen-

erating a sense of shame in the child about the parent. In many Jewish homes, as in the Pressman's, Yiddish was spoken and often the children did not learn it sufficiently to enable easy communication with their parents. Consequently, when "the father no longer finds intercourse possible with his sons," a Jewish father reported to Young, "[m]uch is left unsaid." It was not that most Jewish parents would have preferred it another way. The "sickening invocation of 'Americanism' in the public schools, the word itself accusing us of everything we apparently were not," Kazin reflected, suggested to him that both our "families and teachers seemed tacitly agreed that we were somehow to be a little ashamed of what we were. And that there was shame in this was a fact that everyone seemed to believe as a matter of course."[7]

Thus, second generation Jews often developed ambivalencies. In order to assimilate fully into America, they had to reject and even be somewhat ashamed of their heritage as Jews, the more fully the better. At the same time, doing so did not satisfy many. Their ethnic heritage, no matter how they felt about it, or how they tried to leave it behind for periods in their lives, was a part of themselves to which many ultimately returned for comfort. Again, Kazin put it most eloquently: "So it was: we had always to be together: believers and non-believers, we were a people; I was of that people. Unthinkable to go one's own way, to doubt or to escape the fact that I was a Jew." "The American Jew is torn between two sets of values," wrote political sociologist Charles Liebman, "those of integration and acceptance into American society and those of Jewish group survival. . . . [The] behavior of the American Jew is best understood as his unconscious effort to restructure his environment and reorient his own self-definition and perception of reality so as to reduce the tension between these [incompatible] values."[8]

Lee Pressman's life and career epitomized these tensions. As Harry and Clara Pressman prospered, they were able to take a comfortable, middle-class apartment on the edge of the Lower East Side. The Pressman millinery factory was in the heart of New York City at 24th Street between Sixth and Seventh Avenues. Harry, a slight, quiet, and gentle man, primarily occupied himself with his business and "had very little to do with his children," Irving recollected. Clara's role as child rearer and guardian of the family's social advancement expanded. Irving Pressman remembered his mother as "a very forceful woman" who constantly pushed the children to excel in education, buying chairs and desks to ensure the ability to study fruitfully. Her role as primary overseer of the children was a common one. Immigrant Jewish mothers "particularly look upon" the children "with great pride," wrote Young in her study, "and welcome the newer family ideals which command greater respect for women than traditionally enjoyed by them in the old country." "My mother took care of the children," according to Irving, "and she was very intimate with us" emotionally, despite her forcefulness in certain matters.[9]

This was the case even more so with Lee, her eldest, than Irving, for in his early years young Lee contracted infantile paralysis that withered the muscles in one of his legs. "I might say that there was an affinity between my mother and my brother," Irving reflected, "because as a young child he had polio . . . and she didn't want to have him with crutches" that would make him feel inadequate. "So she carried him everywhere he went."[10]

The doctors had told Clara Pressman that her firstborn son "was never going to be able to . . . use his legs," according to Lee Pressman's oldest daughter, Ann Pressman. Clara, though, "was bound and determined to figure out a way that he would be able to walk. She went everywhere she could think to go, and to every doctor she could go to" for help, until she found a surgeon who performed a tendon transplant enabling Lee to walk. For the first five years or so of his life, though, Clara, physically robust in her youth but barely five feet tall, literally carried her child everywhere the family went. As a result, the bond between Clara and Lee was even deeper than the normal fondness for the firstborn. "Every firstborn Jewish son is always a potential Messiah," to the family, remarked Lee Pressman's middle daughter Marcia, years later. The affliction of his early years and Clara's maternal commitment to her son strengthened their feelings for each other even more.[11]

Evidently, Clara also bequeathed her forcefulness, determination, discipline, and zest for life to Lee as well. "She and Dad both had a real little sparkle in their eye," Ann recalled, "so when you talked to them, they had this little light, this sparkle. . . ." Clara's aspirations for Lee did not stop with walking unaided. Her pressure for educational achievement was intense on both sons, Irving noted, though she did not have to press Lee to study and read as much as her youngest son. While the surgery enabled him to participate in a few street sports, the polio and surgery had left "one leg considerably less formed" than the other. This left young Lee with a limp as a child—an affliction which he always consciously attempted to hide in later years—and which subjected him to the taunts, name-calling, and meanness of other children. "I think . . . he suffered extremely acute humiliations as a child," Marcia judged. Irving seconded this opinion; as a youngster he remembered his older brother as a studious bookworm until he attended Stuyvesant High School, where he engaged in a few track events and made the swim team, "despite his adversity." Lee Pressman himself claimed parental pressure resulted in his academic advancement. "The folks were rather strict about" keeping him focused on his school progress, and tried "to follow a path of keeping a youngster reading, tending to his studies, and looking to college and into a profession." "The natural result," Lee observed, "was considerable reading."[12]

In fact, his studiousness put him in high school at an early age as he graduated from grammar school at age twelve and a half. In high school he took violin lessons and, for a period while studying for his bar mitzvah, became intrigued by Judaism. Irving remembers his brother putting on the phylactery bindings for prayer every day before going to school. However, Lee later told an interviewer that for most of his life he had not taken his religious training very seriously, and, in fact, when asked if he ever believed in an omnipotent God, responded "I should say not really." The early flirtation with his religion's traditions could not have come from either Clara or Harry, according to both Irving and Lee, as both parents were essentially secular Jews in America and were not especially observant. "I just went through the typical training for preparation for the bar mitzvah, and after that no actual training, just an occasional attendance of synagogue, at special holidays, with my father," Lee later recalled. The family did, however, participate in celebrating the holidays from time to time.[13]

In 1919, shortly after Lee entered high school, the Pressman family left the Lower East Side. They moved to a Jewish section of suburban Bensonhurst in Brooklyn, acquiring along the way, as evidence of their rising standard of living, a Stutz automobile. The detached Bensonhurst house on 80th Avenue was built of stucco and was roomy, leading to a pleasant change in living conditions for the Pressmans. The neighborhood kids played stickball, football, and skated in the streets; it was rare, though, to find gentile playmates. While he could have transferred to a different school, Lee insisted on completing his high school studies at Stuyvesant in Manhattan. Nor did he expect that his studies were finished when he graduated. He knew that his mother ardently wished him to pursue a professional career, either in law or medicine. The latter profession did not appeal to him. They did not consider a career in the family business. "That topic never came up in our family discussions," Lee told an interviewer years later. "It was always assumed that I would go to college and to a professional school. Business had too many vagaries, too many ups and downs. It was always the aspiration of a Jewish parent to have something better" for their children. When he completed Stuyvesant in 1922 at the age of sixteen, Pressman entered New York University's Washington Square College, later transferring to Cornell University.[14]

Entering college at sixteen probably reinforced Pressman's personality bent toward discipline, hard work, and achievement, which had been instilled by his mother. He did quite well academically. Because "I was rather young in the classes that I was in," he reflected, "there wasn't as much social activity or sports as one would find if he were at a natural age in physical development." Not that Washington Square College, located then on the fourth floor of the American Depository Book Company, was a sports powerhouse. In those years the school remained small; Lee's class was the first large class to come in, with approximately 150 to 200 students. "Most of the comradeship was done on the fourth floor," Lee's friend Jacob Rabkin recalled. "It was a very intimate group of people because we were thrown in together on the fourth floor and we saw each other very often" during class changes and locker socializing. Rabkin remembers Pressman as being very handsome, charming, and articulate. Evidently Lee's potential for academic achievement caught the eye of Dr. Munn, a professor of English literature who went on to become dean. Munn encouraged Lee to consider transferring to Cornell for his sophomore year and assisted the young man in obtaining scholarship money.[15]

Despite their general middle-class status, business fortunes limited the Pressman family's ability to help financially with their eldest son's higher education. This was especially true after the early 1920s, when the elder Pressman sold his garment business and undertook a partnership in a restaurant–hotel across from Madison Square Garden. The restaurant business was one that Harry Pressman knew nothing about, according to his son Irving, but perhaps he hoped it would be less volatile than garment manufacturing. The struggle to make the new enterprise a success, combined with the tuition and rooming costs needed for Lee to attend Cornell, forced his parents to seek outside help. In 1925, the year before he graduated from Cornell, Lee applied for and received the George C. Boldt Memorial Scholarship. In his application he noted that his part-time dishwashing work and summer work as a counselor, with the assistance his parents were able to afford, totaled approximately 50 percent of the money he needed for his tuition.[16]

CORNELL AND HARVARD

Thus, Lee Pressman, firstborn son of immigrant Jewish parents of modest income, began his academic work at Cornell. Lee's experiences at the school over the next two years brought him two passions: his wife and his life's work. Sophia Platnik (nicknamed Sunny) was, like Lee, a Jew from New York's Lower East Side, but from a poorer family. In terms of other riches, though, Joseph and Minnie Plotnick's daughter had been blessed. "My mother was a very beautiful lady, very feminine," recalled daughter Marcia. Lee himself had matured into quite a handsome man by the time he had turned twenty. Standing six feet tall and weighing 175 pounds, he had the upper body muscularity of a wrestler, dark curly hair, angular features, and slightly arched eyebrows that sharpened his gaze; he was then, and remained afterward, very attractive to women. In this case, however, he was the pursuer of the romance and the infatuated lover, Sunny, for a time, the reluctant but interested target of his affections. A woman of great intellectual and artistic talents, who often kept them hidden, she studied languages intensively—Russian, French, and especially Hebrew. "She was one of the few first generation children born in this country that pursued her Jewish studies to the extent," Marcia said. She essentially completed the essentials of a rabbinical training though, as a woman, she could never become a rabbi. Once she decided that she too was interested romantically in Lee, the couple spent a considerable amount of time together, both on campus and as summer camp counselors. When Lee graduated from Cornell in 1926 and moved on to Harvard Law School, Sunny stayed at Cornell until her graduation in 1928.[17]

In terms of Lee's additional passion—his profession—Cornell also provided the intellectual seed that eventually bore fruit in Pressman's later career as a lawyer representing the labor movement. During Lee's years at Cornell, labor economist Sumner Slichter taught at the school. After taking his course in elementary economics in his sophomore year, as a junior Pressman signed up for the professor's course on the history of trade unionism. "He was a very excellent teacher," recollected Lee years later, "and got me really basically interested in the activities of trade unions." In his senior year he became a grading assistant for the professor. "In terms of my life activity," Pressman recalled in hindsight, it was Slichter and Cornell, not Harvard Law School, that gave him a focus and an outlet for his social idealism.[18]

Obviously, something about Slichter's course and the subject of trade unionism struck a responsive chord in Lee Pressman. As a young adult his personality contained evidence of a romanticized social idealism; this found expression in his desire to have his life's work accomplish something positive about the injustices of the world, certainly not an uncommon trait in young people. His brother Irving remembered that Lee was always intellectually interested in economics and political–economic reform, even in high school.[19]

On the other hand, intense parental demands for career success also shaped his personality. He felt a responsibility to the family to succeed as a Jewish son of Jewish immigrant parents. This resulted in a driving ambition intense enough to put some people off. Years afterward, when the FBI began investigating his role in the Hiss–Chambers case, agents interviewed an anonymous source who appeared to be an acquaintance of Lee's at Cornell. Pressman, he recalled, was "a brilliant student and one who was respected for his ability," the source said. The informant, however, "disliked the subject's personality" because he thought he was "an opportunist" in the pursuit of academic and professional success. This also was not an uncommon reaction in Jewish children in whom immigrant parents had instilled such ambition, ambition that sometimes put off non-Jews and enhanced their anti-Semitism. As an Anglo–Saxon teacher reported to Pauline Young, "Mentally the Jewish children are the backbone of my class, but they can be an unsufferable nuisance because of their constant desire to distinguish themselves, and that's why they are not very popular" among their schoolmates.[20]

It was quite likely that Pressman encountered such anti-Semitism at both Cornell and Harvard. The Anglo–Saxon-dominated world of professional schooling was uneasy with the professional ascension of Jews; many institutions of higher learning at the time, especially the Ivy League schools, even began imposing restrictions on their admission. At Cornell, the rural residents of upstate New York regarded Jews from New York City as taking "their" slots at the school, since they believed it was their lobbying that had resulted in state funding, entitling them to special consideration. This anti-Semitism extended into social life as traditional fraternities refused to recruit Lower East Side Jews, no matter how bright, articulate, and ambitious.

Therefore, Lee, as did twenty-eight of his urban compatriots, joined the local chapter of *Omicron Alpha Tau*, a Jewish fraternity. In the fraternity, some noted Lee's developing political idealism. Pressman and a number of his fraternity brothers were regarded as somewhat "pink," an FBI interviewee who knew Pressman in these years recounted later. These students were "described as intellectually interested and somewhat 'starry-eyed' about Socialism, Marxism, and Leninism and the Soviet experiment," the bureau investigative report detailed. They "would indicate their feelings and sympathies for the most part at 'bull sessions,'" according to the informant, who did reflect that such interest among college students was perhaps not all that unusual. He "wished to point out that his statements as to the 'pinkish' group should be considered in the light of the times and should also take into consideration the age of the students." Thus, first generation Jewish students were never far from social tensions grounded in ethnic, class, and perhaps even ideological considerations. "While they have the same civil privileges and encounter no legal restrictions," wrote Pauline Young, "they find it frequently impossible to conceal their origin. The attitudes of other people are such that they compel them to realize that they are Jews, and that they belong 'where they come from.'"[21]

The physical affliction of polio—which sensitized him to the injustices the world can heap on the innocent—and the parental demands for professional success—which gave him a driving ambition difficult to hide—combined to make it appear that Lee Pressman was a young man who was interested in doing something to rid the world of injustices, even as he benefited himself. Further, his quick mindedness intimidated people and sometimes led him to become impatient with the slower witted. His intellectual talents, however, did not usually run to original thought. Lee Pressman processed information strategically, and his thought naturally ran to tactical questions. His was a mind that could see well in advance the possibilities inherent in a situation and what one could do to achieve one's objectives. "Fundamentally, you can classify Jewish minds in two groups," remarked Pressman's close work associate Harold Ruttenberg, himself a Jew. "One is the deep prophetic intellectual mind. The other is the operational mind. Pressman was the operational mind. . . . [H]e was intellectual in a way, but he wasn't intellectual in that his interests were catholic. They were specific and narrow."[22]

When Pressman entered Harvard Law School in 1926 he thus had qualities well suited to the professional world of law. He chose Harvard, he later told an interviewer, largely because it was one of the few law schools requiring an undergraduate degree for admission, and this exclusiveness seemed significant. Even for a bright student, a Harvard legal education proved challenging, requiring a tremendous amount of work and self-discipline—even more so for Pressman because he had to tutor other students for tuition money, as he had at Cornell. He excelled at such discipline, though, and finished second in his class academically. He also served on the *Harvard Law Review* in his second and third years, a coveted position; he became case note editor in his senior year, the second most influential position on the *Review*. An acquaintance at the time "found him to [be] very active and very able," FBI agents wrote of their investigative interview with someone who knew Lee during his time at Harvard. "He stated that he was energetic and showed a great deal of ability to stick with a hard problem until he reached a conclusion on it." There were many such problems for the aspiring lawyer. "[P]ractically your entire life during your second and third year revolves around the law review," he remembered years afterward. "Your ordinary course work you take in stride." Aside from frequent courtship letters to Sunny, he had little free time. When "you're at Harvard Law School and you're trying to make the Law Review and then you're on the Law Review there are very few interests outside of your law school work that you become involved with." Even so, he occasionally did find a bit of time for family visits. "He saved up enough money from his tutoring to invite me to come to visit him at law school for one of the football games," remembered Irving, who arrived chaperoned by a female cousin. Lee proudly gave him a tour of the school's campus. [23]

However, at Harvard, Lee also found social exclusion based on ethnicity and class. He did not find the same acceptance—as a Russian Jew who had to tutor to make ends meet—as the sons of the non-Jewish, old wealth elitists or the gentrified Americans who were staking out their places in American society, students, for example, such as Alger Hiss. Hiss served with Pressman on the *Harvard Law Review*, and the latter in fact directed his work on the *Review*. In later interviews, Pressman made it known, with visible feeling, that he and Alger did not travel in the same "social circles" at Harvard. Hiss became a pet of Professor Felix Frankfurter. He had descended from a Baltimore family that had social pretensions even though it was, before and during Alger's day, suffering downward social mobility for a number of reasons. Pressman, obviously, was not a part of the same "shabby-genteel" social strata as Hiss. Frankfurter, a German Jew, was a nortorious social climber. While he could sometimes form bonds of sponsorship with lower-class Jewish students who fed his ego with intellectual idolatry, Frankfurter did not take to Pressman as he did to Hiss and a few other Jewish students. For years afterward, Pressman felt this sense of slight.[24]

Despite his interest in unions and the labor movement, Pressman had not had the opportunity to take a labor law course, since the school only initiated such a course in his third year. By then he was far too tied up with the *Law Review* work to take it. He had had Professor Frankfurter for administrative law, however, and Frankfurter—the celebrated defender of Italian anarchists Sacco and Vanzetti—had garment union ties and had written a book on the antiunion use of judicial injunctions. Lee approached "the most colorful and controversial member of the faculty," as Alger Hiss later characterized Frankfurter, for advice on how to start a law practice focusing on representing unions. Outside of one or two firms representing the garment unions in New York City, there were hardly any labor-side law firms in the country in those days. Frankfurter, however, had participated in litigating several Amalgamated Clothing Worker cases involving labor injunctions and had ties with several New York City lawyers that he had worked with on those cases. "About my second or third year I called on Felix and told him I wanted to go into the labor law field and did he have any idea about what I could do to get into such a field. He said, 'My advice to you is very simple. First, get to be a good lawyer and then you'll have no trouble, if you want to, representing labor unions.'" He did give Pressman a letter of recommendation to the New York firms handling the garment union cases, but nothing came of it.[25]

Other than this contact, Pressman was not one of Frankfurter's inner circle of favored students. Frankfurter had a reputation as a Progressive, but "his didactic style was challenging, even confrontational," wrote Hiss. Moreover, he "was cocky, abrasive, and outspoken." As a result, he "was not popular with the majority of his students. . . ." Hiss came to Harvard bearing a letter of introduction from William Marbury, a lawyer and friend of the Hiss family who knew Frankfurter. "As a result, I got invited to the Sunday teas" at the Frankfurter residence on Brattle Street, a highly prized badge of acceptance for those legal students aspiring to become part of the progressive legal intelligentsia. The teas were in fact semiorganized sessions of intellectual discourse, with Frankfurter acting as the "impresario and catalyst," bounding "from book to book, magazine to magazine" in his library, "like an adult Peter Pan" searching for a well-turned quote. Hiss's genteel bearing clearly attracted Frankfurter. "I remember Alger Hiss best of all for a kind of distinction that had to be seen to be believed," Pressman told journalist Murray Kempton years later. "If he were standing at the bar with the British Ambassador and you were told to give a package to the Ambassador's valet, you would give it to the Ambassador before you gave it to Alger. He gave you a sense of absolute command and absolute grace and I think Felix felt it more than anyone. He seemed to have a kind of awe for Alger," Lee observed. According to Harold Cammer, also a Harvard Law School graduate, Frankfurter's social climbing tended to cause him to favor non-Jewish students from what he perceived was the American gentility. He made an exception here or there for a poor Russian–Jewish student who fed the renowned professor's ego with adulation. Pressman, though, clearly one of the brightest of the class of 1929, and interested in pursuing a reform-minded legal career in an area in which Frankfurter had expertise, never received a Brattle Street invitation.[26]

Despite the slight, Pressman valued his training at Harvard—not so much for the substance of what he learned, but for the analytical skills imparted. "It wasn't the content of the course you were getting that was important," he later remarked. The analysis of cases and the Socratic teaching method practiced at the Ivy League law schools forced the students to separate facts from assumptions and relevancies from irrelevancies. He recollected that in his first year, one professor focused on a medieval case for an inordinately long time. "For three months we had been giving him our statement of facts and he would point out that we were overstating it or understating it. You would say, 'This is a fact of the case,' and he would say, 'Where do you find this?' 'Well, I assume this,' you would say, and he would say, 'I didn't ask you what you assumed. I asked you to state the facts.' When we got through with that case," he remembered, "every single person in that class had been trained. If he were ever given a statement of facts to read, he could tell you what the facts were." As a by-product, the "second important lesson, at least for me[,] was that you learned to distinguish the relevant from the irrelevant," an ability that he prized for the rest of his life. "[I]t's been my guidepost—in your ordinary relationships, in your professional relationships," he informed the interviewer. "And by and large I have found that when you see a person who can" separate relevancies from irrelevancies, "you have a person with a fairly clear mind."[27]

Thus, Harvard Law School bequeathed to Pressman analytical skills that served him well professionally for the rest of his life. However, that mindset from time to time could also lead him to be too coldly analytical and excessively devoted to logic and rationalizations. Even so, the mastery of those analytical skills were what many law firms were looking for when hiring young graduates from the first-rank law schools. Like many others in his class, he made the rounds of the big Wall Street law firms in New York around Christmas of his senior year. "These big firms snap up the *Law Review* men," Pressman remembered. "You can take your choice of the one you want." Pressman found his home at the firm of Chadbourne, Stanchfield, and Levy, "at what we considered then . . . a very fancy salary." The bar exam followed in June, and he started work in September 1929.[28]

WALL STREET LAW PRACTICE AND THE DEPRESSION

The Chadbourne firm specialized in corporate reorganizations and receiverships, but also had a varied general corporate practice representing such large companies as Anaconda Copper and American Tobacco. Pressman at first found himself doing "a little bit of everything," except that there "was no trial work attached to it." Shortly after he arrived, the firm assigned him to a senior lawyer for mentoring. That attorney was Jerome Frank. In the following year, Frank would become a leading light of the "legal realism" movement—an academic school arguing that "law" was socially determined and not rationally divined—with the publication of his treatise *Law and the Modern Mind*.[29]

Jerome Frank, originally born in New York City of German–Jewish heritage, grew up in Chicago. By 1928, he had become a prominent lawyer in that city and "quickly came to be recognized as one of the nation's leading corporate reorganization lawyers," according to his biographer Robert J. Glennon. In spite of his corporate law practice, he always maintained broad artistic, intellectual, and progressive political interests. Family concerns, however, caused him to return to the city of his birth. He moved to New York City "out of concern for his daughter, Barbara, who suffered intermittently from a psychosomatic paralysis of the legs," and who was then undergoing psychoanalysis with a New York doctor. Frank encountered the young Lee Pressman not long after arriving at Chadbourne. "After I had been there a few weeks he wrote a memorandum and gave an oral statement about an intricate legal problem that quite delighted me," recollected Frank. He resolved then to take "him on as my cub."[30]

Frank, a man with "bright, piercing blue eyes, a broad mouth, a high, sloping forehead, an olive complexion, and sparse-medium brown hair" was a very charismatic figure to young lawyers, recalled John Abt, his "cub" at his Chicago firm. Even so, from the first, his relationship with Pressman seemed to run in the opposite direction, with Frank somewhat fascinated by the young man. "I would say that he" was "probably the best lawyer that I've ever met," Frank reflected many years afterward. He "was the quickest legal mind I ever encountered . . . quick, sure, and ingenious. As it turned out, he was also a man of great executive ability." Thus began a relationship between Pressman and an older sponsor that was to find replication in later years with his ties to John L. Lewis and Philip Murray. He "always had somebody behind him who was pushing him" professionally, observed his brother Irving. As a youth he had had responsibilities far in advance of his chronological age; he was always in advance of his age group in school and later professionally. Indeed, it was remarkable that Frank, himself something of a *wunderkind*, could be so enamored of the young Lee Pressman.[31]

On a more personal level, Lee and Sunny continued their long courtship and engagement. After returning to New York, Pressman lived at home and turned over his earnings to his mother, who saved a nest egg for him. Harry Pressman's restaurant business, however, had fallen on tough economic times a year or so before Lee had graduated from Harvard. According to Irving, the enterprise collapsed due to his father's lack of experience at managing that type of business. Nevertheless, the family was somehow able to make ends meet, and on June 28, 1931, Lee and Sunny were married. Since the bride's family did not have enough money to pay for the wedding, Lee's mother arranged to have the reception held at the St. Maritz Hotel. The young couple moved to the Flatbush section of Brooklyn, visited with the Frank family at their home in Croton-on-Hudson, and generally settled into the lifestyle suitable for an up-and-coming Wall Street lawyer.[32]

The advancing economic depression, however, interceded. Through the early 1930s, financial hard times had left Lee Pressman and others like him generally untouched—corporate receivership and reorganization work was, after all, plentiful at that time. Even so, many of these young professionals could not ignore the human miseries around them and those groups that were among the first to try to do something about the misery—groups such as the American Communist Party, for example. As Alfred Kazin recalled the streets of New York City in the depths of the Great Depression, he often encountered "the nude shamed look furniture on the street always had those terrible first winters of the depression. . . ." We "stood around each newly evicted family to give them comfort and the young Communists raged up and down the street calling for volunteers to put the furniture back and crying aloud with their fists lifted to the sky." Pressman, with his own sensitivity to injustice, must also have glimpsed more than one scene where communists seemed to be the only individuals trying to rectify the misery of the helpless.

Increasingly, the events that surrounded young lawyers—particularly those from Pressman's social milieu—began to force them to question the viability of the political and economic system as currently constructed under capitalism. Everyone, even young Wall Street lawyers, as Pressman's friend Jack Rabkin later recalled, searched for answers to the economic apocalypse that ground down millions of people. In that kind of context, corporate law practice began to become burdensome to attorneys motivated by some sense of social responsibility and idealism, such as Frank and Pressman. Frank, in particular, disliked the "factory" atmosphere of the large Chadbourne firm and questioned the ethical standards of some of its practices. Lee as well had come to believe that this type of legal work was not for him. Intellectually, he continued to pursue an outside interest in labor law through a loose association with a small legal publishing group, the International Juridical Association (IJA).[33]

The American branch of the IJA owed its existence to Carol Weiss King, a Progressive lawyer long active in representing radicals and immigrants. The group's preamble clearly set out its focus: to combat "legislative, administrative, and judicial tyranny" against political dissenters by assisting progressive lawyers to more effectively represent clients—such as workers and unions, among others—who experienced wholesale violations of their civil liberties. This work was done largely through the publication of the *IJA Bulletin*. The publication contained "extensive coverage of political/constitutional cases and movements" and combined both "theory and practice" for those attorneys struggling to represent the downtrodden and the oppressed, according to King's biographer and IJA historian Ann Fagan Ginger. For the next ten years, the *Bulletin* chronicled many of the political, legislative, and legal events of the New Deal era.[34]

More important, the IJA placed lawyers of a Progressive mind-set into more intimate professional contact with each other. Many had started in corporate practice in New York after law school, but as a result of the Great Depression found themselves increasingly troubled professionally. Pressman's involvement came "probably through Shad Polier who was a classmate of mine at law school," he later thought. In addition to King and Polier (who became IJA Director), Joseph Kovner, "a very bright, able, decent and compassionate person among the sharks of the New York legal world," soon became the *Bulletin's* editor. Kovner (who later served Pressman as an assistant general counsel in the CIO), recruited Nathan Greene (also a Pressman classmate from Harvard, as well as a Frankfurter favorite) to help him do the major editorial work on the *Bulletin*. Pressman, among the earliest group of young attorneys recruited to the cause as "founding editors" of the IJA's publication, noted that the association "was no organization" when he started to work with the group. "It was just a little bulletin that was put out by the two persons at that time. . . . [W]e had about three or four of us . . . reading decisions of courts involving labor injunctions." In addition, "It was the only bulletin that was being put out . . . covering or concentrating on labor—on opinions and decisions of courts pertaining to labor problems," he commented. According to Pressman, "They worked as if they were working on a law review for a law school. They would submit law reports on important labor and civil rights cases" of interest to attorneys of a Progressive bent. The IJA's first published issue arrived on May 1, 1932, featuring discussions of both the *Scottsboro* civil liberties case and an analysis of the recently passed Norris–LaGuardia law prohibiting labor injunctions and "yellow-dog" contracts.

The bulletin soon attracted others. The IJA quickly became an influential networking association for progressive, civil liberty, labor-minded attorneys. Alger Hiss, then working in New York, also became involved, as did Pressman's friend and later law partner Nat Witt. Although Pressman and Witt had both attended New York University (NYU) in the early 1920s, Witt had not gone to Harvard Law School until about the time Pressman graduated in 1929; it was at the IJA where he and Pressman first became friends. Additional legal luminaries connected to the IJA included Tom Emerson, later National Labor Relations Board attorney and subsequent Yale law professor, and future Supreme Court Justice Abe Fortas. All, in one way or another, wrote Ginger, had "been near the seats of power at Harvard and Wall Street," and therefore "had confidence in the power of their intellect to help bring about basic social change."[35]

While some of those affiliated with the IJA were in all likelihood communists, at this time it did not appear to others that Lee Pressman had more than a liberal orientation tinged with "pink" colorings. IJA member Jerome Hellerstein told Hiss defense attorneys years later that Pressman and Witt, whatever their later activities, "were not Communists, at least at that time." Similarly, Pressman's personal friend Jack Rabkin, who lived in the same neighborhood and knew Lee during those early years in New York City, supported this observation. "I don't think he was dominated by a leftist philosophy at that time," he recollected years later. Nevertheless, the group brought him into closer contact with much more radical streams of political and social opinion than he had probably been heretofore exposed, except perhaps briefly at Cornell. Nat Witt, for example, had been radicalized significantly earlier than Pressman due to the Sacco–Vanzetti case. Combined with the social agony of the advancing Great Depression, along with Pressman's own underlying personality, the IJA experience was an important step in preparing Pressman for the further activist commitments he was to make.[36]

The election of New York Governor Franklin D. Roosevelt in the fall of 1932 profoundly affected the career directions of both Jerome Frank and Lee Pressman in short order. The banking crisis and downward spiraling economy promised that the new Roosevelt administration was going to be one of legislative innovation and reform. In early 1933, Frank had been in contact with Pressman's old law professor Felix Frankfurter, who was then serving as a prime recruiter for the staffing of the early New Deal agencies. First promised a general counsel's job in the Department of Agriculture solicitor's office, a political patronage debt knocked Frank out of the competition. However, he had turned in his resignation at the Chadbourne firm so he had little choice but to remain in Washington and angle for another position. Shortly afterward, Frank began working with New Deal brain truster and Columbia professor Rexford Tugwell to shepherd the Agricultural Adjustment Bill (later Act) through Congress. Soon he began anticipating an appointment to that agency."[37]

It was clear that when Jerome Frank left for Washington he intended to take Lee Pressman with him, should he find a position in the New Deal. Once

Frank left, his "cub" moved over to another small law firm, Liebman, Blumenthal, and Levy, because of dislike for the Chadbourne style of law practice. However, both Pressman and Frank knew the move was temporary; the chance to work on the anticipated social and economic reforms in Roosevelt's first hundred days was the prime objective for each. "The job is going to be even more interesting than I anticipated," Frank wrote to Lee in April 1933. "I suggest . . . that you send me letters showing your education experience, etc. Tugwell knows I am hoping to have you here with me and approves." He also asked Pressman to check with Alger Hiss and Nat Witt to test their eagerness to make connections in the coming New Deal. Pressman responded that he had informed both Hiss and Witt, "who are considering the matter. From the short experience I have had away" from the Chadbourne firm, he wrote to his mentor, "I am fully convinced that both you and I are never going to have, if possible, any similar yoke around our necks."[38]

From the Liebman firm Pressman handled a number of Frank's personal legal matters and waited for his invitation to Washington through the spring of 1933. "I am sitting on edge just waiting for news from you as to what's occurring," he wrote Frank in May. If nothing opened up in Washington, Pressman hoped something would develop nearer to home. In June he wrote Frank about a possible appointment with an anticipated U.S. Department of Labor investigation into labor racketeering among New York City AFL unions. "You know how much I am interested in getting into this phase of the investigation," he reminded Frank. Explaining that he had written one of the special attorneys appointed to work on the investigation—"offering my services in this connection"—he informed Frank that he had been told that staff assignments came through the Department of Justice headquarters. Perhaps Frank's new Washington contacts could help make that assignment come Pressman's way. "Is there any possible way of my getting into the task somehow?" he asked Frank. "I'd love to spend the next few months really hard at work on this problem since it really has been the most interesting available to date."

Still, the delay in starting up and staffing the Agricultural Adjustment Administration, to which by now Jerome Frank had been appointed general counsel, became increasingly difficult for Pressman to endure. "I understand what the situation probably is in Washington about new assistants," he wrote Frank in July 1933, "but I am exceedingly anxious to get to work with you." That chance finally came later that month. Frank "called me that I should come down" to Washington "and then when I came down . . . I became the assistant general counsel" in the AAA, Pressman remembered. He received a raise of several thousand dollars and, more important, he had moved into the swirling currents of American Progressive reform in the early days of the New Deal. Although long desired and much anticipated, this career move would have a profound impact on Lee Pressman's future life. Pressman, the first American-born son of Russian–Jewish immigrant parents, had overcome a difficult social milieu and climbed to personal and professional advancement in the United States. He had fused his quick-witted intelligence, extreme self-discipline, driving ambition, sensitivity to injustice, and romantic social idealism into a professional reward. He achieved what he thought would be a true position of power, a position that surely implied, if only subconsciously, some aspect of social acceptance. He soon learned that power in the New Deal was not what or where he had thought it would be. Ultimately, he would conclude that the capitalist system had generated political power inequities so great that real change would be impossible, as long as that system prevailed.[39]

TWO

CERTAINTY IN HUMAN FORM

When Lee Pressman arrived at the AAA in Washington in July 1933, Jerome Frank quickly took advantage of his young aide's talents. Journalist Gardner Jackson, a Progressive Era ally of Felix Frankfurter in the Sacco–Vanzetti case, who himself joined the AAA's Consumers Council division, judged "that Lee had an almost abnormal domination on the personal level over" the older attorney. In "the business of decisions on tactics, on appraisal of individuals through whom you had to work, fellows in other departments, fellows up on the Hill," Pressman, Jackson believed, always was "decisive in persuading Jerome as to when and how he should work to further a proposal, or an idea," Jackson later recollected. When later asked by New Deal historian Arthur Schlesinger Jr. to explain his own similar reaction to Pressman's personality, Jackson noted that it was a question of psychodynamics. They had both "found a great deal of comfort operating with . . . such a confident human being." "I actually think in retrospect that Jerome and I were very similar people," the journalist told an interviewer. "Jerome was a highly trained intellect" and could "master his tool of the law to a high degree. But I think he was emotionally so uncertain of the direction he was taking, as I certainly was, that he did very much what I did with Lee. . . ." "We found comfort," Jackson thought, "in being associated with a certainty in the human form in Lee Pressman."[1]

Beneath the veneer of this overweening certainty, however, Pressman experienced a good deal of the psychic confusion and doubt that plagued many in his generation. They came of age in an era of profound world historical crises—the cataclysms of total war the rise of fascism and inexplicable

23

economic collapse. These events loosened social moorings considerably. Pressman came to Washington to escape the social sterility of a Wall Street corporate law practice. He hoped to become a soldier of reform in the army of the New Deal, but found over the next two and a half years in government service that true reform was terribly difficult to achieve from within. As John Abt characterized it, "We thought here was an opportunity to have our hands close to the levers of power. To really do something to bring the country out of the situation it was in." Sadly, they discovered they were wrong. Powerful business interests reasserted themselves behind the scenes within all the new governmental agencies charged with their regulation. As John Abt observed about the efforts of elite New Dealers to bring about change, we "very soon found Washington gave us a quick political education that we were nowhere near the levers of power."[2]

Under capitalism, Pressman concluded in the end, there could be no lasting fundamental change. This key verdict combined with the matrix of his personality, ethnicity, and previous life experiences to lead him along the path to political radicalism. In addition, the AAA experience ironically gave Pressman the skills he used later to shape governmental policy from outside the state bureaucracy. Although Pressman may have exhibited "certainty in human form" to others, underneath it all he too had insecurities that made the all-encompassing political ideology of American communism quite seductive.

THE AAA EXPERIENCE

Pressman's work for the AAA started in July with a temporary appointment, just as the agency began operations under the oversight of the U.S. Department of Agriculture and its new secretary Henry Wallace. The top agency administrator was George Peek, later replaced by Chester Davis. Both had strong ties to the agribusiness community and owed their appointments to the party patronage system. Pressman began work in Jerome Frank's general counsel's office as Assistant General Counsel in charge of the division's section of marketing, codes, and licenses. Almost immediately, internal disagreements about the law's proper administration surfaced. Pressman and his colleagues envisaged the AAA as being the agricultural counterpart of the National Recovery Act (NRA). They should try to do for agriculture what the NRA allegedly was trying to do for the industrial economy. What historians have come to call the "First New Deal" under Franklin Roosevelt attempted to rectify the problems of the economic crisis by encouraging and allowing businesses to combine and share markets without being threatened by antitrust litigation. In exchange for that freedom, businesses had to develop codes of self-regulation protecting the public interest and preventing overproduction, which most economists at the time believed caused the Great Depression. A protected business structure in every industry would therefore be able to able to revive the American economy, claimed proponents.[3]

The Agricultural Adjustment Administration would do the same thing for the sorely depressed agricultural economy by controlling the production of staple commodities such as wheat and corn, and the processing of various other farm goods. Pressman's marketing section handled the legal end of the processing activities. "We dealt, for example," he later explained, "with the field of processing of milk, the processing of fruits and vegetables, of meat. The objective on the processing end as it was on the staple crops was to try to limit production and regulate distribution to bring supply and demand into some degree of relationship." In effect, these marketing agreements, codes, and licenses were similar to the NRA's "codes of fair competition" in the industrial sector, but applied to large agricultural processing businesses and distributors. Pressman directed the "drafting of these marketing agreements and licenses," along with their administration and enforcement. Quickly, the workload became intense and Pressman struggled to find sufficient legal talent to accomplish the agency's essential legal tasks.[4]

As the workload increased, rifts developed between the administrator's office, dominated by officials with agribusiness orientations, and the more reform-minded attorneys of the legal division—Frank, Pressman, Abt, and Hiss foremost among them. The disagreements focused on policy issues, with the latter group often supported by FDR brain truster and Undersecretary of Agriculture Rexford G. Tugwell. To the former group, regulation meant to "eliminate the overproduction, curtail the production if you can, and let the processors make as much money as they possibly can, and in that fashion some of it will siphon back," Pressman observed. Frank and his young legal reformers, on the other hand, believed that regulation by the AAA meant a balancing of agribusiness desires, consumer protections, and small farm–farm laborer interests. Over the next two years, most of the internal bureaucratic wrangling centered around these two orientations. The agribusiness group within the agency resented the Progressives. George Peek's oft-repeated criticism's of the legal staff reflected this discomfort: "There were too many Ivy League men, too many intellectuals, too many radicals, too many Jews," he insisted.[5]

No sooner had the agency begun its work than the administrator's office called the activities of Frank's staff into question. "As I told you I was greatly surprised at your comment this morning to the effect that members of the legal staff have been unwarrantably expressing themselves on policy questions," Jerome Frank wrote to Peek's assistant Charles Brand, in apology. Even the Assistant General Counsel was not immune. "In response to your memorandum," Pressman wrote to Wayne Taylor, Peek's executive assistant, "we wish to advise the farmer as an individual has no status under the National Recovery Act." Pressman had been exploring the concept whether farmers, as employers, would be required to meet the standards of the NRA as it pertained to their employees. "The purpose of the Agricultural Adjustment Act is to raise the farmer's proportion of the national income," and did not relate to any other legislative requirements, Taylor wrote. "The farm laborer belongs to a group not intended to be covered." If farm prices went up, so eventually would farm laborer wages. "The farmer has enough problems at this time without being further burdened with this extremely difficult question of farm wages and hours," he peevishly closed.[6]

In the beginning, nevertheless, it was uncertain as to who would come out on top in the AAA bureaucratic struggle. Frank believed he had the sympathies of not only Rexford Tugwell but of Agriculture Secretary Henry Wallace as well. Despite Frank's protestations to the contrary, he and his young colleagues did indeed intend to shape agency policy in a way favorable to the interests of the most downtrodden in rural America. It was this possibility, after all, that had attracted them all to New Deal government service in the first place. In this, Pressman, Abt, and Witt, among others, tended to be more insistent and less desiring to be politically circumspect than was either Frank. We "looked down our noses at Jerome because he was a waverer," recollected Abt years later, because he "didn't stand up against the pressure of the right."[7]

Thus they sought to buttress the Progressive thrust in areas outside the general counsel's office. In the fall of 1933, for example, Pressman and Nat Witt, who had arrived at the agency a month after Lee, arrived unannounced at the Chevy Chase home of Progressive journalist Gardner Jackson and tried to recruit him. "They simply said they wanted to meet me, that they had heard a lot about me," recollected Jackson. In an effort to charm Jackson, Pressman asserted he had sat in on Jackson's Sacco–Vanzetti Committee Hanover Street meetings when he was in Harvard Law School in 1926 and 1927. They expressed "profound admiration" for the long years of Progressive work Jackson had done and "laid it on thick with the most silky kind of" approach. Perhaps Jackson would consider giving up his newspaper work and join the AAA's soon-to-be created Consumers' Council Division, they asked. Here was a chance to do good again! Pressman and Witt "saw an opportunity doing great things in reforming our economic and social organization through government," the journalist maintained.

Lee Pressman, especially, intrigued Gardner Jackson. "Because I was never sure of myself, and never had the absolute answer, I found in this young guy, on that first visit, with his absolutely precise, convinced expression of possibility and all the rest of it, a personality that was so confident that he gave me something to tie to," Jackson recalled Pressman's impact. He later believed that Pressman's recruiting intentions had reflected a well-thought-out strategy. "Lee thought he saw in me a kind of guy who would be very use-ful in his designs," Jackson speculated, "primarily because of my gregarious nature and my liking people so much, which he did not. He could guide me into a teamship with him in such a way that I would be a complement to his operation."

Whatever Pressman's intentions were toward Jackson, his and Witt's efforts to charm worked; shortly afterward, the journalist joined the AAA's Consumers Council Division staff. Thus, the reform-minded lawyers in Frank's office nurtured their vision of the agency by placing allies where they could, though the nerve center of idealism remained in the Legal Division. As John Abt later remarked, "For better or worse, it fell to the lot of the AAA gen-eral counsel's office to give voice to the millions of . . . farm workers" suf-fering most horribly under the Great Depression. Whether they would be able to outmaneuver the Peeks and the Davises depended, in large measure, on their success at defending their act before the federal courts.[8]

Many court observers, however, reckoned that experimental nature of economic regulatory schemes such as the NRA and AAA would have tough sledding before the nation's economically conservative Supreme Court. To develop trial strategy and present the AAA's case, Frank hired John Abt and Arthur Bachrach, Abt's brother-in-law and an associate of Frank's from Chicago. Pressman assisted them and exercised his talents for operating behind the scenes in order to help develop a workable litigation strategy. In December 1933, for example, Pressman visited the home of his old constitu-tional law professor from Harvard, Thomas Reed Powell. Powell had invited several friends over to socialize, including Gardner Jackson and his wife Dode. Powell, like Jerome Frank, believed that the judicial personality, including the judge's social and economic philosophy, had much more to do with determining how a justice would vote than any legal "principles" that could be divined from past case precedents or, as Pressman later put it, "It would be far more realistic in trying to evaluate what was going to happen to look at those Justices and try to determine what do they think in terms of spe-cific modern events. . . ." than how a set of established case precedents might force them to rule. It was a lesson that his law student Lee Pressman learned well. In a letter to his faculty colleague Felix Frankfurter, then in Cambridge, Powell mentioned Pressman's visit. "Later in the evening Lee Pressman and Bachrach came in," he reported. The two traveled to Boston with Jackson to participate in the New England milk code hearings of the AAA. Powell wrote that after "the Jacksons had left I had a long talk with Lee and Bachrach. Lee is much concerned about the particular form in which litigation arising out of the A.A.A. will get before the Court," and how it best might be approached.[9]

In fact, Pressman had been working on this problem for some time already. In the early days of the New Deal, Justice Louis Brandeis held frequent teas at his home for the New Deal liberal intelligentsia. "It was a field day for Harvard Law School" alumni, Pressman later remarked, because so many agencies had one or more Harvard lawyers in key policy positions. "So when you went around to these teas, you'd be meeting yourself," so to speak. At one of these social occasions, Brandeis inquired "about my work in the Triple A. I was explaining to him about . . . how we were attempting to regulate and curtail the production[,] and how we were trying to fix the prices[,] . . . and his only response after hearing me out very nicely and patiently was, 'There's something wrong with these big agencies.'" Clearly such a criticism from Brandeis signalled danger for the New Deal; the AAA's lawyers had little hope if they could not secure the support of one of the court's most pronounced liberals.[10]

Consequently, Pressman pressed Powell for his thoughts. "He says that Brandeis is very strongly opposed to much of what is going on because it is making for control of the big fellows and suppression of the little fellows. Lee wanted to know if I would be willing to give him a guess on the attitude of various Justices toward different features of their work," he informed Frankfurther. In doing so, perhaps Powell would provide "a view . . . to guiding them in determining what cases to press and what cases to postpone." "I inferred, also, that he hoped that I might give some kind of suggestions, presumably on a judicial-psychological basis, which might serve as . . . leverage to influence the policy of the Agricultural Administration. I gathered that he thought the person in charge was altogether too favorably inclined to the big people and that in this respect his attitude was different from that of Wallace and Jerry Frank."

Powell suggested that the AAA should pursue its policies without regard to what the Court might do. He agreed Brandeis was uncertain, but was not so sure of his ultimate hostility. Brandeis "had so often written in favor of legislative experimentation and of judicial respect for the judgment of the legislature that he would be badly back-tracking if he didn't live up to those professions," the professor judged. Overall, however, he "told Lee that I thought that the problem of lining up the Justices in advance was so difficult and that any conclusion would be so precarious that it was much better for them to go ahead and put into effect the policy they thought best[,] without regard to an effort to imagine which would be more palatable to a majority of the Court." He did agree to write memorandum on the problem if Pressman would put the queries to him more specifically, "on paper."[11]

Even as the AAA attorneys plotted their strategy on if, when, and how to sustain the act's constitutionality before the courts, tension within the agency rose. Agribusiness-oriented critics increasingly voiced their distaste for the general counsel's personnel to the Roosevelt administration, damning them as "city slickers," ignorant about farming. As Alger Hiss wrote in his memoir, as "conservative opposition to the New Deal developed in later months, we young lawyers became a conspicuous target for Roosevelt's opponents." Though Hiss was Anglo–Saxon, he remarked that the popular reference to them as being Felix Frankfurter's "Happy Hot Dogs" only thinly disguised a racial slur. "We were well aware that the epithet was a demogogic appeal to anti-Semitism, the printable version of the sally in some businessmen's clubs, 'the Jew Deal.'"

In response, Pressman and his colleagues increasingly evidenced deep skepticism about the intentions of the business interests facing them. During the milk hearings in Boston, according to Gardner Jackson, Pressman seemed "the most cynical fellow sitting up at those hearing tables," he thought. He "would talk under his breath to me all the time, wisecracking at the 'lying sons of bitches' representing" the milk companies, and "would get bored with the whole procedure and have a hard time sitting at the table." And as 1934 progressed, Pressman found himself reacting ever more stridently against what were coming to be perceived as intransigent enemies. Lee started with "a very pronounced focus on the dispossessed of our country in agriculture, and elsewhere," commented Jackson. Later he wanted more and more to participate in "the effort to stir that up as hard as could be stirred up." In so doing, Jackson thought Pressman developed a "complete cynicism, as manifested at milk hearings, about the corporate mind, the corporate intention, the chicanery in accounts, all that sort of business." During those years of the Great Depression, Jackson admitted, those were attitudes shared by many Progressives, including himself. In addition, Secretary Wallace, whom they assumed to be a kindred spirit, proved to be of little help when they needed assistance at resolving interdepartmental disputes.[12]

Indeed, in the end, the internal relations within the AAA itself presented the most confounding problem. As a Pressman memo for Rexford Tugwell, written in 1937, recounted, "it was undoubtedly" the marketing agreements, and more particularly Frank's policy attitudes toward their functioning, "which led to the most bitter disputes within the AAA." "The basic issue which was raised in the marketing agreements was whether the AAA would use the instrumentality of the license to check the books and records or the corporations that would receive the benefits of the marketing agreements[,] in order to make sure that the farmers would receive a fair share of the benefits arising out of the crop control[,] and that a fair share of the benefits be passed along to the consumer." If stabilization resulted in higher profits to processors, why should those profits be entirely apportioned to the processors? The Secretary of Agriculture should be authorized to inspect the "books and records" of the enterprises to guard against unfair profit taking, Frank and his assistants believed. The "books and records" issue "raised the basic question whether the instrumentality of marketing agreements and licenses would be used . . .

to regulate[,] or whether the government would merely be a cat's paw for the processors."

Pressman noted how the milk producers and distributors allied with each other against effective regulations, in effect, keeping retail prices high while preventing mass distribution of milk. "The marketing agreement and license which the AAA could issue for this industry could have been used to clean up the entire industry," he wrote to Tugwell "and really [would] have eliminated all the abuses and permitted the people to have milk at a much lower price. . . ." However, the Agriculture Department "refused to buck the milk producers' cooperatives" and the industry got its way. A similar struggle occurred over the meat packing agreement, where Frank's fight to have a "books and records" inspection clause inserted into the code resulted in no agreement at all. And, in the fresh fruits and vegetables segment, the general counsel's office faced large-scale processors who were also farmers. "As such, and acting in a dual capacity, they pleaded for aid to the AAA as.farmers. But[,] they fought viciously against the introduction of the books and records clause in their capacity as processors," Pressman pointed out, probably because such an inspection would show "huge profits . . . without any resulting benefits to the public by way of lower prices." In the final analysis, the "books and records" issue stimulated the most profound battle within the AAA and the Department of Agriculture to that date, and ultimately resulted in the firing of Jerome Frank and Lee Pressman. "Well, my God, the Civil War was a picnic compared to this issue as it [was] raised from the lower echelons up to the top," Pressman recalled, "and down again and up again and down again and up again. It went up and down that ladder about five times a day, over a period of weeks." The whole concept that a government regulator should have effective oversight of profit "was anathema to a man like," Peek's successor, Chester Davis.[13]

Finally, in February 1935, Davis resolved to put an end to the conflict. He used a dispute over a legal memorandum written under Alger Hiss's direction, which ruled that under the cotton code, landowners could not remove land from production if it would result in widespread poor farmer displacement. Davis believed the memorandum was not just faulty, but an effort to superimpose the general counsel's policy preferences. The AAA administrator had positioned himself well by this point, arranging critical southern political pressure on FDR. Consequently, Secretary of Agriculture Henry Wallace assented to the dismissals of Frank, Pressman, Jackson, and two others. Somewhat surprisingly, the AAA "purge," as it later came to be known, did not strike at all of the "radicals" and it left Hiss, who oversaw the drafting of the opinion, untouched. The choice whose "heads would roll" puzzled John Abt, for he escaped discharge as did several other agency leftists, even as Davis asked a few apolitical attorneys to leave.[14]

After his dismissal, Pressman maintained the "hard" and cynical demeanor he had displayed within the agency once he had lost faith in its efforts to reform. The dismissal letters came after a lunch between Pressman, Abt, and other attorneys, wherein all speculated who would be the most likely to fall first. Immediately after finding Wallace's dismissal letter on his desk, the emotional Gardner Jackson remembered charging into Pressman's office, letter in hand, unaware that Pressman and others had also received similar communications. The journalist asked Pressman if there were any legal grounds on which he could fight the discharge. "Lee opened the letter and read it very calmly and deliberately." He refolded the letter and calmly handed it back to Jackson and said he did not think there was a legal basis to fight it. Visibly upset, Jackson made for the door when the others called him back as they collectively pulled their own discharge letters out of their pockets. "Pressman was the first to reveal his letter. He was obviously getting a saturnine chuckle out of the whole thing."

Later, twenty AAA staff members crowded into Frank's office, benumbed but still doubtful that their ideological confrere Henry Wallace had actually approved of the firing. Pressman scoffed. "I can remember[,] visually[,] Jerome walking back and forth behind his desk and turning and looking out the window at the vista down the Potomac," Gardner Jackson reminisced. "He kept saying over and over again, 'This cannot be. We have worked so closely with Wallace. . . .' He was interrupted two or three times by Lee Pressman," Jackson recounted, "who with complete cynical composure said, 'Jerome, you're crazy. Of course this has been approved by Wallace. It's obvious that it has. You're a romantic. If I were in Wallace's position, I would approve it. The political necessities are such chat he can't follow any other course.'" That evening, Jackson and his wife Dode encountered Lee and Sunny Pressman, with whom they socialized from time to time, at Washington's Shoreham Hotel. "Lee [was] taking . . . [the firings] with complete amusement and cynicism as just an inevitable stage in the fight we were making," according to Jackson.[15]

Nevertheless, for a brief time afterward, on the surface it seemed that Lee Pressman harbored a belief that government work within the New Deal could result in change. Using the good offices of Josephine Roche, a businesswoman and New Deal official he had recently met, he approached Secretary of Labor Frances Perkins. He told her he had heard she needed a new solicitor. Roche had recommend him as very "admirable, very able, very intelligent, very broad-minded, very well-posted, and extremely presentable and a good negotiator," Perkins recalled. Unfortunately, Pressman's efforts to charm appeared transparent. He told her "how much he admired this, that and the other thing" about Perkins's former social welfare work, and "that was his first false step." Why, she asked herself, was a young lawyer making such an effort to tell a middle-aged lady "how much he admired her and all her works?" "He didn't have to do that," she thought. "I wonder why he does?" Pressman explained his desire to become a part of the Department of Labor, and how he thought that labor in the United States and how it would develop in the next ten years "was the key to American civilization." The secretary needed the right acute legal advice because the Department of Labor was obviously the critical government agency to guide how it would develop. "He laid it on a little thicker, always with the most unctuous manner," he recalled. He was "super-respectful, super-polite, more polite than you need to be, [and he used] more utilization of your title than is absolutely necessary. . . . When he stood" to leave, she said, "he bowed from the hips." That "turned a screw in my mind," Perkins claimed. She judged that he was too "fancy," a New York Progressive Era characterization implying political radicalism.[16]

Concurrent with the Perkins initiative, Pressman cobbled together additional work representing important New Deal figures and agencies. Within a few weeks of being bounced from the AAA, Pressman received a call from Roosevelt advisor Harry Hopkins, then director of the Federal Relief Emergency Administration (FERA), later to become the Works Progress Administration, or WPA. In their first meeting, the administrator told the lawyer exactly what role he expected him to play. "He called me over and asked me if I wanted to come into his show, and I said all right. But he said, 'I have only one instruction for you. You won't get instructions from me often. The first time you tell me that I can't do what I want to do, you're fired. I'm going to decide what I think has to be done and it's up to you to see to it that it's legal.'"[17]

This was the kind of work Pressman was made to do. He had only met Hopkins twice before, but quickly came to admire the official's forcefulness. "In a conference, he was very agile-minded, very swift and given to practically no folderol or hypocrisy. He would go straight to the heart of a problem" and refused to "tolerate any phony or irrelevant discussion . . . [or] excuses of why things couldn't be done because of administrative problems . . . person-nel[,] or somebody on the outside whom you had to deal with. He just didn't want to know when there were obstacles in your path." Hopkins "horrified anybody who dealt with customary government procedure," Pressman noted with approval. When Hopkins said he would put so many thousands of people to work, that was what would happen; when people had to be cut from the rolls, that was also what would happen. "All the administrators around him would weep and cry," and he would just tell them to stop and do it.[18]

Showing men in power how to get things done legally was of course a skill at which he excelled. Pressman set to work analyzing the budget request that would transform FERA into the WPA, laying out in detail just how other agencies and courts might interpret the legislative language. He suggested how the phrasing could be amended in ways that would most efficiently accomplish what Hopkins wished. Subsequently, he carried through the negotiations necessary to get the relief projects the FERA director wanted through the general accounting office. "Pressman was very smart and a clever operator, made for this kind of work, which was essentially political persuasion," reflected John Abt. Pressman had brought Abt—an "unpretentious, reserved, mild-spoken fellow, with terrific precision in his utterance"—in Gardner Jackson's characterization—into the WPA as assistant general counsel. Abt later charged that Pressman intentionally limited the former's access to important officials. "Though he was one of my closest friends," he wrote of his relationship with Pressman, "he was also a man of great ambition and a sense of competition, always protective of position and prerogative."[19]

By mid summer 1935, Pressman also became general counsel of Rexford Tugwell's Resettlement Administration (RA), splitting his time between FERA/WPA and the RA for the rest of year. The RA "was a hodgepodge," Pressman recalled. "Every conceivable thing that Tugwell had in mind, or Roosevelt had in mind came in the Resettlement Administration." It experimented with residential "greenbelt" projects, suburban areas ringed around cities to provide green space. It bought submarginal land and paid residents a sufficient price for it to get them to move to better, more productive land. It resettled sharecroppers from the south to Alaska and helped them establish cooperatives. Finally, it loaned sharecroppers money at low interest rates. He "never [had] had such manifold, diverse legal problems" to deal with, he recollected, "or tried to think through so many gimmicks to try to handle them."[20]

Though he continued to serve Hopkins and Tugwell part time until 1938, by late 1935 it had become clear to Lee Pressman that the New Deal was still the old deal. The firings confirmed a conclusion Pressman had been moving toward for some time. Writing to Tugwell in 1937, Pressman informed him that his AAA experience had stimulated much reflection. "The most interesting problem raised under the AAA is whether the regulatory device is possible where it comes in conflict with the major controlling financial interests." He indicated that the only time the agreements had worked was when the financial interests had been able to seize effective control of the code and manipulate it to enhance their power. "Rarely . . . [has] the regulatory body been able to exercise its discretion in such a fashion as to weaken control of those in power."[21]

This view coincided with author John Strachey's contemporary analysis of New Deal reformism under capitalism in *The Coming Struggle for Power*, first published in 1932 and republished in an American edition in early 1935. According to Jerome Frank, Strachey's popular and engaging Marxist polemic on capitalism's socially destructive economic dynamics influenced Pressman's thinking a great deal. Though Strachey focused largely on economic history and European developments, he provided his American readers with a commentary on the New Deal's reform efforts in an addendum to the American edition. Writing in April 1934, Strachey dissected the Roosevelt administration's reformist program, arguing that it had little chance of success, for it would be captured by the forces it intended to control, forces that were part of the move toward another world war. "For even if, as I believe it must, the New Deal 'fails,'" he wrote, "in the sense that it will never give to the vast majority of the American people tolerable conditions of life, it may well for a time at any rate, succeed in giving a very great deal to particular interests and persons." "The remorseless law of the concentration of capital is everywhere at work. It seizes the very policies, such as the New Deal, which were intended to remedy the devastation it had wrought, and makes use of them to accelerate its march." Pressman, having viewed this process intimately from inside the Agricultural Adjustment Administration, had come to the same conclusion, and felt he had been given an object lesson in the exercise of social power. A "very serious question arises as to whether regulation is possible at all because of this basic situation," he concluded. Unbeknownst to Tugwell, Frank, or Hopkins, the situation and the main problem, increasingly for him as it was for Strachey, had come to be capitalism itself.[22]

THE WARE GROUP YEARS

Sometime in the latter part of 1933 or very early 1934, Lee Pressman secretly joined the American Communist Party along with a number of his other AAA colleagues. In August 1948, *Time* magazine editor and former underground communist emissary to this group, Whittaker Chambers, became the first witness to disclose publicly the formation of this clandestine unit of New Deal government employees organized by Communist Party operative Harold Ware. Chambers charged that the purpose of the group, at the time he was associated with it, had been to shape government policy, if possible, along lines favorable to party's preferences. In addition, if the opportunity presented itself, the Party also hoped to place some of the brightest and most able of this group of New Dealers-turned-radicals into even more important government departments.[23]

But why did Lee Pressman join? Since that time, many pages have been written about the Ware Group and the individuals involved in it. Many thousands of pages more have been written by and about people who converted to American communism in its "heyday" during the 1930s and 1940s, both by those who stayed in the Party and by those who left. Ironically, in all of this avalanche of words, two of the most acute analyses of why many people came to the Party are those of Whittaker Chambers and Vivian Gornick, the first writing from the perspective of a bitter enemy, and the second from the perspective of a lover yearning for what has been lost. Both singled out the inner emotional life of the convert as the most common motivating factor. And each analysis has a resonance that helps shed light on the probable reasons Lee Pressman made such a fateful decision.

Despite having become embittered toward communism, Whittaker Chambers' autobiography *Witness*, first published in 1952, explores with serious reflection the psychological dimensions of why he, and in his judgment many others like him, converted. "How did it happen that this movement, once a mere muttering of political outcasts, became this immense force that now contests the mastery of mankind?" he asked in an imaginary open letter to his children. "Even when all the chances and mistakes of history are allowed for, the answer must be: Communism makes some profound appeal to the human mind." That appeal was the seductive faith of rationalism. "It challenges man to prove by his acts that he is the masterwork of Creation" by ending "the bloody meaninglessness of man's history—by giving it purpose and a plan" in order to achieve "order, abundance, security, [and] peace. . . ." It becomes in effect a secular religion. "An educated man peering from the Harvard Yard, or any college campus, upon a world in chaos, finds in the vision the two certainties for which the mind of man tirelessly seeks: a reason to live and a reason to die."[24]

It was for this reason, particularly among intellectuals with whom he was familiar, that communism had such a deep emotional tug, given the two cataclysms of the twentieth century, total war and economic crisis. While one or the other may be more important to a certain individual, both affected all converts deeply. And both belonged to the "greater crisis of history for which Communism offers a plausible explanation and [to] which it promises an end. When an intellectual joins the Communist Party," Chambers insisted, "he does so primarily because he sees no other way of ending the crisis of history. In effect, his act is an act of despair. . . ."[25]

Communists rarely joined the party for personal gain or sheer intellectualism. "I have met few Communists who were more than fiddlers with the dialectic," Chambers noted. "But I have never known a Communist who was not acutely aware of the crisis of history whose solution he found in Communism's practical program, its vision and faith." "Under the pressure of the crisis," Chambers observed, "his decision to become a Communist seems to the man who makes it as a choice between a world that is dying and a world that is coming to birth. . . ." Those who come to communism do so because they have an intense will to survive and no other answer seems possible. To Chambers, communism "offered me what nothing else in the dying world had power to offer at the same intensity—faith and a vision, something for which to live and something for which to die." "It demanded of me those things which have always stirred what is best in men—courage, poverty, self-sacrifice, discipline, intelligence, my life, and, at need, my death."[26]

Though Vivian Gornick did not explicitly identify those two social causes in her book, *The Romance of American Communism*, she similarly emphasized the emotional basis of the communist appeal, and how at certain historical points, particularly during the 1930s and 1940s, those appeals became increasingly convincing. She too agreed some of the roots of the communist connection resided in a sense of inner emptiness. Intellectuals, "[p]ossessed of talent, education, economic freedom," she wrote, "nevertheless experienced profound spiritual disconnection" during those years. "Marxism touched—and healed—that wound in the soul, and made them Communists." Passion to achieve reconnectedness and reintegration, she insisted, was "at the heart of the Communist experience. "There are, it seems to me, a number of stable hungers in the human psyche. . . ." One of these hungers, beyond question, is the need to live a life of meaning. The motive force is the dread fear that life is *without* meaning," she wrote, echoing Chambers. "This fear-hunger speaks to a need not of the flesh but of the spirit, a need having to do with the deepest definitions of what it is to be human."[27]

While parts of Gornick's analysis coincided with Chambers' on communism's attractiveness to intellectuals, she also commented on other themes of the communist conversion experience that had special relevance for Lee Pressman. Immigrants, especially Russian–Jewish immigrants, no matter how successful at apparently achieving upward social mobility, came from a culture possessed of a deep sense of not belonging—both in Russia and in the New World. "These people had no external nationhood; nothing in the cultures they had left, or the one to which they had come, that had given them anything but a humiliating sense of outsidedness," Gornick wrote. This climate of exclusion in turn stimulated a need to belong to something greater than oneself, to belong to a larger collectivity. "The more each acknowledged his or her condition as one of binding connectedness, the more each one pushed back the darkness and experienced the life within." Communism could bring that sense of "binding connectedness" as little else could in an age that had lost confidence in other faiths, other answers.[28]

Moreover, Jewish culture in New York City provided fertile soil for communism's appeals. First, that culture did not dismiss as alien conceptions of social revolution. "The idea of socialist revolution was a dominating strand woven through the rich tapestry of unassimilated Jewish life." Ideas about revolution "were as natural apart of the stream of being on the Lower East Side, and then later in Brooklyn and the Bronx, as were Orthodox Jews and Zionists. . . ." A second generation Jew might reject those ideas, or support them, or ignore them, "but he did not in the deepest part of himself disown them, or find them strange or alienating creatures. They were there, they were recognizable, they were *us*." Second, Jewish culture had forever stressed the moral need "to become." "This strain runs with subterranean force through most Jewish lives regardless of what other aspects of experience and personality separate them," according to Gornick. "Thus, Jews "'became' through an intensity of religious or intellectual or political life. In the highly political twentieth century they became, in overwhelming numbers, socialists, anarchists, Zionists—and Communists."

In combination, then, it is perhaps easier to understand how Lee Pressman could come to embrace communism. Writing about another Jewish communist lawyer she interviewed for her book, Gornick eloquently described his path to radicalism during the depression years in a way that must have been quite similar to Pressman's. The stock market crash began "a stunning descent from" the height of his pursuit of middle-class social mobility and "an uneasy sense of retribution began to permeate his being. . . . Slowly, the 'hedonism' that had taken hold of him began to evaporate and in its place there appeared an arid, wasted sense of things." This attorney began practicing law in New York City in the early 1930s—a time when Pressman himself began to experience increasing discomfort with the Chadbourne firm and intensified his interest in a socially meaningful career path. Gornick's interview subject saw "all around him stun and misery, all around him the sounds of a new language beginning to push against the internal silence he now lived intimately with. The language was Marxism. Bit by bit, the language overtook the waste, bit by bit the hungry mind and soul turned away from the passivity of depression and faced toward the activating renewal of fresh understanding." This must have been all too similar to the journey that Pressman himself began in New York and continued in Washington in the AAA. Thus, when CP organizer Harold Ware, who "floated" around the halls of the Agriculture Department, Pressman recalled, approached him, it gave practical form to those largely inchoate feelings.[29]

And so, Lee Pressman decided to accept, for reasons probably unknown even to himself, Harold Ware's invitation. Harold Ware had invited him to lunch, asked if he would like to join a communist group, and indicated that he was "to go to a meeting on a certain date." Pressman was one of the earlier recruits to the Ware Group, as his attendance predated John Abt's, and Abt dated his joining in June 1934. "Tall and lean, in his early forties, Ware appeared professorial," Abt wrote, "down to his wearing of pince-nez." Whittaker Chambers described "Hal" "as American as ham and eggs and nearly indistinguishable as everybody else. He stood about five feet nine, a trim, middle-aging man in 1934, with a plain face, masked by a quiet earnestness of expression. . . ." Ware habitually wore an "off-color brown suit of some heavy fabric, carefully pressed, and a brown fedora hat, carefully brushed. . . . He might have been a progressive county agent or a professor of ecology at an agricultural college."

He was, however, not that at all. Ware had a long lineage in the Communist Party—his mother was the legendary "grand old lady" of American communism, Ella Reeve "Mother" Bloor. After graduating from Penn State College of Forestry, he had farmed, but when the "Bolsheviks came to power in Russia, Hal began to raise money for the purchase of farm implements" for the new Soviet Union. He then spent the next decade trying to bring farm mechanization to the new socialist mecca. No less a personage than Lenin had "acknowledged that his work 'was more helpful than that of any other American'" to the Soviet cause, according to Abt. "I was to learn that Hal was shy and retiring before large audiences," he remembered, "but most effective and persuasive in small committees and living rooms with a flow of colorful talk and stories."[30]

According to Pressman, during his period of association with the Ware Group, it remained largely a Marxist study circle, reading and discussing communist literature provided by Harold Ware, and later his superior, Joszef Peters (during the Hiss case often simply called J. Peters, one of his many aliases). To the FBI, Pressman "described this group as one which would meet together to discuss problems and would analyze the usefulness of the AAA program in connection with the plight of the sharecroppers. The bulk of analysis consisted of criticisms of the defects in the policies of the AAA. . . ." At the outset, the group included himself, Witt, Kramer, Abt, and Ware, Pressman claimed, but not Hiss, whom he said may have left before he joined. They would usually hold their meetings by rotating to each other's homes. Ware distributed literature, instructed them to read the party's newspaper the *Daily Worker*, and then the group would discuss issues of ideological importance to all good communists. Pressman further indicated that Ware "used to ask if in connection with their employment with the AAA there was anything of importance that would be of value to the Communist Party." Pressman said he told him "nothing that was not already known by the public." Ware, however, "used to insist that there must be something of importance that was not being disclosed to the public." Ware would then collect the tithe-level party dues as evidence of their commitment to its mission.

John Abt confirmed Pressman's characterization of the work of the Ware Group. Occasionally, someone in the group would write a memo for Harold Ware if "there were developments we thought were particularly interesting or important." That information, he surmised, was then "passed . . . on to the national [party] leadership in New York for its consideration in estimating the direction of the New Deal and what might be done to influence it." He denounced the charges that the Ware Group as "having been engaged in espionage," though. "That we met privately and that we did not openly reveal our membership was used to portray us as a conspiratorial group engaged in disreputable and treacherous practices," a fact that was untrue. "As it developed it had no sinister aspects to it—espionage and all that—God knows what kind of espionage could be taking place in the AAA," Pressman informed Daniel Bell.[31]

Still, as early as 1950, a fuller portrayal emerged about the activities and personalities in the Ware Group, one which, while not explicitly disputing Pressman and Abt's characterizations on any specific assertion, tended to buttress Chambers' portrait. In *Witness*, the former journalist and underground communist emissary recounted how upon his arrival in Washington in mid-1934 Ware and Peters had spoken to him of the personalities in the group, including Alger Hiss. The party had "separated" Hiss from the group because of his transfer from the AAA to head the Senate's Nye Committee investigation into war munitions profiteering—a post of critical importance for an underground communist. After briefly meeting Hiss in Ware's and Peters's presence, Chambers claimed that that evening Ware took him to his sister's violin studio on Connecticut Avenue, adjacent to Dupont Circle, to spend the night. The violin studio became one meeting place for the group.[32]

Chambers identified an additional gathering spot—the St. Matthews Court apartment of Henry Collins Jr., also a leading member. In addition to Pressman, Collins, Abt, Witt, and Kramer, the underground party operative named Collins' National Recovery Administration associate, Victor Perlo, as part of the group, and of course Hiss, prior to his separation. Each of these leaders, Chambers believed, also developed parallel groups of their own, each with twelve to fifteen adherents of government employees. "St. Matthews Court was the only place in Washington with a touch of Greenwich Village," Chambers wrote. "It was a mews that lay between M and N Streets, just off of Connecticut Avenue. The court was flanked by two- or three-story brick houses with window boxes and gay shutters. . . ." It was, to Chambers, "a little too conspicuously picturesque for an ideal underground headquarters." Collins' second-floor quarters "was a big, sprawling, attractive apartment. The entrance . . . led into a small hall. To the left was a big living room," or rather "two rooms, shaped roughly like a reverse L. . . . Collins was all that Princeton and Harvard can do for a personable and intelligent young American of good family," Chambers wrote. "To some, he seemed a little chilly and diffident." "But he was persistent, very tenacious and held at least his political convictions, with a fierce faith," he judged.[33]

The Ware Group, while "not primarily a Marxist study group," did not focus on espionage, according to Chambers, though some members later participated in such activities. "Its functions, if less sensational, were scarcely less important." It recruited communists into the underground and assisted placing them in government agencies. "The real power of the Group . . . was a power to influence, from the most strategic positions, the policies of the United States Government," he claimed, "especially in the labor and welfare fields." Under Ware's leadership, prior to his death in a car accident in August 1935, the group eventually came to be "a tightly organized underground, managed by a directory of seven men. In time," Chambers asserted, "it included a number of secret sub-cells whose total membership" must have included lose to seventy-five people. Lee Pressman was a part of that leading directorate.[34]

In later years, two other members of the Ware Group, Hope Hale Davis and Nathaniel Weyl, both of whom abandoned the communist cause, provided additional support for Chambers' account. Neither of them, though, ever met the journalist. Weyl's FBI account insisted that when he had joined the group in its earliest stages, Alger Hiss was among its members. He had been actively in left-wing politics at Columbia, and after he came to Washington to work in the AAA in June 1933 he "was contacted by an individual, subsequently known to him as Harold Ware," Weyl's FBI report noted. Ware informed him that he knew of his communist background and that an underground group had formed in Washington and that he was to join the group. From his first association with the group, Lee Pressman, Alger Hiss, John Abt, Nathan Witt, Henry Collins, John Donovan, and Victor Perlo were there, with Charles Kramer joining shortly after Weyl. He "stated it appeared to him that this underground group, with the exception of Charles Kramer, had been organized prior to the time Weyl joined, although he stated it was conceivable that he had attended its first organized meeting." Prior to his departure from Washington in mid-summer 1934, he "estimated he attended fifteen or twenty" weekly meetings of the group, all held in the violin studio of Ware's sister. He claimed that "Lee Pressman was present at about ninety percent of the meetings he attended, and that he has a fairly clear recollection of Alger Hiss and Lee Pressman being present together at some of these meetings," the FBI statement continued.

Weyl then went on the characterize his perceptions of the personal qualities of various members of the Ware Group: the hard-drinking old-time labor radical Donovan, a founder of government unionism at the National Recovery Administration, who later went to work for the labor movement; the moody, difficult, and somewhat neurotic but logical Kramer; the elitist Collins; the enthusiastic, "good-looking, mild mannered rational" Perlo; the "very hard and bitter" Nathan Witt, who was the "caricature of a radical"; the "quiet and intelligent" Abt; the "well informed and very sure of himself" aristocrat Alger Hiss; and, of course, Pressman, who "was a convivial type and at least superficially had a great deal of warmth for his friends." He thought Pressman had been a sincere Communist but not nearly so devoted" as Hiss, the FBI statement indicated. Weyl had no memory of meetings at Collins's apartment, nor of any associations with Chambers or Peters, as their connections occurred after he left Washington in mid-1934.[35]

In 1980, another former member of the Ware Group, author Hope Hale

Davis, recounted her associations with the Ware Group in an autobiographical article written for the *New Leader*. She later wrote a full-length memoir, *Great Day Coming*, of her years as a communist, to come to grips with the reasons she had joined the cause. These two writings render a firsthand portrait of the nature of the meetings themselves and the internal workings of the Ware Group. Davis participated in the group from 1934 through 1937, when she left to move to New York. Indeed, in her *New Leader* piece, she described a meeting of "15 comrades" at what she believed was the Pressman residence in 1935, of which about six were leaders of units. . . . The rest of us made up a sort of semi-social elite, privileged to be in on any exciting event. . . ." "Attending weekly unit meetings was a comrade's first duty," Davis wrote. "After a day of the frantic activity then going on in all New Deal offices, it could become a long, toilsome evening. Part of the time was spent in discussion of our current job situations with advice on strategy of whether to try to influence policy or simply to achieve promotion—a primary goal," she remembered. "We were all encouraged to maintain an outwardly conventional bourgeois household and help ease our way upward by entertaining the right people, the more conservative the better."

"Next on the meeting agenda was a survey of world news, with an analysis by one comrade of a specific event. Listening to these earnest, laborious reports, I tried not be reminded of Christian Endeavor meetings, but the similarity was inescapable," she wrote with irony. "I can see Victor Perlo now, young and ardent, drawing a map of China on a child's blackboard with a different color of chalk for each province as he traced the route of the Long March being led by Chu Teh, Chou En-lai and Mao Tse-tung. We all tried to become as sure of the location of the Huang Ho and the Hang-shui as of the Mississippi and the Hudson." Finally, Davis reminisced that the evenings closed with the sale of communist literature and dues collection. "Any secret directives—for purloining official documents, making contacts with Party operatives elsewhere, or the like—were given to individual comrades after the general meeting broke up." She knew such directives occurred because they were given to her husband Karl, and to herself at various points.[36]

Thus it appeared that at least some times Ware Group members surreptitiously gathered documentary information for the Party, although not all of them did so and perhaps some were unaware of the requests given to others. It is hard to avoid observing that this type of activity represented a level of commitment beyond that typically found in a literary society. The Party had come to represent for most of these people their way to affect the world positively, to make the wrongs right. Like Davis, all of them fought against "a nagging awareness of the false values I was using my talents to sell" in their professional lives in the middle-class world. "And most of the world, it seemed, was hungry and out of work. All I was doing about that," Davis

remembered, "was buying an apple each morning from the unemployed architect who waited at the entrance of my building. Meanwhile miles of makeshift
shacks . . . [and] slums, [were] festering with crime, disease and racial injustices. So many problems! What could one person do? Where would you
start?" The answer for the members of the Ware Group was to join the communist cause. Better yet, join it in an *underground* fashion—and even purloin
unclassified though unauthorized government documents for it—for that
added an intensity and a sense of danger to the experience, and helped quiet
their sense of collective helplessness.[37]

Finally, we should consider Pressman's least-guarded declarations
about his reasons for joining the CP and the Ware Group. Years later, in 1956,
in an oral history with political sociologist Daniel Bell, then working on a
study of American communism, Pressman struggled to come to terms with his
decision and its underlying dynamic. The emotional complexity of the communist appeal—highlighted by both Chambers and Gornick—resulted in near
inarticulateness. Even when removed from the direct threat of red-baiting and
direct personal danger, Pressman's notoriously precise legal mind became
notably imprecise in illuminating the underlying causes of what came to be a
seventeen-year political commitment of some depth.

Bell asked him why communism had attracted him. "I've never been
able to frame that answer for myself," he replied. Some press reports "refer to
the fact that I was concerned about Hitler, and the depression. I can't talk
about the depression," he noted, "because I never felt it in any real sense."
Becoming affiliated with either the Socialist or Communist parties did not
"assume the sense of importance that it" did in the 1950s, he pointed out. "As
for me, I don't think that up til [sic] that moment I had any political contacts."
He agreed with Bell that "[c]ertainly for almost anyone joining one or the
other[,] it would be an important event," but did not know whether Bell could
"appreciate someone for whom it assumed no such importance. You might
even say it was on the level, for me, at least, of joining a literary group—say,
a Mark Twain Society."

Joining an *underground* communist group, even in 1933, was hardly on
the level of becoming involved with the Mark Twain Society, though. Inter-
spersed with his rambling comments in response to Bell's question, Pressman
eventually touched on at least a part of the ideology's seductiveness. "I'll
make this observation," he said to Bell, "how many people were there [in
Washington] at that time that were getting any information whatsoever about
what was happening in China. You wouldn't find it in the *New York Times*,"
he pointed out.

> You know it does something to someone when you're about that age
> and someone gives you something to read about events happening in

China—on the Yangtse [sic]—of the social and political unrest—the plans to overthrow Chiang Kai Shek—that you knew nothing about before—inside information of world shaking events—it's fascinating. You're in with somebody who tells you what's going on. . . . And they [the Communist Party] were working . . . with groups in Iowa and Minnesota and Nebraska in connection with the stopping of foreclosures of mortgages and things of that sort, as I say, if you were given literature by a group that tells you about activities [that] are going on—of a stirring kind—it is conceivable that you continue going to meetings, discussing these very problems.

Therefore, according to Pressman, the allure of "stirring" emotional appeals to action pulled him toward the Party, not the logic and rational argument that formed so much a part of his life as a lawyer, nor the precise intellectual arguments of *Das Kapital*. "I am not one steeped in the classics of Marxism. Frankly, I've never read a book by Karl Marx," Pressman proclaimed. Clearly, then, whether he realized it or not, it had been the emotional dimension that had bonded him to the communist cause. Indeed, despite his cold, cynical, and superior demeanor at times, the lawyer "had very very deep feelings although he said very little about them in words," according to his daughter Ann Pressman. His middle daughter, Marcia Pressman, agreed; he was and remained for all of his life, "very uncomfortable about acknowledging his own feelings" or those of others. Even so, he "was very passionate in his feelings," she believed, despite his struggle to control and articulate them. For that reason, perhaps, the Ware Group could be nothing more important to him than "a literary society" with whom he had a type of social flirtation. Somehow, somewhere inside him, though, Lee Pressman felt a passionate and intense desire to rectify the injustices of the world, perhaps arising subconsciously as a result of the humiliations of childhood polio, suffering through episodes of ethnic exclusion, or both. Communism provided him with an answer as to how things became wrong and with a vision of how to make the world right again, of how to achieve social justice. "What I remember most deeply about the Communists is their passion," Vivian Gornick wrote. "It was passion that converted them, passion that held them, [and] passion that lifted them up. . . ." Thus had Lee Pressman come to accept the Communist cause.[38]

PRESSMAN'S RETURN TO NEW YORK

Through 1935, ideologically transformed but professionally at large, Lee Pressman still faced the problems of how best to earn a living after his separation from the AAA. "I haven't heard anything the Labor matter," he wrote in reference to his Perkins initiative in a personal letter to Gardner Jackson while vacationing in Miami with his wife Sunny and young daughter Ann, who had been born in 1934. Consequently, he was "quite convinced that it is a closed matter." From press reports it appeared that the Resettlement Administration had budget difficulties, and this "has convinced me that an early departure from there would be in order," and not only because of money. The "Resettlement Administration in its present state is a shrieking disgrace," bogged down in "appalling confusion and worse," due to administrative incompetence. Therefore, now seemed a good time to leave. "In considering where best I can be *useful*, it seems to me that" legal work with some AFL national union or a NLRB-related job would be attractive. "Could you do something in that connection?" he asked. But, "I think the foregoing is more than enough of my problems," he wrote. "For yourself, Pat, I have a feeling that you have cleared any [and] all obstacles in the path of the determination of *what* should be done" to help the sharecroppers Jackson currently advised. "In my opinion, your efforts in connection with the sharecroppers have been invaluable," he told his former AAA colleague, with whom by now he had obviously struck up a personal friendship. "The only person I have sought out and spent many hours with is Lee Pressman," Jackson wrote to Felix Frankfurter in late October 1935. Pressman "stands the test of all Dode's and my standards better than any other individuals with whom we have been thrown in the New Deal," he enthused. "His mind, his heart and his self-control make a combination to which we are devoted." Early in their AAA association, Jackson later recalled, Pressman "made overtures very openly to me" that we "would make a wonderful combination. He even went to the extreme of saying that my flat face and blue eyes were in contrast to his aquiline Jewish face," Jackson recalled years later, "and that that, even on the surface, [we] would make a fine combination to function around together. . . ." Pressman admitted to the close relationship, though later the two had a falling out. The journalist seemed to him like "when you put a piece of sodium on water, and it scoots all around. That's Pat Jackson. He's like a flea on a hot stove. Give him a compelling motive for doing some social good, and he'll be up there on a hot stove doing social good. But," Pressman continued, "he can create more issues at different spots which require some alleviation than any good being done. . . . For some strange reason he gravitated toward me, and thought of me as a person—I gather—who was more stable than he was and a little more calm than he was. We maintained a very close relationship, and I became very fond of him, became very friendly" on a social basis.[39]

By late 1935, Pressman had fully resolved to return with his young family to New York City and practice law privately. Shortly before he did, at a turbulent American Federation of Labor (AFL) convention in Atlantic City, an angry, hulking, man leapt "over a row of chairs . . . [and] jabbed out his right fist" at Carpenters' Union President William Hutcheson, himself equally hulking, bloodying him and sending the latter "sprawling against a table," wrote astonished news reporters. The attacker was United Mine Workers of America (UMWA) President John L. Lewis, an industrial union champion, whom Hutcheson had just called a bastard for his defense of the rights of the incipient industrial unions delegates from the auto and rubber industries. After thus "informing" Hutcheson that he had taken great offense, labor journalist Edward Levinson described how "Lewis casually adjusted his tie and collar, relit his cigar, and sauntered slowly through the crowded aisles to the rostrum. . . ."

In AFL councils, Lewis had been the foremost promoter of organizing the unskilled workers in mass production. The labor federation's craft-oriented approach had failed over and over with these semiskilled and unskilled industrial workers. Still, because of depression-fostered pay cuts and seeming government support for collective representation, these workers had feverishly appealed to national unions for help in organizing for self-defense. Once more, the federation would only support plans that parceled them out, once unionized, into one of many of the older craft unions. The nascent industrial unionists realized the only hope of successfully establishing collective bargaining with huge corporations such as General Motors was to organize on an industrywide basis, and had come to the convention to fight for such a plan. As Lewis biographers Melvyn Dubofsky and Warren Van Tine note, the Lewes–Hutcheson altercation produced political theater on a grand scale. It symbolized Lewis's decision to break forcefully with the federation, if necessary, and lead an independent effort to organize these millions of restive industrial workers. The fight grabbed headlines, and three weeks later, in November 1935, Lewis and a few other similarly minded union leaders announced the creation of the Committee for Industrial Organizations, originally intended to operate as a caucus within the AFL that would work to foster industrial unionization.

Although busy with the details of relocation to New York, Lewis's dramatic punch and subsequent initiatives drew the attention of Lee Pressman. As he expressed to Frances Perkins, he truly did believe that the labor movement's course of development promised to be the motive force behind a good deal of America's future. "[B]y God, that's the kind of situation you ought to be in on," he later recalled saying to himself. Observing Lewis's initial actions from afar, he started to look for ways to connect with the CIO leader. He turned to Lewis confidante Josephine Roche, who had arranged the Perkins interview. Although he did not know it at the time, in a little over a year he would be at Lewis's side in historic negotiations that would at long last establish the first successful industrial union movement in the United States.[40]

THREE

HAMMER AND STEEL

L ee Pressman, his younger brother Irving recalled, had always been moved to do something "economically . . . for the benefit of the country and everyone else." While he had thought he might be able to inaugurate true reform as part of the New Deal, the quick massing of conservative forces changed his mind, as did his growing intimacy with communism's insistence on the impossibility of meaningful reform coming from within. This meant that pressure would have to emanate from outside the bureaucracy of the state. Surveying the political landscape of late 1935, most observers would have agreed that the increasing demands of nonunion industrial workers for collective bargaining was, in effect, the most realistic opportunity for developing that outside pressure.

While Lee Pressman may have not waded through the volumes of *Das Kapital*, in Ware Group discussions he surely learned the historic role that Marx and Lenin assigned to workers and workers' organizations in bringing about revolutionary social change—and also of the importance of the guiding vanguard of intellectuals of which he was a part. Pressman correctly judged that the legal apparatus of the growing New Deal state would critically affect what the leaders of this new industrial union movement would be able to achieve. And, in his three years of government service, Lee Pressman had become an expert, albeit a frustrated one, on how outside political pressures shaped the government's policy decisions. Now he would become part of those outside forces, he would become "useful" to Lewis, as he had to his former employers. He would harness his considerable executive abilities and organizational talents in a dual pursuit of justice; publicly, as John L. Lewis's *consigliere*, and clandestinely, as an adherent of the CP within the high councils of the industrial union movement. Soon, the whirlwind that was the CIO would sweep over the U.S. industrial landscape and the results of the clash of labor and capital would be profound for the modern American state. And during these years, to use journalist Murray Kempton's eloquent phrase, the news was filled with the "imagery of combat between armies which give and ask no quarter, a war whose resolution is unforgiving violence[,] and in which John Lewis was a great hammer and Lee Pressman a piece of steel."[1]

INTO THE CIO

Upon his return to New York, Pressman angled for a Lewis introduction with Josephine Roche, whom he had met while working for the Resettlement Administration. He knew that she had been a Lewis confidante for years, and told her that "he would love to meet Mr. Lewis because there might be a possibility of my getting into this new labor movement." At first she appeared reluctant, but because of her evident fondness for him, she said she would see what she could do. In February 1936, not long after he had returned to New York City, Pressman received a call from Roche indicating that Lewis would meet him.[2]

"We met for lunch," Pressman later remembered, "which lasted about an hour or two and I suppose he was just sizing me up. . . . " "I was sort of an aggressive person," he said in an understatement, "and told him I was very anxious to get into the labor movement." In particular, Lewis's initiation of the CIO intrigued him. "It looked like it had tremendous possibilities" he said to the UMWA president. Lewis, Pressman reminisced, did not say much, but mentioned he would keep him in mind in case anything turned up. Two or three casual luncheons in New York followed this initial meeting, in which Pressman elaborated on how his services could be of assistance.[3]

The ambitious attorney impressed the older man, in various ways probably reminding him of himself. According to Pressman's later CIO associate Harold Ruttenberg, the lawyer and the union leader "were two peas out of the same pod. They both were cold blooded, analytical and could separate their personal emotions and themselves from decisions involving other individuals, other human beings, and Lewis would have liked him from day one." Soon their relationship would ripen into a personal friendship, with Lewis maintaining sincere regard for Pressman's strategic acumen and operational ability, and Pressman becoming more and more fascinated with Lewis's innate sense of the use of power and the almost overwhelming dominance of his personality. "He once explained to me that in all these conflicts with employers, government and otherwise," Pressman admiringly said of Lewis at one point.

He "had a very simple policy—create a crisis—and then proceed on the assumption that the other man's nerve will break first. And he said, 'You can't lose.'"[4]

In March 1936, with growing impatience, Pressman wrote to Lewis volunteering to prepare legal memoranda on the injunction aspects of the Goodyear Rubber strike then in progress, one of the first CIO-related engagements. "In connection with the organization work to be done in the mass production industries, mass picketing in strikes will probably be of vital importance," Pressmad pointed out, though few legal cases had heretofore dealt specifically with the legal issues surrounding mass picketing. Therefore, he believed that "the wide sweeping injunction granted by the Court in connection with the . . . strike may have far reaching importance as a legal precedent," having an impact and "considerable significance on all future mass organization work. I should be glad to prepare some legal material on this problem," he offered, "if this could be of some use to those persons who are conducting the appeal . . . or if such material would be of value . . . to the Committee for Industrial Organization. . . . " Pressman's letter reflected his typical influence technique; he strove very quickly to become "useful" to a potential mentor, divining what he would soon find a need for and then putting into operation the necessary developments to fill that need. At about this time, Pressman came at Lewis from another direction. Learning of Lewis's longtime policy reliance on economic consu tant W. Jett Lauck, he wrote the latter trying to arrange a meeting, hoping to press his case through another route. Finally, John L. Lewis recontacted Pressman and arranged for him, in the company of Lauck, to meet with John Brophy, a former UMWA associate of Lewis's whom he hired to be the CIO's administrative director.[5]

"'John, there's a young attorney I'm going to send over to you one of these days,'" Brophy recalled Lewis's statement years later. "'I want you to look him over and let me know what you think of him.'" Several days afterward Lauck arrived with Pressman in tow at the CIO's first office in the Rust building in Washington, D.C., and introduced Brophy to the attorney. After some preliminary discussions about the organizing directions of the new CIO, Pressman moved swiftly to make his case that the leaders of the nascent industrial union drive had to have sound legal advice on tap at all times. He "moved into a very extended discussion of the future of the C.I.O and the need for specialized assistance," Brophy told an interviewer, "such as an attorney could give, with his training and experience. I listened for a while and then raised doubts as to the utility of all this." Brophy thought the job at the moment was primarily promotional, a job of generating publicity to attract workers, currently being well performed by the dramatic John L. Lewis, whose speeches and public letters denouncing the do-nothing executive council of the AFL created drama and excitement. Pressman countered that he saw "many places where legal paper work can be of advantage" and they continued for several hours debating whether or not there would be a need for the work of outside professionals such as himself. Brophy, a short, slight Irishman with a ruddy face and a nervous laugh, thought that the only time labor leaders needed a lawyer was when those leaders got into trouble with the law or into a controversy with an employer that dragged them into the courts. "But otherwise, no. We did our own negotiating. We did our own publicity. We did our own organizing. Still, Lee Pressman "was very insistent that I would find out that as we moved into this situation, there would be increasing need for technically equipped people." Brophy believed that when the CIO got to that point, those types of people could be engaged ad hoc, if necessary. Lauck, for the most part, listened intently to the debate, presumably reporting the gist of it to Lewis.[6]

Brophy maintatned that he believed the experience subconsciously "built up a certain amount of resistance . . . because I felt I was being pressured" to agree to the hiring of Pressman, although clearly that determination would come from Lewis. "Lee was too persistent a salesman," he reflected. "I didn't like it." As he later commented in his published memoir, *A Miner's Life*, Brophy had come quickly to resent Pressman's "manner of lecturing me for my own good." Nevertheless, Lewis inquired as to the results of the interview several days later. Brophy reiterated the same points he had made to Pressman. The mine workers' president, however, was perhaps more interested in the lawyer's personality and street smarts than in his legal scholarship. "Well," Lewis persisted, ignoring Brophy's arguments about when and where a labor leader might need an attorney on hand, "what do you think of him?" "'He's very persistent,' I said. 'Lot of drive and persistence there,'" although he had no way to tell about his legal abilities, he told Lewis. Lewis evidently agreed, and tried to assist Pressman in making connections with incipient industrial unions.

In May 1936 he recommended Pressman's legal services to James Carey, president of the newly minted international union, the United Electrical and Radio Workers (UE), which emerged out of a number of directly affiliated "federal" local unions the AFL had chartered in the turbulent 1934–1935 period of labor unrest. At this point, the CIO still existed as an internal AFL committee; thus, unions such as the UE started as AFL unions and later moved into the CIO when it became a freestanding labor federation. "You may recall my conversation with you at the [Heywood] Broun dinner," Lewis remarked, "when I said I was anxious for you to meet Mr. Lee Pressman . . ." who "is in every way an attorney of ability and promise, with a fine liberal outlook. It is my opinion that your organization could do no better than to have him become associated with you as counsel. I doubt that Mr. Pressman is materially interested in the question of financial retainers," Lewis thought. "He is rather imbued with a sincere desire to make a contribution to the cause which you represent." Carey remembered the uncharacteristically "flowery" letter years later, though the recommendation came to naught. Shortly afterward, Lewis apparently decided to secure Pressman's services himself.[7]

Pressman's own accounts of his hiring do not mention the Brophy interview and date his first formal invowvement with the CIO, after several meetings with Lewis, to mid June 1936. He received a call from Lewis, he said, asking him if he would like to become general counsel for the soon-to-be-created Steel Workers Organizing Committee (SWOC), the first formal CIO-directed organizing effort in a mass-production industry. "I'd like it very much," Pressman responded. Lewis directed him to appear the next day in the Commonwealth building in Pittsburgh and meet with Philip Murray, a vice president of the United Mine Workers and Lewis's most trusted lieutenant. Lewis had tapped Murray to take over the direction of CIO organizing in the largely nonunion steel industry.

Pressman boarded a train early the next day and dutifully arrived on schedule. The lawyer introduced himself to Murray, who informed Pressman that the first order of business would be a meeting with officials from the Amalgamated Association of Iron, Steel, and Tin Workers (AA). This was the AFL union that held formal trade union "jurisdiction," or territorial control, over the industry, due to its AFL charter. Lewis wished to gain the agreement of the AA to cede that jurisdiction over to the SWOC and the CIO, the latter of which at this time was still formally within the AFL, but operating independently. This was important to Lewis, for he had to hold the support of the other union presidents, such as David Dubinsky of the International Ladies Garment Workers Union (ILGWU), who might assist him in industrial organizing but who had no interest in leaving the AFL.

Murray instructed Pressman to draft a formal agreement between the AA and the SWOC clarifying the agreement previously reached with AA officials. That agreement gave the SWOC organizing rights to unskilled workers in the steel industry in exchange for Lewis's promise of a $500,000 grant to the AA for organizational purposes. "I drafted an agreement there that day between that committee and the Amalgamated Association that would authorize the committee to organize the Steel Workers to set up their own locals," Pressman remembered, "and someplace down the road, the locals chartered by SWOC would work out some arrangement" with the AA. Immediately afterward, Pressman firmed up his hiring arrangements with Lewis. The UMWA president told him that he had "checked him over" in regard to his legal skills and had received good recommendations. He would be general counsel of SWOC on a part-time retainer, plus expenses. "And," Pressman simply recalled, "I was in business."[8]

THE LEWIS–PRESSMAN RELATIONSHIP AND THE EARLY CIO

Until the eruption of the Great Flint Sit-Down Strike in late December 1936, Pressman's initial activities with the CIO predominantly involved the SWOC organizing campaign. The SWOC members and staff included David McDonald, Murray's UMWA assistant since 1923, who became secretary–treasurer of SWOC; Van Bittner, also a hard-bitten UMWA official, who became SWOC Western director, based in Chicago; Clinton Golden, a former Brookwood Labor School instructor, Amalgamated Clothing Workers organizer, and NLRB regional director, who became Eastern director of SWOC, based in Pittsburgh; and finally, William Mitch, still another UMWA officer, who became SWOC Southern director, based in Alabama. Joining Pressman as part of the SWOC "brains trust" of professionals were Vince Sweeney, former labor reporter for the *Pittsburgh Press* and soon-to-become editor of *Steel Labor*, as publicity director, and Harold Ruttenberg, a college-educated intellectual-activist, who had been deeply involved in the militant Rank-and-File Movement within the Amalgamated Association in the steel industry during the period 1934–1935, as research director.[9]

The committee faced considerable problems. Ever since Andrew Carnegie's general manager Henry Clay Frick defeated the Amalgamated Association at the historic Homestead Steel Strike in 1892, unionization had been nearly extinct in the U.S. steel industry (though not in the related iron industry). The World War I years proved to be an exception, when the first National War Labor Board, needing uninterrupted war production, established a typl of collective bargaining representation. That anomaly disappeared in 1919, when organized labor tried to institutionalize the war gains by sponsoring an organizing drive among the hundreds of thousands of immigrant steelworkers now dominating employment in the industry. Despite a massive recognition strike, the AFL's attempt collapsed in the face of unrelenting corporate hostility and state-sponsored political repression. Once again, the industry reverted to unchallenged management domination over employment policies. In the prospersus 1920s, the steel companies practiced an effective form of welfare capitalism—the payment of high wages and the provision of other types of benefits—that continued to dampen union sentiment.

After 1929, however, the Great Depression eroded the high profits necessary for an effective practice of welfare capitalism, as wages and employment declined precipitously over the next five years. The 1932 election of Franklin Roosevelt, and more importantly—the passage of FDR's National Industrial Recovery Act's (NIRA) section 7, providing state support for the principle that workers had the right to choose collective representatives without management interference, touched off pockets of unionization drives all over the country. Rising union militancy within the steel industry was propelled by the insistence of the AA's Rank-and-File Movement, begun in 1934 and tethered to local organizations of the old AA. At the same time, companies expanded their establishment of company-oriented employees' associations, or Employee Representation Plans (ERPs), to stave off further agitation for an independent voice mechanism. By 1936, though, ERPs were, in many places, themselves becoming restive, with ERP leaders increasingly confronting their smployers with member grievances.[10]

Thus, even though the Rank-and-File Movement and escalating independence of the ERPs gave hope to SWOC's founders, they faced a daunting history of defeat and disappointment in this most basic of American industries. If the fortress of mighty steel could not be scaled, there was little hope that a lasting industrial union movement would ever take root in American soil. "The problem immediately facing us," Philip Murray said at an early CIO meeting in November 1936, was

[h]ow to overcome the traditions of a half century of successful resistance on the part of the owners of the industry to Unionism; how to create in the minds of the workers confidence in the members of our staff; how to get them to understand that every possible effort would be made to protect them in their jobs, safeguard the fact that they would become enrolled as Union members from the knowledge of the bosses so as to prevent probable reprisals in the form of discharges and subsequent blacklisting; how to neutralize and overcome the atmosphere of suspicion, fear and terrorism that has hung over the industry almost continuously since its inception more than half a century ago.

"So," Lee Pressman simply said, "we set out to organize," starting in late summer and continuing through the fall.

And from the start, Lee Pressman exercised organizational influence. Early 1936 CIO executive board minutes reflect little direct commentary by Pressman, other than to request the board members to forward him the names of trusted local attorneys in various regions whom he could contact, if needed, about local problems. Yet Pressman was shrewd. "He had all the street smarts that eventually I developed," recalled his colleague Harold Ruttenberg. The "role that Pressman played . . . was very significant because he was aggressive, assertive and very vocal," but only in a suitable manner, even in the founding meeting. "Lee Pressman was a pro, and I learned from him, that you can say anything you damn well want to [to a labor leader] . . . one on one, with nobody around." Typically Pressman would wait until the meeting adjourned, and then he buttonholed either Lewis or Murray in a corner. In the early CIO years, Lee Pressman's "relationship was more that of a lawyer for Lewis, a lawyer for Murray, than it was as the head of the legal department" of the CIO, thought James Carey, who not long afterward became secretary–treasurer of the organization. "That came later." As Pressman himself later put it, his job with this new labor movement was broad scale. In "all the years I was with Lewis or with Murray—I don't think I ever got a specific instruction." "I had an extraordinary relationship—both with Lewis and with Murray. And I was never confined, that is, not what you'd call restricted[,] to the legal end. . . ."[11]

Indeed, John Brophy also agreed with that assessment. "Pressman was an able, energetic, [and] very adroit person," he pointed out, "and . . . he went all out to make himself very useful to Lewis. He didn't confine himself to legal questions," according to the SWOC director. "[I]n fact, I think he did a minimum of that. His interest was organizational, and administrative on the highest levels—that is, in the formulating of papers and policies. . . ." "Lee was a cool[,] deliberate operator, who knew precisely what he was doing, who had an eye for the main chance," Brophy judged. "He acted almost as the grand vizier. . . . There's one thing sure, he knew where power resided very quickly, and he devoted himself to that and serviced Lewis . . . faithfully and well, for Lewis's ends." Within a year "it became evident that he had the complete favor of the big boss. . . . "The relations were very, very intimate—very, very personal—between Lee and John L." "Lee was willing to do all the leg work and arrange things . . . to do a lot of the detail work if necessary, so that Lewis began to depend on him very much for . . . specialized work." Consequently, Lewis's old UMWA political opponent believed, "[t]here was an acceptance of Pressman—as the fellow who had the ear of the big boss," Lewis, within the CIO staff, and who thus operated as "more than being a lawyer, more than being a negotiator" for the new labor movement.[12]

What Lee Pressman experienced over the next four years with John L. Lewis as chief of the CIO affected him profoundly. As a personality, of course, the UMWA president was in many ways larger than life, and his magnetic leadership of the industrial union movement became the perfect match of person, place, and time. He had the capability to quote Shakespeare and the Bible with equal facility; his hulking frame and overgrown beetle-browed eyebrows often scowled opponents into submission and, if his hypnotic glare failed, very few could match the withering epithets he hurled at adversaries, corporate and political. Certainly in those years no one in the labor movement equaled his ability to mobilize unionists' organizing energies on such a grand scale.

So, understandably, Lewis's persona fascinated many. But for Lee Pressman, that fascination ran deeper than most, intrigued him, filled him with admiration, filled him with pride at being associated with labor. Lewis's willingness to confront, to engage, to battle his enemies in a righteous cause, stirred similar feelings in the young attorney. At just thirty years old he had moved into an important leadership position in what apparently had the capability of becoming a broad social movement of the American working class. That movement, if it succeeded, would encompass within its realm not only the economic unionization of the mass-production industries but political mobilization. Pressman observed this human dynamo with awe, even reverence, as Lewis strode through the American industrial–political landscape in the late 1930s, seemingly knocking aside all opponents.

In fact, Lee Pressman psychologically responded to John L. Lewis in a way not unlike that of Chicago social activist and community organizer Saul Alinsky, a friendly Lewis biographer and one of the few people who ostensibly maintained a close personal friendship with Lewis. Interestingly, the early family life of Alinsky and Pressman had intriguing parallels. Both, for example, had unforceful men as fathers. Alinksy's father—a Russian–Jewish immigrant who ran a tailor shop and achieved modest financial success, not unlike Harry Pressman—"appears to have been a withdrawn, passive man," according to Alinsky biographer Sanford Horwitt. He was also a man who never could seem to fit into the wider community beyond his business activities. And Alinsky's mother, Sarah, was "a survivor . . . demanding, self-centered, and manipulative. Her coarse energy and drive were expressed in an Old World Yiddish style"; she was the archetypical Jewish mother "who took no prisoners," writes Horwitt. But toward her son Saul, she "was protective." The similarities to Clara Pressman's child-rearing dominance seem partially similar, as well as her own protective cloak around Lee during and after his bout with infantile paralysis.

Likewise, Alinksy biographer Sanford Horwitt notes that the social activist had an affinity to Lewis in terms of his own personality style. Alinsky, like Pressman, admired "the aggressiveness; the gamesmanship, the deliberately provocative challenges and insults to opponents; first the promotion of conflict, then the negotiated resolution of it to win political advantage; the use of power." And for both Alinsky and Pressman, the bond developed into more than leadership admiration; it grew into one of deep psychological identification. In Horwitt's judgement of Alinsky's reaction to Lewis, "it came down to a question of manhood. The measure of a man was his bravery, his fearlessness, his courage, his strength." And again, like Pressman, those qualities had become important for Alinksy to cultivate because his "own father was such a weak, forlorn figure. . . ."

The result was "an almost starry-eyed relationship with Lewis," commented Horwitt, wherein Alinksy, although thirty years younger than Lewis but similar "in personality, style, and inclination," saw himself in the labor leader. "Lewis's great nerve, the pleasure he took in assuming a defiant stance, his projection of intellectual superiority" in tandem with "the romantic attraction of a great movement and its great leader" proved deeply seductive to Alinksy, as it did to Pressman. Moreover, Lewis's innate sense of strategy and tactics for interpersonal dominance endlessly fascinated both younger men, as did the union president's belief "that there was no fun or skill in merely waylaying an adversary; one had to use some imagination" in bringing about their downfall. Pressman had a similar bent. As Lee's daughter Susan commented about her father's later life, he "enjoyed getting even. You could see it formulating in his eyes."

Lewis's adroit interactions with President Roosevelt captivated each as well, and formed the basis of their later reputations as raconteurs. These oft-retold incidents, repeated by both with relish for years, were more than mere entertainment though. While the incidents "were the kinds of small stratagems that many people might have found merely interesting or amusing," writes Horwitt, Alinsky—and Pressman—"found them important as tools for manipulating and controlling events and people. Tactics and power—even at a seemingly mundane level—went hand in hand, and there were few better practitioners to watch and to learn from than John L. Lewis."[13]

This analysis is supported by the observations of others as well. Donald Shaughnessy, who interviewed Pressman for the Columbia Oral History Project and maintained a social relationship with the lawyer afterward, indicated that while he himself had grown up admiring Lewis, "Lee doted on him. If Pressman ever had a father figure, John L. was the man. On a few occasions, I had an opportunity to share a glass of sherry with Mr. Lewis," Shaughnessy wrote. "This was long after he and Lee" had ended their relationship. "Lee wanted to know everything about him. How he looked, what he said, how he said it, and so forth. Hungry for the last and least important detail."

The intensity of the Lewis–Pressman psychological bond can perhaps be gleaned from the following passage from Pressman's Columbia University oral history interview. Shaughnessy's had asked a question about the relationship between John L. Lewis and his daughter Kathryn, who served as the union president's personal assistant. In passing, Pressman described her physical appearance and mentioned briefly that she had her father's attractive facial features, and then, without prompting, moved, almost in the manner of a free association, into a quite personal reaction to Lewis's own physical appearance:

> Very pretty face, I might say, with the features of John L. Lewis, who has very sensitive features, you know. They're usually hidden by your looking at his eyebrows most of the time and his bushy hair, but his ordinary features, his nose and his mouth, are very, very sensitive features. The ruggedness is given by virtue of his jowls, but look at each individual feature, when he smiles, his eyes, his nose, his mouth are the features of a very sensitive soul.

Pressman romanticized Lewis down to the most personal level; to him, the latter was at once the avenging angel of justice, smiting—often effectively one might add—the partisans of economic privilege on behalf of those suffering injustice. At the same time, Lewis was the compassionate soul, whose sensitive feelengs were grounded in the cares and concerns of the common people of the country. Lewis merged both masculine strength and sensitive compassion into an attractive image of maleness for Lee Pressman, an image that perhaps he believed instinctively was the correct one for a man, but one that he found lacking in his own father and first generation immigrant childhood. Perhaps in Lewis he had found complete what he had been searching for in his other mentoring relationships—first with Jerome Frank and lateri- with Philip Murray—a powerful and yet caring father figure who would teach him how to right the world's wrongs.[14]

But the flowering of that relationship would not have occurred had Pressman not eventually lived up to his sponsor's expectations. Until the eruption of the Great Sit-Down Strike in Flint, Michigan, in late 1936, he worked at various projects trying to increase his usefulness to Lewis. His first litigation involvement in the SWOC organizing campaign came in September 1936, when he was called to Portsmouth, Ohio, to assist members of an AA lodge charged with murdering two strikebreakers supplied to the Portsmouth Steel Company by the Bergdorf Detective Agency. The plant had mostly shut down as a result of the organizing campaign, Pressman recalled, but the strikebreakers would run a dinkey engine, a kind of steel transporation cart, between plants "to make the pretense that they were operating. . . ." Most of the striking workers were Appalachian and excellent marksmen, and someone from the overlooking hills shot two of the strikebreakers accompanying the dinkey engine "like little rabbits, right through the eyes." The sheriff arrested about twenty of the strike leaders, despite the fact that the specific perpetrator was still unidentified. The incident divided the town and created an especially tense social situation when Pressman arrived, with trepidation, to represent the incarcerated steelworkers.

"My God," he thought to himself, "here I am, the only legal practice I had had up until that business . . . [had] been with some corporate reorganizations on a very high level in New York where you walk into a court room with all the dignity and backing of a big law firm in New York, and government practice," he recalled years later. And "here I am, down in Portsmouth, all by myself, in a town hotter than a firecracker" due to an unpopular strike, with twenty people about to be charged for murder and depending on him for help. He secured the assistance of an Ohio attorney, Ted Lamb, also a Harvard graduate, and together they fended off some of the indictments and succeeded in avoiding conviction on the others, which was, "frankly, . . . an achievement for me" in his first legal crisis. Moreover, the strikers held firm, assisted by this legal aid, and supplied enough pressure to convince the company to negotiate and sign a contract.[15]

It was, however, the kind of excitement and experience that Lee Pressman had long sought—dramatic and emotional, a battle of right against wrong. Increasingly, as the months went on, his high profile within the SWOC-CIO became a resource for other Progressives equally eager to enlist in the industrial union cause, such as Gardner Jackson, who eventually came on board as an official of the Lewis-inspired Labor's Non-Partisan League (LNPL), an electoral organization that Lewis hoped would maximize labor's political clout in the upcoming 1936 presidential elections. To make that happen, the UMWA president had funded the LNPL with an unprecedented half a million dollars from the United Mine Workers tresury.[16]

Indeed, a LNPL connection showed how quickly Pressman moved to assert his personal influence in policy areas. The organization marked a departure in politics for American labor. For years, the AFL's political policy had been to reward labor's political friends and punish its enemies. It did that by giving or withholding its official endorsement on a nonpartisan basis, and little else in terms of electoral action. The LNPL aimed to render significant electoral aid, however. Although in name "nonpartisan," in reality Lewis tied the LNPL closely to Roosevelt and the New Deal forces. "Dear John," Pressman wrote to Lewis in October 1936, "I haven't had much contact with the Labor Non-Partisan League in connection with the present political campaign" and consequently, he said, he somewhat reluctantly offered his observations. But on a recent Washington trip, he had come into "contact with several incidents which were disturbing and suggested certain problems to me." He had "discovered" that requested administration appropriations for emergency employment relief were going to decline, with certain projects slated for extinction. Furthermore, the White House refused to make funding available to the Department of Labor to implement the provision of setting up minimum wage standards under the Walsh–Healey law. "The foregoing leads me to wonder," Pressman advised Lewis, "whether the President, in spite of the fact that his [expected] victory will have been made possible only as a result of the combined efforts of organized labor and the otes of both organized and unorganized labor, will not, after election, carry through policies which may be detrimental to the interests of labor and the under-privileged farmers." "Shouldn't the speeches which are being made to the numerous labor rallies," in which Lewis participated in all over the country, "indicate what the leaders of organized labor are going to demand of the Administration after the election?" he asked. "In other words, by indicating such specific demands, at the present time, the rallying of labor votes around the President on the basis of such speeches can be effectively pointed to," he wrote, "to bring about the various measures that will be necessary to protect the interests of labor."

He counseled that mention should be made of the funding necessary, as well as assistance from federal authorities to ensure against state and local government violations of worker civil liberties in union organizing and collective bargaining. "I appreciate that the argument will probably be made that it might interfere with the chances of the President for reelection, if the labor leaders now come out with specific proposals that may be attacked by the Republicans," he admitted. "However, it seems to me that such specific proposals and several more which you may have in mind will result only in securing more votes for Roosevelt . . . [and] prevent any misunderstanding between the President and labor as to what will be expected from the Administration within the next few years." If Lewis agreed with his observations, he closed, "I should be only too glad to come to Washington at any time you want me to to help in preparing some paragraphs, along the foregoing lines, for the speeches that you will be making during the next few weeks." Lewis responded with uncharacteristic caution, indicating that he had consulted with others and thought a public aggressive stance might not be best. But the letter reveals how soon into his employment with the CIO Pressman felt comfortable in approaching the country's most prominent labor leader with policy-shaping suggestions in a critical presidential campaign.[17]

Pressman's role as the CIO's prime legislative policy advisor–implementer expanded in the wake of President Roosevelt's landslide reelection in November 1936. Lewis and Murray interpreted the election as a working people's endorsement of Roosevelt's claimed support of unionism, and as such they desired to obtain federal and state legislative gains for their support. And from the first it was clear that Pressman would be in the forefront of this effort. Early in December, Pressman wrote Amalgamated Clothing Workers of America (ACWA) President Sidney Hillman regarding industrial unionism's state-level legislative program. "Mr. Lewis, Mr. Murray and I have discussed the specific which might be suggested for introduction in . . . several states as the state legislative program for labor," based upon several draft bills drawn up by the attorney. They aimed first to push through their legislative agenda in Pennsylvania. Included was a state version of the Norris-LaGuardia antiinjunction act to prohibit state courts from issuing injunctions in labor disputes. In addition, they planned a state-level "baby" Wagner Act for employers falling outside of the jurisdictional scope of the federal National Labor Relations Act (NLRA, or Wagner Act). By definition, that law could only apply to businesses with an impact on inter, as opposed to intra, -state commerce, so supplementary state laws were needed. Also important to future CIO organizing campaigns was a statute prohibiting corporations from paying compensation to law enforcement officials for the mass appointment of deputies in strike situations—a technique often used to break strikes. This proposal also included public "show cause" provisions binding officials who undertook such appointments to prove their necessity to keeping the public peace. Similarly, other suggested bills centered around protections of the right to organize: protections from civil liberties abuses by local authorities; prevention of the abuse of evictions to undermine worker support during labor disputes; licensing control of private detectives engaged in labor spying; and restrictions on the purchase and possession of industrial munitions and tear gas for use in connection with businesses. Pressman suggested that Hillman might want to promote a similar agenda of state-level reforms in New York via his leadership in the American Labor Party, a Progressive labor alternative to the machine-controlled politics of New York's Democratic Tammany Hall contingent.[18]

All of these concerns were in the forefront of public knowledge at the time, due to the public hearings of the senate's LaFollette Civil Liberties Committee. This senate investigation, launched by supporters as an adjunct to CIO organizing initiatives, had publicized the history and current use of corporate and local government collaboration designed to break strikes and undermine support of unionization by workers. Pressman's former AAA/Ware Group colleague John Abt directed the government's investigation into violations of worker civil liberties. Always competitive, according to Abt, Pressman initially had ambitions to be chosen as chief investigator and lobbied for the appointment despite what would have been a clear conflict of interest. Further strengthening the CIO's ties to the senate committee was Gardner Jackson's role in promoting its establishment along with the National Labor Relations Board. Interweaving the connections further, Pressman's IJA/Ware Group friend Nat Witt had become secretary of the National Labor Relations Board, the agency created to administer the provisions of the NLRA. It was to have the power to determine questions of union representation and to investigate and set right employer unfair labor practices inhibiting unionization, but had been stymied by business opposition. Therefore, such a senate investigation seemed to be a way to bring about compliance with the law.[19]

These interconnections made Lee Pressman particularly "useful" to Lewis for the policy-level tactical advice he could develop from this network of New Deal elite. That usefulness would soon give him entrée into policy areas within the American labor movement, previously rarely entered by middle-class professionals. And, while he was becoming more and more valuable to John L. Lewis, collaterally he also was increasingly becoming more and more "useful" to the American Communist Party.

THE POST-WARE GROUP CP CONNECTION

The exact nature of Pressman's CP involvements in New York prior to 1938 is still murky. In his public testimony before the House Un-American

Activities Committee in 1950, Lee Pressman said he had been a dues-paying Communist Party member during the period 1934–1935, but cast aside his Party connections when he left government work in Washington and returned to New York. "When I left the City of Washington I advised the [Ware] group—and I believe on that occasion Mr. [J.] Peters may have been present—that I was leaving the . . . Federal Government, and I was disassociating myself from the group, or the Communist Party, or any group of the Communist Party," he testified. When asked if he told the group members his reasons, he carefully responded that, "I preferred from that moment on, at least, in my private practice, not to have organizational relationship with the Communist Party, such as being a member of the Communist Party."

He admitted, however, that that statement did not indicate that he had severed all ties. "Over the past number of years I have had contacts and dealings with known leaders of the Communist Party, whom I have met from time to time," he continued. He told the committee members that the CP officials with whom he had met, basically party labor secretary Roy Hudson and legislative representative Eugene Dennis, "would discuss with me their viewpoints, their recommendations, and suggestions, with respect to organizational activities of the CIO while I was counsel for the CIO. I discussed those problems with these people. When they made recommendations or suggestions which I deemed to be of assistance or helpful to the CIO," he indicated, "I accepted them." However, he went on, "I state here now, as categorically as I can, that at no time from 1936 until 1948 did I take instructions or directives from anyone, including these leaders of the Communist Party, which were contrary to the established policy of the CIO."

Representative Richard M. Nixon inquired further as to the nature of his "organizational" break with the party. Pressman elaborated by stating that his reason for the disassociation was because he did not want to consider "myself a member completely committed to all the policies and doctrines of the Communist Party." Nevertheless, when Nixon asked if it was an "ideological" separation, Pressman reluctantly responded, "I would say not completely." Thus the essential thrust of his testimony was that he had remained ideologically supportive of communism subsequent to his departure from the AAA while general counsel of the CIO. He met with Party officials after 1938 to discuss CIO matters, "but . . . while I met with them and dealt with them, they did not direct my activities or my opinions and beliefs."[20]

Others offered a different picture. Pressman was quite aware that Whittaker Chambers had testified to before the HUAC, and he knew of Chambers' 1939 meeting with Undersecretary of State Adolph Berle, shortly after he defected from the CP. Chambers had privately informed the New Deal official of the Ware Group's existence and of Pressman's CP involvement that included activity during the period 1936–1938. In his best selling memoir *Witness*, published in 1952, Chambers outlined a deeper association by Pressman with Party activity after he left the Ware Group and before he became the full-time general counsel of the CIO. And in private statements to the FBI, Chambers claimed that is was he who had ordered Pressman to take the CIO post, after the central committee had expressed qualms about the Party's ability to control the lawyer. The most detailed version of what Chambers said had occurred came in a series of FBI statements he gave to the bureau, beginning in 1945, resuming once again from January through April 1949, and then continuing through October 1950. In these recollections, the former communist underground operative alleged minor Pressman activity in underground Party matters, at least through the end of 1936, and perhaps into 1937.[21]

Chambers said in 1949 that during one of the Ware Group meetings he had ordered the lawyer to grab the opportunity to work for Lewis. According to the recollections of the former *Time* magazine editor, in the "latter part of 1935 or early 1936 . . . on one of my meetings with Lee Pressman in Washington, the latter informed me that he had an opportunity to become general counsel for the CIO. Pressman was rather agitated," he claimed, "because he said the Central Committee of the Communist Party, USA, had informed him that he was not to accept this position." J. Peters, chief of the U.S. Party underground, who had taken over direction of the group after Harold Ware's death, filled Chambers in on the reason for the central committee's decision. This Hungarian-born Communist was a man with the demeanor "of a minor commissar—a little more humble than the breed, for he had a sense of humor," Chambers observed, "—but [basically] reserved, innately distrustful, [and] secretive." He told Chambers afterward "that the Party felt that Pressman was a lone operator and impulsive and the Party was afraid that if he took this job, that they could not control him."

The attorney asked Chambers' advice about what he should do. "I informed Pressman that he should go ahead and take the job and that I would personally take the responsibility in the event that there were any repercussions from the Communist Party," Chambers stated. "I took this action, because I was convinced that the job of general counsel for the CIO was of first importance to the Communist Party. Therefore, I was willing to take any consequences that might follow from this flouting of the decisions of the Central Committee." No consequences followed, however.

That very night he and Pressman "drove in Pressman's automobile to the latter's apartment located on Connecticut Avenue in the vicinity of the Washington Zoo." Chambers told the FBI that the lawyer's "wife and child were not present when I visited the apartment on this occasion. I did notice," he said, that "it was a rather large apartment and contained modernistic furniture. I think that the conversation between Pressman and myself on this occasion dealt with the difficulties Pressman was having in financing his younger brother's way to law school."[22]

Setting aside the issue of the truthfulness of Chambers' recollection, his observation that the general counselship of the CIO would be a key position was on the mark. With the eruption of the sit-down strike wave in the auto industry in early 1937 and the subsequent emergence of the CIO as a potent economic and political force, Pressman's importance increased tremendously. Those events had placed him in a policy-related position that Party leaders regarded as critical to American communism's future. Since 1935, both internationally and in U. S. politics, the CP had pursued its Popular Front policy, essentially a decision to align with liberal, middle-class, nonsocialist forces against fascism's advances. For a time, Party leaders judged that this meant they should attempt to expand their influence within established, old-line AFL unions, as the CIO seemed at first to threaten a Popular Front strategy. However, the opportunity to become influential in the effective unionization of the mass-production industries provided an unparalleled opportunity for the CP to become a significant political player in American life for the first time. And upon further consideration, Party leaders decided that an expanding, dynamic, and militant labor movement could only help further Popular Front strategy.

Lewis needed scores of zealous organizers and therefore willingly accepted Party members into these jobs; collectively, they became a group that even enemies acknowledged added tremendous organizing zeal to industrial unionism's drives. Eventually a few Party members and fellow travelers would rise to top-level status in a number of new CIO international unions. Perhaps more importantly, though, the Party, largely through Pressman and Publicity Director Len DeCaux, maintained a presence in national CIO offices. Pressman's value as Lewis's and Murray's "left-hand man," so to speak, far outshone any other contribution he might make in clandestine but insignificant CP activity. This became crystal clear in December 1936, when autoworkers in Flint, Michigan, the heart of the giant General Motors manufacturing complex, engaged in the most dramatic, important, and successful strike in the history of American labor. And Lee Pressman was soon drawn into the thick of it.[23]

PRESSMAN AND THE CIO'S FIRST VICTORIES

For many years, unionism had existed in pockets of the auto industry, but its limited scope resulted in little effect on employee relations policies. As in other industries, the depression changed workers' sentiments toward unionization, though many still feared the loss of their jobs, should favorable attitudes become known. By August 1936, many remnant AFL auto unions coalesced into the United Auto Workers (UAW) and affiliated with the CIO. Since June of that year, UAW organizers Wyndham Mortimer and Robert Travis, had worked to recruit a small band of committed autoworker unionists in General Motors (GM) home based in Flint, Michigan. More extensive organization seemed impossible due to the corporation's total dominance over the community and the fear of unemployment.

The landslide reelection of President Roosevelt, and more importantly, the gubernatorial election of liberal Democrat Frank Murphy, a former pro-labor Detroit mayor, indicated to Flint UAW organizers that external conditions had possibly taken the direction needed to break the pall of corporate control. Additionally, with the CIO affiliation, the fledgling auto union accessed the seasoned leadership of John L. Lewis. And during the previous spring and fall, the well-publicized hearings of the LaFollette Civil Liberties Committee revealed an extensive corporate network of industrial munition-eering, strikebreaking, and antiunion espionage. These and various other civil liberties violations of worker's rights to free assembly had created a negative public reaction toward General Motors and other large corporations.

Throughout the fall, the UAW had called on GM to negotiate, but top corporate officials responded that wage and working condition matters were the province of local division and plant management, who also refused to meet with union representatives. On December 28, a group of workers spontaneously began a sit-down strike in the corporation's Cleveland Fisher Body plant. Using the sit-down strike tactic that proved so effective during the earlier 1936 rubber industry strikes, workers prevented strikebreakers from being brought into the plant by simply remaining on the premises, but refusing to work. Then, when GM laid plans to remove several critically needed auto body dies from Flint for security reasons, UAW militants in Flint emulated their brothers and sisters in Cleveland and launched the Great Flint Sit-Down Strike on December 30, 1936.

Because of the integrated manufacturing processes of the auto company, a shut-down in even a small number of critical facilities could close down all production. To accomplish this, workers on the premises had to maintain control of the plants for at least a reasonable amount of time and somehow prevent eviction for trespass. And those eventualities depended on their own courage and willingness to resist local police authority and unjust local court decrees. Their success also depended on their access to outside assistance—food and information, most importantly, of course—but also to labor leaders capable of at least demobilizing active public hostility to trespass and labor militancy. It was here that the negotiation expertise of the CIO's John L. Lewis and, to a lesser degree, the tactical legal acumen of Lee Pressman and UAW attorneys, counted.[24]

Pressman's analysis of how legal issues would quickly come to the fore in the CIO's struggles for mass unionization proved correct in the GM situation from day one. The legal interconnections between the tactic of the sit-down, the law of trespass, the developing labor law of the National Labor Relations Board, and civil liberties law violations played significant roles in the dispute. Though no one could claim any great litigation victories were won during the course of the strike, Pressman's abilities as a shrewd legal tacticias and his presence at many of the critical points during the CIO's involvement in the struggle worked to the industrial union movement's advantage. In truth, a convergence of forces and the efforts of many individuals resulted in the UAW's stunning defeat of the world's largest manufacturing corporation. A good many of those forces involved labor law—common, statutory, and administrative—and the ability to judge how that law could be used in the union's favor. Union attorneys constantly counterposed workers' rights to freedom of association for collective bargaining to the employer's legal right to the use of property. They argued that employer claims of the sanctity of private property were undeserving of primary consideration, given the corporation's violations of workers' civil liberties. These endeavors assisted the struggle in two ways. It gave pro-worker politicians the "wiggle" room they needed to work strenuously for a negotiated settlement rather than an armed confrontation, moreover, the pubcic articulation of these rights helped shore up the morale and determination of the sit-downers themselves.

Pressman, along with John Brophy, Adolph Germer, and Powers Hapgood—the latter two men Brophy associates brought onto the staff to assist in CIO organizing—initially shared liaison duties with the UAW. The CIO general counsel's first brief involvement in Michigan came in early January 1937, when he received word in Pittsburgh that Genessee County Judge Edward Black had issued an injunction against the sit-down on Friday, with an order to the union to show cause on Monday. Pressman called his partner Walter Liebman in New York, whom he assumed owned some GM stock, and asked him, "just on a hunch," to go immediately to the GM building and check whether Judge Black owned any GM stock. "Anybody up around Flint, Michigan, and that part of the woods . . . probably . . . [had] some stock," Pressman surmised. "And sure enough, I find that he has some stock."

Subsequently, Pressman left for Detroit to discuss the injunction with local UAW attorneys Maurice Sugar and Larry Davidow. According to Sugar's biographer Christopher Johnson, Pressman admired Sugar for his many years of committed involvement on behalf of the labor movement and Socialist Party, greeting him "'like a novitiate greeting a master.'" Further discussion ensued regarding whether an effort to get Judge Black to recuse himself due to his financial interest in the auto corporation was advisable, and Pressman asked Sugar to confirm whether Michian law would mandate

Black's removal, as the Harvard lawyer well educated in corporate and financial law suspected it would.

The next day, even as Pressman and other CIO and UAW traveled to the state capitol of Lansing to present the union's side alongside Governor Murphy's, the UAW convened a press conference outlining Black's financial interests. Quickly, the initial injunction lost its public acceptability, and company lawyers soon decided to seek satisfaction from another jurist. The delay gave the union more time to hamper production and reveal to the public the nature and extent of GM's dominance of the Flint community. Still, even with the intercession of Governor Murphy, who had offered to mediate, the union could not get a face-to-face meeting with management, a fact that threatened union morale. The CIO simply could "not permit the public to understand that we were so weak we couldn't get a meeting" with the corporation, Pressman pointed out. The situation was critical as well for the new industrial union federation, for "the success or failure of the Auto Workers strike meant the success or failure of the building of the C.I.O," Pressman said, and "[t]he loss of that strike might have been the end of the C.I.O."

Matters remained for a time in a stalemate. Returning to Washington after the unsuccessful meetings in Lansing, Pressman—the student of the use of power—admiringly observed how the deft maneuverings of John L. Lewis created a situation where the Roosevelt administration appeared to be considering stepping up its interventions in the conflict. One morning, before a meeting between Lewis and Assistant Secretary of Labor Edward McGrady, the CIO leader noticed in the papers that McGrady had been scheduled for an afternoon briefing meeting with President Roosevelt. McGrady was reporting to the president in the absence of Secretary of Labor Frances Perkins, and Lewis had known McGrady for years, since he had been a former union official. Lewis therefore arranged for an additional meeting with McGrady to occur that night at 8 P.M. at Labor's Non-Partisan League offices in the Willard Hotel. At Lewis's instruction, CIO press functionaries privately informed news organizations that there would possibly be an important development in the GM strike announced at the Willard that evening.

At the appointed hour Lewis and Pressman returned to a hotel suite to await McGrady's arrival. When the Assistant Secretary showed up, he encountered a throng of over one hundred reporters and photographers hungry for what they assumed would be news of a message being conveyed from Lewis to the White House and then back again to Lewis. After a few mild protestations by McGrady at being used in this fashion, and several hours of discussing toe sit-down situation in a general way, Lewis and McGrady each left the suite solemnly stating, "No comment." "The next morning the papers were just filled [with speculations] that this was some secret proposition, that Roosevelt was laying a basis for doing something to General Motors: to take over the corporation," Pressman recollected. He noted that most industrialists intensely disliked Roosevelt and the New Deal. "Roosevelt was the big black ogre to them and they assumed that anything that Roosevelt had the power to do, if the CIO would ask him to do it, he would do it. There was a great difference between the fact and what they thought," however, he pointed out. Nevertheless, Lewis succeeded in creating the *appearance* that the administration was going to do something soon regarding the strike, and perhaps to the corporation's disadvantage.

Lewis's ploy worked. Given the working-class support FDR had received in the 1936 election, the administration could not state publicly that the meeting was really about nothing at all, so no statement about the McGrady incident came from the White House or Perkins. "It wasn't long after this incident that Murphy arranged for a meeting between the corporation and the union" on a face-to-face negotiation basis, Pressman observed. He believed that the McGrady flap, along with workers' success at fending off local police eviction, combined to convince GM executives to come to the table for truce negotiations in mid-January. In addition, Murphy's decision to only call out the National Guard for general peacekeeping and not eviction helped. Not long afterward, Murphy announced a tentative truce agreement between the parties.

The Murphy-UAW-GM truce resulted in the union agreeing to vacate the plants with the "understanding" that the company would negotiate over collective bargaining rights with the UAW *prior* to any other organization, and would not resume production. The union began the evacuation when by circumstance a reporter discovered a company telegram indicating it intended to invite delegates from an antiunion citizen's group to participate in the discussions, ostensibly to represent non-UAW GM workers. The friendly reporter informed the CIO office in Washington, which instructed the UAW to stop the evacuation. "The non-evacuation of that one plant saved the UAW," reflected Pressman years afterward. With the prior agreement in ruins due to the company's bad faith, "of course, bedlam broke out and Murphy, again, was right in the middle of it," Pressman recounted.[25]

Despite the efforts of Murphy to increase the involvement of the Roosevelt administration, the corporation seemed determine to wait the strike out. Realizing this, strike leaders Robert Travis and Roy Reuther implemented a daring and dramatic seizure of yet another critical adjacent plant to the ones they held, one that produced engines for all Chevrolets. A successful taking of this facility might break the deadlock in the union's favor, they reasoned; at the very least, it would shift the crisis into high gear.

Shortly before that secret event was to occur, Pressman made plans to return to Detroit to appear in court with Sugar and Davidow on GM's new injunction pleading. Writing to Davidow, Pressman gave instructions on the types of affidavits they would need, and commented on the likely unsuccessful result, which they all knew going in. "Of course the injunction will be granted," he wrote, "but it is up to us to make a splendid record of the position of General Motors" in its refusal to obey the National Labor Relations Act. "I expect to be in Detroit Monday morning, and will proceed . . . to Flint with you and Maurice. I should also like to participate in the argument before the Court," he requested, which was sure to be the most critical labor litigation activity in which he had yet engaged. In preparation for the argument, he called on his network of Progressive lawyers, particularly legal scholars Nathan Greene and James Landis, who tried "to put together some rationale to make the legality of a sit-down strike" into a workable legal argument. And Pressman well knew that this was more than "a little difficult."[26]

The appointed time had arrived for the lawyers. As UAW publicist Henry Kraus recalled the scene, "[T]here was drama here, too, for the partisan [union] audience . . . [had] packed the courtroom and hallways outside." The arguments before Judge Paul Gadola in Flint began the afternoon of February 1, coinciding with the still largely secret effort by the sit-downers to capture the additional plant. Sugar, Davidow, and Pressman knew that their primary aim was to achieve further delay and sensationalize the growing negative public image of General Motors as an unrepentant violator of federal labor law. Nevertheless, as Christopher Johnson notes, Sugar, Pressman, and Davidow asserted important arguments about law and morality that deserved consideration, even in spite of their unlikely acceptance. In court, neither of the parties addressed the issue of the legality of the sit-down strike directly. The corporation's counsel simply based its pleas on the primacy and sanctity of property rights, citing precedents as far back as 1898. The union attorneys centered their arguments against the injunction on the fact that in injunction proceedings, the applicant must come before an equity court with "clean hands," that is, free from any wrongdoing, an approach that Sugar had used to defend labor unions for a number of years. That tack allowed the lawyers to introduce into the record information of company malfeasance relating to the National Labor Relations Act and violations of workers' constitutional liberties regarding freedom of assembly and association.

During the hearing, as Pressman was making one of these "highfalutin" legal arguments—"You'd think we were [before] the Supreme Court" he fondly recalled—he claimed that the judge should view the case from the perspective of modern economic conditions in 1936. Gadola stopped him, pointing out that they were not arguing economic issues. Pressman held his ground. "'We claim that we can show that the action of the management was of a nature which would forfeit their right to the plants,'" he insisted. "'Do you mean that you claim the right to seize property as you see fit?'" the incredulous judge returned. "'We mean that we can show a most ruthless and blatant disregard for the laws of the United States as they concern relationship between worker and employer,'" Pressman countered. So, one wrong justifies another, asked the judge? "'No,'" the CIO general counsel ended his point, "'but I do claim that to get an injunction the appellant must come into court with clean hands, free from any blame or illegality.'"

After four hours of such "pretty impressive" legal fencing, during the midst of which the court was informed of the new plant seizure and incorrectly told that there had been deaths involved, the result was as expected. "[W]hen we're all through" Gadola "pushes some books aside and picks a piece of paper from the desk all typewritten and reads his opinion all prepared—granting the injunction," Pressman recalled, amused. The opinion thus fit nicely with the pre-prepared injunction order quickly handed to him by the company's attorneys.[27]

That night Pressman called John L. Lewis in Washington and advised him that, given the existence of the new court order and the new plant seizure, he expected renewed pressure on Governor Murphy to use the National Guard to enforce the order and evict the strikers. It was perhaps time for Lewis to personally take over the union's negotiations, he thought. Lewis agreed and made arrangements to come to Detroit. "I'd gotten the distinct impression," no doubt conveyed by Maurice Sugar who had known Murphy for years since law school at the University of Michigan, "that Governor Murphy was a man who had a very great compassion, [a] very sensitive person and the possible violence would have quite an impact on him." Pressman thought they should work this angle. Prior to Lewis's arrival and the potential order of the National Guard into the plants to enforce Judge Gadola's decree, Pressman sat "down with two or three other fellows in the headquarters of the autoworkers" in Flint and wrote "out a telegram ostensibly signed by the sit-down strikers and addressed to Governor Murphy." The lengthy telegram stressed the probable violence and deaths that would flow from an effort to remove them, Murphy's potential responsibility for it should he order in the National Guard, the reason for their fight against the corporation, and their determination to see it through. "Every other line referred to martyrs who had died for a cause," the CIO general counsel reminisced. "We knew our man—[as] a very sensitive . . . person to whom the very thought of violence" disturbed greatly. "We knew we just had to keep those guards away from that plant and the only way was to appeal to his sensibility." The strike leadership had the telegram approved by the sit-downers in the plant and sent to the governor that evening. Murphy "told us subsequently" that "this was the most excruciating moment for him," Pressman said later. It was his "horror at the thought that he should be the cause of bloodshed and deaths" that convinced Murphy to redouble his efforts to negotiate a settlement, and that Guard troops would continue to be used, at least for the time being, to keep the general peace.[28]

This was a personality reading that Pressman also conveyed to his new mentor, John L. Lewis. The story of the critical negotiations in Detroit's Recorders Court building from February 3 to February 11, when General Motors and the UAW-CIO finally reached agreement, has been told often and in detail elsewhere. Once again, Lee Pressman perceived the business arrogance he had so often observed during his work in the AAA. The company's representatives—William Knudsen, Donaldson Brown, and John Thomas Smith—"wanted to make you feel as if you . . . how can I put it? That we should be on bended knee. They'd walk into a room with us" as if "this was the most outlandish thing that they ever heard, that they should be sitting within a few feet of us" in the cramped and unadorned judicial chambers of Murphy's jurist brother, George.

Indeed, the governor faced a formidable task; the scions of American corporations had had little experience in directly negotiating with union leaders heretofore and resented it terribly. During the course of the negotiations, Lewis's bluff and bravado, often undertaken spontaneously, proved instructive to the young attorney at his side who, along with UAW officers Homer Martin and Wyndham Mortimer, represented the union. At one critically tense point Lewis unexpectedly started to walk out of the meetings when Murphy brought up AFL claims reghrding the representation of GM's skilled workers. This move dumbfounded Pressman, who believed the CIO leader was throwing away the opportunity to meet face to face with top corporation officials, an opportunity for which they had struggled for some time to achieve. "I didn't have an idea in my head" on how to react to the AFL claim," Pressman recalled. Lewis then rose, reached for his coat, and methodically made for the door, with his bewildered aide hastening to follow. At the very last moment, Murphy plaintively asked where he was going and Lewis ludicrously informed the governor that if he truly believed that the AFL could help reach a settlement in this crisis, he may as well also call in Ethiopian President Haile Selassie—then prominent in the news of the 1930s—into the negotiations, for it would have about the same impact. "You couldn't have said a more ludicrous thing," Pressman remarked in appreciation of Lewis's skill and dramatic flair. "The three arrogant industry men burst out laughing," where up to that point "they had never cracked a smile." Murphy quickly made amends and assured Lewis that the negotiations would proceed with the parties as presently constituted.

Pressman's conveyance of Sugar's sense of Murphy's aversion to violence was also a tactic the CIO chief used repeatedly, according to Lewis's biographers Melvyn Dubofsky and Warren Van Tine. Pressman recalled an impromptu private meeting between the two at Murphy's sister's residence in Detroit one Sunday morning in the first week of February, at which the issue of potential violence erupted once again. Sooner or later, as Michigan's chief law enforcement officer, Murphy would have to enforce the court order. The constant responsibility that Lewis continued to lay on Frank Murphy's shoulders persuaded the governor to try one final time to achieve a settlement prior to ordering in the National Guard for eviction.

Even so, the corporate negotiators would not discuss anything substantive prior to a union evacuation of the plant. Here, once again, the sit-downers themselves moved the parties toward a settlement they could not have achieved without rank-and-file action. Lewis, according to Pressman, knew that the workers would find some way to move the dispute forward, and held to that belief during the negotiations. When GM made one last effort to force the strikers out by turning off the steam heat in the plants, the sit-downers reacted by unexpectedly opening the windows, making the plants' sprinkler systems vulnerable to freezing, and thereby vitiating fire insurance protection of the buildings and machinery. The chagrined company executives had to ask Murphy to request Lewis to get the sit-downers to close the windows, which they did. This simple act of two-way communication, Pressman thought later, finally broke the logjam in negotiations and subsequently things moved swiftly toward a conclusion.[29]

The historic agreement between General Motors and the United Auto Workers, drafted by Pressman who worked the details out with John Thomas Smith, was signed on February 11, 1937, in the presidential suite of Detroit's Statler Hotel. Lewis had taken to bed ill with a respiratory ailment, but oversaw the final details from his sickbed. The company assented to recognize the union as the exclusive collective bargaining agency for its members for six months, and to negotiate with it looking toward execution of a contract, without discrimination toward the strikers or union members, and to drop all legal claims. In exchange, the union would leave all plants, and then its members would return to work. It was a resounding victory for the union and a giant leap forward for the CIO. A proud Lee Pressman stood over Murphy's shoulder as the UAW's officers signed the pact. Lewis, Pressman noted, had "lived for this moment"—the founding of a viable national industrial union movement. It had been a dream of his "for years and years and years," this "organizing mass production industries" and consequent decline of corporate arrogance.[30]

Though Pressman's role as CIO general counsel had not been critical to the outcome of the strike, he did make significant contributions. He engaged corporate attorneys at their own professional level, sensed the limits of New Deal politics, understood the role of the CIO in court, and tactically emphasized Murphy's abhorrence to bloodshed. All proved of great value to Lewis. He also made a positive impression on Lewis with his own negotiating abilities. In his oral history for Columbia University, Pressman recounted how at one point he had worked over William Knudsen, the least strident antiunionist of the GM negotiators, on a particular issue, while Brown and Smith had briefly left the room. "I started talking with Knudsen . . . and I was asking him whether there couldn't be a solution [to a particular problem they had been discussing] along these lines. Lewis was watching me," he noted. "So he let me alone, and in a few minutes Knudsen was agreeing with me on this solution, which was what we wanted, and practical. It made sense." Retlizing that they had left Knudsen alone, the other two GM negotiators burst back into the room after about four minutes, and "practically yanked him from under his hair. . . ." Lewis and Pressman "had a jolly laugh" that this high-priced executive was apparently unable to be left in a room to speak for himself without "guidance." The CIO chief's fondness for the young Lee Pressman grew as a result of this incident and his other activities during the spring of 1937, and also Lewis's desire to impart to his young charge, by example, some of his own innate mastery of the negotiation process. Lewis would again press his general counsel into action in short order.[31]

Taking advantage of the pro-union conclusion of the GM strike, the dramatic Lewis almost immediately dropped another bombshell on corporate America by secretly negotiating an agreement with U.S. Steel Chairman Myron Taylor for recognition of the Steel Workers Organizing Committee. After a chance dinner encounter between the UMWA president and steel executive Myron Taylor at Washington's Mayflower Hotel in January 1937, the two began highly secret meetings aimed at discussing the possibility of voluntary union recognition. Taylor had carefully watched the developments in Flint and more particularly the government's reaction and, given the rising orders for steel and promising business conditions, the first in a long time. He concluded that unionization in the current political climate was perhaps unavoidable and should be accommodated into corporate strategy. By the end of February 1937, the two had struck a deal.

Pressman received a phone call from Lewis instructing him to meet him, along with Philip Murray and Sidney Hillman, in New York. When all three arrived, Lewis told them that he had just met with Taylor and put the finishing touches on an agreement between the SWOC and U.S. Steel, to be executed two days later at the Pittsburgh offices of U.S. Steel President Benjamin Fairless. Over the weekend, once again, Pressman drafted the essentials of the agreement as indicated by Lewis: the company would recognize the SWOC as the collective bargaining agency for its members. There would also be a ten cent per hour wage increase, a commitment to a straight forty hour work week, and further negotiations looking toward a fully articulated labor contract. On the appointed days, Murray, Golden, Pressman, and other SWOC directors arrived at the Carnegie building in Pittsburgh where the "doorman almost dropped dead when he saw us." Murray presented Fairless with the document Pressman had drafted, and they both signed. The "fortress" of mighty steel had fallen without a shot by the beginning of March, three weeks after the end of the GM strike. With those two acts, within a month the CIO had made itself into a going concern and a realistic rival to the AFL for dominance of the American labor movement.

But it seemed the forward momentum had just started. Lewis's final victory of spring arrived in April 1937. Emulating their Flint brothers and sisters, Chrysler autoworkers had begun a Detroit-centered sit-down strike in March. Once again, Governor Frank Murphy interceded as mediator; Lewis and Pressman, along with UAW President Homer Martin, represented the union side in negotiations at the governor's in Lansing. Walter Chrysler headed the company team, joined by corporate officials K. T. Keller, Nicholas Kelly, and Tex Colbert, a Pressman Harvard Law School classmate, as counsel. Chrysler, as company founder and titular owner, influenced the negotiations but was not as strongly antiunion as perhaps some other businessmen. But he shared control of the company with the corporation's financiers, as represented by Kelly and Keller, who seemed able to veto any agreement not to their liking. A key issue for the company officials was that while they would agree to negotiate and bargain collectively, they would do so only after the strikers left the plants. After a number of days, with Lewis again blustering and threatening, this time Murphy adopted a harder line, indicating that he would be willing to use the National Guard to remove the strikers, if necessary. The CIO chief took what he could and signed an agreement similar to the one at GM.[32]

Thus, within several months after Lewis had him appointed as general counsel to the SWOC and the CIO, Pressman had started to perform functions within the industrial union movement that clearly had policy-shaping implications. His services as a legal draftsman and rescuer of incarcerated strikers charged with murder were important, but his value went beyond that. In time, Lewis, Murray, and even Hillman would listen to him carefully on political and legislative matters, and particularly so on those matters pertaining to the government's legal protection of the right to organize. Additionally, in the first four months of his employment, he had proved his "usefulness" in a variety of ways in Flint and Lansing as the eagle-eyed Lewis no doubt analyzed his protege in Pressman's varied interactions with corporate executives, corporate lawyers, and politicians. Subsequent to the wrap-up of the Chrysler agreement, Lewis proved his fondness for the younger man when he invited him into the usually sacrosanct and insular world of mine worker collective bargaining, allowing him to draft a few contract proposals. "I was the only lawyer that Lewis ever brought into a coal miners" collective bargaining meeting, he recalled. He thought Lewis seemed to be saying to him, "Look, toodle along, will you. Let me show you how this thing works."

While lawyers historically had played a markedly minor role in policy determination within the American labor movement prior to the birth of industrial unionism, Pressman's emergence as CIO general counsel seemed to signal a new era. He, and soon many other attorneys like him, would be key actors, serving as liaisons between industrial unionism and the New Deal, staff people who could mediate and shape the relationship of labor with the growing administrative state. The CIO's birth, growth, and subsequent consolidation during the late 1930s through the late 1940s would be intimately interconnected with this new "administrative" state and its transformation of Americans' assumptions about government involvement in economic life. The ability to utilize a middle-class professional such as Pressman to apply requisite outside pressure on the administration of laws by labor-related government agencies would prove crucial at key junctions. Pressman's capacity to "arrange" various aspects of agency policy determination and supply government administrators with the logical arguments and public rationales they needed to rule in the CIO's favor was a talent that heretofore organized labor had largely ignored or thought unimportant.

And for Lee Pressman, the opportunity to become the "steel" for John L. Lewis's "hammer" in the early months of 1937 also realized deep personal goals. An anecdote originating with Saul Alinksy, and popularized by Murray Kempton, may reveal how Pressman himself internally reacted to Lewis and the exciting, almost earthshaking, economic and political events in which he had been involved since becoming CIO general counsel in June 1936. Saul Alinksy, interviewing Pressman in 1948 for his Lewis biography, was apparently taken by a story Pressman told of a negotiating ploy Lewis used to shake the confidence of Chrysler's K.T. Keller, who had been sitting during the negotiations for two days with an arrogant smirk on his face. At one point, Keller commented that Lewis had not said much, and asked for his reaction to a matter. A glowering Lewis turned slowly and dramatically in his chair toward his adversary and said that what he would really like to do was to wipe the incessant smirk off of Keller's face. The very aggressiveness of the comment stunned the group into silence. After a short break to relieve tension, Pressman claimed, the negotiations began to move forward in earnest.

Alinsky, however, quoted Pressman's words in the following way. He thought, he told Alinsky, his witnessing of that scene had been "the high point of his life":

> It is impossible to put into words just what everyone felt at that moment. Lewis, the man, was not threatening Keller, the man. Lewis's voice at that moment was in every sense the voice of millions of unorganized workers who were exploited by gigantic corporations. He was expressing at that instant their resentment, their hostility, and their passionate desire to strike back. There just was no question that Lewis's threat was not against Mr. Keller as a person, but against the Chrysler Corporation

and every other giant, soulless corporation in the country. It was a moment of real greatness because Lewis transcended his own person and was speaking out of the deep yearning of millions to force a great, sneering, arrogant corporation to bend its knee to organized labor. I cannot remember when I have been so moved in my life. I have never before experienced anything so completely devoid of individual personality, for those two voices of Lewis and Keller were really the spokesmen of opposing fundamental forces.

Murray Kempton, repeating the Pressman anecdote, judged that "this shining moment in his memory may speak volumes" about Pressman's own personality. "History was a war of contending classes, and its hero attained his peak when he transcended himself and became the impersonal embodiment of the class for which he spoke." Considered from the perspective of the young lawyer's participation in the dramatic labor events recently won, the first months of 1937 could surely have seemed this way. It would not be surprising that Pressman's oft-concealed idealism and romanticism, fired by his identification with Lewis as a father figure and avenging angel of the working class, would have resulted in such an emotional reaction. Perhaps never again would Pressman's heightened feelings reach the apogee they did when Lewis cowered Keller into submission in the abstract. At that moment, at least, the future must have seemed, as Kempton wrote, "without limit; for such a captain and his followers, there are no walls too high and frontiers too distant."[33]

FOUR

MOBILIZING THE ADMINISTRATIVE STATE

I n April 1937, industrial unionism's future must have looked rosy to Lee Pressman. Three of America's largest industrial corporations—General Motors, U.S. Steel, and Chrysler—had succumbed to Lewis's CIO in quick succession, and one of these without a strike. As the fear of employer retaliation against union membership lessened, the SWOC and other CIO offspring began to grow. In steel, the SWOC numbers shot up by leaps and bounds; by April, it had negotiated over fifty contracts and claimed 280,000 members. Moreover, on April 12, 1937, the labor movement received some critical help from a place where it least expected it. Unexpectedly, the still largely conservative Supreme Court issued its historic *Jones and Laughlin* decision, holding the National Labor Relations Act constitutional. This made the previous business policy of essentially ignoring the Act's provision because of their alleged unconstitutionality no longer viable. Even so, in the coming years, such hard-boiled antiunionists such as Tom Girdler of Republic Steel and Henry Ford vigorously fought CIO organizing efforts.[1]

Thus, though the CIO had achieved critical success, important competitors of employers already under contract remained unorganized. Leaving these businesses to undercut the wage costs of the organized companies threatened the long-term survival of the CIO itself. The new industrial union movement had no choice but to complete the unionization of all of its key industries. If a few industrialists engaged the new federation in no-holds-barred industrial warfare, though, and won those contests, where would the fledgling organization find the morale-building resources necessary to sustain

75

a fight for its continued existence? What tools could it use in this economic struggle other than labor's historic reliance on its own ability to strike?[2]

The answer lay in the relationship of the working class to the New Deal, and how that working class could be mobilized to exert influence. FDR owed his resounding election victory in 1936 to working-class votes—and he knew it. And, in these years, at least, to what extent that working class vote was separable from the intentions of the leadership of organized labor, often remained uncertain to politicians. Over the next ten years, the political relationship between New Deal forces, the CIO, and the AFL held the key to the potential growth and consolidation of a rising labor movement. It would take a concentrated effort to marshal the support of a broad array of New Deal administrative agencies concerned with a variety of labor questions, however. From his government experience, Lee Pressman knew that there was law and there was administration of the law. Politicians could easily backtrack in the face of the countervailing pressures that business would provide. Pressman had learned that a good law without a progressive administration of that law would lead to frustration, disappointment, and apathy, if not defeat.

From 1937 to 1947, it would fall to Lee Pressman to become the CIO's key mobilizer of the political–legal structure of a pro-industrial union New Deal administrative state. More than anyone else, he possessed the type of personal talents and social networking skills necessary to position CIO concerns favorably to the legal elites administering agencies and developing policy. Absolutely critical among these activities was his 1937–1940 oversight of the legal effort to utilize the NLRB to salvage the CIO from the defeat it experienced in the 1937 "Little Steel" strike. In addition, Pressman also worked to mobilize administrative New Deal state resources in other contexts and forums. He had correctly conceptualized the potential underlying a symbiotic relationship between the legal aspects of the state and industrial unionism at a key turning point in U.S. labor history. While his remark refers explicitly to the CIO general counsel's NWLB "Little Steel Formula" cases in 1942, Harold Ruttenberg's observation of Pressman's political–legal operations could be applied with equal force to his pre-war service to industrial unionism as well. "Lee Pressman was the chief of staff under Lewis and under Murray . . . in that whole campaign, which was enormously successful. He was the fountainhead of it, no question about it."[3]

THE CIO LEGAL DEPARTMENT

The legal and political work of the CIO would have quickly overwhelmed Pressman had he not been able to add two other attorneys to what was soon to become the general counsel's office. In late February 1937, he hired the scholarly Joseph Kovner, a Yale Law School graduate, who had worked as editor on the *IJA Bulletin* in collaboration with Carol Weiss King. Kovner recommended Anthony Wayne (Tony) Smith, also from Yale. A former aide to Pennsylvania Governor Gifford Pinchot from 1934 to 1937, Smith had been affiliated with William Donovan's law firm on Wall Street, where Nathan Witt had also spent a brief time. In 1937 he started to represent New York unions in collective bargaining and in cases before the National Labor Relations Board, where he first encountered Pressman, then still operating out of the law firm of Liebman, Robbins, and Pressman.[4]

Together, until Pressman and his two assistant general counsels parted ways acrimoniously in 1941, the three formed what became the Legal Department of the CIO. From the first, Pressman viewed his role as assisting in the formulation of high-level policy for the industrial union federation. Kovner and Smith were the legal technicians he hired to do the necessary scholarship that would support policy implementation in organizing and collective bargaining. "It was a relation in which we were the lawyers but Pressman was the power guy. He was the man who would push things on the power front. He would take a position and go forward with it and we would catch up with the law," recalled Kovner. In fact, very often Lee Pressman "did not operate from the point-of-view of the law." He either disliked, or had little patience with, the careful research needed for writing legal briefs and he "knew that." While Pressman recognized and appreciated a good legal argument, he was not a legal scholar but a man of action. He had a tremendous ability "to press a position on his client's side; [to] push it very hard," Kovner maintained. This was a view of Pressman's legal talents that John Abt shared. "He was a far better negotiator and political operator than he was a[n academic] lawyer," he wrote of Pressman in his memoir. "He didn't have the necessary patience to do the thorough analysis required in tackling a difficult legal case." "[P]utting together a brief requires lots of careful, and often dull, research, which was beyond Lee's tolerance," thought Abt.[5]

By April 1937 it became obvious that the legal–political work of the CIO had grown precipitously, and Lewis instructed Brophy to put Pressman on a full-time salary, plus expenses. The CIO general counsel realized that his brutal travel schedule between New York, Pittsburgh, and Washington would be lessened by once again returning with his family to the Washington, D.C., area, where of course John L. Lewis's UMWA and the CIO had headquarters. In 1938, Lee and Sunny, now with two young daughters, Ann and Marcia, left New York life and rented a series of modest, middle-class homes in the district's tranquil suburbs.[6]

THE LITTLE STEEL STRIKE AND THE NLRB

In the late spring of 1937, Lee Pressman found little tranquility in work. After the signing of the agreement with U.S. Steel, the SWOC stepped up its efforts to organize the hardened antiunion flank of the steel industry— Youngstown Sheet and Tube, Inland Steel, Bethlehem Steel, and Republic Steel—collectively known as the "Little Steel" companies. While among their number the Jones and Laughlin company had agreed to a representation election, which the SWOC won, the executives of these other corporations, led most forcefully by Republic's Tom Girdler, insisted on keeping their companies union free. The seemingly irresistible CIO momentum had led, unfortunately, to a seething militancy among the SWOC rank-and-file converts in many places, putting pressure on the SWOC's chief, Philip Murray, to take action, even though overall membership gains had not been impressive in many places. Without consulting Lewis, Murray, smarting personally from Lewis's domination of the Murray-directed steel organizing drive to that point, called a strike that began on May 26, 1937. Four days later, on Memorial Day, 1937, ten Chicago workers lay dead, shot by Chicago police who allegedly were protecting a Republic Steel plant, victims of the infamous "Memorial Day Massacre," as the shooting came to be known. Not long afterward the CIO would experience its first serious collective bargaining defeat, becoming, in CIO historian Robert Zieger's phrase, a "fragile juggernaut." It would lay with Lee Pressman's General Counsel's office to attempt to salvage what it could from the Little Steel engagement through the mobilization of the only weapon that seemed to remain in the industrial union movement's arsenal—the New Deal administrative state.[7]

"Before spending the rest of my life dealing with John L. Lewis," declared Republic Steel President Tom Girdler, "I am going [to retire] to raise apples and potatoes." Although Girdler made that statement in 1934, by 1937 there had been little change in his determination to avoid unionization. The fitful progress of the SWOC organizing among the Little Steel companies continued to vex Lewis, Murray, and other CIO leaders. The companies' employee representation plans had largely gone independent, but often proved problematic vehicles for unionization in Little Steel; sometimes serving to insulate workers from the SWOC's entreaties, sometimes forming a basis for inroads, depending on the area and the company involved. As the course of organizing accelerated after the U.S. Steel contract and the Supreme Court's *Jones and Laughlin* ruling, the SWOC's leaders realized future gains would depend on the decisions and administrative rulings of a reinvigorated NLRB and how far the courts would go in support of the agency.[8]

Pressman's Assistant General Counsel Joseph Kovner succinctly made this point in a report to CIO officials even before the strike began. The

Supreme Court's decisions in the *Jones and Laughlin* NLRB cases had only started the process of legal evolution in several key areas, he noted. Subjects such as the extent of board jurisdiction—the many dimensions of potential unfair labor practices, the depth of likely court review over NLRB rulings, and the problems of how to deal with labor activities beyond the board's jurisdiction—would take time to flesh out. In particular, Kovner indicated that the recent court decisions did not deal with the questions of company union status. Moreover, they only mentioned the issue of majority rule in a supporting reference to a previous Railway Labor Act decision favoring the concept. "However," he pointed out, "many problems involved in the cases such as the unit of bargaining and minority rights were not answered. A wide realm of difficult problems is still to be determined."[9]

From the first, it was apparent to Pressman that dealing with the Little Steel representatives would be at least as difficult as negotiating marketing agreements with business leaders in the AAA, and perhaps even more so. At a negotiation conference with Youngstown Sheet and Tube officials on April 28, 1937, for example, Philip Murray, accompanied by Pressman and other SWOC officials, informed the company's general counsel that SWOC had signed up a majority of its employees at its Youngstown and Indiana Harbor plants. Therefore, Murray requested, according to a memo prepared afterward by Pressman, that the company's officers sit down and negotiate collectively with the SWOC, as required by law, and he submitted a proposed contract similar to the one recently struck with U.S. Steel.

The company officials protested that they had no way to know if the SWOC did indeed represent a majority of employees at those plants. Even so, they "state[d] that regardless [of] how many employees of the company were members of the Steel Workers Organizing Committee, whether we had 100% or 90% of the employees as our members, the company did not intend and would not sign a written agreement with the Steel Workers Organizing Committee in regard to wages, hours or working conditions." The company would generally adhere to the terms and conditions "as set forth," in the U.S. Steel agreement, but would not put the deal in writing with the union. The other Little Steel companies took similar stances in a calculated strategy to meet the letter of the law without establishing a relationship with an independent labor organization.[10]

By May 20, when Republic closed its highly organized Massilon, Ohio, plant in order to avoid signing a contract, rank-and-file SWOC strike sentiment had climbed. According to Pressman, the SWOC's organizers advised the leadership to press forward while their signed-up members supported the organization ardently. In response to this militancy, Murray set the strike to begin on May 26, 1937. After several more or less peaceful days of picketing after the strike began, confrontations escalated. On Memorial Day, Chicago police fired point-blank into a line of marching strikers moving to picket a Republic plant's gates after a mass rally, leaving ten dead and scores more in the hospital, all of it captured for history and congressional investigation on newsreel film.

During the month of June, the companies began to use every time-tested antiunion weapon available, including developing an intense public relations campaign against the strikers, fomenting potent "back to work" movements in various areas and resuming production, where possible, with strikebreakers toward the end of the month. The SWOC tried to set in motion the New Deal political forces that had worked to its advantage so well only months before. Little by little, however, facilities began to resume operations, and strikers, disheartened, began to return, or try to return, to work. Sporadic violence continued through the end of July. By the end of the summer, it had become clear that the union had suffered a terrible defeat.[11]

Perplexingly, the assistance from those New Deal political forces just simply did not seem as easily forthcoming and as determinedly resolute as during the GM strike. Various liberal governors with plants in the Little Steel states attempted to mediate, virtually to no avail given the unflinching stance of Girdler and his colleagues, who seemed as expert at mobilizing public opinion against political elites who tolerated disorder and trespass as against the SWOC. Moreover, even a national official such as Secretary of Labor Frances Perkins could not make progress toward a settlement. At high-level mediation sessions begun in mid-June 1937, a prominent panel of federal mediators worked hard to get the parties to settle. Meeting with the SWOC group first, which included Lewis, Murray, McDonald, Bittner, Pressman, and Sweeney, the mediators explored avenues of settlement that might be acceptable to the unionists, who pointed out the companies' continued unwillingness to execute a written agreement embodying the conditions SWOC requested.

Before convening the companies' representatives, however, a local judge in Warren, Ohio, announced an injunction limiting SWOC picketing and ordering authorities to guarantee plant access to Republic and Youngstown plants. Swiftly, corporate executives in the affected areas announced their plans to reopen. The mediation panel attempted to dissuade the companies on the basis of the potential for riot and bloodshed. The business leaders demurred, claiming "that they did not feel in justice to their employees who wished to return to work that they could delay any longer. They informed us," wrote the panel members in their report, "that they were assured by the proper officials of adequate law enforcement." Probing deeper regarding the businessmens' positions, the mediators uncovered seemingly implacable hostility to many aspects of what the U.S. Steel contract encompassed. Little Steel industry officials refused to meet at the top level with Lewis and Murray; however, they would direct subordinates to meet with the union if requested in order to meet the letter of the law. Two companies even indicated that they would be willing to "discuss" oral and written agreements. Their "representatives would be instructed not to enter into such an agreement with the S.W.O.C," the federal mediators' report summarized. "We then attempted," they wrote with a hint of sarcasm, "to determine further just what they meant by collective bargaining."

The following morning the mediators again met with the union's negotiators. In these exchanges, John L. Lewis took the leading role. He stated "that the only issue was securing an agreement in which the union spoke for its members," by now a considerable paring down of objectives. The "union representatives stated they were positive there were no terms in this proposal upon which they and the companies could not agree if they met around the table." Lewis offered to withdraw personally if the corporate officials had an objection to him, and promptly followed his own suggestion by departing for Washington. Thereafter, the panel redoubled its efforts but to no avail. "After further consideration the Board decided, in view of the attitude of the companies, that it could not accomplish anything further by way of mediation."

Collaterally, the mediation efforts of various New Deal governors in the Little Steel states met with much the same results. The companies had succeeded in putting enough public pressure on elected officials, for the most part, so that no one was evidently willing to reprise Frank Murphy's role as guardian angel to the CIO. Even worse, President Roosevelt now seemed to wish to establish distance between his administration and the industrial union movement. To John L. Lewis's demands that he rescue the workers that had reelected him, Roosevelt issued his celebrated "a plague on both your houses" comment at a presidential news conference, castigating with equal force the intransigence of the companies and the militancy of the CIO. Therefore, with no political help in the offing, the mediation board's decision to recess implicitly acknowledged that the companies had the better hand in the struggle and wanted to continue playing it.[12]

With the top-level political forces in an unfavorable array, the CIO turned to what seemed the only resource left to it—the National Labor Relations Board. Early in June, shortly after the Memorial Day Massacre, Pressman called on Nat Witt, now secretary of the NLRB, then an influential position for board decision making. Pressman asked Witt to come to Pittsburgh to met with him and Philip Murray regarding Inland Steel's position that it did not have to execute a written agreement if it put into place any understanding with the SWOC after a joint meeting. Murray and Pressman told Witt they needed a quick decision from the board on the issue. "Since Witt knew the presentation of that question to the Board was contingent upon a demonstration by the union that it represented a majority" of Inland employees, according to NLRB historian James A. Gross, "he explored that question with Pressman and Murray." They asserted that the CIO had about 85 percent of Inland's workers signed up and could demonstrate it through a membership list. Witt advised them, then, to petition "not for a members-only recognition, but for exclusive bargaining rights on the basis of its claim of majority representation; and at the same time to demand negotiation of a written agreement." Then, when Inland refused to sign, even with the SWOC offering to demonstrate it represented a majority, the union could then press an unfair labor practice charge for failure to bargain in good faith. Pressman's connections within the New Deal administrative state had now begun to come into play.[13]

Likewise, Pressman and the SWOC turned the NLRB's attention toward Republic Steel, which by now had become the union's chief target. The SWOC, he claimed, wanted to have a representation election. "However, the policy of discrimination, coercion and intimidation which has been followed and maintained by the Republic Steel Corporation since the organizing campaign of this Committee, and continued during the present strike, makes it impossible to have such an election conducted at the present time in a fair, impartial manner. For this reason, we have not formally filed" for a representation election "but rather suggest that there be an immediate investigation by your Board, looking into the charges we have thus made," he wrote to the NLRB's Chairman J. Warren Madden. Despite Pressman and Murray's representations to Witt, and despite the rhetoric of his correspondence to the NLRB, in truth, the SWOC simply did not have the kind of recruits necessary to support an overall majority representation claim at Republic. Therefore, if government pressure was to be brought to bear against the company through the NLRB, the union had to press a large-scale antiunion discrimination claim and hope to resolve it prior to any true determination of union membership. While these were not the ultimate reasons upon which the agency used to proceed against Republic, it did serve to buy the SWOC time in the heat of the crisis. As the steel mediation board discussions showed, the corporations' were as yet not about to be cowed by government interventions.[14]

While Pressman exercised his political connections, it fell to his assistant general counsels, particularly Anthony Wayne Smith, to develop the legal theory that the NLRB ultimately used in its case against the companies. Tony Smith, as he was informally known, had been doing part-time work for CIO unions in New York via his connections with Kovner. By mid-July 1937, Smith was in the thick of the Little Steel fight. "I provided the legal theory upon which we eventually did get" SWOC strikers put back to work, he asserted in an interview years later. With the strike obviously becoming a lost cause, the key issue for the SWOC would be an effort to gain reinstatement for SWOC supporters. "The critical questions was: if your people lost the strike were your people entitled to get their jobs back?" "Nobody at the labor board had any idea what to do; Lee Pressman had no idea what to do" in regard to developing an effective theory upon which the NLRB could proceed, he said. Since the SWOC did not have a majority organized overall and therefore could not claim majority recognition rights, the strikers legally would have no right to return to their jobs, unless some new unfair labor practice against union supporters could be found. If "it could be shown that there was a new discrimination against them, in refusing to rehire workers upon reapplication," then a new unfair labor practice basis for restoring SWOC members to their jobs would exist. However, Smith recollected, "this meant that we would have to show that other men were being rehired and they were not." Pressman sent Smith out into the field in the Little Steel towns to develop a profile of industry hiring and layoff patterns. In subsequent months, he was aided in this work by Joseph Kovner and Meyer Bernstein, the latter a SWOC staff member and close colleague of Clinton Golden.[15]

That work sent Smith and Bernstein out into the steel towns of Ohio and Pennsylvania, trying to reconstruct historical and current patterns of employment. It was quite an experience, Smith remembered. Since in many cases the workers involved barely spoke English, the "all nations" appellation of the old AA lodges was indeed all too true. Interestingly, many of the initial leads regarding employment patterns were supplied by the management of the Jones and Laughlin company, the one steel company with which SWOC had been able to reach an agreement. "With that [information] we constructed a picture of discrimination in new hiring and submitted that to the National Labor Relations Board and they accepted that. And on the basis of those preliminary showings, they picked up their own investigation . . . of the discriminatory pattern."

Afterward, it "became rather a cooperative endeavor" between the CIO–SWOC and the board's attorneys, who of course had staff, resources, and subpoena power. In April 1938, the NLRB announced its decision entitling Republic strikers to reinstate their old positions with seniority rights upon application for reinstatement, much to the horror of Tom Girdler, who immediately declared an intent to appeal. To conform with newly announced procedural safeguards promulgated by the Supreme Court, the board vacated its initial order but reaffirmed it in October 1938. During this time, Smith and Bernstein, under Pressman's general direction, went on compiling documentation about incidents of antiunion discrimination of SWOC supporters as they were either refused rehiring upon application, or suffered disadvantageous conditions imposed on them upon rehire.[16]

What followed over the course of the next three years proved a war of legal attrition, with Pressman and his assistants working diligently to mobilize the NLRB and its staff to keep pressure applied on the corporations, and particularly against Republic Steel, the most irreconcilable of the lot. As Joseph Kovner said, CIO attorneys at the time generally regarded the NLRB, under its first chairman, J. Warren Madden, as essentially doing the work of the CIO. However, there were many points along the way where the preferences of board personnel did not dovetail with the internal organizational needs of the SWOC, especially as they related to court appeals and settlement negotiations. Especially after 1939, when conservatives in both parties banded together with AFL leaders incensed at what they claimed was pro-CIO NLRB bias, the Madden board operated in an atmosphere of increasing political controversy. Enemies of the board even launched powerful NLRA amendment drives in 1939 and 1940. The latter investigation, chaired by conservative mouse Democrat Howard Worth Smith of Virginia, subjected Madden's administration of the board to intense public scrutiny.[17]

Even so, Pressman knew that the NLRB was the SWOC's main chance to win through the New Deal administrative state what it could not in a sheer test of economic strength. While President Roosevelt and other top-level politicians did not see the necessity to put their prestige on the line for the CIO, by 1938 the federal bureaucracy contained many New Deal Liberals and Progressives of various stripes, and even radicals, such as Witt. Here was where it was possible to mobilize sympathies, here was where government policy had the potential to be shaped in a way favorable to ultimate SWOC goals. And thus it was here that Pressman worked to assert the influence necessary to devise strategy and shape that policy, as with his interactions with Witt, among others. Here was where he could supply the logic and backbone needed to prod the sometimes reluctant, and less committed, government personnel into maintaining legal pressure until surrounding conditions had changed sufficiently to work in the CIO's favor.

In order to do that, of course, Pressman needed, at a minimum, fair-minded administrators. He definitely found one in J. Warren Madden, the NLRB chairman. "He did not come into the field, as far as I could tell," recalled Pressman of Madden, "with any preconceived notions or background pertaining to labor matters." He was not prejudiced, he believed, toward either labor or employers. Madden "had a most acute and logical mind" and used the act itself as his guide to administration. It was within the statute itself, Pressman realized, that the potential for labor's administrative law advances lay. The "statute was so good, so specific, so all-embracing, so clear in its purpose and intent and provisions . . . that all labor needed at that time was not a hi-falutin' liberal with preconceived notions who might lose his nerve and say, 'Goodness gracious, I can't go this far, or that far.' What labor really needed . . . was precisely a Warren Madden" whose sole administrative touchstone was enforcement of the NLRA as written.[18]

Thus the board's October 1938 decision holding that the strike against Republic Steel grew out of the company's new post-strike unfair labor practices proved a critical victory for the CIO. The board ordered the corporation to reinstate all strikers in the State of Ohio with back pay from the date of each striker's voluntary application for reinstatement, and to discharge whatever replacements had been hired in order to do so. The NLRB also ordered Republic to disestablish its company unions. This was a decision of tremendous significance, for it involved the back pay of over 5,000 strikers, and more importantly, buttressed morale among the SWOC's adherents and led to financial pressure on Republic. Other Little Steel companies had NLRB cases pending also, but they had not engaged in the same magnitude of post-strike discrimination, as did Republic. Still, the Little Steel companies remained adamant in their refusal to sign a contract with the union. Because, as Pressman noted in his memos to SWOC leaders and district directors explaining the complex administrative procedures necessary for the union to undertake to meet with the board's specific requirements under the decision, the company intended to go to the Court of Appeals. "If the decision is adverse to the company, it will doubtless try to appeal to the Supreme Court of the United States" and would probably get a stay of any order pending a decision by the top court. Therefore, they could expect it would be some time before final implementation.[19]

By early 1939, it had become clear to Pressman's staff that NLRB personnel could vary in their enthusiasm for promoting the CIO's position, even given the board's decision, depending on the regions and people involved. As Meyer Bernstein wrote to subregional director Nathan Cowan, "The Labor Board recently has been bending over backwards in an effort to appease company lawyers. It has sustained no charges unless they have been uncontrovertably [sic] supported by the best kind of legal evidence. There must have been a history of antiunionism in the particular persons involved in the case. The worker must have been almost 'Simon pure' in order to get reinstatement and the Labor Board is now beginning to demand that we furnish proof that someone else was given the job vacated by the discharged man. The courts are going even farther [sic] than this," he wrote in exasperation. "They miss no opportunity to throw out as many cases as they can." And, in the negotiations with Youngstown Sheet and Tube involving the NLRB and SWOC, over and over again "company representatives lapsed into their old thumb twiddling habits," Bernstein reported to Pressman. "They refuse to concede anything," he wrote. "Never during the course of our negotiations have they admitted a single charge. Never have they agreed, in conference, to reinstate this man or that. They may call the men back, and have—but we never know about it till after it is done."[20]

The difficulties involved in pressing the cases forward caused discomfort, even for Philip Murray. One large problem with the Republic decision was that the board's order for reinstatement covered only Ohio facilities, necessitating additional case filings. "The decision handed down by the Labor Board on October 19, 1938, against the Republic Steel [company] excluding among others the Buffalo Plant from participation has created a local situation unfavorable to our present organizational efforts," Nathan Cowan informed Assistant General Counsel Tony Smith. "The men feel that they have been neglected and there is a feeling of pessimism among our people which is very difficult to combat," he noted, suggesting perhaps separate local NLRB proceedings. As the additional SWOC charges against these non-Ohio facilities wound their way slowly through NLRB channels, rank-and-file anger climbed. "Dear Sir," wrote Secretary Ignatius Maryanksi of Local Lodge 1743 in Buffalo to Philip Murray in July 1939, '[a]t our last meeting . . . I was authorized [sic] to write to you and find out what is wrong that after 26 months of struggle against Republic Steel Co. there is nothing being done here in Buffalo in our case. All we hear is promises and we are pretty well fed up on them. What we want is action, and action soon. You are settling other matters like the Automobile workers and others,'" Maryanski wrote in a reference to Philip Murray's and Sidney Hillman's well-publicized mediations in a United Auto Workers factional struggle, "but you are not doing anything for us. We feel that you are not doing your duty to your organization the S.W.O.C. as you should being at the head of it." Murray's peevish reply outlining the cases' legal status reflected his sensitivity. "Your charge with reference to my not doing my duty is absurd, and did [sic] you know anything about the activities of the officers of the organization with regard to the conduct of its affairs, I am quite sure that your local organization would not do what it has done." Clearly, if the SWOC had any hope to breathe life into the stalled organizing progress it had made in the Little Steel industry, the importance of a favorable eventual outcome to the many complexities of the board's decisions was crucial.[21]

But as time went on the legal context surrounding the Republic case grew even more convoluted. Girdler's appeal on the main NLRB Ohio-based decision had by now reached the Third Circuit of the Court of Appeals. To ensure SWOC concerns received due consideration, Pressman filed as an intervenor, even though the NLRB was formally the defending Party. In another forum, Republic began an antitrust suit against the SWOC stemming from events surrounding the strike, pleading for treble damages running into many millions of dollars. In response, Pressman filed similar counterclaims on behalf of the CIO and attempted to persuade the Justice Department to initiate its own antitrust prosecution against the company. In addition, several Republic stockholder groups had filed a mismanagement case against the corporation, even further clouding many legal issues now involved. The Court of Appeals handed the NLRB a victory in November, and all parties expected a Supreme Court appeal. Early in 1940, Pressman informed Murray that the appeal had been logged in at the top court, with both the NLRB and SWOC filing briefs "in opposition to the Supreme Court assuming jurisdiction." "In addition, we have been in constant touch with the officials of the Labor Board[,] in an endeavor to have them send out representatives to the Ohio steel towns obtaining the necessary information and preparing records for the enforcement of the Board order after a final decision has been obtained from the Supreme Court. The Board is now preparing the necessary forms which they have worked out with us and we expect to have their representatives in the field very shortly," he reported to the SWOC chairman. With the legal per-ambulations about to untangle, events overseas also began to impinge on the contest.[22]

With the beginning of World War II in September 1939, U.S. defense preparations accelerated. For some time, Lewis and Pressman had been attempting to gain legislation prohibiting the awarding of government con-tracts to labor law violators. When Roosevelt began to rely more and more on Sidney Hillman for production–labor relations issues, appointing him to a series of public commissions, committees, and boards, Lewis began to pres-sure Hillman, whom he now considered a rival, to effectuate a policy denying government contracts to companies violating labor statutes. In mid-June 1940, Hillman, then sitting on the National Defense Advisory Commission, won FDR's agreement to a set of such labor policies for mobilization, which were promulgated in August. By October, Hillman claimed that Army and Navy contracts thenceforth would not be granted to labor law violators. Lewis quickly pointed out a number of deficiencies in the policies that Hillman worked out. Even so, executives and stockholders of the Little Steel corpora-tions could not take for granted that loopholes would allow them to continue to handle labor relations as in the past and still win federal defense contracts.[23]

While NLRB delays continued to frustrate—formal complaints for Youngstown Sheet and Tube and two of Republic's plants had still not been issued as of May 1940, and the case at the Buffalo plant had been delayed as well—Pressman persisted without fail, constantly pressing the agency for-ward on unsettled matters. "I had a conference yesterday with Charles Fahy, General Counsel of the Board," Pressman informed Murray in May 1940, to resolve the dispute over the date from which the board would request back pay. The conference pleased Pressman indeed. Fahy offered a solution that he found quite workable. The board would immediately issue a complaint secur-ing the back pay date to be the date that the board originally issued its Ohio Republic decision, or when all the strikers at the plants in question had made application to return, whichever was earlier. "On the basis of what Fahy claims that the Board is prepared to do, it means we get immediate and quick action in all pending cases." While there might be a basis for some minor con-cerns, overall it was a good offer. "On the whole," Pressman advised Murray, "I think the foregoing is an equitable solution and one which we should not criticize."

The impending Supreme Court decision, the situation involving government contracts, and the languishing NLRB cases at last moving forward evidently prompted an unexpected response from Republic Steel. In June 1940, Pressman informed Murray that "Charles Fahy called me today to advise that Mr. Patton of the Republic Steel Corporation" wished to "initiate discussions looking toward settlement." Pressman told Fahy that they would need more accurate information about the gross amounts owed prior to any discussions; at the present time, the union did not have it. "Furthermore, I pointed out that we would consider it an extremely unfortunate thing if the Board entered into any discussions or if the Board, pending such discussions, permitted any postponement to be made" of the outstanding cases. Fahy "indicated that for the time being they were not going to give any postponements," but he did feel obligated to conduct discussions with Patton, if requested.[24]

But the NLRB persisted in trying to stimulate settlement talks, and by the fall of 1940, negotiations between the SWOC and both Youngstown Sheet and Tube and Republic had been undertaken under the agency's auspices. With Pressman and Smith representing the SWOC, Ernest Ballard and Ralph Bowers representing Youngstown, and NLRB Regional Director Oscar Smith representing the board, the parties confronted each other in a settlement conference on October 30, 1940. Oscar Smith began by reading a proposed settlement by the company. One of its provisions was that certain individuals were excluded from the agreement, and Pressman queried why this was so, if they had not been convicted of crimes. Ballard claimed the company had evidence of such, and that those individuals could be convicted if tried. "Mr. Pressman objected, [noting] that in the Republic Steel Decision handed down by the Third Circuit Court" the court stated that "the Labor Board was not a criminal court and that it quite rightly disqualified strikers from reinstatement only after a decision from a qualified court." The company claimed that it could have them arrested and convicted without difficulty, if that was what the union wanted. "Mr. Pressman said, 'that is up to you, but we will not agree to their exclusion simply because you say you have evidence that they engaged in crimes,'" the conference minutes recorded.

Conversation shifted to a number of other individuals and controversies surrounding their reapplication dates. The company also offered to post watered-down notices on the disestablishment of the company union; at this point, NLRB official "Oscar Smith insisted upon working the notices to the effect that the Company Unions are through." After a luncheon break, the SWOC parties watched carefully as the company and NLRB reprised former discussions on how any settlement, if reached, should be executed. Here Pressman's suspicions were aroused. "Mr. Pressman then requested to know whether the settlement proposal which was transmitted to us by Mr. Halliday [of the NLRB] was something upon which the Board and the Company had jointly agreed. He wanted to know whether we were being presented with a fait accompli." Regional Director Smith admitted that that was partially true, at least in regard to some of the principles of settlement, which "had been gone over with the Board." Pressman, however, would not buy into such an agreement. "Mr. Pressman then stated that we object to the manner in which the thing had been handled," the conference minutes chronicled, "and the principle on which the settlement had proceeded. He pointed out that we had an entirely different theory in mind." That theory was the one used by the board itself in Republic's Ohio and Buffalo cases. The conference concluded with the company indicating that it might be willing to change positions and asking SWOC to put together a counterproposal.[25]

Pressman held out for more and applied counterpressure to the agency. In a sharp letter to NLRB board members in Washington, he stated that after further analysis regarding the board's suggested settlement principles, "We have come to the conclusion that the proposal is fundamentally inadequate and unsatisfactory and that we cannot accept it." Outlining the many inequities contained in it in detail, the CIO general counsel ticked off the SWOC's objections to the deficiencies of the company-NLRB basis of settlement. He noted, moreover, that it "was definitely understood between SWOC and representatives of the Board[,] as the result of several conferences over a period of many months[,] that the instant case would be tried on the same theories" as in the Republic cases, which had much more just back pay determinations. In conclusion, Pressman listed a litany of his and the union's objections to the NLRB's role.

> This case is now three and one-half years old. . . . As a result of clerical errors on the part of the Board, for which we were not responsible, no action was taken on them until the Spring of 1938. At the Board's instance, we entered into settlement negotiations shortly thereafter, which came to nothing as the result of the company's recalcitrant attitude. A month or two later, we perfected our charges and again sought the issuance of a complaint. We allowed ourselves to be drawn into settlement negotiations again this Fall, but without substantial results. Thereafter, in instance after instance, we sought prompt action by the Board on a theory which would make recovery possible for the men whose individual suffering has been in no sense their fault nor the fault of the organization which has represented them in these proceedings.
>
> We have been lead to believe[,] that if we were patient and permitted thorough preparation by the Board, a preparation which has now consumed in its final stage the better part of a full year, it would soon be possible for us to go to trial or effectuate a settlement on a sound basis. We are now met with a proposed offer of settlement, which

appears to have some support on the part of Board representatives, which is entirely inadequate, and which it would be utterly impossible for the union to accept or to undertake to present to its membership. We wish to make a very firm protest against the acceptance of any such proposal by the Board, and renew our request that the Board proceed to trials on this matter on the basis of a complaint covering all the charges and making possible by its allegations and by the theory of trial a full recovery of back wages lost by the workers. . . .[26]

The SWOC's decision to hold fast, along with the other increasing pressures, evidently prompted the company to move further in the direction of seeking settlement by February 1941. Ballard called Oscar Smith and indicated that he had "changed his ideas on the case considerably. He is willing to go much further in settlement than ever before," a file memorandum recorded. Ballard pressed Smith to arrange a negotiation session, who informed the union that based on his talks with Ballard the "whole question of back wages is now open. . . . " At a following conference, recorded in the SWOC minutes, the company outlined its new proposals and made significant concessions. The union also compromised on a few issues of concern to the company. By the end of March, the parties had worked out final details on stipulating an end to the cases and claims. In addition, the company soon agreed to a procedure to obtain union certification through a cross-check of dues-paying members with company payrolls. If the SWOC demonstrated a majority in both company divisions, a satisfied Pressman informed Murray in July 1941, "The company agrees to negotiate with the SWOC representing all of the employees of the company as a single collective bargaining unit[,] and to execute the signed contract upon the consummation of the negotiations."[27]

Similarly, the SWOC engaged in settlement discussions during the fall of 1940 with Republic, the company that had by far the highest back pay exposure. Pressman, Smith, and Bernstein met with Republic's Patton and the NLRB's Robert Watts to explore an overall settlement of all related claims generated by the cases. One issue of clear concern to Republic was a number of personal injury and false arrest suits brought by individual steelworkers against Republic's officers, as well as a stockholder suit against Girdler and other corporate executives. "Mr. Pressman said that the damage and false arrest suits are being handled on a contingent basis" by another law firm and that the SWOC was "not a Party to them." Therefore, he could not officially include these cases in the settlement discussions, but as an added incentive he offered "that he would be glad to use his good offices to help secure an amicable adjustment. . . ." The company then offered back pay dating from mid-1939. "Mr. Pressman pointed out that a trial examiner's report had already been issued in the Buffalo Case and that in this report the trail examiner had recommended full back pay from the time of first application for reinstatement," which dated from September 1937. While the union might accept a date of the NLRB decision of October 1938 as a basis, it could not do more, the conference minutes indicated. "However, Mr. Pressman very carefully pointed out that there was no room for compromise between" that date and the company's suggested 1939 date. Patton suggested the pending trial in the case the company's Monroe plant should probably be suspended, given the settlement negotiations. Pressman obviously wanted to keep all of the financial pressure that he could on the company, so he "said that the case had been delayed so long and postponed so often that we were under moral obligations to commence proceedings."

At a second conference the following week, Republic stated it could not accept the SWOC's proposed offer of October 1938, and Pressman held out against a May 1939 date. Eventually, negotiation proposals emerged that indicated that a settlement using the median date of all workers' actual reapplication dates in 1938 might work. Pressman then took Patton aside and explored the possibility of company recognition of the union and the execution of a contract, which Patton promised to take up with Girdler. Between this conference and the next, however, Philip Murray imposed a mandate that any agreement had to treat the workers in all Republic facilities the same, in regard to back pay computations. Having reached another impasse on back pay dates, Pressman indicated that little more could be done at that point. "He said he was quite sure Mr. Murray would reject" the solution they had been exploring "unless he—Pressman—had an opportunity to go over the matter at length. "Pressman asked for a few moments privately with Patton," the conference minutes reported. "Taking up the question of a signed contract Patton said that Girdler said to wait until the Supreme Court acts on the" NLRB's Heinz case, which would determine whether a willingness to sign a contract when an oral agreement had been reached was a basic element of good faith bargaining. The implication, of course, was that if the Court so held, Girdler would finally sign an agreement with the SWOC. Certainly Girdler's attitude was quite a change in heart—or at least in mind—from 1937.[28]

By early 1941, Pressman convinced Murray to continue Republic negotiations pending a survey of all outstanding areas in which the SWOC had cases pending. In March, Tony Smith and Meyer Bernstein assembled the needed information, and the parties seemed ready to accept a November 1, 1938, date of back pay for all non-Ohio cases. By July 1941, Pressman had worked out stipulations with the company, putting to rest the many tangled issues, claims, and cross-claims emanating from the four-year legal struggle. Ultimately, the settlement terms awarded back pay, what the replacement worker on that striker's job earned "during the period for which the striker is entitled to back pay." The company also agreed to disestablish its company union, to drop all claims in its antitrust suit, and to allow a similar union dues-payroll cross-check for SWOC recognition. A satisfied Pressman wrote to Philip Murray on July 22, 1941, that this "completes our arrangements with the Inland Steel Company, Youngstown Sheet & Tube Company, Bethlehem Steel Corporation, and Republic Steel Corporation. All four corporations have now entered into stipulations providing for cross-check (elections in the case of the Bethlehem Steel Corporation)," the attorney informed Murray. The SWOC now had "arrangements for signed contracts where we can demonstrate a majority. In addition, we have established the practice that all of the plants where we demonstrate a majority in the case of each company will be embraced within a single collective bargaining unit."[29]

While the victory might not have been quite as picturesque and emotionally inspiring as that of the Flint GM strikers marching jubilantly out of the plants in 1937, it was every bit as significant in terms of the long-term survival of the CIO as an institution. It lessened the threat of major unorganized employers continuing to put downward pressure on already established contracts and standards. And of course it brought thousands of new recruits within industrial unionism's circle. Of course, the changing economic circumstances brought about by the defense preparations played a large role in restoring the CIO's forward momentum. But for that to happen, Pressman and other labor attorneys had to work to buy the time necessary for economic conditions to change from the disasters experienced during the Roosevelt recession during the period 1937–1938. Luckily, by 1940, the economic context had changed in the SWOC's favor because of the European war. Had they not, the CIO might have become just another ephemeral and short-lived industrial union uprising, so common in U.S. labor's past. Now, as the nation approached war, the CIO, having survived the challenges of the late 1930s, was once again being presented with an opportunity to grow.

Much of this must have been on Lee Pressman's mind as he stepped up to the podium of the Transport Workers Union (TWU) convention in New York City in September 1941, not long after the SWOC struck the final agreements with the Little Steel companies. TWU President Mike Quill informed his members that if "there ever was a friend to this organization, a sound worker and a great legal mind, it is the next speaker, the General Counsel of the CIO, Lee Pressman." The delegates rose as the attorney strode to the platform and applauded enthusiastically as Quill pinned a convention badge to his lapel. Pressman lost no time in relating the CIO's most recent accomplishments to the challenges facing the TWU in its struggles against New York City's municipal government. He recalled that four years previously he had spoken to TWU officers during affiliation discussions. "That evening I told you about our [steel] negotiations" and our first contract with U.S. Steel. "I also had to tell you that evening that after we had taken on the United States

Steel Corporation, the Steel Workers Union took on a few other steel corporations in Little Steel," he continued. "In 1937," he added frankly, "those Little Steel corporations whipped us. They beat us in that strike."

However, while the CIO had lost those particular battles, it had been able to win the war. "Today, four years later, I take great pleasure in bringing to you the news that last week the representatives" of SWOC and the Little Steel companies had met "and in short order we expect to get written contracts" he announced, arousing the delegates' delighted applause. "Now, what we were able to do to Tom Girdler of Republic Steel Corporation[,]" the TWU should be able to do to the Board of Transportation. It was all a matter of showing employers and the government "that you mean business, that you insist on getting your rights, that you insist on getting and keeping the conditions that you have and that you mean to improve them."[30]

And in a way perhaps the Little Steel NLRB cases were nothing if not a sustained performance at legal insistence. Pressman and his colleagues in the general counsel's office had persevered in their assertion of the SWOC members' rights under the National Labor Relations Act. They had presented agency officials with the theory needed to press the case, had mastered the economic complexities necessary to arrive at a just settlement workers would support, and had navigated against the currents of political missteps along the way. Pressman's ability to determine overall operational strategy, to stay the course once having decided on it, and to influence policy shapers in the top echelons of the NLRB created a countervailing pressure on board personnel. Such officials might have been likely to accept the companies' positions on key points in order to settle the cases without the CIO general counsel's agitation for the CIO position. In the end, that the SWOC achieved what was necessary to begin moving forward again in organizing the steel industry was not only a testament to Pressman's operational skills, it also was a testament to his commitment to the many thousands of Little Steel industry workers who had been fired, beaten, or killed for the simple act of wanting to join a union to improve their lives.

ADMINISTRATIVE, LEGISLATIVE, AND JUDICIAL FORUMS

From 1937 to 1940, Lee Pressman's Legal Department also engaged in other activities besides the Little Steel effort. Most visible was Pressman's role as CIO "point man" in political and legislative matters, under both John L. Lewis and his successor Philip Murray. Less visible, but no less important, was his representation of CIO interests before a variety of New Deal agencies and his litigation activities in the area of civil liberties. Pressman's operational initiatives and defensive strategies added to the complex web of developments necessary to put the CIO on firmer footing, preparing the industrial federation to lobby for equitable national labor policy for influence during the war years.

While a broad array of legislative concerns occupied Pressman's time during these years—the CIO's interests in the evolving New Deal administrative state were fundamental, after all—two in particular required the most attention. Both of these issues dealt with making sure that the newly won rights granted under the NLRA, and recently etched into the fabric of national law by the Supreme Court, could withstand the rising opposition to CIO advances. In 1938, this played out in an effort to mobilize administrative-legislative backing for a policy prohibiting government contracts for labor law violators. And, during the period 1939–1940, Pressman and his assistant general counsels directed the CIO's campaign to prevent a potent NLRA amendment drive from eviscerating the law that all industrial union leaders realized was critical to their future. Moreover, Pressman's keen grasp of the potentialities of administrative law was a representational area in which he excelled, and in which he realized presented the greatest opportunity to aggressively assert CIO interests. It "was a period for which the C.I.O. should be given considerable credit," Pressman asserted in his Columbia oral history reminiscence, "in using every conceivable instrument or device we could put our fingers or hands on, to assist ourselves. Not just going out [and] butting your head against the wall . . ." but finding a statute and saying, "'Let's use it, let's try it, give it a whirl. All we can do is lose.'"

Pressman reviewed the specific statutory language of the Walsh–Healey Act, for example, which mandated that federal contractors adhere to minimum wage levels in a locality in order to obtain government contracts. It occurred to him that there was no reason why that law should focus only on the textile and building trades industries. These were two economic sectors that had incessantly experienced wage undercutting from nonunion bidders but were also noncapital intensive. Why not try to employ that approach to the capital-intensive industries, especially those resisting the CIO?

Pressman approached Lewis and Murray about filing a petition with the Public Contract Board under Walsh–Healey, a petition that would target the steel industry. At the time, nonunionized steel producers such as Bethlehem—the only steel manufacturer in many of its localities—paid significantly less than the now-unionized U.S. Steel facilities in Pittsburgh. Both leaders doubted that the government would establish a rate that would in any way affect Bethlehem. Pressman's challenging rejoinder was, "'Who is going to say . . . what is [a] 'locality'?'" He went to work on the briefs and as always maneuvered behind the scenes to put together the argument that the steel industry was an economic "national-local community." The CIO general counsel's ability to work the system and arrange for a persuadable trial examiner, an official "of the stripe of the New Deal days," that is, a "good" New Deal liberal, resulted in an initial pro-CIO ruling in November 1938. The decision created four "local" communities for the steel industry and brought Bethlehem wages up to U.S. Steel levels, creating positive momentum for the SWOC's Bethlehem organizing campaign. "Up until that point," a self-satisfied Pressman recalled, "nobody but the textile industry" had been able to use Walsh–Healey to such an advantage. Similarly, not long afterward, contemporaneous study of the Fair Labor Standards Act of 1938, at a time when he had just taken a trip out West saw an open pit mining operation involving considerable worker travel time from the rim to the mine face, led to another initiative. Wage and hour administrator regulations, he pointed out to John L. Lewis, required wage payments for that time. "What are you up to?" his inquiring principal asked. "I'd like to start a hearing on this [under the] Wage and Hour Law," and try to get a "ruling that that [time] constitutes work." Pressman filed for hearings, developed his administrative law arguments, and won his case. The UMWA later used that precedent to press litigation for portal-to-portal pay in underground mining.[31]

Clearly, then, Pressman was always on the lookout for opportunities to mobilize the power of the federal government, particularly its executive-administrative power, where leverage could be exerted with the least opposition. He and Lewis therefore approached President Roosevelt on the wider and thorny problem of granting government contracts to corporations with continual violations of the National Labor Relations Act. The ever-careful FDR refused to accede to Lewis's request to issue an executive order against the issuance of such contracts. "At that time," Pressman noted, "we were advised that such an executive order would not be legal" and therefore, while preferring the executive or administrative agency route, the CIO was forced to go to Congress for enabling legislation."[32]

After first reviewing the idea with Attorney General Frank Murphy, who gave his support for Pressman's draft bill, the CIO general counsel worked the Hill and ultimately convinced Senator Robert Wagner to introduce the proposal. After some adept legislative maneuvering by Pressman with the Senate Labor Committee, the bill moved to the floor and passed. In the House, however, it ran into tougher sledding, because the leadership referred it first to the Judiciary Committee, which was not strongly pro-labor.[33]

The CIO general counsel then orchestrated a set of hearings in an effort to move the proposal forward. In his own testimony—the first time he spoke substantively before Congress on a labor issue—he laid out the case for the measure to a not-wholly enthusiastic panel. Under the proposed bill, he informed the legislators, if a company had been found to be a labor law violator by the NLRB, it would then notify the U.S. Comptroller General of that fact, and thereafter the company would not be "entitled to submit bids to the

United States Government. In other words," Pressman paraphrased the intent of the bill, "the Government says, 'I am a purchaser of materials. I have on the one hand an administrative agency that I have established. It has a certain definite policy, and I say to those people who want to deal with me that they have got to comply with the orders of that administrative agency that I have set up.'" Arguing the case that the government should not continue to support—indeed, even provide rich benefits—to those companies like Bethlehem Steel and Ford Motor that repeatedly ignored NLRB rulings in the process of long-drawn out appeals, Pressman encountered resistance. Unfriendly representatives charged that under this type of legislation, the NLRB, if it were biased in favor of the CIO, could then in effect "blacklist" any company that refused to deal with an affiliate of the industrial federation. Even more significantly, the Judiciary Committee members noted that such a law would no doubt complete the partial organization of many industries that the CIO as yet had only begun, to which Pressman readily agreed.[34]

After mobilizing intense constituent pressure on Judiciary Committee members, the CIO finally broke the bill loose from the Committee's stonewalling efforts. However, it then went to the House Rules Committee, chaired at the time by an old Roosevelt nemesis from New York, Representative John J. O'Connor. Lewis and Pressman made a personal lobbying visit to O'Connor, and even attempted to cut a deal by promising CIO reelection support for the congressman. O'Connor agreed to move the bill forward, then quickly "reneged on his promise to us," Pressman recollected, largely due to adverse "press commentary."

The attorney believed it had been a defeat with long-range consequences. If it had gotten to the House floor, Pressman judged that it had enough support among the general public to pass. In an era of defense buildups, large industrial corporations could not afford to forego bidding on the growing volume of lucrative government defense contracts. As a consequence, more likely than not the organizing job of the CIO in the major industries would have been completed prior to World War II. Pressman's frank answer during his Committee testimony drove the point home best. Where a collective bargaining agreement had not yet been established, "This bill will give it to us." This would have made the industrial union federation a far stronger organization going into the war years, and arguably would have enabled it to wield more political and legislative clout in the creation and implementation of wartime labor policies. "We came that close to getting that kind of law through. . . ." he mused later. "Had we gotten it through at that time . . . it would have made quite a difference in the history of labor relations."[35]

While the CIO took the political offensive on the government contract issue, the campaign to prevent amendment of the National Labor Relations

Act was a rearguard action. Despite numerous CIO complaints that the board under Chairman J. Warren Madden proved too easily swayed and affected by AFL criticism, no one in his or her right mind in the industrial union movement seriously wanted the Act opened up for amendment. There was perhaps no more important political-legislative issue to the CIO than the preservation of the statute and Madden's NLRB. "The leadership of the C.I.O.," Pressman declared, "knew the importance of the act, and enjoyed the importance of the act to their own movement," although sectors of the AFL leadership obviously did not.[36]

Speaking in retrospect, years later, Pressman heaped considerable praise on NLRB Chairman J. Warren Madden for the Act's administration during its early years. "He had a most astute and logical mind," he recalled of Madden, though no background in labor matters. And that being the case, the agency chairman simply carried out the pro-union language of the statute as then written. In his many times of defending the board before Congress, Madden "would prepare a statement that was literally unassailable, and the Congressmen couldn't do a thing to him" except deny the truth, of which more than one was willing to do. Thus it "was a matter of profound importance to the labor movement, as to who was a member of the board," and particularly so as to who was chairman. The years of the Madden board, 1935 to 1940, were "in my judgment . . . the best I've every seen of an honest administration of an outstanding statute. Most extraordinarily honest in administration," Pressman concluded.[37]

Certain segments of the AFL, though, especially a handful of national leaders in Washington, saw things differently. As the "dual union" rivalry between the federations heated up after 1937, the NLRB soon found itself caught in a cross fire. True, board members such as Edwin Smith clearly without doubt philosophically favored industrial forms of organization. Madden, on the other hand, tried to keep the agency on an even keel with the labor movement. As charges of "pro-CIO" bias in bargaining unit determinations and multiunion elections emanated from both employers and the AFL, the chairman tried to quell the criticisms. He crafted the "Globe Doctrine" policy that would allow craft severance from an industrial bargaining unit under certain conditions in 1938. However, in turn, this doctrine provoked Pressman into countercharges that the board had caved in to unwarranted carping. The CIO general counsel later realized that while at the time he was sharply critical of this board policy, he realized that Madden's evenhanded attempts to resolve the craft-industrial rivalry was about the best that could be done in this intense public policy battle.[38]

The end result of the interunion warfare came to be an odd political alliance of the AFL national leadership and business organizations such as the National Association of Manufacturers (NAM). Both now wanted to open up the act for amendment. After the failure of President Roosevelt's efforts to "purge" his Party of conservative obstructionists of the New Deal in the 1938 congressional elections, the amendment drive picked up steam. Labor committees in both chambers began lengthy hearings into the administration of the law by the Madden board, posing a danger to the statute. "I can't describe" adequately "all the details and the anger and the frustration, on the part of the C.I.O.," when we "saw that by virtue of this fight[,] and what the A. F. of L. was doing, . . . was just simply cutting the throat of the institution that was so important to both of us."

Indeed, for the CIO, a developing organization without an extensive infrastructure of resources, the capabilities of the U.S. government proved a boon to its organizing. Board personnel, although reluctant allies at times, had the responsibility to carry through complaints to hearings if the dispute could not be settled, once the union or employee as the charging Party proved a prima facie case. Union attorneys could participate wholeheartedly, if they chose, as CIO lawyers did in the critical Little Steel cases. But during these early years, as Pressman noted, "In every way that you could conceive of, you were always trying to invoke Governmental machinery." With labor board staff pressing the issue, from "that time on, it was the United States Treasury versus these corporations." The legal detail work and the assembly of proofs did not fall, unilaterally, on the shoulders of the union's counsel. The "extent to which union attorneys might participate would vary and depend on the tricks of the trade," Pressman observed, "how important it was, how much you were immersed in something else." While the government "had the corporation busy on that front, you were also initiating some other proceeding to take care of the corporation on some other front." Thus, the NLRB was exceptionally useful in waging these multipronged organizing-bargaining initiatives.[39]

So the CIO had to do its utmost to keep the statute intact and the board friendly. By the spring of 1939, the CIO General Counsel's office was deeply involved in orchestrating the industrial federation's testimony against the AFL and business charges against the NLRA. Assisted by Tony Smith, Joseph Kovner, and Meyer Bernstein, Pressman directed the preparation of statements by CIO officers, handling John L. Lewis's and his own personally. He also garnered as much information as possible from affiliates regarding their experience with the board, emphasizing wherever possible how the agency had been effective in assisting labor and employers in achieving stable industrial relations. Strategically, the CIO hoped to drag out the hearings, advising affiliates to insist on making detailed statements orally to the committee. In addition to buying time, these statements would assist in getting industrial unionism's side of the dispute before the general public in a way in which no other tactic could.[40]

Although Pressman eventually testified before both chambers' labor committees, his Senate testimony in late August 1939 came first and provided the essentials of the CIO's indictment of NLRA–NLRB critics. Citing the extensive involvement of his office with the board and its personnel, and his and his associates' consultations with other union legal counsel across the country, Pressman told the committee that we "think therefore, that we have something substantial to say about the problems" before the committee. And while attempting to project an aura of "reasoned" discussion, Pressman's testimony would from time to time edge over into strident denunciations of the CIO's opponents and "enemies," a seeping out of anger grounded in his deepening reidentification with his working-class roots. Despite priding himself on his emotional control, to express anger when opponents attacked the interests of what he liked to call the "common people" of the country was one feeling he could never quite totally hide.[41]

Pressman's statement, as CIO general counsel, dealt with a number of issues. He first confronted and dismissed head-on alleged NLRB bias and the real reasons for industrial unrest. Later he dealt more explicitly with CIO objections to the various amendment bills before Congress—the AFL-sponsored Walsh bill protecting craft prerogatives—and the many business-backed measures. And from the first, there was little doubt about his assessment of where all the "fog, and the noise," all the "deliberate misstatements and absolute distortions" about the board came from. While he did not spare the AFL from his barbs, more than anything corporate arrogance underlay the amendment drive, he charged. The act was no more one sided than any other law that regulated a social evil; no fair objection could be made that antitrust laws, designed to prevent business monopoly, were "one sided" because they did not also regulate small businesses. What was truly one sided, Pressman argued, was the tremendous power that employers held over workers. What the NLRA meant to do, was "to prevent a particular kind of offense of which employers only . . . can be guilty. The offense is the utilization of the employers' economic power over his workers to deprive them of full freedom of association in unions of their own choosing. . . ." Workers did not have any similar power over the employer, a power which "can hardly be exaggerated. . . ." "Moreover, that power was exercised "as ruthlessly and as brutally and as unscrupulously as the management of such corporations alone can exercise such power." Critics complained of "petty violations of municipal ordinances and local laws occasionally indulged in by individuals in labor organizations, frequently under bitter provocation," the attorney pointed out. "To begin to compare the two, and to pretend that the Federal regulation of one requires Federal regulation of the other is to lose all sense of value and proportion."

Existing law covered those offenses well. Indeed, "that irresponsible and tyrannical court-made [injunction] law" which "labor and progressive opinion" had still been "unable to bring fully under the control of the representatives of the people," was well known to have been repeatedly applied to such types of disputes, despite the Norris–LaGuardia Act. Under these conditions, it was foolish to think that the Wagner Act needed more "balance" to control labor offenses. No serious critic could contend that local police authorities did not enforce such laws. "Only persons totally" out of touch with the "realities of industrial warfare as it is inflicted by corporate interests on the workers of this country can pretend any such thing."

And then Pressman's passionate identification moved him to his most eloquent indictment of labor's enemies.

> It is the workers, and not the officers of the corporations, who are crammed into disgusting and unsanitary jails and prisons during every labor dispute of significant proportions. It is they who are beaten up, and assaulted, and gassed, and shot and killed. It was not the police, and it was not the employers, and it was not the strikebreakers, and it was not the company unionists, in the little steel strike who were shot in the back, and who had their skulls broken, and who spent long days and weeks in prison for no offense but the assertion of the rights which the law of the land had conferred upon them.

Given this context, the labor board's strictures against employer unfair labor practices were mild; indeed, "the regulation of employers is gentleness and light in every sense." Employers only had to stop their illegal behavior and suffered few penalties, and even that after having had ample opportunities to contest the board's findings and appeal to the courts. Unless the employer continued to disobey a direct federal court order, the most that would happen is the dispersal of back wages for having violated the law of the land. "The contrast between our methods of regulating the conduct of individual workers[,] on the one hand, powerless and helpless save as they are aided by their own organizers, and on the other hand[,] the conduct of the money lords and the ruthless dictators who direct the destinies of our large corporations[,] is so great as to make the charges of inequality directed at the act both ludicrous and tragic," Pressman charged.

The real reason for the opposition to the board could be found elsewhere. Any labor lawyer knew the disadvantageous position he faced defending his clients' interests in court, going "in [with] the full expectation that he must fight a losing battle all along the line." The judge's views almost always "harmonize[d] completely with that of his opponents." Conversely, employer counsel arrived with the confidence "that they need only lay their case before the judge to obtain a decision in their favor." Pressman continued that "employers have grown so accustomed to this state of affairs that when they are confronted with a tribunal which administers the law fairly and without bias, they think they are being discriminated against and oppressed."

Thus did Lee Pressman carry forward his continuing public and private battle with the country's economic royalists. Testifying afterward in the House, he came under more intense scrutiny, especially by conservative Republican representatives. Nevertheless, since FDR did not favor the amendment, opponents could not generate enough political energy in the 1939 sessions for the bills to get out of committee. Enemies of the NLRA and Madden NLRB, however, soon tried another tack. An alliance of frustrated Southern Democrats and Republican conservatives, employers, and the AFL pushed House allies to sponsor the creation of a special committee to conduct an oversight investigation into the NLRB's implementation of the Wagner Act. Chaired by conservative Democrat Howard Worth Smith of Virginia, it was charged with looking into the claims of NLRB "bias" in administration. For most of 1940, this committee's highly publicized and politicized hearings would be the focus for anti-CIO/NLRB forces. Strategically, Pressman and the CIO largely eschewed trying to convince this implacably hostile committee directly and left it to the board members to reiterate the case that they had made before the labor committees. The CIO general counsel did, however, mobilize the federation's efforts to develop anti-Smith committee pressure at the grassroots level in industrial union strongholds. While Smith's amendment bill passed the House in mid-year, President Roosevelt, to whom the Madden NLRB had become a political liability because of the AFL, tried to put the issue to rest by tilting board policy toward the craft federation on key issues.

The easiest way was through the appointment process. Consequently, FDR refused to reinstate Chairman J. Warren Madden when his term expired in 1940 and appointed Harry Millis, an academic and labor relations practitioner, in his stead. In tandem with his previous appointment of William Leiserson, a like-minded academician, the NLRB now had a majority of pro-AFL members who quickly put into place policies to satisfy the craft union critics. "In the course of that fight," Pressman later recalled, "the net affect was that the caliber, the standard of effective administration of the statute as it was intended to be administered, was constantly being decreased, because whoever continued to effectively administer the act was flying against the opposition of the employer, the opposition of the newspapers, the opposition of the A.F. of L. . . ." While this proved disappointing to Pressman and the CIO, who had lobbied for Madden's reappointment to no avail, it did enable the NLRA to remain statutorily intact until 1947.[42]

Hectoring the National Labor Relations Board to press the Little Steel cases forward on one hand, and publicly defending the board and the law before Congress on another, certainly occupied much of Pressman's time and talents from 1937 to 1940. But other legal venues and forums could not be ignored. Up until this point in his career as CIO general counsel, he had engaged sparingly in traditional litigation while representing CIO interests prior to the 1940s. One reason was the sheer press of time: the NLRB and attendant political controversies surrounding its existence were so important to industrial unionism that those endeavors had to take first priority. Another factor was that fledgling CIO affiliates and converts from the AFL often had their own general counsels who initiated litigation on various issues, with Pressman and his assistants only becoming involved in the latter stages of the case or on appeal, and sometimes even then only peripherally. In truth, until the domestic influence of the New Deal began to wane after the period 1937–1938, the traditional litigation demands placed on the industrial union movement were limited; administrative law representation required much more attention. From time to time, though, the CIO general counsel's office would be in the thick of both offensive and defensive court battles, an activity that expanded in the 1940s as the new federation became more institutionally settled.[43]

Obviously, Lee Pressman had always realized the potential significance of court litigation, even as he struggled with ambivalent feelings about its overall impact on the CIO. Early in his CIO tenure, proud of his heightened stature after the GM strike, he initiated contacts with his former professors from Harvard Law School to get their advice on court approaches. He had no problems with his constitutional law professor, Thomas Reed Powell. "Thanks for sending me the card which announces your new firm," the latter wrote in a personal note. "I trust that your members will cooperate amicably together and that none will indulge in a sit-down strike," he continued in jest. "We professors fortunately have the privilege of sitting down without striking, and we take full advantage of our opportunities." Powell, with whom Pressman had cultivated a friendly relationship, mused about the President's court-packing plan that had brought the constitutional scholar an increase in speaking engagements for his ruminations about the constitution and the Supreme Court. FDR's plan had also "established that one of the Justices at any rate is not too aged to be agile in turning somersaults," Powell amusingly observed, in reference to Justice Owen Robert's switched vote on the NLRA. "Perhaps now you can accept the distinction that I once made," he wrote to his former student, about how court decisions can often "easily be reconciled on the ground that one went one way and other went the other."[44]

But with Felix Frankfurter, Pressman once again had difficulty connecting at the social level, though it very much seemed he continued to want to try. "[S]o you have been 'importuning' Felix to let you come and see him, have you?" wrote Gardner Jackson to Pressman in the fall of 1936. Jackson, of course, knew Frankfurter well from their joint fight in the Sacco–Vanzetti case. "He asked me what the hell you wanted to see him about, and, of course, I replied, 'How should I know? Haven't heard from Lee all summer.' To which he answered, 'Why, I thought he was one of the fellows you counted on more than anyone else.'" To this Jackson readily agreed. However, "what with you up to your neck in the struggle" it should not have surprised Frankfurter as to Jackson's lack of contact. Then he went on to caution Pressman about the legal scholar and soon-to-be Supreme Court associate justice. "I just want to warn you to take Felix with more than a dose of salt as far as point of view goes. If it's technical judgement you're seeking, nobody better in my opinion," Jackson wrote, "but my experiences with him this summer have brought me all around the circle to where I was when I started with him ten or more years ago. He's the most consummate opportunist I know, and when I try to pin him down to attitudes and opinions he has expressed to me in the past I might just as well be trying to pin down a bubble of mercury."[45]

Pressman, though, continued to try to cultivate the same kind of relationship he had with Powell. In a personal letter to Frankfurter in May 1937, Pressman wanted to probe the legal scholar's mind regarding the labor law problems facing the CIO, and seemingly to overcome Frankfurter's continuing coldness, for whatever reason, toward him personally. The tone of the letter had all of the earmarks of a former protege writing to a former mentor, attempting to show how much he had achieved professionally. "Dear Felix," Pressman began, now on a first-name basis, "After I called you from Lewiston, Maine, I became engaged for the following few days in conferences with Governor Barrows. . . ." on the shoe industry strike then in progress, Pressman wrote, confident that Frankfurter knew of the high-profile counsel he had provided to Lewis during the GM and Chrysler sit-down strikes. Unfortunately, the shoe industry negotiations concluded without result, "as you probably have seen in the newspapers. . . . The real reason for the letter, he wrote, was "to explain that the reason I didn't call you after my last call was that I was called away from Maine in a hurry to come to Pittsburgh in connection with the" critical Jones and Laughlin-SWOC union representation election. Pressman also noted in distress the response of legal liberals to the problems of labor organization, about which, perhaps, he wished Frankfurter to offer thoughts. "I must confess that I was very seriously disappointed in the reception which I received from some of the so-called liberal attorneys in Boston. I certainly become more and more discouraged as to their attitudes and practices when any serious issue arises. . . . I would certainly enjoy an opportunity to talk to you for awhile, in the near future, as to some of the problems which have come up[,] and I can anticipate [that] will come up . . . in regard to our labor organization drive," he closed. Despite the effort, Pressman never breached Frankfurter's indifference, an attitude the CIO attorney probably returned when Frankfurter turned into a conservative jurist upon his elevation to the Supreme Court.[46]

By late 1938, two litigation areas seemed particularly crucial to the CIO's future. The first was an effort to defend against treble damage antitrust suits brought by employers engaged in disputes with CIO affiliates. The second was a more proactive thrust designed to enshroud labor union activity with constitutional civil liberties protections in order to ward off the increasingly hostile reaction to CIO militance by state and local governments.

Perhaps because the hard-bitten unionists that founded the CIO did not expect much federal court protection in the area of civil liberties, the antitrust suits appeared to be the greater immediate danger to the movement. The lead case in this area became *Apex v. Leader*, a 1937 dispute of suits and counter-suits arising out of a company's refusal to recognize and bargain with the CIO-affiliated hosiery workers union. The bargaining breakdown led to a violent sit-down strike against the corporation, which later won damages of over $200,000. Under the Sherman Anti-Trust Act, the court then trebled the award. Soon, Republic Steel started a similar suit against the SWOC, claiming $7,500,000 in damages.

The ramifications of the unfavorable 1937 lower court decision in *Apex* momentarily stunned the top-level leadership of the CIO. While the Clayton Act of 1914 and the Norris–LaGuardia Act of 1932 had ostensibly narrowed the union-related injunction scope of antitrust actions, neither statute had explicitly contained language that said unions could not be conspiracies in restraint of trade by virtue of their actions in a labor dispute. Hence, this made them still subject to damage suits testing the law's interpretation. Characteristic of the CIO leadership's concern, Philip Murray requested a special report from Pressman on the progress of the appeals at the federation's executive board meeting in June 1939. Similarly, the union lawyer outlined the seriousness of the case in his 1939 report to the convention.[47]

Pressman and the general counsel's office, however, did not play a lead role in the appeals. They assisted the union's own counsel, Isadore Katz, in the appeal's brief writing. The national office's attorneys also filed as *amicus curiae* on the Supreme Court appeal to lend the authority and weight of the larger federation to its affiliate's case. "I enclose a copy of a brief which we have filed in the Supreme Court," Pressman wrote to Lewis in March 1940. "For the first time we are presenting . . . a complete [and] exhaustive legislative history of the Clayton Act" he informed the CIO president, arguing that the legislative history clearly showed Congress intended exemption of unions. Pressman and his colleagues based their theory on the legislative history of section 6 of the Clayton Act, contending that when acting in their own interest, the law exempted unions from antitrust laws. The CIO brief did admit that if unions conspired together with employers to raise prices, for example, their exemption would not be appropriate. Although the Supreme Court's 1940 majority decision did not key in on the CIO's *amicus* argument explicitly, as many progressive attorneys had hoped it would, the judgment did go in the hosiery workers' favor. The court held that legitimate labor activity interrupting commerce, such as a strike or boycott, even if involving violence, did not automatically fall under "the prohibitions of the anti-trust laws." Thus, although Pressman did not receive the pristine statement of exemption he desired, the reversal of the lower court judgment in the *Apex* case put to rest not only that appeal but also the Republic case and the challenge to the SWOC treasury.[48]

The CIO litigation involving civil liberties issues unfortunately lasted much longer than the antitrust suits, for it involved not a focused area of federal law but a panoply of unfavorable state and local restrictions. Ever since the LaFollettee Committee had popularized the connection between labor organizing and civil liberties, labor lawyers increasingly viewed constitutional law as a way to challenge antiunion state legislation and local ordinances. This, of course, was nothing new; the AFL in fact had pursued a similar course at times throughout its history. Nevertheless, in the late 1930s, the CIO's organizing energy still outstripped that of the older federation's, and wherever the battle was joined, employers' ability to influence the local legal environment often proved critical.[49]

There was no better example than Jersey City, New Jersey. The political machine of Democratic Mayor Frank Hague let it quickly be known that CIO organizers were not welcome. "We will not permit these Communists to come in there and destroy the friendly relationship which has always existed between legitimate labor and the city government," Boss Hague said of the CIO in 1936. Using his extensive control over city government, Hague passed ordinances barring picketing, handbill distribution, and mass meetings without permits, and even used the police to "deport" CIO organizers from the town. The CIO's city central affiliate retained attorney Abraham Isserman to seek injunctions against the restrictions and, in 1937, to start another suit challenging ordinances of their face and as applied, using eminent lawyers, with impeccable nonradical credentials, as counsel.

The challenge incensed Hague. As he told his city's Chamber of Commerce during a meeting in 1939, "[W]e hear about constitutional rights, free speech and the free press. Every time I hear these words I say to myself, 'That man is a Red, that man is a Communist.' You never heard a real American talk in that manner." By the time the case reached the Supreme Court in 1939, prominent civil libertarian attorney Morris Ernst directed the litigation effort, and Lee Pressman had signed onto the brief on behalf of the national CIO. Once again, the industrial federation won a victory with a 5 to 2 vote, holding that Jersey's City's actions had been unconstitutional, a decision that evoked much public comment. It proved a surprise. As Pressman's 1939 CIO convention report observed, it "is a little surprising that after all these years[,] in which the courts have been used to protect property rights, a decision uphold-ing human rights is greeted with acclaim and triumph as being the first of its kind in the annals of the American judiciary."[50]

And indeed, it would have been quite difficult to find someone more skeptical about the judiciary in labor disputes than Lee Pressman. In a reveal-ing 1940 presentation before the National Lawyer's Guild (NLG), Pressman launched into an analysis that was as insightful about the interconnectedness of power realities in American economic life as it was denunciatory about judicial "nullification" of beneficent labor laws. His topic centered on the impact of the Norris–LaGuardia Act and National Labor Relations Act on the legalities of picketing and boycotting. "I would like to concern myself with the task of setting this problem in its place in a broad perspective of labor law," by commenting on the hostile judicial reactions to those laws, as well as the general antiunion sentiment commonly found among legislative and exec-utive authorities. These perceptions, he charged, were no doubt stimulated by the "superior" economic power of employers. Arrayed against these combined forces, he believed, "the laws [themselves] are helpless."[51]

Indeed, the current criticisms by opponents of labor's newly won legal rights, he argued, threatened the "future achievement by it of complete equal-ity of a matter of law and fact in the economic and social life of the commu-nity." The anti-NLRA campaign then in vogue, based on charges of the alleged "one-sidedness" of the law, had used "every channel of influencing public opinion [and] has dinned into the ear of the American people" that labor had "not only an equal, but . . . a superior status," to employers. "Skilled special pleaders," he charged, "mantled in the robes of columnists and com-mentators, have erected an elaborate structure of misstatements and half truths upon this lie." By taking provisions of those laws that favor labor in one small aspect or another and sensationalizing them, opponents drew away the focus from "the overwhelmingly superior power and legal protection which the employer otherwise enjoys" in any labor dispute.

Few other conclusions could be reached given the proclivities of the American judiciary. Even if provisions of those two laws did indeed favor labor, Pressman argued, judges made sure via their interpretations and rulings that those small advantages in statutory language provided little comfort. "I want to be clear on the point that my criticism is directed to the fact that the courts simply refuse to allow labor to exercise its right to collective bargain-ing, to form unions, and to carry on union activities by way of strikes, picket-ing, and boycotts." "The judicial analysis of the conflicting interests of a union and an employer made in" various court decisions, the CIO attorney charged, "reveals the basic nature of the restraints imposed upon labor that still confine it to an inferior positions in our society." Any action taken by labor to further its interests obviously harms the business interests of the employer against whom it is directed, and as such, "courts are constantly curbing both the degree and the kind of pressure" that unions may exert. Even when top-level courts decide in labor's favor, the problem does not disappear. "Labor lawyers are accustomed to the fine disregard of strict precedents which the lower courts practice in labor cases," where oftentimes "[e]ven the influence of the Supreme Court is slight. . . ."

New Jersey, California, Washington State, Illinois, and Massachusetts lower courts, for example, "still insist that labor may not interfere with an employer's business. Pressman observed that "[b]y juggling concepts of unlawful means or unlawful purposes, the courts can avoid the requirements" of statutory language if necessary. He cited the recent *Meadowmoor* decision of the Illinois Supreme Court as only one instance: the judges ruled the union's picketing illegal because it hampered the employer's right to do business. "To this court, the right to property is 'inherent,' while the exercise of free speech is simply a 'privilege.' The union can exercise its constitutional rights," Pressman said with his sarcasm rising to the surface once again, "so long as it does not interfere with the employer's 'sacred' rights." "These decisions can only be understood as judicial attempts to confine labor action to the least possible effectiveness."

Judges, he believed, were only part of the problem. "Equally serious, perhaps even more so, are the host of state and local laws and ordinances imposing criminal penalties that are used upon labor" in disputes over picketing, literature distribution, and mass assembly. No federal labor relations law reached into that realm, he noted. Nor was there anything in those laws "that can touch the employer's use of the press, the radio, temporary shutdown of his business, or the removal of his business to other communities to defeat organized labor." This "kind of conditioning of the ideas and sentiments of a community by the employer is so interwoven into the texture of our society," he aptly pointed out, "that it is simply beyond the reach of the law." "It is this combination of legal doctrines ignoring labor's interests, of legislative enactments utilized to impose criminal penalties upon labor action, and the domination of social institutions by the employer group as a class, which gives us a complete picture of labor law in the United States." In truth, the "comparative legal status of the employer and the union is clear. The remedies of the employer are numerous, they are swift, immediate and extremely effective. The legal remedies of the union are few and slow in operation."

Against this very pessimistic view of the labor law situation as it stood in the late 1930s, Pressman did see one ray of hope. While judges and politicians all too often gave the collective economic rights of workers short shrift, there was one area of U.S. law that stood, at the very least, on an equal footing with property rights in the pantheon of hallowed legal traditions. That area was constitutional law, as it related to civil liberties. "The one legal approach to labor action which may well prove useful," he advised his audience of Progressive lawyers, "is the growing realization and acceptance of the fact that labor action is nothing more or less than the exercise of constitutional rights." Picketers and leaflet distributors were simply "exercising the right to freedom of speech; union meetings represent the right to freedom of speech and assembly." Recent Supreme Court decisions seemed to be moving in this direction. "The simple protection of these constitutional rights will solve many of the complicated legal problems that are involved in the exercise of labor's right to picket and to boycott," he closed on a hopeful note. He urged his audience to help in the "establishment of the legal doctrine that labor is justly entitled to the full enjoyment of the federal Bill of Rights, and the full enforcement of the federal civil rights statutes against lawless public officials and private individuals."

Thus, as the New Deal judiciary increasingly centerpieced civil liberties protections in labor cases, Pressman began to temper his strong views. As early as his 1938 report to the CIO convention, in fact, he "stressed the importance of affirmative legal action to protect the rights of workers. . . ." "Legal aid to labor organizations . . . can be made much more useful than it has been in the past," the general counsel informed his industrial union brethren. "More intensive and affirmative action on the part of labor organizations can be taken to test the legality of local ordinances and state statutes purporting to prevent workers from holding meetings, distributing leaflets, and prohibiting picketing. Injunction proceedings as an offensive measure," he proposed, "might be instituted against corporate activity interfering with the right to organize and against public officials for violations of civil liberties." Union counsel may want to consider utilizing federal civil rights laws in this endeavor. However, Pressman warned, ultimately the "conditions which result in a denial of civil liberties to workers can only be remedied by vigorous trade union activity in the political and industrial sphere." The rights workers currently possessed, he pointed out, "have only been won through the continued insistence upon them in the face of the most reactionary and violent opposition."[52]

While Pressman had court litigation primarily in mind in the civil liberties area, he again turned, almost instinctively, to the federal government to complement industrial unionism's litigation resources in the fight for unionists' civil rights. At the end of 1938, he had become aware of several Reconstruction Era civil rights statutes he believed the federal government could use to intervene in areas where local authorities had engaged in wholesale violations of worker civil liberties during organizing campaigns. He therefore broached the subject with John L. Lewis, then locked in a seemingly unending war with employer-dominated authorities in Harlan County, Kentucky. The general counsel suggested that the CIO attempt to persuade recently appointed Attorney General Frank Murphy that the Department of Justice

(DOJ) ought to have a unit working to guarantee those statutory rights. Both well knew that this type of activity would find favor with the civil libertarian-minded ex-governor of Michigan. After initially corresponding with Murphy about the idea, Pressman followed up with a personal meeting. He found that his idea had evoked a warm welcome from the new Attorney General. Much to the labor attorney's pleasure, in early 1939, Murphy announced the formation of the Civil Liberties Unit (CLU) at the Department of Justice.[53]

Pressman hoped that after only a few such criminal prosecutions, hard-core antiunionists would tone down the level of their hostilities, enabling more effective union organizing. He wrote in thanks to the Attorney General and offered his services. "I wish to express the appreciation of this Organization of the momentous step taken by your Department for the protection of civil liberties of the people which should go a long way in strengthening the foundation of Democracy in this country." The CIO's Legal Department would, of course, be glad to be of any assistance and would forward the investigation requests of affiliates to the Department of Justice.[54]

Unfortunately, while of use in several significant engagements, the CLU never measured up to Pressman's enforcement standards. "Thus far the work of the division has not come up to the expectations of organized labor," the general counsel informed the CIO convention delegates in 1940. While the DOJ utilized labor complaints to force local officials to "abandon" offending statutes and ordinances in several notable instances, in all too many others "the division has failed to act in situations where the CIO organizers have been subjected to assaults, beatings, unlawful arrests, and persecution by local officials." Moreover, lack of funding and inadequate personnel resources—local FBI agents and district attorneys were the frontline enforcement officers—hampered CLU work.[55]

Thus, while helpful, by 1940 it became clear that the CIO could not rely exclusively on the Department of Justice to augment the union's own resources in the way it had with the NLRB in the Little Steel strike cases. Consequently, civil liberties cases from localities moved forward on the CIO's own initiatives, often in tandem with AFL-initiated suits. The most significant, of course, were the companion cases of *Thornhill v. Alabama* and *Carlson v. California*, the former brought by the senior federation and the latter by the industrial organization. Both of these cases dealt with the issue of picketing as a form of constitutionally protected free speech. And ironically, the Supreme Court's newest associate, Justice Frank Murphy, wrote both decisions. But *Carlson*, which Pressman argued orally at the same time the AFL's Joseph Padway argued *Thornhill*, has been eclipsed in historical fame by the latter decision and opinion. *Thornhill* became the landmark as the bulk of Murphy's reasoning on the issue largely appeared in that decision, with *Carlson* receiving only a brief restatement of the rationale expounded in *Thornhill*.

Due credit, though, should be given to Pressman and his co-counsel for their parts in establishing elements of their theory in the majority justices' minds.[56]

In some ways, according to legal analyst Margaret Broadwater, the *Carlson* case "appeared to raise more broadly applicable issues about free speech as related to picketing than *Thornhill.*" Consequently, at the time it attracted other organizations to file amicus briefs, pro and con, because appellant John Carlson's picketing occurred on a public highway adjacent to a tunnel project in Shasta County, California, and not on private property. For this infraction of the county ordinance, sheriffs arrested CIO partisans, Carlson, and twenty-nine others protesting the contractor's refusal to hire them because of their union affiliations. Throughout the dispute, the picketers behaved peacefully, and the messages on their signs displayed temperate language designed to inform passersby of the labor dispute. Still, the local court imposed both jail terms and fines, and Carlson himself served more than a week, prior to his release. Moreover, while a labor activist, he was not an employee of the employer being picketed. Taken together, these facts had the potential to broaden the scope of the free speech-picketing protections related to labor issues beyond the strict employer–employee nexus and the site of the dispute.[57]

California labor attorneys Richard Gladstein, Aubrey Grossman, and Benjamin Margolis lost the *Carlson* case at the trial and appeal levels in California. As it then moved forward to the Supreme Court, Pressman and his assistant general counsels stepped in to direct the Supreme Court litigation because of its broad significance—much as the Solicitor General's office did in cases brought by U.S. government agencies to the highest court. Collectively, the six lawyers authored a brief that challenged the picketing restrictions of Shasta County's ordinance as a violation of the First and Fourteenth Amendments. Pressman then presented oral argument in his first Supreme Court case on March 1, 1940, along with *Thornhill* disputants.[58]

Much as in the *Hague* case, the CIO brief argued that peaceful picketing in public places to advertise a position in a labor dispute fell under constitutional protections. It was an expression of opinion, grounded in the rights protected under the National Labor Relations Act, and therefore bound up with the rights of free speech and assembly. The brief cited recent high court decisions such as *Schneider* and *Hague* as precedential, as well as the court's own recent acceptance of the implicit connection between constitutional civil liberties and labor law articulated in its *Jones and Laughlin* NLRA decision.

The union advocates did not argue that any type of picketing behavior found protection in the Constitution, but simply that there had to be evidence of activity presenting a "clear and present danger" to the state before laws could prohibit speech. Indeed, in Shasta County's case, the ordinance was so broad in its prohibitions that it forbade any type of picketing at all in labor disputes, out of fear of fomenting mob violence and riot. Even were that so, the

CIO brief insisted that the "danger to the state arises not from the picket line but from the vigilantes who would suppress the picket line by force and violence. To avoid this danger, the law of Shasta County steps in to stop, not the lawless vigilante mob, but the peaceful pickets." In effect, "the authority of the state is wrapped about the private interests of these parties to a labor dispute, to strike down the exercise of civil liberties by the Union." The high court, they argued, should once again point out to local authorities their true responsibilities. In *Schneider*, the court said the city had to clean the streets or arrest those who littered, but could not arrest the leaflet distributors. And in Jersey City, Mayor Hague was told to "suppress any disorder that might occur at CIO meetings, and not the meetings." Therefore, the duty of Shasta County officials was "to control mob violence, not to suppress picketing."

Justice Murphy's opinion for the majority agreed, at least in part. While he did not specifically address the argument connecting the NLRA's protections with the Bill of Rights, he agreed that the ordinance, in its entirety and as applied, given the peaceful nature of the picketing and the truthfulness of the signs, violated constitutional protections of civil liberties. "The sweeping and inexact terms of the ordinance disclose the threat to freedom of speech inherent in its existence," Murphy wrote. "The carrying of signs and banners, no less than the raising of a flag, is a natural and appropriate means of conveying information on matters of public concern." For the reasons he listed in Thornhill, the justice once again declared that peaceful "publicizing [of] the facts in a labor dispute[,] . . . whether by pamphlet, by word of mouth or by banner, must now be regarded as within that liberty of communication which is secured to every person by the Fourteenth Amendment against abridgement by a state."[59] While the *Thornhill*, and especially *Carlson*, decisions proved a great satisfaction to Pressman, it was not long before the high court began to narrow its picketing as free speech doctrine. In a legal memo circulated by Pressman's office about a year after the picketing decisions came down, the CIO's attorneys justly pointed out how the decisions at first "had a persuasive influence upon the state courts and, with few exceptions, have been accepted as the rule." Unfortunately, however, recently the high court itself had begun to erode and qualify the civil liberties protections, particularly so in the *Meadowmoor* decision, they said, where the majority opinion by Justice Frankfurter affirmed local legislative authority to restrict disputes where picketing comingled with a history of violent confrontations. So all was not as rosy as it seemed a short while ago, the CIO's attorneys warily concluded. Even so, clearly the New Deal judiciary had at least started to transform itself from the *bete noire* Pressman had so denounced. In the years ahead, as the Roosevelt, and then Truman, Supreme Courts developed, the CIO general counsel would have many more opportunities to test the liberal judiciary's commitment to economic justice and civil liberties for workers.[60]

Thus, on balance, Lee Pressman could look back at his first three years as general counsel of the Congress of Industrial Organizations with a sense of fulfillment and pride. In the trench warfare of administrative law, he emerged relatively victorious, though scarred, by the qualifications and compromises of the battlefield. Before the NLRB he salvaged the Little Steel strike for the SWOC. Before Congress, though CIO legislative offensives moved nowhere after 1938, Pressman's defensive mobilizations fought off opponents from both within and without the labor movement, preventing NLRA amendment. And in court, cracks in the edifice of judicial hostility to labor activity widened enough for him to participate in securing newly defined civil liberty protections for labor activists, protections that other types of political activists would be thankful for in the future. He now turned to the most significant of his accomplishments—guiding the CIO through the perils of national labor policy making during wartime.

FIVE

❧◈❧

ESTABLISHING THE
COMMONWEALTH OF STEEL

A t the Liberal National Lawyers Guild (NLG) convention in 1937, then-U.S. Solicitor General Robert Jackson told the delegates that all rights depended on the achievement of economic security for the mass of citizens, as all other rights, political included, depended on "economic independence to assert and defend those rights." Lee Pressman, who may well have been in the audience at this early NLG Convention, surely agreed. The pursuit of justice in the context of the New Deal era meant legalism could not be divorced from the great issues of the day. There would be no justice in the halls of the legislatures or stately courtrooms if society did not confront the stark contrast between those who had and those who had not. Indeed, it had been Pressman's sense of injustice and his questioning about how a lawyer could and should help pursue economic justice that channeled his energies, enabling him to rise to public prominence in the liberal Bar, even as he expanded his commitments to the American Communist Party.[1]

In truth, there existed two political "personas" in Lee Pressman's life— the Liberal New Deal-oriented labor lawyer, pursuing economic justice in political, legislative, and court forums; and the radical underground Communist cadre member, dedicated to an ultimately more satisfying pursuit of justice through economic and social transformation. In the more public persona, Pressman seemed like many other New Dealers of this period, perhaps Left leaning but certainly with "respectable" mainstream positions on the issues and controversies of the day. Within this public arena, Pressman directed the enormously successful administrative establishment of the maintenance-of-membership form of union security during World War II through

113

an NWLB initiative, and as a result, all of labor grew tremendously during the war. This effort to win governmental approval for the "disciplined democracy" of union security, as the board euphemized the compromise, assisted in establishing the "Commonwealth of Steel," wrote the author of the decision. The "commonwealth" made it possible for organized labor to remain sufficiently strong enough to fight off a conservative resurgence at the end of the war, a key turning point in modern U.S. history. But that achievement was not enough. In his private persona, Pressman maneuvered, at considerable risk, to try to adapt CIO policy in ways that the American Communist Party leadership thought would directly enhance the fortunes of American communism, which, he believed, might ultimately result in a more lasting social justice.

Reconciling the demands of living out these two "personas"—the general counsel of the militant industrial union movement and the underground ideological supporter of American communism—proved difficult. Pressman had to maneuver around the intrigues of internal CIO politics, the quickly shifting labor relations policies of the U.S. government, and the even more quickly shifting labor policies of the American Communist Party. One thing was certain: none of the time he had spent on accomplishing these tasks had been boring. While the pre-1940 period had seen the birth of industrial unionism, at which Pressman attended, the defense and World War II years, the period of its adolescence and growth, during which he helped guide the CIO to organizational maturity, turned out to be just as exciting. In later years, critics would charge that the expansion of wartime union security provisions so bureaucratized labor leaders that the organizations' militancy atrophied. Others noted that given the expected conservative effort to roll back union gains of the New Deal at the end of the war, the compromise was understandable, and so it must have seemed to CIO leaders at the time. At least through the end of 1942, Lee Pressman, like a proud parent, could reflect on his and the movement's many accomplishments on behalf of American workers, and look with hope toward the future.[2]

LEE PRESSMAN, LABOR, AND NEW DEAL LIBERALISM

As a leading member of the liberal Bar, and as someone well known for his aggressiveness, Lee Pressman expectedly did not shrink from professional controversies. This included internal NLG executive board disagreements as well as external conflicts in which he thought liberal lawyers should be involved. In short order, he, along with associates such as John Abt and Nathan Witt, among others, became part of the "radical" wing of the new professional association, often pressing issues far beyond what less strident liberals such as NLG leader Morris Ernst preferred. Two incidents in particular reflected both Pressman's confrontational personal style and, to be fair, his honest concern that if the liberal Bar was to become a potent professional force, it must not be afraid to take militant positions.[3]

The first incident involved what the fraternity of legal Progressives should do about a threat to one of their number. In August 1937, Pressman's associate, Ted Lamb, faced possible disbarment for alleged unprofessional conduct for his alleged too-vigorous representation of a union client's interests before an anti-labor jurist. Pressman, as did many others in the guild, rushed to Lamb's public defense. Some other NLG leading lights, such as Liberal attorney Morris Ernst, thought Lamb should simply apologize.[4]

When Pressman learned of that fact, he wrote to Ernst in protest. "You appear to be still impressed with the idea that the judge was without fault in the matter and that Lamb owes him an apology," the CIO general counsel wrote, "and that a national committee would embarrass any attempts to settle the case." Noting that Lamb had been denied the most elementary fairness in presenting evidence about his theory against the issuance of the court's injunction, it "therefore became necessary for Lamb to insist most vigorously and aggressively for the right to present evidence in support of his contentions." How could he do else, Pressman asked? Surely Ernst, who argued the *Hague v. CIO* case before the Supreme Court, should appreciate "that judicial prejudices against the interests of labor unions are cloaked in the hypocritical mantle of legalistic doctrines." Further,

> To explain away the differences between Lamb and the Court on the basis of a mere difference in law can only result in a humiliating submission to these prejudices. The very patient attitude on the part of the Court is only a polite way of describing a kind of judicial arrogance and obstinacy which is even more provocative to counsel facing it than forthright expressions of judicial intolerance.

Ernst's views, Pressman continued, "ignore the provocations and look only to the heated words," thereby condemning "the attorney and not the Judge." That, he maintained, could only encourage other jurists in their "intolerance." As an attorney, Lamb had shown his commitment to unions and liberalism many times, even to the point where he had been twice subjected to "physical attacks upon him." The powers pressing the disbarment case did not want a simple apology, Pressman thought, they wanted labor attorney capitulation.

A formation of the national committee could help offset the negative publicity Lamb had received to date. Otherwise, without such a committee generating offsetting publicity, "Lamb would be left with a blot upon his reputation which would be totally undeserved." Even worse, other lawyers would think twice about how vigorously to represent unpopular causes. If an unwarranted judicial attack had been made against either him or Ernst, Pressman argued, a national defense committee was a procedure he believed both of them would like to see established on their behalf. Outlining how he thought the "mechanics" of such a national defense committee should work, he implored Ernst to join in the effort or, if not, to at least forego attempts to dissuade other prominent legal Liberals who might be willing to serve. "In this particular situation," the CIO general counsel closed, "a man's livelihood and future life are involved. He has asked us to carry through this job. We certainly should join together and start our program."[5]

In a similar vein, Pressman rushed to the defense of newly appointed associate Supreme Court Justice Hugo Black. Not long after the former Alabama senator's appointment to the high court, press accounts circulated questioning Black's juridical capabilities, reports citing "authoritative" court sources. Therefore, when Chief Justice Charles Evans Hughes commented offhandedly before the American Law Institute about judges' of "conspicuous ineptness," the remark attracted note, and many pundits assumed he had been referring to his new colleague on the court. In the Senate, Black had been a strong labor supporter, an economic populist, and a literalist on constitutional protections of First Amendment civil liberties. Indeed, he was one of the few jurists for whom Pressman maintained an unwavering admiration for much of his career.

Quickly, the CIO attorney dashed off a draft of a letter of defense and sent it to his former mentor Jerome Frank for comment. Frank had moved to the Security and Exchange Commission but was still active in liberal politics. The "enclosed may not be completely artistic," Pressman admitted to Frank, "but the question is whether we can get some prominent fellows in the Government to support the sending of this letter . . . very soon, if at all," in order to counteract negative publicity.[6]

Pressman's draft was generally couched in politeness and circumspection, understandably, but it was also to the point. "To permit the belief to be widely entertained[,] that the Chief Justice of the United States has taken the unprecedented step of deliberately and publicly reflecting on the ability, if not the character, of a member of the highest judicial tribunal" could be extremely damaging to public confidence in the institution, Pressman pointed out to the Chief Justice. Perhaps in reflecting on that possibility, Hughes might note that the general public had little capability to critique, professionally, the job a jurist was doing, and thus was especially susceptible to accepting press commentary without question. "Perhaps few laymen appreciate that Mr. Justice Black has, insofar as one may judge from the quality and quantity of his opinions, plainly demonstrated a grasp of legal principles and a competency of judicial technique[,] which suffer in no respect from comparison with the capacities" of current or former Supreme Court judges. In fact, only Hughes had exceeded Black in the number of written decisions. "More important," Pressman continued, "Mr. Justice Black is, in the opinion of many members of the bar, an outstanding jurist, who is infusing the work of the Court with a keen appreciation of the social and economic problems which, to an ever increasing extent, come before it for decision." This "vigorous contemporaneity of approach" had to be of great value to the highest court, the CIO attorney offered, as the court itself had recently begun to shift to a more modern perspective. And, though many of Black's opinions had been dissents, experience had shown that the great dissenters in Supreme Court history often were expressing an "advanced point of view" that eventually the majority of the court embraced.

Thus, for all of these reasons, the anticipated (but then unknown) signatories of the letter, as individuals or on behalf of the National Lawyers Guild, were sure that the Chief Justice would want to consider clarifying the meaning of his comments before the institute. Therefore, they "respectfully suggest that a proper consideration for the relations between the public and the judiciary requires the issuance by you of a public statement which will effectively dispel any misconceptions to the purport of your address." All in all, it was indeed an aggressive Lee Pressman who took the lead in agitating for such types of response to controversies in which he felt a liberal legal professional association should be taking part, even if, as it did here, it exposed individual lawyers personally to the approbation of the Chief Justice, who might of course some day sit in judgment over one of their cases.[7]

Collaterally, in his political work for John L. Lewis through 1940, Pressman advanced other issues on the Liberal agenda. As a labor spokesman, he held forth on the need for a national health care plan before a national conference of public health specialists, in the process sharply criticizing the policy positions of the national medical professional associations. "[T]he upper hierarchy of these medical associations," he charged, "simply refuse to give adequate health service to the people of this country" by obstructing any proposals increasing the supply of medical services, making them more readily available to the people of the country. Pressman also assisted Alabama lawyer Crampton Harris, who was representing the Southern Conference on Human Welfare, in trying to put together a litigation campaign attacking the Southern poll tax and its conservatizing impact on national politics. In that effort, he anticipated the tactic later used by NAACP lawyers in *Brown v. Board of Education*. As he told John L. Lewis, they would have a crying need for a socioeconomic brief of depth and force if Harris and he were to succeed. "It is appreciated by all that it will be extremely necessary for a detailed and comprehensive economic memorandum to be prepared showing the complete background of the Southern poll taxes and their impact on the exercise of the democratic rights and privileges," he wrote to Lewis in December 1939. He recommended that the CIO organizations in the South assist in obtaining this kind of information and suggested the federation help underwrite Harris's fees. Even more, he proposed that the federation should attempt to stir up its affiliates on the issue, perhaps through its political arm, Labor's Non-Partisan League. Through this agitation, the CIO might create "enough public attention" so that "when it gets to the Supreme Court it is not merely just another legal case but actually has deep social significance."

Finally, as the war emergency heated up at the close of the decade, Pressman acted as a spokesperson against the indiscriminate imposition of wiretapping by agencies such as the FBI, on civil liberties grounds. "We must not permit any form of tyranny or oppression to seep into our daily lives under the guise of protection of national defense," he insisted before the House Judiciary Committee. Such authority posed a great threat—not to espionage agents who would simply avoid using the telephone to communicate if such legislation were passed—but to citizens "whose economic and political views and activities may be obnoxious to the present incumbents of law-enforcement offices. . . ." Through such activities, Pressman's prominence as a Liberal activist expanded significantly by 1940.[8]

As the election season heated up, it was clear to many inside and outside the labor movement that the central position Pressman played within the CIO had increased significantly with the passage of time. He influenced federation policy and served as an important spokesperson for industrial unionism in many different forums and on many different issues. To Gardner Jackson, it "became apparent that he wanted to, and did in fact, dominate the operations of the CIO headquarters. As far as my knowledge goes," Jackson recalled in his Columbia oral history interview, Lewis concurred generally with Lee Pressman's advice on strategy—"when to make moves, and when not to," especially in legislative matters. And, no less important a Roosevelt administration figure than Rexford Tugwell acknowledged Pressman's potential influence on the national liberal scene. "Saw Pressman on Saturday night," he wrote in his diary in December 1939. The hot political issue at that moment was whether Secretary of Commerce Henry Wallace would be chosen as the vice presidential candidate on the Roosevelt ticket. "Approached [Pressman] very tentatively [as to the] suggestion that Wallace is [the] logical candidate," Tugwell recorded. "But did not advance to suggestion of rapprochement. Lee has vindictiveness and memory of an elephant. Still resents [the AAA] purge of '35 with virulent hatred. But Wallace must somehow be tied to labor if any good is to come of the whole thing; and Pressman is powerful in the CIO."[9]

INTERNAL CIO POLITICAL STRUGGLES

Pressman's growing prominence in the Liberal world and his access to Lewis and Murray no doubt led to interpersonal jealousies and internal national office intrigue, which also soon became intertwined with a left–right ideological political struggle. Ironically, as his reputation as the prime minister of the CIO grew, internally the lawyer's CIO relationships frayed. The first difficulty arose with Gardner Jackson, with whom he had an especially bitter parting of the ways. Later, Pressman explained that their break still perplexed him, and must have had some psychological dynamic. He attributed one reason to Jackson's chronic drinking problem, resultant poor memory, and loose tongue; and it was true that Jackson had a well-known proclivity for starting and repeating gossip that created many potential difficulties among the Liberal power brokers in Roosevelt's Washington. Jackson, for his part, later recollected and attributed one element of the falling out, ex post facto, to Pressman's subterranean radical political agenda "which superseded any personal attachments or feelings."[10]

Jackson had by 1937 assumed the directorship of the CIO-backed Labor's Non-Partisan League (LNPL), which brought him into constant contact with Pressman. At first their relationship continued to be as warm as it had been in the AAA. "I remember one evening very vividly," reminisced Jackson, "arranged at the urgent insistence of Lee Pressman in the home of [NLRB member] Edwin S. Smith in Alexandria, Virginia." "The objective of that supper party at Smith's house—participated in by John L. Lewis, Nathan Witt, Lee Pressman . . . and myself—was to persuade John L. Lewis to exercise his direct personal power and influence on the president, FDR, in behalf of lifting the embargo on the shipment of arms and munitions to Spain. That was a terrific evening," he recalled. "John L. agreed on the rightness of our positions, finally, although asking a great many questions, . . ."[11]

Little by little, however, the Jackson–Pressman personal relationship unraveled. Jackson's suspicions about Pressman's politics became aroused, he said, one evening when at a small social gathering, which included former Ware Group member Charles Kramer, the latter demanded that Jackson turn over foundation money he had obtained to help Southern sharecroppers to a well-known communist front organization. The discussion, well oiled with drink, turned ugly when Kramer and a compatriot, according to Jackson, almost physically turned on him in anger. Apparently, Jackson had hoped his friend Pressman would defend his views, but he did not. "Lee kept very subdued and quiet throughout this discussion, [seemingly] acceded to the requests [of the others], but he himself never made a direct thrust at me in connection with it," Jackson remembered. That incident, and one other, when he "found Pressman absolutely cold in his reaction" to a problem Jackson experienced in relation to John L Lewis and the LNPL, started to make him suspicious of Pressman. "That actually made me, from that point on, have grave misgivings about Lee and his probable associations with the Communists."

By early 1941, an unalterable break occurred. "Many things have happened since we have had an opportunity to converse," Jackson wrote to Pressman mentor Jerome Frank in February 1941, "among them so absolute a differing between Lee Pressman and me that it almost obsessed me for a while. Every conception of the relationship between two human beings with which I was brought up were violated by the consummately ruthless disregard of friendship which Lee exhibited." In Pressman's defense, however, it is quite clear that Jackson's tendency to gossip and to engage in gross overstatements caused many relationship difficulties—and not only with Pressman. Jackson and Jerome Frank, for example, exchanged a series of vituperative letters over alleged indiscreet remarks repeated by Jackson. It is quite possible that the break was substantially as Pressman put it: Jackson created so many of these types of problems that ultimately it became in the lawyer's interest to break off the relationship completely. It also is possible that Pressman's manner in ending the relationship may have been less than sensitive, given his personal predisposition to a lack of awareness of other's feelings.[12]

Even though the Pressman–Jackson split had overtones of personal animosity that perhaps led to harsh political judgements, it was nonetheless true that by 1938, by Pressman's own admission, he had begun acting as a concealed Communist within the CIO hierarchy. Exactly what the impact was between his ideological affiliation, his willingness to meet regularly with Party officials, and the ebb and flow of CIO decision making is hard to untangle. For years afterward, Pressman maintained it had made no difference at all. He had made himself available to CP Labor Secretary Roy Hudson and Legislative Director Eugene Dennis, and discussed CIO and labor-related issues with them and those CIO matters' relationship to Party concerns. But he insisted over and over that he had done nothing in his tenure with the CIO that was not in accordance with federation policy. As he put it in a later interview with the FBI, the Party was fortunate to have had him as a sounding board for its labor policies as they related to industrial unionism. He listened to what the CP officials argued the CIO should be doing. If it sounded beneficial, he would then argue for it within the CIO. If it was not in the federation's best interest, he would not. In this, some of his opponents agreed. No less a detractor than John Brophy, on the right in the CIO's internal factional struggles, concluded that he never saw Pressman give anything but good legal advice on a traditional trade union basis.[13]

On the other hand, there were others, on both the Right and the Left in these ideological struggles for the future of industrialism, who believed differently. The most significant of those on the Left was his Ware Group associate and fellow radical John Abt, who in 1938 took a position as general counsel to Sidney Hillman and the Amalgamated Clothing Workers. Abt, until Hillman's death in 1946, performed the same role Pressman did for Lewis and later Murray in the CIO and United Steel Workers of America (USWA). Pressman, according to Abt, in one way was right about their role, yet in another way wrong. Since during most of these years the interests of the American Communist Party and the CIO were often congruent, the ideas Pressman heard from the Party did indeed prove beneficial as CIO policy initiatives. Yet underneath this statement lies the nub of the issue: What Lee Pressman and John Abt believed the CIO should be doing—what was in the federation's best interests—was highly colored by their ideological proclivities. As Abt himself proclaimed, "I can't remember any time when we disagreed with the Party, although in retrospect I can see moments when perhaps we should have."

It was difficult, therefore, perhaps even impossible, for either of them to be clinically objective. "Within the Party, Lee and I—and others—were 'on ice,'" Abt recalled in his memoirs. "We were never integrated into the Party rank and file, belonged to no Party unit, were largely unknown within the Party, even within the leadership." In an oral history years afterward, Abt acknowledged that both Pressman "and I got a number of ideas of what the CIO ought to be doing from discussions with the Party. Then we could see what we could do to materialize it." Moreover, he said, in commenting on the Party's role, it "had some ideas that hadn't occurred to us." Hence, in reality, the Party had, more often than not, willing activist advocates for its policies within the CIO's top echelon for many years. Abt admitted that Pressman, as well as he, did not attend any Party meetings. "But as far as his relations with the Party were concerned, discussions with the Party, taking leadership from the Party, . . ." Pressman was much more than a semi-involved observer.[14]

Not that Pressman's ideological leanings were any surprise to those in the know in the CIO, not even to John L. Lewis, Sidney Hillman, or Philip Murray. Sidney Hillman knew about Abt's politics; indeed, he valued the lawyer's ability to have the confidence of the Left leadership in various CIO unions and to act as a communication channel to the Party when necessary. Both Lewis and Murray did much the same with Pressman. Secretary of Labor Frances Perkins, for example, claimed that she warned all three of Pressman's "fancy" tendencies early on. After being put off by Pressman's 1935 interview with her, "I had watched his progress" within the CIO during the GM Sit-Down and afterward. "[D]id it ever strike you, Hillman, that there was just a tinge of the Communist in him?" she claimed she told the Amalgamated Clothing Workers president. "Why doesn't he go get himself a good job and practice law for a while, instead of giving so much advice to trade unions. It doesn't seem natural for a young man."

Hillman patronized her, saying he did not believe it was so, and even if it was, he told her he knew how to deal with Communists. "Oh, well, but he's interested in these things. He wants to give his life to these things. He wants to help." John L. Lewis and Philip Murray gave much the same reaction to her warnings. "He may be a Communist," Perkins recalled Lewis musing, "or he may think he is. You can never tell with these young men." Hillman assured the Secretary that they knew how to handle such people. Perhaps Hillman put it to her best as to Pressman's usefulness. "I want to tell you, Madame Secretary, that we can work through Pressman as we can't work through anybody else." "Really?" she asked. "Yes," Hillman responded. "He is able to reach the men and the officers of the union. He has been able to be in touch with some of them in ways that we couldn't without attracting attention. We don't know them, but he's a younger man and he gets along with them well." Perkins did not report Murray's reaction to her as being cautioning, but others have noted his relatively tolerant attitude toward political ideology until his final break with the CIO's Communists in 1948. It does not take too much to read between the lines: the top leaders of the CIO knew that Pressman had Communist connections, at the very least; and even more probably, those connections were some of the most "useful" things about him, notwithstanding his additional talents.[15]

That "usefulness" was sometimes lost on others within the CIO's internal organizational life. On the Left, of course, sat Lee Pressman, comfortably ensconced as Lewis's chief assistant, joined by CIO Publicity Director Len DeCaux. On the Right sat CIO Secretary-Treasurer James Carey, but in day-to-day office routine John Brophy, Gardner Jackson, and, ironically, Pressman's own assistant general counsels, Anthony Wayne Smith and Joseph Kovner, struggled for policy influence. Occasionally, SWOC staffers Vincent Sweeney, Clinton Golden, and Harold Ruttenberg joined the center Right. Fundamentally, it became a contest of which faction would be able to sway the leadership on policy matters. More often than not, Pressman emerged victorious, much to the irritation of the anti-Communists. Brophy, who at one point might have been best able to challenge Pressman, soon chose to not butt heads with the general counsel directly. Their relationship was, recalled Gardner Jackson, "a very singular sort of arm's length relationship. My memory is that John really never bearded Lee Pressman, that he succumbed to the dominant, aggressive personality that Lee manifested in all this period, and that because of Lee's intimate, not only official, but unofficial association with John L. Lewis himself[,] Brophy always deferred to Lee."[16]

Others were not as reluctant. The infighting appeared as early as 1938 and continued for years afterward. With Brophy unwilling to challenge Pressman's influence, Tony Smith took up an active role in trying to offset Pressman wherever possible. He was initially the most aware member of the CIO Right about Pressman's political leanings, as Joseph Kovner admitted it took him some time to come to the same conclusion. Smith had been in the Soviet Union in 1926 and observed with alarm the emerging Stalinist state; he also claimed social contacts with people close to the Party. He therefore strongly opposed what he came to believe was Pressman's all too similar political leanings early on, far sooner than the others who later joined him. Suspicious of Pressman's legal advice during the crucial events surrounding the decision to undertake the Little Steel Strike, he began to interpret Pressman's activity as CP determined. "I regarded him as the centerpiece around which the communist presence in the CIO" coalesced, Smith recalled years afterward. True enough, Pressman's organizing drive and energy were potent, and "he was, as a matter of fact, in control of [CIO] . . . policies" in many areas. The former UMWA staffers that came in to run the CIO were "far too decrepit" in age and keenness of mind to provide any organizing drive, and the general counsel was obviously not.[17]

For Smith and Kovner, much of the factional struggle centered on foreign policy. Smith had a very active interest in labor affairs in Latin America and alleged that he tried to compete with Pressman's influence with Lewis on the issue. The CIO chief was quite taken with the power potentialities of mass Latin American organizing. The Communist Party also was attempting active organization of Latin American workers, and in one incident, where Smith apparently thought Lewis's daughter Kathryn was conveying her father's wishes about a Latin American labor issue, Lewis came to Smith to clear up the misunderstanding. Pressman, John L. Lewis told Smith, was speaking for him on that point and in this matter, as well as in others, "he found Pressman useful." You used, Smith recalled Lewis saying, what you had to accomplish your objectives. After the announcement of the Nazi–Soviet Non-Aggression Pact in 1939, both Smith and Jackson attributed John L. Lewis's actions regarding the Mexican oil deal—helping to get Mexico to sell expropriated U.S. oil supplies to the Third Reich through financier William Rhodes Davis—to nefarious Pressman machinations. Pressman vehemently denied such allegations. To "the outside world . . . [it] looked rather important, but actually it was the work of small people and children at play," he thought.[18]

The period of the Nazi–Soviet Non-Aggression Pact of 1939 to 1941, though, proved quite difficult for many American Communists. For Pressman, the problem was not so much ideological, at least at the time. Since 1935, international communism had called for a united front, with bourgeois democracies in opposition to the growth of the fascist menace in Germany, Italy, and Japan. John Abt claimed that both he and Pressman understood the reasons behind the agreement. England and France clearly had no desire, at that point, to join with the Soviet Union in an alliance against fascism; many claimed that their true hope, in Abt's words, was to convince Hitler "to march east rather than west." As to Lee Pressman, he "accepted . . . [the pact], like I did.

Agreed with it." Despite their Jewishness and Hitler's virulent anti-Semitism, the continued existence of the socialist motherland took precedence over any individual distaste.

Sidney Hillman's response was interesting: he simply cut off his general counsel, John Abt, from certain matters, in essence screening the lawyer out of his growing defense-related activities. For Pressman, however, the pact forced him into an increasingly tricky situation. John L. Lewis's isolationism and obsessive opposition to U.S. involvement in any war now coincided with the Communists' like-minded determination to support the Non-Aggression Pact. Therefore, on the one hand, Pressman found it easy to reinforce those proclivities and at the same time remain true to Communist policy. But conversely, SWOC Chairman Philip Murray, for whom Pressman also worked, eventually moved further and further away from Lewis in support of FDR's desire for U.S. intervention.[19]

For a time, of course, Lewis's position of noninvolvement in foreign hostilities proved compatible with CP objectives. For the Party, it was important to keep the United States out of the war in order to preserve the viability of the Pact and, from Lewis's perspective, to prevent the undermining of labor's power position as a result of U.S. involvement in World War I. That congruence allowed Pressman, both in private and public, to support Lewis's stand opposing the Roosevelt administration's interventionist policies which, while certainly not controlling Lewis's actions, no doubt at least reinforced his innate proclivities.

Shortly after the Nazi invasion of Poland in 1939, for example, he wrote a memorandum for Lewis that focused on the international aspects of U.S. gold policy and its relationship to the hostilities. By raising the price of gold, he argued to Lewis, the "United States Government is financing England and France in its [sic] European war by purchasing gold which . . . is becoming practically valueless as the basis of a world monetary system" due to mass stockpiling. In so doing, this underwriting resulted in a "social program for our domestic problem . . . [being] completely abandoned because of the alleged absence of sufficient funds to carry it through." He suggested a couple of policy alternatives of which he thought Lewis should be aware. Relatedly, he chronicled the results of a high-level negotiation session on an anticipated industrial mobilization plan in which he participated with top officials of the War Department, the AFL, and the National Association of Manufacturers. Pressman's recounting of his negotiation positions evidenced more than a little foot dragging—perhaps also because this is what he knew Lewis wanted to see as well—on his part. He questioned when the best time would be for the CIO to take part in public discussions about industrial mobilization. He believed it was necessary to reserve the right to determine the "appropriate time . . . because of the effect which such discussion may have on the public opinion and the inference that we may be exciting war hysteria."[20]

In public, Pressman also gave voice to the antiintervention sentiments of his chief. In a nationally broadcast radio speech on the CBS network in January 1940, Pressman reviewed the CIO's legislative plan for the upcoming session of Congress. The plan contained "two main ideas," as announced by John L. Lewis, he said. "The first is that nothing must be done that will in any way lead to involvement of the United States in the European War, . . ." since it would cloud the focus of labor on the domestic improvement of the lot of the American people. The second idea was that the gains made by American workers must not be rolled back. "Labor has the least to gain and the most to lose from war," Pressman maintained. "That is why our position on this question, while it coincides with that of most of the American people at the present time, is perhaps the most emphatic of any group."

> On pretexts of economy, more money for war purposes and similar catch cries, the reactionary financial interests and their political henchmen hope to reduce appropriations for the unemployed and for public works, to emasculate labor and social legislation, and to restrict our civil liberties. The CIO is giving a lead to all believers in democratic progress when it refuses to contemplate any retreat before this reactionary attack, but on the contrary calls for a determined advance in adapting social legislation to the needs of the whole American people.[21]

Pressman refined this in two other major speeches. Before the Labor Law Committee of the National Lawyer's Guild at the Hotel Commodore in New York City, he attempted to persuade his listeners on how "under the guise of national defense" conservatives were moving to eviscerate all of labor's gains. Noting that business spokespersons shrewdly in public gave "assurances" that the "gains of labor" would be protected, in the same breath they were only too happy to point out, though, that "in times of stress, or in case of national emergency, all groups must be willing and ready to sacrifice." Business profits, the general counsel stressed, always seemed to be the one area they excepted from sacrifice. "In other words, as soon as you begin to talk about sacrifice on the part of all economic groups in our community, it is taken for granted that such sacrifice must come from one and only one group, namely, the workers, all ostensibly in the interests of national defense." Furthermore, labor militants were all too easily singled out as being saboteurs and treasonous, simply because they struck for decent wages and working conditions, leading reactionaries to propose vicious antistrike legislation. "Isn't it clear to any reasonable mind," he asked rhetorically, "that to unleash legislation of this kind is merely to establish a reign of terror, during which the most hysterical and vicious forces will run rampant, when innocent people will be degraded and repressed in the exercise of simple rights—all under the cloak of preventing sabotage."[22]

Finally, in another nationally broadcast radio address before the May 1941 national convention of the National Lawyer's Guild—only shortly before Germany decided to invade the Soviet Union and abrogate the Non-Aggression Pact—Pressman once more took the opportunity to relate national defense to legislative danger to the labor movement." [O]pen season on union leaders and active members" had finally been declared in Congress, he charged, citing several restrictive proposals' willingness to let employers fire anyone "on suspicion of being subversive" or using "coercive" methods, and mandating repeated "cooling off" periods. Using "a carefully whipped-up war hysteria as a cover" for their antiunionism, such legislation, if passed, would simply let companies have their way in collective bargaining through excessive delays. Workers only struck for the most serious of reasons, he argued quite cogently, yet pundits and politicians treated strikes as the sole fault of workers. "It is the workers who must do the sweating and the toiling in producing the goods which this country needs for its defense and survival," Pressman continued. "To vilify these people without justification, to condemn [them] with ease, merely leads to a destruction of the morale of the common people and the imposition of economic slavery." The CIO would fight to kill any such legislation. Indeed, if the country wanted a real defense program, he suggested that Congress pass a law requiring criminal penalties for those employers who violated the National Labor Relations Act. "With one stroke we should thereby have created the legal machinery whereby we might really put a stop to the sabotage of defense on a colossal scale," he mocked. In reality, a restored protection for workers civil liberties and economic security would be the rational way to underpin true national defense. "It is the duty of progressives everywhere to support this fight," he told his fellow NLG members and the country, "whether they are part of the labor movement or outside its ranks." Only in so doing, he closed with a slightly sarcastic aside to those former friends who seemed to be shrinking from labor's defense in trying times, "liberals and progressives will justify their existence. I know of no other way for them to do so."[23]

The internal political factionalism within the CIO also encompassed the growing tensions between Lewis and Murray, especially as the 1940 election approached. Since 1937, FDR's tepid support for the CIO, his refusal to acknowledge Lewis as political king-maker, and his internationalist foreign policy led Lewis to abandon his previous support. Conversely, during that time, Sidney Hillman grew increasingly close to the Roosevelt administration. Philip Murray, though less inclined than Hillman to be a Roosevelt sycophant, still tended to make common cause with Hillman and the Democrats on national and international political issues. Consequently, of the top three CIO leaders, Lewis's independent stance remained a solitary statement. In October, prior to the convention, Lewis stunned the nation—and most of the CIO—by making a national radio speech endorsing Republican Wall Street lawyer Wendell Wilkie for president. In his speech, he asked American workers to trust his leadership and promised that if working-class voters would not follow him into the Wilkie camp, he would resign as president of the CIO. It was a gamble Lewis lost. Most American workers, as Pressman characterized it years later, recognized Lewis as the leader of the labor movement, and FDR as the leader of their political movement.[24]

Thus, the 1940 CIO convention, held in the wake of the election, was a gathering infused with high drama. Would Lewis keep to his word and resign the CIO presidency? If so, would Philip Murray, the heir apparent, be willing to take up the burden knowing full well he had stood in Lewis's shadow all his life and would likely do so again even if he became president of the CIO? What role would the Left continue to play in the federation? While allied with Lewis on foreign policy at that point, how could they accept and support a Wall Street lawyer for president? How would the CIO handle the growing anti-Communist sentiment, apparent in the country and within labor's ranks as well, that had been growing since the announcement of the Non-Aggression Pact? It was indeed, in Pressman's words, "one of the most exciting, one of the most dramatic conventions the C.I.O." ever had. And he came to it increasingly caught in the pressure of conflicting forces.[25]

Pressman's detractors, such as Tony Smith, were convinced that Pressman lobbied Lewis to change his mind and retain the presidency. Indeed, although later he intimated in his oral histories that he had not agreed with the Wilkie decision, in a personal letter written at the time, a communication infused with honest emotion, the general counsel cast his lot with the CIO founder unreservedly. "I have been, am and will always be convinced that you are the leader not merely of labor but of the common people of this nation," Pressman wrote. He continued,

> I am therefore wholeheartedly in support of your position for two reasons. First, nothing should be left unturned and no effort spared in order to assure your continuance as a leader of our people; and, second, your judgment as to the position which labor should take, based upon the fundamental force which motivates you, namely, the interest of labor and the common people, should be sufficient for anyone interested in the same end.

Pressman's letter was curious in some ways, for CIO trade union communist leaders and their supporters did everything possible to avoid being called on by Lewis to take actions with their membership on behalf of Wilkie. Most likely, it may have been exactly what it seems; a personal, indeed emotional, vote of confidence in John L. Lewis as he truly believed Lewis was a great labor leader, whatever the stand of the CP. Others on the CIO Right believed that Pressman's reasons went beyond an exercise of his own judgment and tied them to his leftist political sympathies. Through the 1940 convention at Atlantic City, Pressman was constantly "at Lewis's abode," Smith recalled. He remembered his arriving and looking "terribly haggard" and "his face was drawn." Not only did he have to deal with Lewis's possible impending resignation, but also, as secretary of the resolutions committee, with the anti-Communist convention resolution proposed and supported by Murray, Hillman, and other anti-Communist forces.[26]

Tony Smith concluded that "Pressman was battling to save his own life, and the Party's life, within the CIO," but that interpretation was colored by his own ideology. Clearly, though, Lewis's resignation speech moved Pressman, himself usually reserved in expressions of warm sentiment. Lewis "was leaving the presidency, leaving the scene of battle. People were in tears. I've never seen people so stirred," Pressman recalled. "He pulled out every stop, clanged on every chord that was available." After an outpouring of convention emotion that nearly developed into a draft Lewis movement, he handed over the gavel to a reluctant Philip Murray. Murray then turned and made what was surely one of the most psychologically revealing speeches in history, knowing full well the imposing Lewis would be looking over his shoulder from the wings. For an inordinately long time "he exhorted the people . . . 'I am a man; I am a man: I am a man.' It was a heart-breaking speech," thought Pressman, because Murray knew that the only way he could ultimately be his own man was to break with Lewis, who could be in no man's shadow. And, in the midst of this high drama was Sidney Hillman, "sitting on the sidelines [and] enjoying it immensely," because he knew that he had far more influence with Murray than he would ever have with Lewis.[27]

 Therefore, as Pressman "escorted Murray to the great stage, there must have been a longing backward glance at Lewis exiting to the wings," wrote Murray Kempton. That was not to be the lawyer's only loss at the 1940 convention; he also had to accept partial defeat on the anti-Communist resolution issue. Lee Pressman, as resolution committee secretary, ironically introduced what was in fact a compromise in anti-Communist language, reluctantly accepted by Party supporters among trade union leaders in the CIO. The resolution denounced the influence of "isms" having their loyalty beyond the labor movement within the labor movement, including fascism, nazism, and communism. Murray had wanted some such statement as a precondition of his accepting the presidency; Hillman supported it as well and made an especially vituperative anti-Communist speech.

Party adherents swallowed hard in accepting language that lumped them together with fascists and nazis, who, except for the pact years, they had opposed for so long. No doubt they hoped, in Harvey Levenstein's estimation, that Murray would end up as "Lewis's puppet" and that his demand for some such statement was primarily policy window dressing. Thus, Lee Pressman steeled himself and did what he had to do. As fellow CP member John Abt and fellow traveler Len DeCaux watched the adoption with disapproval, DeCaux remarked that "[m]y glance fell on Pressman's profile. He stood sternly erect, like a Prussian guard both obeying and conveying command. Some saw arrogance in that profile. I saw something else. . . . 'See I don't shrink,' said his expression. 'This I must do. I do it!'" Thus ended the historic convention. "No one knew where the C.I.O. was heading for," Pressman believed. The coming war would change them all. "What would have happened if Lewis had stayed in," he pondered years later, "no one knows."[28]

But things changed more quickly than anyone might have guessed. When Hitler turned his armies' attention "east instead of west" and attacked the Soviet Union, the American Communist Party cast aside its noninterventionist stance immediately. Opponents used this overnight "about-face" during the post-war Red scare to identify Communists or those with communist sympathies, both within the CIO and without. To Party critics, it seemed the utmost in cynicism, positive proof that what American Communists were about was fealty to a foreign power and not domestic reform. However, no one doubted that Party leaders would be just as energetic now in pursuing U.S. involvement in the war as they had been in trying to quell "war hysteria" during the Pact period.

With Murray's move into the CIO presidency, Pressman's own position within the industrial federation entered a period of indeterminacy. Through parts of 1941, he maintained his ties with Lewis, who still participated in CIO affairs as chair of Labor's Non-Partisan League. Pressman's political-legislative memos during this interregnum kept the founder of industrial unionism apprised of what the general counsel characterized as the growing danger that wartime labor relations legislation would work to the detriment of labor. The fear that collective bargaining might collapse because of interminable delays brought about by imposition of mandatory government mediation predominated in virtually all analyses. Indeed, whatever the CP position was at the moment as to workers' need to commit wholeheartedly to the war production, Pressman never set aside his wariness of business's political power and how that power might shape labor relations.[29]

Pressman did not therefore immediately shift his emotional loyalty, at least in private, after Murray hesitatingly strode into the CIO president's office. But given Philip Murray's overall support for FDR's foreign policy, and the ambiguous role John L. Lewis continued to play within the CIO through 1942, Pressman knew he had to be circumspect. His relationship with

Murray to this point had also been a close one, but of course eclipsed by his psychological identification with Lewis and complicated by Party support of the UMWA president through mid-1941. But over the course of 1941, Lewis and Murray would come to an irrevocable break that no one seemed able to prevent. Once good friends, the two mine workers wrestled with their personal emotions and arrived at the conclusion that their decades-long relationship had ended. Lewis could never exist for long without being the center of attention; Murray, who understandably felt insecure with Lewis lurking at the fringes of CIO decisionmaking, could never feel that he was his own leader. And, of course, they had fundamental disagreements about Franklin D. Roosevelt and the coming war.

"I was right in the middle of it, because I was extremely friendly with Lewis, and of course very friendly with Murrray," Pressman recalled. Initially, he wanted to continue to work for Lewis, even if it meant he had to leave the CIO. But Lewis asked him to stay on with Murray. "I'm entrusting you with the need of staying with the C.I.O. and giving perfect and complete support to Murray and the C.I.O.," Pressman said the former CIO president told him. Therefore, he did, and moreover, for a period during 1941, Pressman acted as a go-between for the two leaders, carrying forth sentiments difficult for prideful men to openly express. "In other words, sometimes . . . you can't tell your friends what you think, that you feel hurt, but you'll tell a mutual third party that you feel hurt, hoping that the friend will talk to the other friend," observed Pressman. Therefore, "[w]hereas normally" he "might be making suggestions or offering ideas," he entered a period of shuttle diplomacy, rather different from his normal role "of trying to offer an affirmative policy which might be suitable to one or unsuitable to the other."[30]

Additionally, internal CIO office politics complicated his relationships with the two men. In many organizations, "Each leader tends to have gravitate around himself a little cabal. There was a little cabal around Murray. There was a little cabal around Lewis. And each little cabal, unnecessarily, taunts the leader, and fabricates and distorts and exaggerates. . . ." The contesting cabals in the national CIO office made it incredibly difficult for him. He insisted he tried to maintain friendly relations with both leaders and maintain their lines of communication, believing that "it would be a very sad thing for those two fellows to break." But his position grew increasingly uncomfortable because of the highly charged nature of the situation. Before long it came to a point where he had to be extremely guarded with Murray about what he said about Lewis, because any admiration expressed came to be interpreted as a threat.[31]

Ironically, his own two assistant general counsels, Tony Smith and Joseph Kovner, were the chief pro-Murray participants in the "cabals," according to Pressman. In his Columbia University oral history, Pressman characterized his break with them as stemming from their proclivities to act as "factionalists" in the Lewis-Murray machinations. He claimed he instructed them to stop trying to influence policy and return to the legal books. He even went to Murray, he said, who told him that running his own department was entirely within his province, and that therefore he should make it uncomfortable enough in the Legal Department so that Smith and Kovner would be encouraged to leave. He did, and they did. Tony Smith moved over to John Brophy's Industrial Union Council department and Joseph Kovner into an assistantship with CIO official Allen Haywood.[32]

Not unexpectedly, both Smith and Kovner had different views of their departure from Pressman's office. Obviously, Smith attributed part of his break with Pressman to divergent philosophies of what the labor movement should be doing, and in that he claimed Pressman was in effect himself acting as a factionalist for Lewis. By 1940, he, along with Clinton Golden and Harold Ruttenberg, were the primary stimulators of Philip Murray's support of "industrial council plans" to increase defense, and later wartime, industrial production. Essentially, the industrial council plans aimed to establish tripartite government, employer, and labor bodies that would oversee various industries in a form of corporatist industrial self-government. In that structure, labor would play a co-equal role to industrial managers, and in fact would be involved to varying degrees in industrial management issues. Murray came to support the concept for a time on paper, although it did not gain significant government acceptance, perhaps because of ambivalent feelings that he did not fight strongly enough for a government commitment. Pressman opposed the industrial council plan within the CIO, Smith charged. According to Smith and SWOC Research Director Harold Ruttenberg, Pressman played on Philip Murray's instinctive trade union hostility toward management in an effort to undermine their progress with Murray. "I had a rather long and reasoned discussion with him about it on one occasion," Smith recollected, regarding a particular conversation with Pressman. Why could he not come to support this form of democratic and industrial self-government, the assistant general counsel asked. Basically, Pressman responded, because labor would only be able to come to true power when the system fell apart. And, "he added, [when it does], we must be utterly ruthless." In effect, as Smith interpreted the comment, because the systemic breakdown was not yet imminent, labor would never be able to come to a true sharing of power with employers under capitalism. Under those circumstances, it was better not to cooperate rather than hold an ersatz form of economic power that would sap the militancy that provided true power.[33]

Joseph Kovner, likewise, laid the origins of his break with Pressman to a dispute over the latter's participation as part of the Lewis "cabal." One critical incident, a conflict over the CIO's stance on FDR's pending "Lend-

Lease" legislation before Congress, led to the disruption of their working relationship. The administration regarded labor support for the bill as important, and anxiously awaited CIO policy determination on the issue. Kovner became suspicious of Pressman for giving, in his opinion, slanted legal advice. Pressman, asserted Kovner, wrote a legal memo to Lewis in which he claimed, as one part of his argument, that the phrase "notwithstanding any other law to the contrary" in the Lend-Lease bill might serve as authorization language for a set-aside of labor laws in war industries.

In opposition to Lend-Lease with Great Britain was the position of the Lewis Left CIO coalition immediately prior to the June 1941 Nazi invasion; Murray was unclear to what extent he could support the legislation, and of course Sidney Hillman, now working for the Roosevelt administration, strongly backed the proposal. Kovner took it upon himself to write a countering legal memorandum to Murray, in opposition to what Pressman had argued, and also circulated a copy to Roosevelt administration officials. In the memo he maintained that the phrase in question was nothing more than legal boilerplate, as Pressman well knew; its meaning was that any Lend-Lease legislation would affect only preexisting laws related to the disposition of U.S. defense production. An irate Pressman charged into his office, Kovner remembered, and threatened his immediate discharge if he did not turn over his Lend-Lease files at once. In the end, it is hard to tell which view of dispute was the correct one. On the one hand, to Pressman, Kovner's move would obviously appear a factionalist thrust into policy; on the other hand, to Kovner, Pressman's advice represented a misuse by Pressman of his position to further his radical political agenda, also a factional move. Depending on one's perspective, they both could be correct.[34]

In any event, as 1941 progressed, Pressman realized the need to distance himself from Lewis and most likely would have done so even without the Nazi invasion. It had become increasingly difficult to have a personal relationship anyway, as Murray's suspicions would be aroused by any continuing connections. Moreover, the new Party line after June 1941 mandated a political position on World War II more in tune with Philip Murray's and Sidney Hillman's. Similarly, Pressman himself began to proselytize publicly for the new line. In his January 1940 radio speech, he had underlined the necessity to stay out of the hostilities. Now, in September 1941, he said at a Transport Workers Union convention, "regardless of what it takes we have got to beat Hitler, we have got to wipe Hitlerism off the face of the earth." In explaining the reasons for his change of mind, he said that workers "have slowly come to realize" over the last two years that they could no longer stand apart from the conflict. He admitted that when the war first broke out it seemed the most important thing for the United States was to stay out of it. Over the course of those two years, though, workers had learned that their enemies in the employer class were of the same ilk as Hitler, though on a smaller scale. When they had come to that realization—that Republic Steel's Tom Girdler was Adolf Hitler writ small—the necessity for an all-out commitment to defeat fascism became clear.[35]

Lewis, however, remained strongly oppositional , and as Pressman took up his new foreign policy stance, their relationship came to an end. The final time he spoke to Lewis, Pressman recounted to Saul Alinksy in a 1948 interview, came shortly after the UMWA president made common cause with Herbert Hoover by signing a public statement that the United States should stay out of the hostilities. "I went in to see him and said to him, 'John, I can't go along with you when the logic of the situation puts you in the kind of company that you're in when you sign that document.' Lewis didn't say anything and I walked out and . . . never came back. I went with Murray."[36]

ESTABLISHING THE COMMONWEALTH OF STEEL

It would be hard to find a more contrasting personality to Lewis than Philip Murray. Pressman regarded Lewis as a great leader, and no doubt Murray less so. But he also realized that the latter was "a very complex human being" who had his own leadership abilities. Murray was a plain, soft-spoken man of the people, a devout Irish Catholic born in Scotland who had come to the United States and joined the United Mine Workers as a young man after a fight with a mine foreman. What "Lewis would do . . . by the roar and the rough gesture . . . Murray did by charm and persuasion" with a soft Scots burr, his confessor, Monsignor Charles Owen Rice recalled. Philip Murray was always more comfortable sitting on a porch swing with old friends in Pennsylvania than in dining with the great and near great at the White House. In the words of SWOC Research Director Harold Ruttenberg, Murray "was, in a quiet, non-bombastic manner, able to develop fierce loyalties in his favor, on a personal basis. . . ." "He was just a good, honest man like Abe Lincoln, with a touch of greatness [and] . . . without any selfish ambitions. . . ." Therefore, in his own way, although no one would use the word "dynamic" in reference to him, Murray had personal resources that led to an inner strength and leadership toughness. "[I] must say that in all my experience I never met another man like Philip Murray," Ruttenberg reflected a number of years after their association ended, "although I met many like John Lewis."[37]

But despite that oft-hidden fount of inner strength, the situation Murray faced at his inauguration as CIO president presented him with many known and unknown challenges. With the advent of the New Deal, the American state had grown precipitously, and the labor movement along with it. Although not anywhere near as strong as people supposed in 1940, the CIO's "fragile juggernaut" had been and was still highly dependent on state labor relations policy, a fact that Murray was much more ready to recognize than Lewis had been. In its alliance with the policy makers of the Roosevelt administration, it had sought to achieve offensive policy initiatives wherever it could. But more importantly, especially after 1937, the CIO's relationship to the New Deal state was designed to stimultate it to intercept and dissipate, wherever possible, rising antilabor attacks by a resurgent business community and political conservatives. Everyone knew that when the country finally did enter the war, the context of labor relations would change fundamentally. But exactly what would those changes be?

No one in organized labor wanted to repeat the experience of World War I. Then, labor's influence had risen, only to evaporate at the close of the war in the face of a vociferous antiunion open shop campaign during the early 1920s. World War I labor policy had only loosely tied workers to union representation through government-mandated works councils. Without permanent union organization—without actually bringing workers into labor organizations as dues-paying members and acculturating them about the value of unionism—employers would find it relatively easy, CIO leaders feared, to roll back union power at the close of World War II. In the past, wars had not only led to temporary increases in union power due to labor shortages, but also to a greatly advantaged business class. As the CIO leadership began to realize, the "dollar-a-year" men who started to arrive in Washington to run the war economy of the 1940s had a very different agenda than the idealists like Pressman, who had come in during the early 1930s at the advent of the New Deal. And the fact that their policy influence within the Roosevelt administration seemed controlling was not lost on labor observers. As Howell John Harris, a historian of business labor policy in the 1940s, observed, "No modern war could be fought without their services and expertise, and they could not be compelled to cooperate."[38]

It was clear, therefore, that changes would come, that they would come swiftly, and when they came, the CIO, in particular, would be highly vulnerable to the resultant labor relations policies. Murray understood the collective bargaining context of his generation of union leaders and to a lesser extent what had occurred under the National Labor Relations Act; he had a less firm grasp on the implications of policy in this rapidly shifting situation. "Murray himself," thought Pressman's new Assistant General Counsel Eugene Cotton, was either a "man of great humility or a certain amount of insecurity. . . ." He needed someone like Pressman who could make quick sense of this yet unknown universe of wartime collective bargaining. Over and apart from Pressman's left-wing union connections, which Murray found as useful for internal CIO reasons as had Lewis and Hillman, Murray, the new CIO president, had few other staffers of "sizable" capacity "to provide continuity on a purely technical level" in the negotiation and administration of contracts. "Lee was undoubtedly somebody . . . he really needed," Cotton believed. "Where Pressman was concerned, Murray respected the man's intellect. And liked him," according to Monsignor Rice. "Pressman could be exceedingly likable; he could be very cold, haughty and arrogant to those who didn't matter, but was very friendly, most charming, where Murray was concerned."

Over time, more and more, "Murray was convinced that Pressman did not give him bad advice," and more importantly, "that the advice Pressman gave him was trade union advice and not communist advice," thought Rice. Perhaps Pressman's real value to Murray was that he was a controllable version of John L. Lewis. Lewis was an action man with strategic vision, remembered CIO Publicity Director Len De Caux. Similarly, Pressman had an innate "understanding of strategy in a moving situation" and was "at his best when events were moving fast, when there were dramatic clashes." He, as his former mentor, could go into an unknown situation, be suddenly faced with a new context, and could "immediately form a conclusion and act on it. Pressman, like Lewis," observed De Caux, "could almost act without pattern or without background in a moving situation." It was just what Philip Murray would need as he came face to face with a "wide range of new labor and political situations."[39]

As defense preparations progressed, 1941 surely saw an imposing array of changes sweep through U.S. labor relations. As the labor market tightened during late 1940 and through 1941, workers and their unions—CIO and AFL alike—took advantage of their increased bargaining power to extract improvements. Even the government-created agencies dealing with disputes were not clear that it was as yet illegal to strike. By now, President Roosevelt had appointed Sidney Hillman as a co-director of the Office of Production Management (OPM). To forestall what he believed would be severely restrictive antistrike legislation, Hillman lobbied for the creation of a government body to settle disputes in war production industries and took that message into the CIO ranks. When the president created such an agency, the National Defense Mediation Board (NDMB), Lewis stood resolutely apart, loathe to give anything away needlessly, skewering Hillman as a toady for the administration's antilabor line. At the time, Lewis believed he could make bargaining advances for the mine workers by holding out for a government grant of union security in his percolating dispute with the steel industry owned "captive" coal mines.

The NDMB ostensibly had a tripartite public, employer, and labor structure, but in reality the public members controlled policy development. Murray also initially asserted the importance of keeping traditional labor rights alive without undue government interference, and wanted to see his "industrial councils" plan tried. Soon, however, he acceded to the NDMB route and himself became a labor member. When the North American Aviation strike of June 1941 threatened war production of planes, the NDMB, in cooperation with the UAW's national leaders, took over the militant local union and put down the strike with federal troops. The government then seized the plant and renegotiated the union contract. As a result, Murray's unease with his NDMB association heightened.

After the North American Aviation strike, the NDMB continued along its rocky pre-war course. In the fall, Lewis pushed relentlessly—indeed striking three times—for union security in the captive coal mines in order to test the government's resolve. When the public members denied his demand, labor members were forced to resign in solidarity with Lewis. President Roosevelt then appointed a special arbitration tribunal that ultimately gave Lewis what he wanted, but its decision went largely unnoticed, coming as it did on the same day the Japanese attacked Pearl Harbor. In effect, the combined captive coal mines crisis and Pearl Harbor had sounded the death knell of the NDMB.

It was widely recognized that some successor agency would have to take over dispute resolution for the course of the war. Shortly after the United State's declaration of war, at an emergency meeting, CIO leaders came to the conclusion that they faced an atmosphere of crisis. Potentially severe legislative restrictions on labor could develop in Congress without the intercession of President Roosevelt, they believed, and they concluded that a strategy of asking FDR to convene a joint labor-management conference to work out wartime labor relations policies would be one way they could sidetrack antiunion legislation. Roosevelt did convene such a conference in late December 1941, at which representatives of the CIO, AFL, and rail unions, along with employers, promised to adhere to a "no-strike, no-lockout" pledge for the duration of the hostilities. At their request, FDR agreed to create a more effective NDMB-type agency, the National War Labor Board, to handle all wartime labor disputes.[40]

The problem facing the CIO and its lawyers in relation to wartime labor relations law, at least as Lee Pressman viewed it, can best be garnered from Pressman's nearly contemporaneous address to a labor law conference of the National Lawyer's Guild. In his earlier September 1941 speech to the Transport Workers Union convention, he put the essence of the issue clearly: since the beginning of the defense crisis, business executives had begun a reascent to governmental power and control, and labor had been unable to halt their growing government influence. "These dollar-a-year men created a super-government and they intended and have attempted to literally take over control of your government and my government, the people's government," Pressman charged. With that control came cost-plus contracts and soaring profit margins underwritten by taxpayers and workers. Therefore, "[f]undamentally, our problem here in America is to get labor into the American government defense setup. Our job is to get that labor representation that we have been talking about during the past few years now." In his NLG address, he elaborated on why achieving that equality of representation had now reached a critical juncture.[41]

Labor, in the age of modern warfare, played a "key role" in the "gearing of the nation's total productive machinery to achieve maximum production," Pressman argued. But, he emphasized that "[l]abor is not a cog in that machinery—it is the vital heart and soul of the machinery." For that machinery to achieve its utmost toward the war effort, he insisted, it was mandatory that the concerns of labor be addressed. "[T]he effective operation of the hands and minds which run the machines, the hands and minds of labor" presupposed that the nation confront the need for equity. Labor recognized its common responsibility with its voluntary forbearance of the strike weapon since Pearl Harbor. It was now time for employers and the nation's policy makers to realize their responsibilities. Labor, representing the voice of the common people, must continue to thrive in order for the country to win the war and defeat fascism. Unfortunately, all too many employers had taken the opportunity to profiteer, as in the last war, and/or to use the crisis to provoke strikes that could lead to antiunion laws. If the conditions of the First World War were allowed to repeat themselves, if the government allowed similar types of obscene enrichments, it would result in a decline in "national morale" and result in a danger to the war effort.

It was for these reasons that issues such as wage control, price control, and rationing now became critical issues with which labor and labor lawyers had to deal. "Labor's problems today are thus as broad as the problems of the war . . . [and] the problems of the labor lawyer have entered upon a new era and a far wider sphere." The concerns of traditional collective bargaining contract and unfair labor practice remained, Pressman argued, "but with vastly decreased significance. . . ." Today's modern labor lawyer had to concern himself "with devising an[d] effectuating [a] means of making labor's voice ever more powerful in the drive toward increased production," not for selfish reasons, Pressman added, but to be able to represent the common interest in maximizing the nation's ability to "defeat . . . the enemy." Consequently, he closed,

> It is that concern that requires him to devise ways and means for adequate care of those displaced by war disruption in our economy. It is that concern that carries him and his labor union client into the field of price control to make certain that the adjustment secured at the wage conference table is not negated at the grocery counter. It is that same concern that must carry him into the sphere of planning and participation in defense activities, into the problem of the proper distribution of the available commodities through effective rationing procedures.

Admittedly, [t]hese are new vistas for the labor lawyer." And, they called "for speedy and effective action in the interests of the nation's war effort."[42]

Therefore, the broader parameters of what the nation's economic policies would be were critical—not only did the survival of industrial unionism depend on them but also the defeat of fascism. Invested with such a heavy burden, Lee Pressman turned his attention toward constructing the first part of the edifice that, in time, would sustain not only the existing structure of the CIO but result in its impressive wartime expansion for all of labor. Once again, the resistance of the Little Steel companies to the establishment of a full collective bargaining relationship with the CIO provided Pressman with an arena in which to exercise his skills.

The difficulties with Tony Smith and Joseph Kovner had left Pressman with the lion's share of the work in constructing his first NWLB case. Under the presidential order establishing the board, the tribunal would have the power to determine appropriate wage increases in collective bargaining and decide bargaining issues in dispute, such as the key question of union security, the very subject that had led to the demise of the NDMB. Though the NLRB still handled representation and unfair labor practice cases, during the war its work took a backseat to the work of the NWLB. All of Washington regarded the NWLB as the flagship agency effectuating basic wartime labor and economic policy, an agency that would not only deal with questions of collective bargaining negotiations, but would also be charged with the control of key macroeconomic stabilization policies, such as wage inflation.

While the Little Steel NWLB cases were not the first to come before the agency, nor even the first to deal with the issue of union security, they were influential. As basic steel production was critical to all war production, any decision in this sector would likely spread to other industrial sectors to foster stabilization, a primary government economic objective. The earlier NLRB Little Steel cases in 1941 had established the SWOC's right to exclusive representation in the various companies; still, by early 1942, each of them resisted signing an actual contract. As the efforts to strike negotiated agreements languished, Pearl Harbor shifted over the arena of negotiations to the NWLB. And here, Pressman again realized that the power realities mandated not only good economic arguments and briefs, but also sympathetic listeners.[43]

"Arthur Meyer and I were very close friends," recalled Lee Pressman in his Columbia oral history interview. Meyer, an "independently wealthy" patrician from Scarsdale, New York, became the chair (as public representative) of the three-member Little Steel case panel. Meyer, according to union research director Harold Ruttenberg, who handled the wage side of the case, "was in Lee Pressman's corner from day one . . . [and] I wouldn't be the least bit surprised that Lee Pressman maneuvered" his appointment with the chairman of the full NWLB, William H. Davis. Pressman admitted as much. "[A] great deal of maneuvering went on, to make certain we had a person as chairman of that panel" who was favorable. "In other words, we just simply took a page out of the book of the companies, which had their way, prior to the New Deal," Pressman recalled. "They knew how to operate in the Federal agencies and in the courts. . . . When the C.I.O. began to operate, we decided to take a leaf out of their book, and we also maneuvered, in crucial places, to see that personnel would be appointed who would give us a fair break, and if we got something better than a fair break," he said with some satisfaction, "we never would object either."[44]

Pressman, Harold Ruttenberg, Stanley Ruttenberg (Harold's brother), Vincent Sweeney, and temporary Pressman assistant Ralph Hetzel wrote the initial brief for the Little Steel NWLB case in Washington and Pittsburgh in February 1942. Philip Murray presented the general introduction at the public hearings; Harold Ruttenberg the wages section; and Lee Pressman the union security arguments. In addition to Arthur Meyer, employer representative Cyrus Ching of U.S. Rubber and union representative Richard Frankensteen of the UAW composed the other two hearing panel members. The CIO's arguments first summarized the intensely hostile historical relationship between the Republic, Bethlehem, Youngstown, and Inland steel companies and the SWOC. It then laid out the economic analysis behind the union's request for a one dollar per day wage increase, as well as the necessity to establish a union shop and associated checkoff provision if the NWLB was to achieve maximum production.

Union security proved the most contentious issue. Pressman noted that the basis of employer opposition to union security was opposition to unionism per se, and not a desire to ensure worker freedom, a fact he argued was well documented in the hearings of the LaFollette Committee and the NLRB. Moreover, he contended, since "the war makes it imperative for the union to forget its trade unionism as usual" approach, the focus of union leadership had to change. "It cannot permit its members to treat the problems in the plant today in similar manner as they were dealt with in the past." Union leaders, therefore, needed union security to help them "re-orient" the membership toward the crisis the country was facing, even more so since in addition they were dealing with employers implacably opposed to unionism. That antiunionism had the potential to lead to severe disruptions on the shop floor if union security did not guarantee the union a stable organizational life span. And, if the necessity for union security was accepted, there could be no logical reason to refuse to grant easily implemented dues checkoff provisions using the companies' payrolls. Such payments were nothing more than the administrative side of union security, and the freedom from having to hand collect union dues would enable rank-and-file leaders to work toward solving the real problems in the plant, such as how to increase production and win the war.[45]

Of course, Pressman and the SWOC did not rely simply on the logical force of their arguments. Even though Meyers, according to Harold Ruttenberg, "did everything he could to facilitate the decision our way," Pressman still had to make sure that the full NWLB would accept the panel's decision. As early as February, when the briefs were being prepared, Philip Murray, no doubt on Pressman's recommendation, wrote a sharp letter to NWLB Chairman William Davis, objecting to certain "strange pre-hearing" statements given by government officials and the companies themselves in the expectedly highly public Little Steel cases. These developments, Murray cautioned, "point to a set pattern to prejudice the public mind, and, if possible, the War Labor Board, against the Steel Workers Organizing Committee." He urged Davis not to let the utterances—economist Leon Henderson's statement against large wage increases and William Leiserson's prediction that the NWLB would fall if it granted union security—bias the NWLB. They should not let these comments "prevent the steel workers of this nation from making their maximum contribution to the war effort. . . ."

And not unexpectedly, Lee Pressman went to work behind the scenes. "Before the war labor board he was an absolute master," recalled Assistant General Counsel Eugene Cotton, who came on staff at the tail end of the Little Steel cases. He shone "because there he was exercising not just technical legal skills, which he had, but . . . exercising skills in maneuver, manipulation, pressure, knowing where the weak and strong spots were and that sort of thing." In general, Cotton believed, Pressman and Harold Ruttenberg had jointly formulated the case theory of the briefs and basis for presentation, which was a critical part of the overall job. "But I have absolutely no doubt that in addition to what went on in the hearing there were direct contacts with War Labor Board members" in order to complete "essentially a selling job, a persuasion job."

> Lee was exceptionally good at that, [and] that went beyond standing before a court and presenting a formal argument, . . . [it meant] sitting down in privacy and pressing hard and persuading that the good of the country [required], . . . that since you have a no-strike agreement . . . it's your obligation to do what is necessary to make the workers feel that they are getting a fair shake, that they're getting reasonable respect for their needs that will justify giving up their right to strike.

And before public members like Davis, whom Ruttenberg recalled, "a man of the old school, honorable" and part of the noblesse-oblige elite, Lee Pressman knew the buttons to push. Even those "who didn't agree with him, respected him, wished he was on their side," Ruttenberg commented in admiration.[46]

But it was hardly likely that Lee Pressman would ever change sides.

When the NWLB finally announced its decision in July 1942, containing the famous "Little Steel Formula," the Steel Workers received not all they asked for, but what they needed. In terms of wage increases, the board found that they should be limited to no more than a 15 percent increase, the amount of inflation that had occurred from January 1941, the beginning of the defense period, through May 1942. Thus the NWLB did not accept employer arguments for wage "freezing," but gave considerably less money than the union had proposed. While this was much less than the SWOC had petitioned for, it was an increase nonetheless. The key element of the "Little Steel Formula" for labor institutionally, though, was the decision's adoption of the maintenance of membership device for union security, along with dues checkoff. Maintenance of membership, as developed by the NWLB, made it mandatory for workers to stay in the union representing their bargaining unit once they had joined and allowed only a brief window period to withdraw as contracts lapsed. Generally, it was a weaker form of union security than pleaded for by the SWOC. The union had requested a union shop—where workers had to join the union under pain of dismissal. Nevertheless, when combined with the dues checkoff, maintenance of membership solved critical organizational solidarity problems for the Steel Workers. The SWOC had been forced to put up dues collection picket lines in many areas to recruit war workers replacing draftees, war workers previously unfamiliar with union representation. Afterward, membership in steel stabilized. And in its decision, the board noted that Pressman's answer to a union security question posed by Meyer had been critical to its deliberations.[47]

But the rendering of that decision did not prove the total answer to the SWOC's problems. The Little Steel Formula's maintenance-of-membership grant touched off intense opposition by employers countrywide, leading employer representatives on the board to renew their on-again, off-again dissents, but with heightened shrillness. Moreover, U.S. Steel, which had voluntarily recognized the SWOC in 1937, had executives who were not at all enamored of seeing union security of any type placed in their company's contract. This meant that Pressman had to convince the NWLB anew that maintenance of membership and checkoff were beneficial and should be extended throughout the industry. But in this instance, he could not rely as readily on the viciousness of the antiunionism of the Little Steel industry corporations throughout the 1930s to argue that granting union security would mean final company acceptance and peaceful labor relations. U.S. Steel could make quite a cogent argument that it had voluntarily accepted the union and bargained responsibly, at least since 1937. And, if Big Steel could not be brought under this umbrella of government-mandated union institutional protection, it was quite certain that many other steel producers not part of Little or Big Steel would fight vigorously to keep union security out of their contracts. As employers realized, no union security would keep unions more "manageable."[48]

Thus, on August 18, 1942, Messrs. Murray and Pressman once again presented a critical NWLB case in the U.S. Department of Labor auditorium, the second round of the drive to establish wartime industrial union consolidation. In the Big Steel case, Pressman, supplemented by Murray's comments, argued forcefully for the application of the wage formula to U.S. Steel, noting the industry's historic efforts to integrate wages among competitors in basic steel production. More difficult, however, was the general counsel's insistence that maintenance of membership should also be granted in Big Steel. Much of the Little Steel brief stressed that segment of the industry's antiunionism from 1937 onward and, given Myron Taylor's agreement with John L. Lewis to recognize the SWOC even before the Supreme Court upheld the Wagner Act, this tactic lost much of its persuasive force. Nevertheless, U.S. Steel also had had an antiunion policy in the past, though further removed. Pressman pointed this out, and Murray himself noted that the company's policies were not much different from Little Steel's, even as late as 1936.[49]

Director of Industrial Relations John Stephens responded for the company. Stephens admitted the past was perhaps not all that the present company management would have wished it to be. He noted, in deference to Murray's reputation as a "good churchmen," that "I also know that it says some place in the Bible that he who repents is particularly smiled on by the Lord." Perhaps the board members would also smile on U.S. Steel. While also stating reasons why the wage formula should not be applied to them, most of Stephens's remarks dealt with corporate objections on the union security issue. There were simply not the same reasons for the NWLB to apply this device to U.S. Steel as in the Little Steel cases. The company had and continued to have good collective bargaining relations with the SWOC, and anticipated continuing to do so. So there was stability and productivity as well; U.S. Steel plants were producing at capacity as it was. Organizational stability for the union should not come at the expense of workers' freedoms, Stephens maintained. "If a union is worthy of employee, employer, and public acceptance, it will voluntarily be joined and voluntarily supported." Though having no objections to the national leadership, he particularly noted that leadership at the local and regional levels could use much improvement. Insulating them from membership pressures for improvement would be wrong. Moreover, if the checkoff were granted as well, it may be true that dues picket lines would be unnecessary, but it would simply be substituting one form of coercion for another.[50]

There was some logic in the company's argument. But by this point Pressman had momentum in his corner. Whatever behind-the-scenes persuasive activities he had engaged in tilted the decision making in the union's favor, at least for the time being. Eight days after concluding arguments, the NWLB issued its decision extending both the wage formula and the maintenance-of-membership provisions of the Little Steel cases to U.S. Steel. Unlike the Little Steel decision, though, all industry members dissented. The board opinion pointed out that the antiunionism of the Little Steel companies had been only one factor in the previous decision. While U.S. Steel and the SWOC "had blazed a trail and laid out the highroad" for U.S. industrial history, that in itself did not mean the SWOC did not deserve maintenance of membership and dues checkoff. The grant of the latter, the NWLB asserted, should not be considered a precedent for other cases, however. Conditions somewhat unique to U.S. Steel argued for its adoption—among them no provision for on-site dues collection, differing languages and ethnicities among the workers, and many far-flung facilities. The form of union security granted protected individual freedom, but more importantly, also "provide[d] for the larger liberty of the members in a secure and stable union." Individual rights always were subject to restriction in any civilized society, the NWLB decision pointed out; indeed, that is what made civilization possible. The struggle to develop and maintain free democratic institutions was at the center of the war. Unions, "[o]ne of the youngest of these free institutions would, by this decision, be made more secure for an all-out effort to win the war. By provision for the freedom and security of this union, the empire of steel becomes potentially the commonwealth of steel."[51]

With these two decisions, the war labor board in effect rescued the CIO from a grave institutional crisis, a fact that Pressman himself readily acknowledged. As he reported at the November 1942 CIO convention, the "role played by the War Labor Board is one of transcendent significance" to the labor movement, given that recent developments had now given it the additional power to mandate all wage adjustments, not just those disputed between the parties. Labor had to proceed with caution, he urged, because getting the board to accept its positions in the future would be as difficult a struggle as what had just been achieved. "[W]e are getting a little cocky today because of the contributions that that Board did make during the past six months and are forgetting the fight that we had to make in the early stages of the Board's existence," Pressman informed the delegates. The future fights would have to be conducted more circumspectly because of rising employer criticism, though. Labor could not afford to contribute to shaping a climate of opinion that in any way would undermine public support of the agency. "That Board is one of the few agencies in government that has direct and full participation of labor," Pressman pointed out. "That is an extremely important fact for us to remember."

Pressman stressed a similar theme at the executive board meetings of the CIO and the newly renamed SWOC, the United Steel Workers of America (USWA), in the same month. We "have to recognize, whether we like it or not, that the life of the union is now wrapped up in this War Labor Board." The accomplishments were to date, as he saw them, the following: "We started out with a Board. We still have a Board that is anxious to make a real contribution to the labor movement. We have gotten this union security, [and] we have gotten the fact over that there is to be no wage freezing. . . ." Those were significant accomplishments, but there were still many problems to be faced, such as widespread wage inequities. In order to do that, all CIO unions had to work together. They had to coordinate NWLB cases efficiently and most importantly, they had to make sure that they had formidable representational power on the scene in Washington to work the system.[52]

But that was a fight for another day, another time. As 1942 drew to a close, Lee Pressman had unknowingly reached the pinnacle of his ability to "mobilize the administrative" state on behalf of organized labor. In the coming years, he would fight just as hard, indeed even harder, but with less positive result as the winds of war decisively shifted the direction of American liberalism and business political influence climbed. For now, though, it appeared that Lee Pressman had once again helped engineer two important administrative law decisions in the steel industry, had put "labor's voice" into policymaking in ways that led to substantial institutional strengthening. With the spread of union influence to many industrial sectors, a watered-down form of corporatism came to dominate the American domestic economy during wartime, symbolized by the NWLB's phrase, the "Commonwealth of Steel." A close examination of what it took to achieve those gains reveals that those victories were reluctantly arrived at, even if eloquently argued for in the language of the decisions. State acknowledgment of the concerns of organized labor under wartime conditions was hardly a given that had to be taken into account after Pearl Harbor. Surely policies more amenable to employer interests—especially on the union security question—would have been the easier road for the NWLB. The CIO's ability to have Pressman—an aggressive, credentialed, and charming New Deal insider accepted by political elites—present its case in public hearings and private conferences had been critical to industrial unionism's success.

True enough, that victory came at a cost as union security provisions sometimes resulted in leadership bureaucratization. Nevertheless, given the context of what had seemed possible to achieve in 1942, the NWLB cases must be counted as a victory for organized labor and a significant turning point in labor history. The CIO had secured through the interpretation of wartime administrative law what it had been unable to win through strike efforts at the height of the 1930s or, a realistic assessment must admit, through a politically sensitive peacetime NLRB. Lee Pressman's 1936 predictions to John Brophy regarding the vital role that labor law and its interpretation would play in advancing and consolidating the position of American labor during the New Deal had fully come to pass.[53]

FIGURE 5.1
Clara and Harry Pressman's wedding photo. Courtesy of Susan Pressman Sragow.

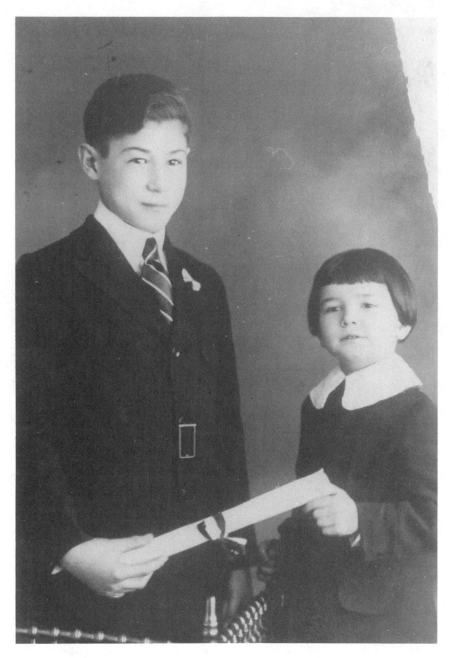

FIGURE 5.2
Lee and brother Irving at Lee's high school graduation from Stuyvesant, 1921. Courtesy of Susan Pressman Sragow.

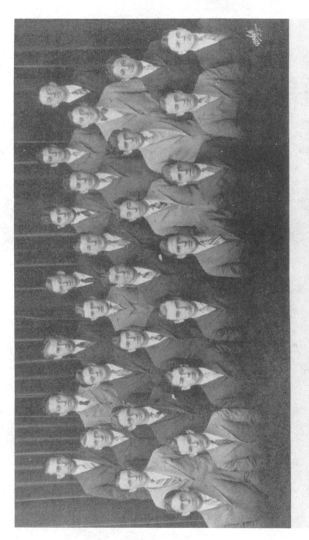

Goldsmith   Coleman   Myers   Schultz   Landes   Leff   Goldstein
   Felmus   Rogoff   Chakin   Rothschild   Weiss   Machson
Delson   Braun   Bluestein   Pressman   Breslau   Fein   Albert
Fishbein   Shapiro   Kreezer   Adler   Erde   Starfield   Wilensky   Thaler

FIGURE 5.3

Pressman in 1925 Cornell fraternity photo. Courtesy of Cornell University.

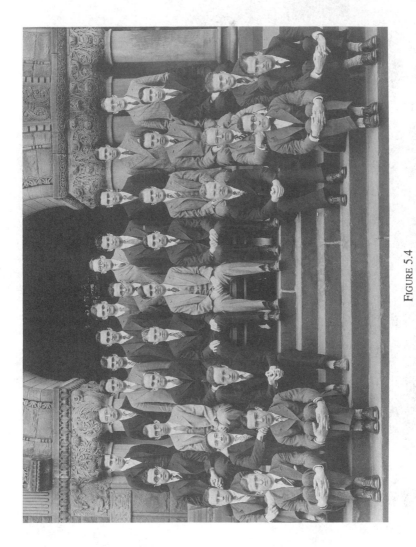

Figure 5.4

Pressman (top row, fourth from right) on *Harvard Law Review*, 1928. Alger Hiss is in top row, fourth from left. Courtesy of Harvard University.

FIGURE 5.5
Lee and Sophia "Sunny" Pressman, circa 1931. Courtesy of Susan Pressman Sragow.

FIGURE 5.6

Pressman (standing, first on left) in meeting with FDR, as WPA/Resettlement Administration General Counsel, 1935. Taken from Pressman's 1948 congressional campaign brochure. Courtesy of Susan Pressman Sragow.

FIGURE 5.7

The CIO signs agreement with the Amalgamated Association of Iron, Steel, and Tin Workers, 1936. Seated on the left are the AA's officers, directly across from Pressman, who is seated on the right. In the center is Philip Murray, with David McDonald to his left, Clinton Golden to his right, and John Brophy standing over Golden's shoulder. Courtesy of Archives of the Catholic University of America, John Brophy Collection.

FIGURE 5.8

Pressman and UAW attorneys Maurice Sugar (left) and Larry Davidow (right) in Judge Gadola's courtroom during GM Flint Sit-Down strike, 1937. Courtesy of Archives of Labor and Urban Affairs, Wayne State University.

FIGURE 5.9

Signing of the historic contract with General Motors. Governor Frank Murphy at desk in center, with Pressman standing directly over his shoulder, 1937. Courtesy of Archives of Labor and Urban Affairs, Wayne State University

FIGURE 5.10

Reprise: John L. Lewis, with Pressman standing over his shoulder, as Walter Chrysler signs agreement with Governor Murphy and the CIO to end the Chrysler Sit-Down, 1937. Courtesy of Archives of Labor and Urban Affairs, Wayne State University.

FIGURE 5.11

Pressman during anti-Taft–Hartley CBS radio interview, 1947. Courtesy of Reni News Service, used with permission.

FIGURE 5.12

Pressman at the SWOC delegate meeting in Pittsburgh, circa 1940–1941. On his left is Harold Ruttenberg, on his right is Philip Murray. Below left is Monsignor Charles Owen Rice. Courtesy of Harold J. Ruttenberg.

FIGURE 5.13

CIO general counsel's meeting in the 1940s. On left, next to Pressman, is Maurice Sugar. Seated on right is Nat Witt. Standing, far left, is Ernest Goodman, with John Abt on far right. Courtesy of Susan Pressman Sragow.

FIGURE 5.14

Pressman during his Progressive Party congressional campaign, 1948. On his left, Senator Glen Taylor, the PP vice presidential candidate. On the right, the enigmatic standard-bearer, Henry Wallace. Courtesy of Susan Pressman Sragow.

FIGURE 5.15

The Pressman daughters, clockwise from top left: Ann, Marcia, and Susan. Courtesy of Susan Pressman Sragow.

FIGURE 5.16

Quieter times at Tavern on the Green, early 1960s. From left to right: Minah Shaughnessy, Marcia Pressman, Donald Shaughnessy (Pressman's oral historian from Columbia University), Susan Pressman (now Sragow), Clara Pressman, Sophia "Sunny" Pressman, and Lee. Courtesy of Susan Pressman Sragow.

SIX

◈

GENERAL COUNSEL

The years from late 1942 through 1945 marked the height of Lee Press-man's public influence and his maturation as CIO general counsel, even as the CIO's ability to influence government labor policy gradually eroded. Pressman inaugurated a series of CIO attorney conferences to coordinate legal–legislative strategy among affiliates, especially at the state level, and joined litigation efforts to lend national weight and significance of his office to these union suits, among them the important labor–civil liberties decisions, *Bridges v. Wixon* and *Thomas v. Collins*. Indeed, his reports to CIO conventions became a bit routine until the challenges of reconverting the wartime economy started to appear. By the end of the period, even as Press-man toasted the defeat of fascism, the survival of the Soviet Union, and the hope of the continuation of the Grand Alliance, even as organized labor reached unprecedented membership heights, even as he and his co-counsels celebrated their Supreme Court victories, Pressman grew troubled. More and more, conservative politicians in both parties held effective power. Thus, he began to find the public members of administrative law agencies, before whom he had been so successful in the beginning, starting to become sensitive to business criticisms and sometimes immune from his influence. By the time of FDR's death in April 1945, the possibility of achieving labor leaders' unrealized vision of a co-equal national economic partnership with business receded even further, and the possibility of a post-war antiunion attack seemed likely. Still, from the vantage point of mid-1945, these troubling observations were as yet only concerns, not overwhelming threats, and might disappear if the Grand Alliance won the war and continued undisrupted into peacetime, inaugurating a liberal, progressive new world order. In order to make that happen, organized labor would have to redouble its efforts to maintain wartime production and begin to help U.S. foreign policy makers restructure the post-war world. Helping the U.S. government foster alliances with world labor movements, the most predominant antifascist force, might even give the CIO leverage on national economic policy.

Luckily for Pressman, the agendas of the liberal and communist worlds once again, for a time, ran more or less parallel. CP policy continued to stress a world scene dominated by a post-war Grand Alliance, as did many Progressives. Pressman could therefore unconflictedly work to ensure war production through administrative rulings. This time, however, the CIO would trust less in the good will of New Deal administrative elites and more on the power of the ballot box by creating the nation's first political action committee, CIO-PAC (Political Action Committee). In all scenarios seeking a revival of domestic New Deal liberalism and an era of international cooperation, a politically powerful labor movement would be the lynchpin. In pursuit of these goals, the Party began to ask Lee Pressman to take considerable personal risks as it sought to influence CIO decisions. As he did so, internal factionalism within the industrial federation increased as Pressman's enemies became aware of his quiet CP-related meetings on CIO policy issues. Pressman's detractors were only too glad to use this knowledge against him in what they perceived was now a fight for the soul of industrial unionism. Thus, even though the official start of the Cold War was still some years off, early warning signs suggested that Lee Pressman's carefully woven skein of public liberalism and private radicalism had started to unravel.

STATE ANTI-LABOR LAWS AND COURT LITIGATION

While the national-level politics never faded far from view, it was the state legislative arena that provided Lee Pressman with the opportunity to direct a litigation campaign and participate in some of his most important Supreme Court cases. With the departure of Joseph Kovner and Tony Smith, Pressman had to recruit new legal talent. Again, through the International Juridical Association network he located Eugene Cotton, and invited him to lunch to explore employment possibilities. "My [first] impressions [of him] were that this was a very hard driving guy," recalled Cotton years later, "not necessarily in an antagonistic way as he related to me, but a guy who . . . bordered somewhat on arrogance." Cotton asked what qualities Pressman sought in an associate, and perhaps with some wartime-induced weariness, "his answer was 'infinite patience.'" "And I suppose there he was talking in terms of what it . . . took to deal with a working group of people," particularly leaders. Pressman was never one to tolerate fools on any level, but there was "an interesting contrast" in his personality, thought Cotton. He "had a certain kind of gentleness or tolerance when it came to the rank-and-file relationships," but often displayed "a real abrasiveness and possibly intolerance in dealing with people at higher levels." Nevertheless, "he was really very bright and . . . good at doing the things that the general counsel of a labor organization is supposed to do. . . . He was a person," Cotton, as had so many others concluded, "of extraordinary drive."

Attracted by the possibility of doing socially useful work, the younger attorney jumped at the chance. In short order, he moved into the CIO building at 718 Jackson Place, where the General Counsel's office resided at the far back end of the narrow building, one level down from the top floor. Indeed, the building itself was barely wide enough for two side-by-side offices; Pressman's sat, perhaps appropriately, on the left, and his new assistant's on the right, with a glass partition separating the two and secretaries stationed in front of each. "That was the Legal Department" of this multimillion member organization, recalled Cotton. He found himself soon caught up in what he considered the most exciting job of his life; he believed in what he was doing and seemed to be on the right side of all of the issues. And unlike Smith and Kovner, Cotton never experienced any kind of professional break with Pressman. He stayed out of internal CIO politics and performed his legal tasks—in the main NWLB, NLRB, and early stage litigation work—well. As a result, he recalled that time with considerable fondness and had little to complain about. Pressman "was good to me," he remembered, as he believed he would have been to any other competent attorney who avoided internal policy issues. Like many other lawyers Pressman worked with, Cotton did not think of Pressman as "a legal scholar." "I'm not saying that there was any defect in his legal abilities," just that the role of a labor union general counsel during these years for the most part did not require such a focus. Pressman excelled where he needed to, in questions of "a negotiatory, legislative, [and] administrative nature."[1]

However, by the early 1940s, it was clear that not all of the legal problems facing the labor movement would be able to be dealt with in that fashion, especially at the state level. Some issues mandated that union counsel initiate litigation, even though as labor lawyers they all knew the hostility courts showed to labor protest. The predominant focus of court litigation through the mid-1940s stressed state and local labor relations legislation and that legislation's relation to the NLRA and federal constitution. In some of the earlier cases, such as *Hague v. CIO* and *Carlson v. California*, for example, the challenges had involved one or more city or county restrictions of the right to assemble, leaflet, or picket, running aground before both the NLRA and the Constitution, CIO lawyers argued.

More often, the suits involved state legislation. The clear preference of the CIO, given the relatively more favorable federal domain, was to insist that federal law dominated virtually all areas of labor relations once the Supreme Court had ruled the NLRA constitutional. In fact, Pressman had made just such an argument in 1941 in the *Allen-Bradley v. Wisconsin Employment Relations Board* case. "We insist that the federal labor policy must be the foundation for any state legislation, we cannot go backwards," his brief cautioned. "The States may not, in the name of the police power or of their right to social experimentation, undermine or challenge the foundation erected by federal law."[2]

Much worse than the events in Wisconsin, however, was what was occurring in the more conservative areas of the South, Midwest, and West. By the early 1940s, state legislatures in these regions had passed all manner of union restrictions—either regulating labor relations or union organizations themselves. As union membership grew precipitously after the Little Steel NWLB decision in 1942, and as the wartime economic expansion into the formerly unindustrialized of the more conservative states threatened to bring unionism to uncharted territory, conservative state political elites reacted with intense fear and passed hampering legislation. By the early 1940s, union leaders realized that laws such as these potentially threatened to stop union expansion into those regions. And, over time, if these statutes dampened the efforts of the labor movement to generalize the level of organization, the laws would in effect create a protective buffer for domestic nonunion competition. This would then erode the wages and standards of the union workers already under contract in other parts of the country and perhaps lead to similar legislative drives by business communities in the already highly organized states.[3]

With this in mind, Lee Pressman began the practice of bringing CIO general counsels from all affiliates together periodically so that they might learn from each other and develop creative answers to common problems. For UAW Associate General Counsel Ernest Goodman, these sessions provided a unique perspective on the developing profession of labor-side legal representation. "[W]e had some excellent discussions there on a variety of issues involving not only just technical legal issues but the broader aspect of the problems" that they all faced, he remembered. And clearly, even though some attorneys, such as Goodman's partner, Maurice Sugar, were Pressman's seniors, the CIO general counsel was recognized by the group as being first among equals, a sign of his maturation as general counsel. "There was no question of his leadership status," Gene Cotton confirmed. "I think that all the other general counsels looked to him for leadership, even though many of them obviously were . . . [strong] personalities in their own right. But they recognized that he was the lead man. They were very easy and useful meetings in the sense that the discussion was [as] free" as it needed to be in order to generate strategies to cope with the developing labor law.[4]

By 1942, then, it seemed that one of the most pressings problems for industrial unionism was the spread of state union-restrictive statutes. Consequently, Pressman devoted one of the earliest of these general counsels' meetings to the question of how to respond. He opened the session by presenting the historical background to the problem as he saw it, Ernest Goodman recalled, and how this "should be appreciated as a real threat not only to the unions and the union movement," but also to "democracy within the country itself," Goodman recalled. Pressman kept his remarks concise and to the point, avoiding all "unnecessary allusions or discussions." And although he "was a person with a great deal of strength," who took explicit positions and fought for them within the general counsels' meetings, he did not attempt domination of his colleagues. Instead, "he used logic, and historical and other means of communication to make his position an effective one. And it was always based upon a reasonable approach," reflected Goodman. "[W]hether we agreed with it or not, his approach was one which was logical within its context."[5]

In the CIO general counsel's view, union lawyers faced two alternatives. They could seek to prevent the implementation of the laws at once by filing federal suits to challenge the statutes' constitutionality, requesting injunctions until the courts spoke definitively on the issues involved. Or, union litigators could take a case-by-case approach: wait for individuals or unions to be prosecuted under the laws, and then challenge the laws in the state courts when the state levied statutory penalties. Pressman favored the former strategy, indicating that unions' legal resources were stretched too thin to take the latter, more atomized route. Despite the historical hostility of courts toward unionism—and here no labor lawyer was more pessimistic about judicial antilaborism than Lee Pressman—since the elevation of a number of liberal Roosevelt-appointed justices to the Supreme Court, unions seemed to be having more success in utilizing federal litigation.[6]

Autoworker general counsels Sugar and Goodman in particular favored engaging the CIO in a more dramatic approach that would publicize the true, class-based nature of the legal struggle. They suggested a good place to start would be to challenge a recent Texas antilabor statute, one part of which required a state license to speak and solicit union memberships. They believed that challenging a law so blatantly unconstitutional on free speech grounds would help unions garner a great deal of public sympathy and thereby additionally aid in organizing drives. The UAW lawyers pointed out that a personal challenge by CIO President Philip Murray would attract the most attention. Pressman opposed, arguing that their approach would be too limited to deal adequately with the overall complexities of the many state laws and related national issues, and the need to define once and for all the appropriate parameters of each. "We had a fascinating argument . . . lawyers got up and talked on one and the other side of it. And most of the lawyers there were very able people who knew how to speak and who had a broad view of the law as well," stressed Ernest Goodman. At one point they took a vote, and only one other attorney supported the Sugar–Goodman preference.[7]

Nevertheless, as an independent affiliate, the UAW had a right to proceed on its own. Sugar and Goodman convinced UAW President R.J. Thomas, a CIO vice president as well, to be the public relations focal point in Philip Murray's stead. Thereafter, Thomas planned a trip to Texas intentionally to solicit union membership at a public rally during a CIO affiliates organizing drive without first obtaining the required license from the Texas secretary of state. As his visit was highly publicized, it came as no surprise that state officials and business forces prepared their response well in advance. When Thomas arrived in Houston two days before a September 23, 1943, Oil and Chemical Workers rally, the outpouring of hostility in the city's newspapers was expected. Soon after Thomas's speech, state officials charged the UAW president with contempt of court for violating a temporary restraining order previously served on him, and then instituted criminal proceedings. Ernest Goodman handled the unsuccessful district court case; the state attorney general convinced the court that the law was legitimate because of the well established state powers to control commercially related activity, within which, they argued, solicitation for union membership fell. The Texas Supreme Court refused to entertain an appeal and upheld the lower court. The next step, of course, was to appeal to the U.S. Supreme Court in Washington.[8]

At this point, Lee Pressman's office directly entered into the case to lend the weight of the national level CIO and thereby enhance its chance of success. Even though Pressman had initially opposed the idea at the general counsels' conference, the CIO's chief lawyer harbored no resentment against the UAW for pushing the challenge and supported the endeavor. And it was critical to utilize Pressman's knowledge and connections. To his credit, Goodman recognized this and acknowledged that Pressman's Washington know-how would be a very important asset. "[O]f course I wanted him in because I had never appeared in the United States Supreme Court," Goodman said. Pressman and his assistant counsels "knew exactly what was going on all the time" in the court, and better yet, "[h]ow to deal with . . . the political divisions in the Court itself." Pressman's personal or professional acquaintance with many of the justices would prove invaluable, he thought. To "know them, and know what might appeal to them, what might not, and how to approach them most effectively was important in the development of that case from our point."[9]

And certainly the U.S. Supreme Court in 1943 differed substantially from the Court of the 1930s. In 1937, President Roosevelt launched an effort to "remake" the economically conservative court of his predecessors. FDR's "court-packing plan" failed, but the threat moved the Court to a more centrist position. The Court then began to move still further to the left as the president had a chance to appoint a number of New Deal justices starting in 1938. Soon the issue of the scope of effective federal economic regulation under the general welfare clause largely disappeared as a disputed issue. Moreover, by the early 1940s, four ardently liberal justices—Frank Murphy, Hugo Black, Wiley Rutledge, and William O. Douglas—formed a distinctly activist sub-bench of the Court, in both the economic regulation and civil liberties areas. Three other New Deal judges—Felix Frankfurter, Stanley Reed, and Robert Jackson—believed in judicial restraint and legislative deference and this often pushed their decisions in more centrist, even conservative directions. In one way or another, Pressman had had some personal connection with nearly every Roosevelt justice except Rutledge, an Iowa law school academic. He had had Frankfurter as a law professor at Harvard, and of course worked with Frank Murphy to negotiate an end to the historic General Motors and Chrysler sit-down strikes. And he had interacted with New Dealers Stanley Reed, Robert Jackson, and then-Alabama Senator Hugo Black in Washington New Deal political circles since his early 1930s AAA service.[10]

Of course, two other Court members, both appointed by Roosevelt's predecessors, significantly affected the balance. One was Chief Justice Harlan Fiske Stone and the other Justice Owen Roberts. Interestingly, while the Roosevelt justices generally agreed that legislative bodies had the right to pass economic-control legislation, when it came to civil liberties issues, they often parted company. The Liberal activist camp of Black, Rutledge, Murphy, and Douglas viewed all legal rule making as being highly idiosyncratic; hence, it did not trouble them to overrule legislative acts conflicting with their view of the appropriate policy. The centrist block of Frankfurter, Jackson, and Reed were loathe to substitute judges' policy preferences for those of supposedly democratic legislative bodies.

It was in the area of First Amendment law that these differences erupted most frequently into long, hard-fought duels over the nature, meaning, and application of what came to be called the "preferred position" doctrine of protecting civil liberties against legislative incursion. In essence, the activists borrowed a 1919 formulation that Justice Oliver Wendell Holmes developed in the *Schenck* case, the "clear and present danger" test. In the latter 1930s, this doctrine seemed to expand via Harlan Fiske Stone's famous footnote in the *Carolene Products* case. Stone asserted the primacy of constitutionally protected First Amendment civil liberties. Thereafter, the court insisted in several cases that states could restrict First Amendment rights only if their exercise could be said to present a "clear and present" danger to an interest the state ought to protect.

The judicial restraint caucus, led by Holmes's former student Frankfurter, denounced the broadening of the test in this way. Felix Frankfurter, in particular, argued that Holmes would never have agreed with its current usage. This wing of the high court therefore often preferred to defer to the determinations of the legislative body if it appeared that those determinations had a reasonable basis. As historian Arthur Schlesinger Jr. put it in a popular analysis of the Roosevelt Court that he wrote for *Fortune* magazine, "[O]ne group is more concerned with the employment of the judicial power for their own conception of the social good; the other with expanding the range of allowable judgment for legislatures, even if it means upholding conclusions they privately condemn." Thus the *Thomas v. Collins* case, involving a question of whether a union organizer, in exercising his or her right to free speech, could ask someone to join a union without first obtaining a license under state law, clearly fell within the context of this swirling intellectual dispute.[11]

By the time it became necessary to file briefs, Pressman and Goodman knew the essentials of their opponents' arguments. Fagan Dickinson, the Texas assistant attorney general who would argue the case, built his theory of the case on the contention that the law was essentially a "commercial regulation" statute. The Supreme Court had long held that states had a legitimate interest in requiring the licensing of occupations involving financial concerns; soliciting workers to join unions to which they must pay initiations fees and dues was essentially a financial transaction. That being the case, the Texas law, as written and applied, simply did not extend to issues of constitutional protection. The highest court had long acknowledged that some types of restrictions on speech were allowable for public protection if the legislature had a reasonable basis for adopting such restrictions.[12]

Thus when Pressman, Goodman, and CIO Assistant General Counsel Eugene Cotton sat down to plan the theory of the case for their Supreme Court brief, they knew the basic arguments they would have to make. Moreover, they decided to go further than make an effort simply to win court agreement that R.J. Thomas, as an individual, had a right to use his free speech protection to ask workers to join a union. The CIO attorneys wanted, or at least hoped for, a much broader definition of constitutional protections. In essence, they requested that if the court found for the union, that it articulate an explicit acknowledgement of the interconnectedness of the individual constitutional rights of workers as a group with the collective process of unionization. If the suit could be made to encompass an assertion of the social value of unionism in exercising, achieving, and protecting workers' constitutional liberties, the litigation might disembowel similar types of state legislation. Even more, it might also act as a catalyst in mobilizing public and worker support for unionism.[13]

In the development of the Supreme Court case, Pressman and his cocounsel challenged the state law on a variety of constitutional grounds. How-

ever, in their brief, they included one particular argument of special significance that had the potential to expand the relevancy of the decision if the
Court should choose to use it as the basis for its decision. In the first section
of their brief, the CIO lawyers argued that a nexus existed between individual
worker constitutional liberties already defined by the court as worthy of protection and the collective right to unionize. And more importantly, it was only
through labor organizations, Pressman and his colleagues maintained, that
employees could truly exercise these important constitutionally protected
First Amendment rights. Begging the court to give "broader consideration" to
this aspect of the case, they pleaded for the decision to confront how far states
could go "in rendering ineffective the rights declared and guaranteed to working men and women" by recent pro-labor decisions such as *Hague* and *Thornhill*. The type of state legislation now in front of the Court, he insisted, posed
a great danger to "the ability of employes to exercise those rights in the only
manner in which, in the main, those rights can be made realistically effective,
namely, through mutual and concerted action on the part of employes."[14]

The rights declared protected in a case such as *Thornhill* were both individual and collective. An individual's right to carry a picket sign informing
the public of a labor dispute thus was "a right which has meaning only to the
extent that an individual employee is free to call upon fellow employes to join
him in the exercise of the right." In the context of labor organization drives,
these two elements were inseparably bound; freedom of association presupposed freedom of speech, and free speech could not exist without the right to
disseminate that speech through collective formations. You could not legiti-
mately "distinguish between the right to think and speak and the right to call
upon others to join in organization for the spreading of thoughts and ideas."
The Texas statute and lower court decisions did not adequately consider that
the very purpose of employee organizations was to effectuate individual purposes through collective activity, and thus the reason for "assembling into
organizations," while individual in origination, had to be collective in effectuation. "Labor organizations exist and act, and the organization for which
Appellant spoke in the present case exists and acts, solely for the purpose of
exercising and effectuating the rights assured. . . ." To exercise their right to
free speech, employees have chosen spokesmen from "their own ranks" to
exercise it for them. It would be physically impossible, for example, for an
individual employee to exercise his or her own free speech in relationship to
all other co-employees of a multiplant employer across the nation, and hence
the necessity for spokespersons who should be free of restraint.

It was therefore impossible for the State of Texas to claim that it had
adhered to the principles of *Hague* and *Thornhill* when its law clearly undercut those rights. How could "a plea to employees to join in common organization for the better effectuation of civil rights . . . be treated in the same cat-

egory as an attempt to sell stock," the CIO attorneys asked. "Solicitation for membership and participation in labor organization is no mere abstract exercise in liberty." Laws and court decisions already recognized the right to collective bargaining, to which the issue at hand was clearly related. "Thus, the freedom of the individual worker to speak effectively through his organization in collective bargaining is, in a very practical and direct way, dependent upon his freedom to solicit his fellow workers to join with him." Previous Supreme Court decisions, the union lawyers insisted, both implicitly and explicitly supported this interpretation.

In effect, the CIO attorneys asked the Court to enunciate, as a component of its decision, the legitimacy of group-related constitutional rights, integrally tied to, yet still distinct from, R.J. Thomas's individual constitutional right to free speech. A bold proclamation along these lines might have effects beyond the individuals involved. First, such a decision basis would support finding other, yet unchallenged, state laws similar in nature to be unconstitutional. Second, an opinion of this type would have moral authority and might stimulate workers to claim their rights, much in the way federal legal assertions prompted successful organizing drives during the period 1934–1935, and *Brown v. Board of Education* for civil rights organizing in 1954.

But it would take more than a brief to convince doubters on the highest court's bench. The attorneys would have to persuade doubters and in this oral argument, along with the briefs, gives legal counsel a chance to tilt the vote in their favor and shape the reasoning of the decision. Pressman argued the *Thomas* case twice, in fact, due to internal divisions—once on May 1, 1944, with Goodman, and for a second time by himself on October 11, 1944. He argued, in essence, that underlying the *Thomas* litigation was a pattern evident in many conservative areas to destroy unionism, and hence the already defined court-protected right to form and join unions. Goodman thankfully recalled that the justices "fortunately . . . addressed the tough questions at" Pressman. "He spoke well. He knew what he was talking about, he was clear and concise, he had a point of view . . . and didn't belabor anything beyond what was necessary to make his points." As a result, "the Court was much more ready to hear him make that kind of historical argument than it would have been for me to have done so."[15]

Shortly after oral arguments, the court deadlocked. The Roosevelt Court's liberal activists neared a majority when Justice William Douglas tentatively switched his vote to support Rutledge, Murphy, and Black. Indeed, Rutledge, who started out at the first conference thinking he would write a minority opinion, soon found it would turn into a tentative majority decision, but Douglas apparently still wavered. Consequently, Rutledge, whose initial minority draft proved quite different from the final majority expression, in the end had to sculpt the reasoning to satisfy his brethren and hold his majority.[16]

From May 24 through June 12, 1944, when the court decided to hear reargument, Rutledge's opinion therefore went through six drafts, with large sections being excised. In Rutledge's first two versions, at least, Rutledge had found where justice lay for him. Pressman's and his colleague's theory of the case had definitely made a deep impact in the first articulation of the constitutional rights involved, as Rutledge gave unions prominent institutional consideration. He stated that legislation could not forbid union officials from speaking freely. Rutledge affirmed that there "is strong reason to support this view when the prohibition includes both general and specific invitation, as it does here, in the fundamental rights of the union as well as those of the individual who speaks. What is basically at stake is the right of unions to existence as well as the right of workingmen to unite for protection of their common and legitimate aims."

Justice Rutledge continued by reviewing the legally protected rights to freedom of association granted to workers under federal statutes and now the Constitution. Although unions were subject to reasonable restrictions, which the Court was not now determining, they had a "basic right to existence which legislation cannot unduly impair" as part of democratic rights belonging to all. "The right of unions to exist includes the right to maintain themselves and thus to secure adherents—to expand within limits which no doubt may be imposed in the public interest." In short,

> It follows that, except for particular disability in special circumstances, the right to join unions cannot be taken away by the state. Nor can the right generally of unions and their members to ask and persuade others to join. These individual rights underlie the very existence and maintenance of unions. And legislation which would forbid them would strike directly at their existence as also at the rights of workingmen to unite and associate, and plainly would be invalid.

Within legitimate limits the state could impose some control, Rutledge acknowledged. However, "there is a right both of existence and of expansion. And those rights are both within the area of free discussion and assembly and within their protections. Although no decision here has put the matter exactly thus, we think it is implicit in the various ones which have marked out some of the boundaries." "Free trade" in ideas was not meant "solely for persons in intellectual pursuits." "'Free trade in ideas' means free trade in assembly and association. It means free trade also in the opportunity to persuade to action, not merely to describe facts," Rutledge asserted. Recent decisions had affirmed employers' rights to free speech on labor matters. And they protected "no less the employees' converse right." "In our system the right of association for lawful ends, except in corporate form, is a common right. But, while varying degrees of regulation will be appropriate for different organizations, there is a core of common right to maintain membership, and thus the institution itself, which cannot be taken away."

Thus, Rutledge had indeed seemed swayed by the general thrust of the CIO's contentions regarding the interconnectedness of the individual and collective rights involved in *Thomas v. Collins*. By the beginning of June, however, as the other justices responded to the drafts, these bold assertions of union institutional protections grounded in individual constitutional rights began to be sloughed off from the opinion. Apparently, there was either no majority consensus on behalf of such language or assertions or one of the justices, perhaps Douglas, strenuously objected to the pitch of the argument. The final draft prior to setting the case for reargument had generally boiled down the issues involved to R.J. Thomas's contempt conviction as it related to his individual constitutional rights.[17]

The nature of the questions propounded to the attorneys for reargument indicated perhaps that a majority believed that the general speech given by Thomas was constitutionally protected, but that his solicitation of an individual worker, which he did as well to test the scope of the statute, might have been properly subject to state regulation. Where unions as institutions fit into the constitutional picture was not forthcoming from the Roosevelt appointees as a group, by this point. We "realized that at that time that the court was split and it was going to be tough going" from then on, according to Goodman. Pressman thought that the swing vote had by now come to be Justice Robert Jackson, which eventually proved correct. While Douglas shaped the language of the decision, it was Jackson who supplied the winning vote.

Pressman opened reargument by indicating that the focus of the justices' concerns propounded to counsel in the reargument notice "raise a fundamental question as to whether a valid distinction can be made between the speech by Thomas and the specific solicitation." Perhaps suspecting that the collectively effectuated free speech argument was having a rough going, Pressman turned to the individual free speech issue. It was apparent to him that the justices were interested in its broader ramifications, but he turned in a way that turned the issue into one of the legitimacy of trade union organization, despite Justice Roberts' protest that it was material outside the record. Union growth required the ability to solicit individually, Pressman began, as during the organizing process such entreaties had to be done in ways designed to "avoid hostile countermeasures" from an employer. This meant beginning organizing efforts were often done through quiet conversations. In "the course of discussing the benefits of trade unionism, no slide-rule test can be laid down as to when you have discussion and proselytization and when you have a specific act or specific words of solicitation," he pointed out. Admitting that that issue would indeed be difficult to determine, Chief Justice Harlan Stone reminded Pressman that such was not the case in *Thomas*, as they had an admitted act of solicitation. Even so, Pressman continued, "by and large, no distinction can be drawn" between general speech touting the benefits of unionism and solicitation and that, taken as a whole, such discussion is merely and only a free exchange of ideas. . . ."[18]

Did the CIO counsel think that the issues presented in the case were similar to passing a statute requiring ministers receiving money for services to register "with a public official," inquired Justice Rutledge. No, Pressman responded, for in doing so in that case, or in requiring newspapers to register, both of which were fairly well settled as legal issues, "no dangers would flow from the act, whereas if applied to [union] organizers many dangers would flow therefrom." That remark provoked the most critical line of comments against his argument from Pressman's former Harvard Law School professor, Justice Frankfurter. Neither of the aforementioned answers were relevant, Frankfurter contended. "Can you say labor organizing is non-commercial?" he asked in disbelief. Pressman responded that even if economic in function, trade unionism involved the conveyance of ideas worthy of constitutional protection. "The psychological factors are the same whether you are promoting a trade union or a commercial product," Frankfurter retorted. Not so, reiterated his old student; the fundamental basis of unionism was an "exchange of ideas" about society, not a commercial transaction.

Pressman continued, saying that he sincerely doubted whether "any distinction can be made against general speech and solicitation." "You are raising the question," Chief Justice Stone remarked, "that the general speech might be regarded as solicitation." To this Pressman agreed wholeheartedly, at least about the statute in question. "If you try to draw a distinction between the solicitation of the speech and the individual solicitation it has this result":

> At the very stage when the organizer addresses himself to individuals[,] and solely to individuals because that is the only means at his disposal, at that point he would not be constitutionally protected; but when you have a mass meeting, when he need no longer be protected, then his speech is protected.

Obviously, the Court was well aware of what had historically happened to union organizers once their identities had become known. They "have been beaten, tarred and feathered, run out of town because the employer and his associates" knew who the organizers were and wanted to chill the desire to unionize. Was not the CIO counsel now bringing in the issue of denial of due process to union organizers, Stone pondered. Again, Pressman said no, the issue was still freedom of speech. "In the case of an organizer, disclosing his name means he no longer has freedom of speech—he does not dare exercise that right."

Justice Jackson, the likely deciding vote, then inquired whether the Texas act mandated that "the organizer . . . reveal where he will operate or limit him in anyway?" Did it locate him geographically, or require that the license be shown to employers? Pressman admitted that it did not, although the license had to be shown upon request to any employee, and employer spies in the workforce were plentiful, and employers could of course get that information directly from the secretary of state. How did the issue of the right to be an "anonymous" union organizer fit into this case, Jackson queried, since Thomas had clearly not been hiding his identity. Perhaps the law was constitutional as applied to R.J. Thomas but not to some other, lesser-known, unpaid rank-and-file organizer? Pressman denied that this could be the case, given the lower court rulings. Both speech and solicitation had been forbidden by the restraining orders, and the lower Texas courts ruled that "both are prohibited without registration and license; if this be so, the statute prohibits speech, which is unconstitutional, and the whole must be unconstitutional."

Upon the conclusion of the reargument, the justices attempted once more to put the case to rest. By now Justices Rutledge, Murphy, Black, and Douglas (the latter with a concurrence) voted the Texas statute unconstitutional on the reasoning outlined in Rutledge's constantly revised opinion. Jackson voted with the group on result, but provided a lengthier, separately reasoned concurring opinion. Chief Justice Stone, along with Justices Frankfurter, Roberts, and Reed, affirmed the law's constitutionality, with Roberts writing the dissent.[19]

Rutledge's January 1945 opinion had by now stripped the issue of unionism almost completely from the case, making it incidental to the constitutional issues at hand rather than integrally related to the controversy. It proved to be, for a number of years, one of the more compelling statements of the "preferred position" view of First Amendment rights. As Goodman years later reflected, "the decision itself . . . was one of the finest dissertations of the meaning of the First Amendment" in that era, finding its way into law classrooms and legal texts. As Rutledge's biographer noted, it became one of a handful of his First Amendment opinions likely to be "read, reread, studied and cited as long as the Republic endures." However, its fundamental thrust dealt with the individual rights of R.J. Thomas.[20]

In reviewing the respective counsels' arguments, Rutledge was quick to lay out clearly the basis of the majority's decision after introducing the parties' perception of the case. Confronted "again with the duty our system places . . . to say where the individual's freedom ends and the State's power begins," Rutledge asserted that is was "the character of the right, not of the limitation, which determines what standard" that should be used. Here the majority adopted the "clear and present danger" test once again. "Only the gravest abuses, endangering paramount interests, give occasion for permissible limitation" of First Amendment rights. American tradition, he contended, made it imperative that the Court should "allow the widest room" for discussion, and the "narrowest range [for] its restriction," especially when coupled with the right to free assembly, as here.[21]

But, in so doing, the Court was not using as the basis for its determination the broader contentions of the parties, either those of Texas or the union. In regard to the latter, Rutledge significantly wrote that the Court should not impose constitutional protections "because . . . interests of workingmen are involved or because they have the general liberties of the citizen." Those factors did not entitle their organizations to what Rutledge now wrote would be special privileges. "In applying these principles to the facts of this case," the liberal justice continued, "we put aside the broader contentions both parties have made and confine our decision to the narrow question" whether the application of the Texas law violated individual First Amendment rights. Thus the Court did not, as he wrote in another section, "ground our decision upon other contentions advanced in the briefs and argument."

Regarding Thomas's rights, the court majority found a constitutional violation. The law restricted him from speaking and his listeners from hearing what he had to say. "The threat of the restraining order, backed by the power of contempt, and of arrest for crime, hung over every word." Regarding the state's contention, that while Thomas had the right to laud unionism in the abstract as long as he did not solicit membership, the majority found no logic. Such a law "compels the speaker to hedge and trim. He must take care in every word to create no impression that he means, in advocating unionism's most central principle"—that workers should unite—that "he not actually ask those present to take action to do so." Freedom of speech would be at an end when "labor leaders" were thus forced only to utter "innocuous and abstract discussion of the virtues of trade unions and so becloud even this with doubt, uncertainty and the risk of penalty. . . ." "Of course," Rutledge went on to clarify, "espousal of the cause of labor is entitled to no higher constitutional protections than the espousal of any other lawful cause. It is entitled to the same protection." Indeed, if "one who solicits support for the cause of labor may be required to register as a condition of his right to make a public speech, so may he who seeks to rally support for any social, business, religious or political cause."

In closing, Justice Rutledge's passion for the First Amendment issues involved enabled him to rise to rhetorical heights unusual in his opinions. While the State of Texas had claimed that the restrictions of licensing were hardly burdensome, he pointed out that the "restraint is not small when it is considered what was restrained."

> The right is a national right, federally guaranteed. There is some modicum of freedom of thought, speech, and assembly, which all citizens of

the Republic may exercise throughout its length and breadth, which no State, nor all together, nor the Nation itself, can prohibit, restrain, or impede. If the restraint were smaller than it is, it is from petty tyrannies that large ones take root and grow. This fact can be no more plain when they are imposed on the most basic rights of all. Seedlings planted in that soil grow great and, growing, break down the foundations of liberty.

Justice Owen Roberts, writing for the minority, expectedly castigated the basis of the decision, insisting that the majority had ruled on a basis other than that pleaded for by Pressman. Roberts capsulized the union argument succinctly: The Constitution mandated "a sharp distinction" between "business rights and civil rights" and that "in discussion of labor problems, and equally in solicitation of union membership, civil rights are exercised." Union organizations "are the only effective means whereby employees may exercise the guaranteed civil rights, and that, consequently any interference" with union solicitation encompasses an infringement of constitutional rights. "Stripped to its bare bones," Roberts elaborated, the contention is that since unions are "beneficial and lawful" and since solicitation for members are necessary to their existence, and since that solicitation is a "liberty of speech," then the act must fall.

"I think this is the issue and the only issue presented to the courts" heretofore, the minority opinion author insisted. And moreover, it was the issue on which the CIO appealed. "The opinion of the court imported into the case elements on which counsel for appellant did not rely." Particularly so, he believed, because "counsel [for the CIO] strove to eliminate [it] in order to come at the fundamental challenge to any requirement of identification of a labor organizer." The majority opinion wrongly focused essentially on Thomas's constitutional right to make a general speech as the basis of its decision to overturn, subsuming the act of solicitation within that activity, even though appellant apparently pleaded for a tighter integration between the individual and collective rights bound up within the case.

While he stated Pressman's contentions more accurately than the majority, Roberts dismissed the idea that union solicitation was anything but an economic transaction. Thomas absolutely intended to test the right to solicit union membership, as the facts in the record proved. This being the case, did the State of Texas have any reasonable interest in passing legislation requiring the licensing of a union organizer, given that the statute as written did not attempt to regulate the organizer's actions, speech, or location? The answer was that it did indeed have such a legitimate interest. "The transaction is essentially a business one. Labor unions are business associations. . . . Men are persuaded to join them for business reasons." Since other paid organizers can be made to identify themselves, so too should union organizers. It "is not our function as judges to read our views of policy into a Constitutional guarantee, in order to overthrow a state policy we do not personally approve, by denominating that policy a violation of the liberty of speech," Roberts concluded.

Thus, in sum, the votes of the majority justices in the *Thomas v. Collins* decision rested, in the final analysis, on their constitutional objections to state legislation that restricted the individual's right to speak freely. As a New Deal lawyer friend of Justice Rutledge, Howard Mann, wrote to him shortly after the announcement of the decision, "Your opinion is a masterful job and one of the, if not the best, thing[s] you have done. Teachers in constitutional law should use this case as governing the whole problem of freedom of speech." Mann informed Rutledge that he had closely followed the case and definitely agreed with the evaluation as it then stood. Ironically, he wrote to the justice, unaware of the early drafts of the opinion, "I had thought from all the discussion that there was more to the case than there is. The arguments made by [the] C.I.O.'s lawyer were certainly broad and sweeping," he correctly noted. Nevertheless, Mann believed that Rutledge had performed a splendid work of judicial craftsmanship. He informed the justice that he should not be too much concerned, as Rutledge often was, with how many opinions he had the opportunity to write. "The history of American jurisprudence will not remember how many opinions you wrote each year," he closed, "but it will long remember opinions of the caliber of this one."[22]

For Pressman and his colleagues, the *Thomas v. Collins* case achieved partial victory. But the failure of the Roosevelt Court to cast its decision in broad pro-union phrasing, as Rutledge had done in his first draft, left an open question regarding the specific constitutionality of myriad other state laws. They did not all have licensing restrictions of this type and would have to be individually challenged, and perhaps appealed all the way to the Supreme Court, on a piecemeal basis. Nor, given its individualistic orientation, could the language of the decision serve as a clarion call for endorsing unionism as the First Amendment constitutionalism of the common man. As legal sociologist Stuart Scheingold notes in commenting on how judicial articulation of rights could serve to mobilize discontented groups, "[W]hether or not people actually learn their rights is less important than that they begin to believe that they have rights." If they are to act collectively, "[W]hat counts is that they cease sublimating their grievances and begin to see redress."[23]

Soon afterward, Pressman tried once again to push forward this constitutional orientation in a related challenge of a restrictive Alabama law. In April 1945, he argued the case of *CIO v. McAdory*, in tandem with an AFL case, wherein he elaborated on the *Thomas* arguments. In his brief, Pressman fleshed out the nexus between union functions and the underpinnings of a democratic society in more detail, stating that the various free speech communications conducted under union auspices "not only vitalize" unions as institutions "but are essential to the effective functioning of a democratic society." At one point during oral argument, he selectively quoted supporting language from the *Thomas* decision, although he certainly must have had ambivalent feelings about using it, since the previous case's overall thrust did not address that particular issue. This time, however, the Court opted to avoid the kind of hard fought wrangling that had occurred in the *Thomas* case; it sidestepped both the individual rights and collective rights issues by tossing the cases out on a technical legal point. *Thomas* had won the CIO and its affiliates an affirmation that union officials as individuals were protected by the First Amendment. However, the CIO had found the most liberal Supreme Court of the twentieth century unable to reconceptualize labor liberty beyond an individual, rights-based nexus.[24]

Pressman's second, and much more public, success before the Supreme Court in 1945 came on the heels of the *Thomas* decision. Ever since the San Francisco General Strike in the mid-1930s, West Coast union leader Harry Bridges had been the object of a seemingly unremitting effort by the federal government to deportment him for his alleged membership in the Communist Party. Bridges, an Australian native, had resided in the states since the 1920s and had built the International Longshoremen's and Warehousemen's Union (ILWU) into a bulwark of CIO strength on the West Coast. After an initial INS ruling against Bridges, a special Department of Labor hearing chaired by James Landis from Harvard Law School ruled that the government had not produced proof that Bridges had been a CP member at the time of arrest, as required by the statute. As a result, Congress then amended the law to ban CP membership at any time and the government, this time the Department of Justice, went after Bridges once more. The U.S. government, on many levels, very much wanted to see Harry Bridges deported. This near obsesssion seemed ironic, for Bridge's antiemployer reputation faded quickly after the invasion of the Soviet Union made labor cooperation mandatory. Still the government persisted, first under then Attorney General Robert Jackson, and later under his successor, Francis Biddle.[25]

As a CIO leader, Bridges drew on the support of the CIO executive board. Most prominently among them, Philip Murray believed that Bridges had been singled out because he was an effective union leader. At Philip Murray's direction, Pressman had been involved with Bridge's legal problems since 1938 by referring Bridges to appropriate counsel. As deportation efforts intensified, Pressman connected the union leader's California lawyers—Richard Gladstein, Aubrey Grossman, and Ben Margolis—with the immigration law expertise of his former associate at the International Juridical Association, Carol Weiss King. She wrote to Pressman, that after reviewing the case law, she felt she could accomplish more working with the California counsel in person, and they agreed. For many years afterward, King remained involved in the Bridges' struggle. Collaterally, Murray protested about the Bridges situation in a letter to President Roosevelt in February 1945, as the case of *Bridges v. Wixon*, the most recent embodiment of the "get-Bridges" effort, neared Supreme Court consideration. Murray entreated the President to halt the government's deportation proceedings on both the basis of equity and the need to continue uninterrupted in the shipping industry, since Bridges had now established good relations with employers.[26]

King recruited Nathan Greene, formerly Frankfurter's student and co-author of *The Labor Injunction*, to write the *Bridges v. Wixon* brief. After he had done so, she congratulated Greene on a masterful job of persuasive legal argument. He declined to share in oral argument, though, and advised that Pressman's position as CIO general counsel made him the most logical candidate to share the argument with Bridges' West Coast lawyers (since King had also declined to share oral argument). At first, both she and Gladstein, who were intimately knowledgeable about the case, doubted Pressman could take the time to become equally familiar. King apparently also had personal reservations about Pressman's well-known ambitious nature. Greene, also an acquaintance of the CIO general counsel, said they needed the best in legal talent, and that, "[Y]ou have to give the devil his due, and Pressman is an excellent lawyer."[27]

The two days of oral argument in early April 1945 were days of high drama, given the prominent personalities active in the Bridges Defense Committee. Solicitor General Charles Fahy—former NLRB general counsel—handled the government's presentation. Gladstein, Pressman, and King sat at the appellant's table, with the first two dividing the argument between them. In essence, the King–Greene case theory argued that a denial of due process occurred because the government had already litigated the case (via the Landis decision), thereby resulting in a form of double jeopardy. In addition, due process was violated since Congress had passed the law under which he was prosecuted *after* Bridges' earlier legal victories. Pressman told the justices that the case involved not only Bridges, but the liberties of 3.5 million aliens, and that, even on its own terms, the government had never proved that Bridges supported the overthrow of the United States. Even if the government's proof about membership was accepted, then the United States had produced insufficient evidence to warrant Bridges' deportation.[28]

In June 1945, the Supreme Court announced its decision, striking down Bridges' deportation, six months after the *Thomas* decision had been announced. The Liberal activists—Doulgas, Black, Rutledge, and Murphy—joined by Stanley Reed this time, overturned the government's order. Douglas's opinion, perhaps to hold Reed's vote, stressed procedural error in allowing hearsay witness testimony into an administrative ruling and treating it as substantive evidence. Moreover, he agreed with Landis's ruling that mere affiliation with an organization did not prove violent revolutionary intent. Justice Murphy produced a separate concurrence, but based his reasoning on constitutional grounds as well, insisting that legally resident aliens were to be protected with First Amendment freedoms under the constitution. In passing, Murphy, in scathing terms, directing his ire at Attorney General Francis Biddle, noting that the government's effort in this whole affair would serve as an unending monument to "man's inhumanity to man." Justice Jackson, who took over prosecution as attorney general after the INS was transferred to the Department of Justice in 1940, recused himself. Of all the Roosevelt appointees, only Frankfurter, along with Stone and Roberts, held out once again for judicial restraint.[29]

And indeed, even though Pressman took little intellectual part in developing the case and remained peripheral to it until it reached the Supreme Court, in the end it had to be regarded as both a personal and CIO victory. The industrial union movement had proved it had the wherewithal and ability to defend one of its own before the land's highest tribunal. That evening, supporters celebrated the victory celebration at a party hosted by Pressman as head of the Bridges Defense Committee at the Lee Sheraton Hotel. While Pressman's press remarks indicated merely that the Court had simply affirmed what the CIO had insisted all along—the deportation proceedings were a harassment effort aimed at an effective labor leader—in private, he was more effusive. "Having been an advocate in the *Bridges* case," he wrote Justice Frank Murphy in June 1945, "I feel somewhat restrained in expressing my personal reaction when reading your . . . concurring opinion. At first I hesitated in writing, but after re-reading the opinion I feel compelled to convey to you these sentiments. One can merely feel a great sense of humility before an awe-inspiring demonstration of the truest understanding of democracy and freedom. . . . What nobler objective can there be than striking down and banishing the fears from millions of aliens which might have prevented them from reaping the full joy of participation in our free institutions. That," he concluded, "is the result of your opinion. May God bless you in your work." Despite Pressman's usual stoic demeanor, from time to time warmer sentiments such as these would well up.[30]

The *Bridges v. Wixon* decision, coming as it did at the high point of civil liberties unity on the Roosevelt Court and on the heels of the *Thomas* decision, also marked the high point of Pressman's success before the Supreme Court. In later years, he had other cases that would make their way to the top court—a key case on portal-to-portal pay would soon be filed, and another critical civil liberties case on the constitutionality of the Hatch Act was then working its way through the lower federal courts, for example. And, in 1948, he would represent the CIO one last time before the Supreme Court, arguing against the Taft–Hartley Act's restrictions on union political activity. Even so, none of the later cases developed in an atmosphere of hope emerging from struggle, of future possibilities of a country and a world in transition.

But the litigation struggles, while critical, were only one forum for the potential pursuit of justice. Lee Pressman, Ernest Goodman noted, "recognized that courts were only one of the places that you could go to, or maybe you had to go [to], in order to achieve social justice. And he recognized that the power, the most important power was in the legislature and in the executive . . . and that this was only one aspect of a much bigger struggle [that was] going on." Indeed, Pressman himself constantly told union activists that, "very frequently what the law is . . . is what you people back in the field, through your mobilization, through your pressure" help define for the courts "what the law should be."[31]

EROSION OF THE CIO's NWLB INFLUENCE

The NWLB's Little and Big Steel decisions in 1942 did not end the controversies facing the board for the rest of its existence. Pressman himself knew that many other issues confronted both the USWA and other CIO affiliates, and that one way or another they would have to be dealt with under board auspices. In fact, he seemed to regard the Little Steel Formula as something of a temporary way station along the road to truly equitable arrangement. His job as general counsel would now turn to expanding the ambit of CIO influence in administrative decision making in order to resolve these lingering issues in industrial unionism's favor.

It would not be an easy task. For one thing, his former mentor had now turned to a campaign designed to break the back of the Little Steel Formula's inequitable restrictiveness, if not the board itself. During the course of 1943, in the midst of the most critical war year, John L. Lewis led his miners out on strike three times in a test of wills against both the New Deal wartime state bureaucracy and, in fact, against President Roosevelt himself. Such demonstrations of militant willfulness enraged public opinion, and strengthened conservative congressional forces so much that they were able to pass the War Labor Disputes Act (Smith–Connally Act) over FDR's veto in mid-1943. Even so, in the end, Lewis had so craftily utilized his rank-and-file's militancy that he won his immediate objectives. Given his psychological bonding with the Lewis persona, Pressman must have muttered quiet praises for the vigor of Lewis's attack, even though his radical commitments mandated adherence to the no-strike pledge. For Lee Pressman, the only way to aggressively reassert union claims of unfairness, while maintaining the latter promise, was to launch once again a legal assault on the labyrinthine structures administrative rule making.[32]

By late 1943, the CIO had become quite critical of NWLB administration, though not as willing as John L. Lewis to risk social condemnation by breaching the no-strike pledge. As always, deep frustration with administrative delays started the process. Indeed, in late 1942, Pressman had told the USWA executive board that, [E]very day I go down to the War Labor Board and go through the corridors" where he often met a local union official with "a sort of sorry look" in his eyes. And, "If you think he is worrying about his decision of the Board, you are mistaken," for, even worse, "he is still worrying about how to get a panel for his case." In essence, as he told the CIO executive board at about the same time, dealing with the NWLB "becomes a matter of hit and miss, can you bring enough pressure, can you yell loud enough to get your piece of paper actually into the presence of the Board?" Furthermore, he found that a lack of understanding for industrial unionism's growing difficulties within the agency was growing. Problems included an unwillingness to assume jurisdiction in some cases, an unwillingness to ask the President to seize facilities not in compliance with board orders, and an unwillingess to order an expansion of fringe benefits, despite employer objections.[33]

But of all the problems, the most critical stemmed from wage issues. The rationale underlying the Little Steel Formula had been the government's desire to control wartime-induced inflationary pressures, mainly through controls on wages. Despite implying to labor that there would be equality of sacrifice, profit control never became a realistic policy option for the Roosevelt administration. As noted before, Howell John Harris has observed "no modern war could be fought without corporate executives' "services and expertise" in industrial production, "and they could not be compelled to cooperate." Assaulting the hallowed concept of profit was not a way to gain their cooperation. Early on, laborites could see their demands for "equality of sacrifice" by limiting corporate profits evoked no response from FDR. Even worse, a related wartime manpower agency, the War Production Board (WPB), charged with stimulating increased production, began moves to get rid of premium pay restrictions and inaugurate incentive pay schemes. Ultimately, CIO officials could see little else they could do and acquiesced in a patriotic effort to produce more for the war.[34]

But CIO leaders could not forever escape the consequences of so doing. Their timidity in confronting the skewed priorities of government wage policy, brought into stark relief by Lewis's 1943 initiatives, finally forced industrial unionists to challenge the injustices of wartime pay policies. Indeed, that militancy had created a number of problems. John Stephens of U.S. Steel, for example, castigated Pressman for an alleged 200 unauthorized work stoppages at company plants in the summer of 1943. What did the USWA plan to do about it, he asked the union's general counsel? "I fear that the steel corporations are making a record of our stoppages and may soon initiate a proceeding before the War Labor Board to test the Board's positions on continued maintenance of membership in the face of repeated stoppages," Pressman warned Philip Murray in August 1943. To the extent that an inequitable national wage policy contributed to restiveness, a CIO-stimulated reformulation might help dissipate some negative energy.[35]

Consequently, in December 1943, the United Steel Workers convened a special National Wage and Policy conference, the first shot in the CIO's administrative battle to get out from under the wage restrictions of the Little Steel Formula. It produced a multipoint program of demands involving revision of wage restrictions, and demands for guaranteed annual wages, severance pay, and group insurance plans. The USWA then notified 500 steel companies of its intent to terminate union contracts in late December, offering to continue work if promised retroactivity on any changes. The companies remained silent, and upon expiration of the agreements on December 24th, the cooperative USWA proved it too was not above briefly casting aside the no-strike pledge. After a quick telegram from Roosevelt assuring retroactivity, the steelworkers returned. U.S. Steel filed its case objecting to USWA demands with the NWLB in January. The board chose a panel in February and held hearings in March 1944.[36]

The fundamental basis of the campaign to break the Little Steel Formula was by then widely known. Despite public assurances, the government had not delivered on its vaunted promises of "equality of sacrifice," the union charged. Workers' wages stayed basically stagnant, while prices and corporate profits rose sharply. Even harder to take, Congress granted lavish government tax breaks and assured business of rich profits under any circumstances. On top of that, the functioning of the Little Steel Formula worked in many places to buttress wage inequalities; workers who did very similar work found themselves earning quite different pay with no hope of equalization, due to the Formula's arbitrary restrictions.

Of all things, the tax subsidy appeared the most outrageous insult. Why, Pressman asked in anger at the 1944 United Steel Workers Convention, had the press not energetically informed the public of the guaranteed tax refunds passed by Congress, with little comment in 1942? Using these refunds, companies that lost money could simply recoup by taking a tax credit for up to two years. "You would think there would be a little discussion on the floor of the Senate when they are turning over a first mortgage on the United States Treasury to American industry," he commented sarcastically. He told the 1944 convention delegates that the new NWLB case would pursue their interests vigorously, and asked them to read and discuss the union's NWLB brief at the local level because it was "not merely a lawyer's brief" but "a steelworker's brief. It tries to present your problems that you have every day in the week, and that is why it should simply not be put on a shelf or tossed away, but should be read." "In our demands we have gone far beyond any other Union that has presented a case either to an employer or to the National War Labor Board," he claimed of the initiative to break the formula. "We have literally marked out paths for all of American labor to follow."

But, cautioned Pressman, securing those gains rested on how well local activists would be able to marshall community support—among church members, local elected officials, and small businesspeople, who were dependent on good wages. Union leaders had to reach out and provide speakers to these forums, for local political coalitions were necessary to restore a rising standard of living for American workers. The union would not win the case by simply filing a brief, however persuasive its logic. "Every night of the week there are men on the radio speaking and preaching the doctrine that our case has no merit," Pressman observed. "All that we have, our great strength[,] is in our numbers and in the justice and equity of our case." Now the rank and file had to bring that message into their communities if they wanted to succeed.[37]

More and more, though, Pressman sensed that that pressure was not forthcoming, and it perplexed him. In June 1944, shortly after the USWA Convention, he informed the union's executive board of the increasingly difficult time he and the officers were having in "persuading" the public members of the panel, now apparently in a far less "persuadable" mood than they had been two years earlier. Indeed, the general counsel believed the steel panel chairpersons thought that the steelworkers at the shop floor level did not care all that much about wage increases. For example, NWLB officials had not received a single local union resolution in favor of the general wage increase, Pressman had been informed. "An individual, or two or three individuals in Washington may see" the panel members "every day in the week and continue to harp on" your points, "but after the first few days you make no more impression." "Why do you think this thing has been delayed the way it has been?" he rhetorically asked the board members. The panel chairpersons "think there is no excitement anywhere. Pressman stands up here and raises hell, and he is just obstreperous, and there is nothing done in the field insofar as bringing it to the attention of these people in Washington."

And, Pressman said, he found the same response over and over again: the union was exaggerating, workers' incomes were rising, FDR officials insisted, referring selectively to government-produced standard of living statistics. "There is no problem," NWLB Chairman William H. Davis responded to a Pressman lobbying effort. He "laughed at us," Pressman recounted. "He didn't take us seriously. . . . 'There is no problem,' he claimed, 'you are greatly exaggerating.'" The union knew that such was not the case; fixed wages were a problem for many workers in the face of rising prices. But for reasons unknown, whether "somehow the rank and file was not being roused, or if they were mad, the leadership wasn't giving them the proper" direction in "outlining for them just what to do." The New Deal political elite in Washington just did not get the message, and this irritated him greatly. When speaking to the National Maritime Union (NMU) in New York shortly after the conclusion of the effort to break the Little Steel Formula, Lee Pressman thanked his hosts wholeheartedly for their invitation to New York. It was "an opportunity that comes rarely to those who have to spend most of their time in Washington dealing with people who even more rarely meet anybody who works for a living," he announced, arousing a round of applause.[38]

Perhaps the real problem, however, was the lesson Pressman said he learned through it all: that while the war had increased union membership, it had also returned business to political power, and for now business had the edge on organized labor. William Davis informed him the board would never be able to grant wage increases because corporations would demand offsetting price increases, which would indeed lead to an inflationary spiral, the *bête noire* of policy makers' concerns. How in the world could the government justify price increases in the face of the fact that corporate profit was currently twenty-four billion dollars, up from four billion dollars from 1936 to 1939, Pressman asked. "He explained to me, and this was my lesson, . . . that of course no price increases would be justified but that they, the corporations, had the political pressure on Congress and the OPA [Office of Price Administration]" of sufficient intensity that it would be impossible to "resist" a price increase in response to any general wage increase. "That was my lesson," Pressman noted sadly, "we have fallen down in our political action," but business had not.[39]

Despite all the effort, in the end the NWLB denied the union's 1944 attempt to crack the Little Steel Formula's restrictions in the fall of 1944. True enough, the USWA came out of the struggle with a gain in fringe benefits, offered by the NWLB to ease the pain of the failure to get wage increases commensurate with the 30 percent price increases that had occurred since the start of the war. But even here the struggle was hard fought. Even on small issues, Pressman commented during a USWA executive board session in Pittsburgh devoted to going over the NWLB decisions in the steel cases, "It took an awful lot of work with those public members after our case was all in." He had spent a great deal of time "explaining how important . . . something which seemed minor to them [was to the union] and the battling that had to go on every day of the week" to convince them. He would see them in the morning and get their agreement, he recounted, and then the steel industry lobbyists would take them to lunch, after which "they had changed their mind and the merry-go-round had to start all over again. . . . And this went on day after day and day after day."[40]

Public member George Taylor, in particular, incensed Lee Pressman with the reasoning he relied on in his opinion denying the Little Steel Formula challenge. Wharton labor economist Taylor said that he would use the benchmark of increases in total worker earnings as a fairer measure of whether workers' incomes had kept pace with price increases, and on this basis it nearly did. "Now, it is perfectly clear that what Taylor has done is one of the most dishonest—and I use that word very deliberately—one of the most intellectually dishonest jobs that has ever been done," Pressman charged privately before the CIO executive board meeting in November 1944. Earnings included such things as merit increases, increases for productivity improvements, and shift differentials. None of those things had been a part of the original Little Steel Formula, which focused on capping basic wage rates. Rate increases since January 1941 stood at 18 to 19 percent, earnings at 28 to 34 percent, commensurate with the inflation rate. Essentially, Taylor changed "the rules of the game," and even worse, did "not even justify" it.[41]

In truth, by the war's closing years, business political influence grew every day. As a consequence, the CIO had become—and not wholly unwillingly—a partial captive of the web of bureaucratic entanglements within which it had sought both protection and advancement, but now found burdensome. Pressman and the CIO thus had ambivalent feelings about the experience. The NWLB had been the only place in government wartime policy where anything more than a pretense of tripartitism existed. Moreover, the threat of having no union security while under a no-strike pledge was a serious enough issue that argued for a labor effort to shape that administrative policy struggle. But now, it seemed to CIO leaders that they were left with a fairly distasteful situation. "I find that more and more, in working with the Public Members of the Board," Pressman told the United Steel Workers directors and officers not long afterward, "we find ourselves with our hats in our hands[,] as beggars for little things we're are entitled to," which, while the union might sometimes get them, obscured that fact that the big things have been settled to its disadvantage. Even worse, "as a beggar you are not entitled to argue about important things" because the members "are more concerned about the criticisms they may get from the industry." "That is what gets me around there," he fumed. "They sit there in their ivory tower, handling these cases one by one," a disgusted Pressman told 1948 NMU convention delegates, "and with an eye-dropper they drop something out every now and then to a group of workers to take care of a little inequity." But that was all. "I must confess that six, eight or ten months ago there were some members on the Board that you could go to and deal with and talk to in terms of fairness and equity," he informed the USWA executive board in July 1945. "Today you just throw your hands up" in futility.[42]

The only answer left for the leadership of industrial unionism was to restore the pre-war political situation which, while full of troubles for labor, was distinctly less amenable to business needs. It was for this reason, of course, that the CIO had undertaken a reanalysis of its political operations in the wake of the many political defeats in the 1942 elections. In 1943, that reevaluation had fostered the creation of the federation's Political Action Committee (PAC), a significant step forward in effectuating meaningful political action. Chaired by Sidney Hillman, with John Abt and Lee Pressman serving as co-counsel, the PAC had an observable impact in the 1944 presidential election, helping reelect Franklin Roosevelt in one of his closer races.

To what extent labor had power to influence the overall political landscape, however, was a crucial question that the future would have to answer in more detail. For now, it was enough to laborites that it at least seemed possible that their political futures were on the upswing. As the CIO moved into the uncertain politics of reconversion after V-E Day, the contest for political control of the economic landscape during the post-war era moved to the center ring, a fact that Pressman underlined in his speech to the 1945 NMU convention. "Never before has the need for political action been as strong or as poignant, as it is today," he said. Therefore, the CIO was reasserting its vision of a tripartite corporatist state by calling for government orders mandating a 20 percent wage increase, a minimum wage increase, a ban on wage cutting, and supplemental unemployment benefits. "[I]f we teach the common people there is tied in with this [wage] demand the basis for full employment and full production through the reconversion period," Pressman said, "I am convinced . . . that nothing can stop the CIO and the common people from marching forward to a decent world, one full of peace [and] . . . unity among the nations of the world." Only in that new world can "we really . . . enjoy the freedom and democracy" for which we have fought, he closed, to prolonged applause from the mariners. Whether or not such visions were to be a part of the future in the world where "Hitler" was "finished[,] and not democracy," and indeed whether there would be peace between the two countries left standing as superpowers at the war's end, would be policy terrain just as difficult as any the CIO had yet traversed.[43]

REAPPEARANCE OF INTERNAL LEFT-RIGHT CIO FACTIONALISM

Though the intense internal CIO left-right tensions abated after the German invasion of the Soviet Union in June 1941, that did not mean they had disappeared. Throughout the 1940s, each side continued to jockey for influence with Philip Murray, whom they no doubt sensed was more "influenceable" than John L Lewis. During the war years, James B. Carey, CIO secretary-treasurer, began to carry the hod for the anticommunists within the national office, assisted predominantly by Clinton Golden, and aided and abetted at various points by Gardner Jackson, Tony Smith, and Joseph Kovner. On the Left, of course, Pressman more than counterbalanced Carey, with the able assistance of CIO Publicity Director Len DeCaux. Minor players on both sides, as well as outsiders such as Monsignor Charles Owen Rice, literally Murray's confessor and an active anticommunist CIO lobbyist, also occasionally figured into the mix.[44]

So, though Murray, like Lewis before him and Hillman as well, knew what he was dealing with in Pressman, he remained the constant object of ideologically inspired hectoring by the lawyer's enemies. For example, early in Murray's CIO presidency, Jackson telegraphed Murray that the CIO resolution committees had been "shockingly stacked with left-wing boys," according to his confidants Smith and Kovner. Jackson, by now a confirmed anti-Pressmanite, for personal as well as ideological reasons, objected to Pressman's selection as resolutions secretary, "and other members are similar to Lee" on the committee. Tom Kennedy, the conservative mine worker chair of the resolutions committee, "will have one hard time dominating" the group, given this state of affairs, he thought.

Later, during the war years, the anti-Pressman offensives continued. "That breakfast was a deep satisfaction," the effusive Jackson wrote to Philip Murray in 1943, obviously after they had shared a morning meal. "I may— and do—differ profoundly with your reliance on the guy with whom I saddled you," Jackson continued, again alleging responsibility for Pressman's sinecure with the CIO, "no matter how indefatigable a worker he is and no matter how skillfully he may have protected [the] CIO from legal difficulties." But, he informed Murray, he had come to understand why Murray felt "compelled to place that reliance in him." Obviously, more people than Pressman were guilty of attempts at ingratiation and internal politicking.[45]

Pressman, however, clearly continued to prove the most valuable staff lieutenant for Murray. Moreover, the CIO president had a history of political tolerance and needed a communication channel to the CIO left-led unions. Since Pressman was usually ingenious about tying his advice, whether CP in origination or not, to traditional trade union rationales, most of the time he insulated himself from such attacks. Even so, according to Harold Ruttenberg, who stated Murray assigned him the job of gathering "intelligence" on Pressman's personal politics, the CIO president operated out of the assumption that Pressman had close ties to the Party, which, for whatever reasons, he resolved to tolerate, much to the irritation of the right-wingers. Clinton Golden remarked in an interview with Daniel Bell, years later, for instance, that "Murray had a deep loyalty to Pressman," a relationship that Golden envied, as Murray always remained distant from the latter on a personal level. "It's quite evident that Golden carries a distinct hatred for Pressman," Bell wrote in his interview notes, "and that this runs far back." "'How can you and I be friends?'" Pressman once asked Golden in his office, the CIO functionary recalled to Bell. The latter's curt reply to the lawyer was "'by [you] staying away from me.'"[46]

Pressman's personality tendencies also heightened the underlying ideological disagreements. From the start, he had irritated a number of people, and this did not abate during the war years. "Posture, profile, manner, contributed to the impression of arrogance," in Pressman, his friend Len DeCaux judged. "Lee just couldn't slope modestly. He was so uncompromisingly erect as to create a well-tailored effect." "His mannerisms on the phone and with business visitors [were ever the same]—abrupt, always and at once to the point—an organized response, with a 1 and a 2 and a 3." The impression extended even to his physical surroundings. "An uncluttered desk—in his case a table-type without even drawers—created an aggressive executive impression, all cleared and polished for action."

According to CIO Publicity Director DeCaux, who had been hired by John Brophy, the lawyer's "seeming arrogance annoyed some CIOers." "From some camera angles Lee's profile looked surly" and he "had an abrupt manner, which some took personally." Moreover, Pressman took little time to ingratiate himself with those he had evaluated that did not matter. Most internal staff he regarded as "just part of the help." "If anyone from the CIO office might rarely lunch, or otherwise hobnob, with one of The Three [Lewis, Hillman, or Murray], he drew many jealous glances. Then to have Pressman arrive, and at once hobnob regularly with Lewis, Murray, or Hillman, [or] sometimes all three!" was more than some staffers could bear. John Brophy, who hired DeCaux, early on told the labor journalist that Pressman's Left politics were grounded in his personal ambition, and when the winds shifted the attorney would abandon them and turn Right, not that he had anything personally against him. "It would have been un-Christian for Brophy"—at that time favoring an alliance with the Left—"to hate Lee," DeCaux thought. "[B]ut nothing in faith or doctrine said he couldn't boil inside when Lee looked right over his head." "As to [Brophy's] predictions," commented DeCaux, "when our leftward sailing [in the CIO] . . . hit storms, Brophy abandoned [ship] . . . 10 years before Lee."[47]

With this subterranean psychodrama of personality and politics playing out in the CIO's national office, it is perhaps not surprising that sooner or later the FBI would find sources only too willing to offer negative information about Pressman. Director J. Edgar Hoover's well-known aversion to political leftism caught Pressman in its web, as it had so many others. Apparently, the FBI first opened its investigative file on the lawyer in February 1941, reflecting initial investigative activities conducted since December 1940. The early file documents contained the usual types of information on "radicals" of all stripes contained in the FBI files of these years: hearsay, innuendo, guilt by association with "tainted" organizations, and so on. Pressman spoke at a UAW Victory Rally in Detroit for Stanley Nowak, a Michigan state legislator and laborite with close ties to the UAW and the CP, who had been unsuccessfully prosecuted by the U.S. Justice Department. There, among a crowd of "approximately 135 persons who were predominately foreign born," the FBI's summary report ominously asserted, the CIO general counsel, flanked by UAW officials and fellow labor attorney Maurice Sugar, pointed out how "the power of the people strongly organized had resulted in the quashing of the indictment" against Nowak, And, he closed, they "should take satisfaction in the fact that they played such a vital role in vindicating one of labor's champions." Pressman's September 1943 speech at a Hotel Roosevelt dinner meeting of the Joint Anti-Fascist Refugee Committee even drew special attention from J. Edgar Hoover himself. In a subsequent letter to FDR aide Major General Edwin M. Watson, Hoover called attention to Pressman's apparently offensive [to the FBI] remarks, his criticism of the State Department's policy of coddling Spain's General Francisco Franco, and his call for international labor solidarity.[48]

By 1942, however, the first intimations of what was to become public during the *Hiss* case began to appear in Pressman's investigative file. Whittaker Chambers' allegations regarding the existence and activity of the Ware Group within the AAA had become known to the FBI in 1942. The FBI then reactivated its investigation and upgraded the file status to a "tentative dangerous custodial detention classification." Meanwhile, the police agency continued a background information investigation into Pressman's childhood, family, education, and professional practice.[49]

Thus, by 1943, the FBI had stepped up its investigative activities related to Lee Pressman, as he now appeared to represent something more than just another left-wing union functionary esconced in a key position. From May 1943 through April 1945, the FBI tracked eight Pressman meetings with either Roy Hudson, Party labor secretary, or John Williamson, Hudson's successor. Pressman conferred with Hudson prior to and during meetings and conventions of the CIO but also, according to the FBI's files, met to discuss other matters such as the internal politics of other CIO unions.[50]

By far, the most significant meeting of which there is a detailed record occurred in conjunction with the CIO's 1943 convention in Philadelphia. It was here that the FBI secured, by accident it seems, what one can assume was a fairly typical interaction between Pressman and Hudson. Hudson, who obviously was a figure of considerable interest to the FBI, had been under close surveillance for some time. On the afternoon of October 31, the CP official made his way to Philadelphia from New York and checked into the St. James Hotel. A microphone surveillance had been installed in his room prior to his arrival—later euphemistically referred to in Bureau memos as an informant "who was in a position to report the matter in considerable detail." That evening, upon the close of the resolutions committee meetings, Pressman appeared at Hudson's hotel room for a brief discussion. Pressman then apparently left. Hudson afterward met with three top officials of CIO unions (one of whom was later revealed to be Harry Bridges) to go over the events of the executive board meeting that day. Pressman returned to Hudson's room at 9:45 P.M., as prearranged, bringing with him the draft language of the convention resolutions already voted on by the committee.

As the two talked, FBI agents sat in an adjoining room taking independent notes. In a summary memo to Hoover, an FBI official reported that those agent notes "show that Hudson spoke to him as 'Lee.'" Hudson and Pressman launched into a "detailed discussion" of the resolutions "and Hudson changed the language" on some of them. "For instance," wrote Ladd, at . . . [one] point . . . he told Pressman: 'Eliminate phrase and such shackling effect'" and then "dictated to him" replacement phrasing.[51]

The substance and phraseology of the resolutions was of intense interest to Hudson, and on this it appeared, if the FBI records are accurate, that Pressman had opened himself completely to the direction and leadership of the Party. Of primary importance to Hudson was the wage policy resolution, for obviously breaking the Little Steel Formula through NWLB procedures had become a paramount concern due to John L. Lewis's contemporaneous success after he abandoned the no-strike pledge. Pressman suggested certain phrasing that Hudson negated, with "the final proceedings," reported the FBI, containing "almost verbatim the phrases and sentences Hudson directed Pressman to include." Relatedly, the reaffirmation of the no-strike pledge resolution was ordered by Hudson to be brought up prior to the wage policy resolution, even though Pressman pointed out that Murray "had indicated to him that he wanted the wage policy resolution brought out first." Pressman somehow accomplished this feat as well, for the wage resolution was not brought up until the second day of the convention. And, on international labor solidarity, "Pressman allegedly was told to encourage Philip Murray to regard this question as of paramount importance and to see that the British and Russian trade unions were informed by the Convention that the CIO was in favor of a world labor conference."[52]

Amusingly, at the time, the surveilling FBI agents did not know the "Lee" was Lee Pressman. In the days following the October 31 events, they approached other—this time actual—informants at the convention, who reported the noticed changes in the phrasing of the resolutions. On November 1, 1943, Hudson unexpectedly left the St. James Hotel. When he returned to the city, the agents did not place a microphone in his room at a different hotel because "they could hear as well by lying close to the break under the communicating door between Hudson's room and that occupied by the Agents." Whether or not Pressman remained in contact with Hudson at this point is unclear, but on November 5, 1943, Hudson phoned Pressman's room at the Bellevue Stratford at 1:40 A.M. and arranged to meet him for breakfast at Thompson's Restaurant the following morning. It was only through actually seeing Pressman at this meeting, and later identifying him through photographs "several days later," that the agents positively connected the voice they had heard with the face of Lee Pressman.

Clearly, this "cloak and dagger" activity surrounding the 1943 CIO Convention posed a tremendous personal risk for Lee Pressman. There is little doubt that if Philip Murray had been presented with proof positive that Pressman had participated in allowing an outside force to shape official CIO policy statements, he would have fired him on the spot. Interestingly, both James Carey and Clint Golden became aware of the influence of Hudson in short order, and each claimed they took the matter up with Murray. In fact, Carey alleged in a 1955 interview with Daniel Bell and William Goldsmith, with typical exaggeration, that he himself had had both Hudson's and the FBI agents' rooms bugged. He claimed his spying revealed that "Hudson [was] . . . treating [Pressman} . . . like a schoolboy[,]" and criticizing "Pressman for not doing a good enough job" in promoting CP positions. More than likely, however, Carey's information may have come from his later contacts with the FBI, or possibly through third parties such as Liberal anticommunist attorney Morris Ernst, who had developed a fawning relationship with J. Edgar Hoover.[53]

Even assuming that Carey and Golden took what they knew to Murray, the CIO president did nothing and allowed Pressman to stay. Why would this be so? One reason might be that Pressman had for so long been the object of internal red-baiting that it had by now insulated him to a degree, especially when Murray knew that the people raising the point were on the CIO Right and no personal fans of Lee Pressman. In addition, since the FBI was conducting an authorized but illegal microphone surveillance, Hoover would not readily release memoranda detailing the specifics of the Hudson–Pressman discussions to nongovernment sources. Of course, it is quite possible that he would communicate the substance of what the FBI knew to others if it served his purposes. In combination, perhaps both served to protect Pressman; unless Hoover released the details of the surveillance to Philip Murray, there was no "smoking gun." When asked by Bell and Goldsmith why the changes in the language of the resolutions, solely in control of Pressman after having been voted on, had not been enough to convince Murray, Carey pinpointed the gist of his problem. "'There were no main changes . . . but in the text there were many changes in shading. You'd have to be an expert at the time to know the difference between the Communist line and the CIO line.'"[54]

Ultimately, a summary of this episode did find its way to the White

House. About nine months later, in a FBI memorandum routinely updating President Roosevelt on CP activities, the bureau reviewed the events surrounding the 1943 CIO Convention somewhat abstractly. The intelligence memo wrote, "Hudson is known to have dictated to an important CIO official portions of resolutions which later were adopted by the Convention in the exact wording Hudson had used." Citing Hudson's post-convention statements, the FBI analyst quoted the CP labor secretary as proclaiming "that although the Communist Party controlled only about one-fourth of the delegates, it had succeeded in realizing over three-fourths of its objectives." The anonymity of the memo thus continued to shield Pressman from exposure from anyone except the CIO Right.

And, the FBI determined, Pressman continued to maintain close contact with Hudson. In September 1944, the two spoke regarding an effort to orchestrate a defeat of the anticommunist forces of UAW Vice President Walter Reuther. Reuther was then making noises about weakening the no-strike pledge, anathema at the time both to Communist leaders and the CIO. Couched in the vague language of conspirators who knew their conversation might be overheard, Pressman informed Hudson that "his guy" (presumably Philip Murray) had informed UAW officers "that unless they agreed on a program, he was not going to inject himself into the situation. In other words, Pressman said, he was not going to push them" to take official convention action to deal with a problem undefined in the memo. Instead, Pressman reported that "(his guy's position) was" that other UAW factions should "go out and 'lick this guy Walter Reuther'" in elections. "Pressman stated that 'his guy' had expressed those views 'today.'" One can assume with some justification that this information made its way to the Left, anti-Reuther coalition in short order.[55]

It would not be long, though, before Pressman's identity came to the attention of government policy makers beyond the Department of Justice. In the tremendous swirl of events occurring in 1945—the death of President Roosevelt, the defeats of Germany and Japan, and the founding of the United Nations—the significance of Pressman's intimate connection to American communism temporarily got lost. By December 1945, though, the critical challenges of reconversion labor relations, epitomized by the beginning of the great strike wave of the period 1945–1946 resulted in President Truman convening a national Labor–Management Conference. The high publicity given to the conference, along with the growing international tension with the Soviet Union, resurfaced the issue, this time with additional clarity. J. Edgar Hoover, perhaps sensing that the current occupant of the White House would be more appreciative of information regarding domestic Communist activity, resolved to draw the President's direct attention to the CIO general counsel's history and, more significantly, to his recent wartime activities. "Considerable information has been brought to my attention," Hoover wrote to Truman military aide Brigadier General Harry Vaughn on December 5, 1945, "which tends to indicate that Lee Pressman, General Counsel of the National CIO, who attended the recent National Labor–Management Conference as advisor to Philip Murray . . . is subject to influence if not actual control by the Communist Party of the United States. I thought," the FBI director closed, "the President and you might be interested in this matter. . . ."[56]

SEVEN

THE ROAD TO GIDEON'S ARMY

From 1945 to 1948, Lee Pressman and the CIO struggled to come to grips with a new world order in the making, along with most New Deal liberals and radicals. Indeed, at the beginning of this period, little still separated the two groups. At the war's close, it "almost seemed possible that men of good will would work together for peace, plenty, social progress, [and] an end to ancient oppressions," recalled radical Len DeCaux, nothing short of a continuation of the Grand Alliance into peacetime. It was a view New Deal liberals held to closely as well, especially former Vice President Henry Wallace, now serving President Truman as Secretary of Commerce. Pressman too echoed these hopes. But, over the course of these three years, liberals and radicals saw this grand vision threatened by the hostile stance of the new Truman administration toward the Soviet Union and its apparent abandonment of the New Deal's domestic social welfare agenda. By the beginning of 1948, many came to believe that only through an independent contest for political power could Progressives look forward to a new golden age arising from the ashes of the last conflagration.

Lee Pressman came to agree wholeheartedly with this conclusion. During 1945, while visions of international U.S.-U.S.S.R. cooperation dominated political agendas, he served as one of the CIO's representatives to the meetings that helped found the World Federation of Trade Unions (WFTU). Along with John Abt, he co-drafted the organization's constitution and then traveled to Europe and the Soviet Union late in the year to view the ashes of the last "hot" war firsthand. Soon, however, beliefs that international peace would control began to dissipate as international tensions between the United States and the Union of Soviet Socialist Republics rose. And, during the early stages of the Cold War, domestic conservatism, reborn during the course of the war, reasserted itself with impressive strength, resulting in a Republican capture of Congress in 1946. In 1946 and 1947, through the massive post-war strike wave and related collective bargaining struggles, Pressman worked with grim determination to protect the CIO against the anti-labor legislative onslaught that eventually resulted in the Taft–Hartley Act. Afterward, he would presciently analyze the ramifications of the new law and then fight in the Supreme Court to undercut new legislative restrictions the law placed on organized labor's political expression, due in no small part to the presumed past success of the CIO-PAC. All the while he had to sidestep threats from the rising tide of anticommunist sentiment within the labor movement, stimulated by the international situation, and with a CIO president determined to keep the federation politically aligned with the Truman administration.

By 1948, it seemed to Lee Pressman as though events had reached a watershed. If there was to be a progressivism of the future, he and many others judged, it would not be found in the presidency of Harry Truman. Yet Philip Murray, appalled by the possibility that Republicans would capture the White House, insisted that the CIO and its affiliates avoid splitting the Democratic Party's strength by supporting an independent Progressive candidacy. Matters were brought to a head when Henry Wallace offered himself as the candidate of a potential new Progressive political formation, and he issued a clarion call for Progressives of all stripes to join his "Gideon's Army," as his quixotic candidacy came to be called. Given Murray's determination and Pressman's own deep disappointments in Truman's Democratic Party, the lawyer found he could no longer square the circle. He decided to answer the call of Wallace as Gideon, as did many liberals, socialists, communists, and nonsectarian Progressives. Thus, with uncharacteristic emotion that spoke eloquently about how much his work with the CIO had meant to him, he bid farewell to his position as general counsel and became an important advisor to the Wallace campaign. In that truly critical year for the future of American politics, Pressman believed, as Murray Kempton wrote in another context, that he "had come to that golden time for any man who has given himself hostage to history, those moments when his own self-interest and the dictates of history seem to be running the same way."[1]

THE CIO, THE COLD WAR, AND INTERNATIONAL LABOR

Late in 1944, the British Trades Union Congress (TUC), responding to pressure from its left-wing unions, called for the reinvigoration of a new world labor movement to be founded at the war's end, a movement that would potentially play a large role in shaping the post-war political economy. Led by aristocratic Sir Walter Citrine, the TUC issued an invitation to both the AFL and CIO in the United States. The anticommunist AFL, certain that the new organization would invite the participation of the Soviet Union's All-Trades Union Congress, declined to participate. For the CIO, though, the invitation acknowledged that industrial unionism had achieved a political parity, of sorts, with the AFL on international labor issues. It therefore jumped at the chance to help found the new World Federation of Trade Unions (WFTU).[2]

Pressman, certainly ever since his association with the Ware Group, had maintained an active interest in international affairs, though he did not take a lead role in this area as some other CIO officers and staffers did. He would, however, make a speech from time to time. Thus, at a conference of the Inter-American Bar Association in Mexico City in August 1944, he gave a quintessential anti-U.S. imperialism speech. He strongly endorsed Franklin Roosevelt's Good Neighbor Policy and pointed out how the CIO had worked to ensure U.S. war contracts in Latin America that would contain wage increases for Latin American workers. Given Pressman's interests and his role as a general advisor, then, it was not too surprising that Philip Murray would request his general counsel to serve as part of the CIO delegation to the founding of the WFTU. To lead the delegation, Murray nominated Sidney Hillman, long interested in international affairs, with CIO Secretary-Treasurer James B. Carey filling the second highest officer slot. John Abt, as Hillman's general counsel, joined the entourage too, as did other officers and staff members, seemingly balanced between the Left and Right on the industrial federation's political spectrum. Of course, to some, the appointment of Pressman, Abt, and other trade union leaders sympathetic to the CP was a windfall for the Soviets. State Department analyst George Kennan, in fact, thought the Soviets regarded the WFTU as a potential tool of Russian foreign policy more useful than the national CPs. Many leaders of national labor movements were Communists; their friendliness to the Soviet Union's international ambitions, as well as the Soviet Union's own trade unions' participation, would give the new organization a pronounced Left influence.[3]

The WFTU started with an initial conference in February 1945. "Never before in history was there so representative, so all-inclusive a gathering of the leaders of organized labor around the world," John Abt wrote. In attendance were 204 delegates representing labor bodies with a membership total of nearly 60 million workers. Watched closely by U.S. diplomats, this initial gathering endorsed a panoply of social welfare economic reform measures, de-nazification of Germany, and the right to participate in all international discussions regarding the economic and political structure of the post-war world.[4]

Pressman had not been able to attend the initial London conference, but soon joined the subsequent discussions. Toward the end of April 1945, as the founding meeting of the United Nations in San Francisco neared, the WFTU's steering committee, which included both Murray and Hillman, met nearby in Oakland to plan the WFTU founding convention for that fall. The nearby location of the labor meeting intended to signal labor leaders' determination that international labor meant to play a role in shaping post-war policy. "What we discussed there," Pressman recalled, "was the basic framework of the constitution for the organization, the method of representation, . . . the basic problems pertaining to an organization were . . . worked out. And there weren't too many disagreements." Hillman, according to Abt, again utilized the radical politics of the two lawyers by arranging for them to be the drafters of the WFTU's constitution, thereby helping to win Soviet assent to a compromise he had worked out on organizational structure and voting rights.

Philip Murray, discomforted at first with the thought of sitting down with Communists, soon bonded with the Soviets top official, Vasselli Kuznetsov. Kuznetsov had met with the CIO executive board en route to California and had immediately put Murray at ease. The Russian diplomat had spent time at Carnegie Mellon and had worked in a Ford auto factory before returning to the Union of Soviet Socialist Republics. To Murray, in several ways Kuznetsov seemed quite like all the Slavs he had known back home in Pennsylvania. And although Kuznetsov was a Communist, he was also a trade unionist, and this commonality with Murray smoothed over ideological tensions. Even so, the Russians could not resist pointing out the difference status accorded labor in the two countries. Upon eventual arrival in Oakland, Kuznetsov gently tweaked the U.S. and British labor delegations about their lack of official status at the United Nations (UN) conference, whereas Kuznetsov was part of the Soviet government's official delegation to the UN as well as to the WFTU. The "American and British delegations" to the UN conference, Pressman noted, simply stated that they "weren't prepared to give that kind of status to organized labor." Even if, as Sidney Hillman wrote in a magazine article about the WFTU later that year, "[h]ere were men who knew that the answers being sought across the bay in San Francisco cannot be left to governments alone" and "would come rather from the earth's common people."[5]

For Pressman, however, the most exciting days of his involvement with the developing international labor movement came during the WFTU's founding convention in Paris during October 1945, and his subsequent trip to the Soviet Union. Most of the trade union leaders he encountered had served in the underground resistance during the war. "Well, when you meet a collection of that kind," he recounted, it "was a very exciting experience." Under no direct guidance from the U.S. CP, Pressman and Abt caucused with leftist trade unionists in the CIO delegation and with the Soviets as well. Trade unionists from Norway, Yugoslavia, Central Africa—from everywhere—had been liberated not only from fascism but, they soon made clear, from the vestiges of imperialism. In addition to the convention issues, the social whirl was extraordinary, even more so than in San Francisco the previous spring, where Pressman and Abt had secured the duplex of Henry Kaiser on Nob Hill and threw a magnificent cocktail party for the WFTU and United Nations attendees. Now, once again, in Paris "they were giving [and going to] receptions and balls and cocktail parties until you nearly went mad, small ones, big ones, medium-sized ones," all of which came upon each other's heels with little time left for sleep.[6]

To memorialize the significance of the CIO's visit for U.S. union members, Publicity Director Len DeCaux wrote a series of travelogues that effectively captured the spirit of the moment. From Newfoundland to Paris, with a stop-off in London, the delegation absorbed the impact of the war close hand. "Hunger stalks the lovely streets of Paris," DeCaux wrote, though "the people you meet on the street still have their French vivacity." "[H]ere, as in England, the big hope of the people is in labor." With the French trade unions strongly organized and a growing membership, led by "young and vigorous leaders" who honed their skills in resistance struggles against the Nazis, French labor had recently experience a marked "resurgence of labor political activity." Impressed at the variety of working-class parties and their "scores of daily papers covering every district of the country," along with the visibility of their propaganda, DeCaux judged that fascism and business reaction, in the form of monopoly capitalism, would soon be pushed out of France, and a broad array of social welfare reform ushered in. Subsequently "the industrial workers and farmers will occupy the predominant position" in the nation.[7]

Perhaps most moving to Pressman, Abt, and DeCaux, along with the other CIO leftists, had to be their visit to the Soviet Union. Arriving in Moscow on October 11, 1945, the CIO delegation members were treated as VIPs which of course, given the foreign policy overtones of the trip, they were. Met by photographers and reporters at the airport, the industrial union emissaries, as evenly balanced a group of "strange political bedfellows" as there ever was, uniformly prized the experience no matter what political conclusions they drew from it. As Hillman could not make the Soviet leg of the trip, James Carey served as top officer. He had more than enough like-minded compatriots from the organization's anticommunist wing, such as Allen Haywood, to offset the Pressmans and Abts. Carey recollected in his Columbia University oral history interview that the CIO Party had had a "lively discussion" on the plane between those individuals who thought they were going to see "paradise" and "democracy in action," and "those of us who didn't expect anything like that." Almost laughingly, Carey seated himself in such a manner that he could block Pressman from being the first speaker to disembark from the plane, figuratively preventing him from "kiss[ing] the soil of Mother

Soviet Union" on behalf of all American labor. Occasionally, though, he too heaped praise on his hosts when the diplomatic politics of the situation seemed to call for such a statement.[8]

Of course, given their ideological predilections, Pressman and his brethren on the Left could not have been other than favorably impressed with what they saw. "It was a great experience for both of us. Terrific," Abt enthused over forty years later. The group first saw the "Palace of Culture," a facility capable of accommodating five or six thousand workers at one time, with space for dramatics, sports," and other cultural, family, and recreational activities for workers. They moved on to Leningrad, again touring the extensive social welfare programs administered by Soviet Trade unions—child care centers, libraries, chess rooms, adult education classes, and a variety of arts and entertainments. The reason for many Soviet workers' high morale during the war, DeCaux wrote, was the "cultural work carried on by the trade unions. . . ." This work the Russian unions performed in lieu of shop floor representation and collective bargaining, since in the Soviet Union they alleged a complete mutuality of interest in enterprise matters since there were no capitalists to exploit the workers. Toward the end of their stay, the CIO visitors explored the headquarters of the Soviet Union's national trade union center, the All-Union Council of Trade Unions, a bureaucracy employing some twelve hundred workers. The CIO delegates must have at least subconsciously compared it to their own modest "national center" in Washington. They investigated department after department—Wages, Organizing, Social Insurance, Housing, Cultural, Rest Homes, Sanatoria, and Hospitals—and heard Russian trade union leaders extol the virtues of their system's lack of industrial relations conflict. At one point, recalled Abt, "I said to Lee, why don't we ask them for the legal department?" With tongue in cheek, Pressman responded out of mock concern for his own job security: "Don't raise the question. They probably don't have a legal department." Overall, the trip made a deep imprint on the CIO communists and fellow travelers. "Most of the CIO delegates were deeply impressed with the wide scope of trade union activities in the USSR," wrote Len De Caux in his travelogue, with the democratic character of their organizational setup; with their independence and initiative in all matters that affected the workers' welfare. . . . " Like his ideological brethren, De Caux had obviously filtered what he had seen through rose-colored glasses, even as the CIO's anticommunists had their most cynical judgements confirmed because the unions they saw did not bargain or represent workers at the point of production. As a result, both sides had left with their prejudices strengthened. The tinderbox of internal CIO left-right factionalism was once again ready for the spark that would ignite it.[9]

Indeed, the ideological war seemed to erupt before the delegates departed. The visit abroad had shown how the linchpin that held the CIO internal solidarity—wartime alliances now quickly eroding—had slipped free. Carey recalled one late dinner when, after much drink had flowed, he had to excuse himself for a brief time. When he returned, he found Allen Haywood "in a big battle with Pressman" over the relative merits of the United States and the Union of Soviet Socialist Republics. The former's intellect, of course, was no match for Pressman's razor-edged debater's mind, a mind well suited to "whither" opponents if he wished. At one point, Carey remembered, they seemed "about to swing on each other." Pressman, seeing Haywood's rising temper, demurred, concluding their debate by drolly observing: "'Why . . . Allen, you promised me you wouldn't start the counterrevolution until we got off Soviet soil.'"[10]

The counterrevolution within the CIO, however, was in fact well under way by early 1946, and directly tied to issues of foreign policy and domestic legislation. The Truman administration, lurching from one domestic economic crisis to another in the reconversion period, found a "get-tough" foreign policy approach toward the Soviet Union a welcome diversion from its ineptitude domestically. As tension between the United States and the Union of Soviet Socialist Republics mounted over their suspicions of each other's motives and intentions regarding national security needs and the shape of the post-war world, anticommunist forces, both within the CIO and without, quickly found they could tap into a rich vein of antiradical rancor. In this way, they added leverage to their efforts to purge "unwanted" influences from industrial unionism.

But, for a time during 1946, exactly which way Philip Murray would lean was not at all clear. Truman's early performance caused him great consternation; the President's seeming hostility toward labor militancy, his hesitancy on meaningful price controls, and his appointment of conservatives did nothing to suggest that Roosevelt's New Deal was dead. Anticommunist Catholic trade unionists had been chiding Murray on the internal CIO–CP influence issue and had made a bit of progress; still, the CIO president needed internal unity as the economy reconverted. For this reason, he adopted a tolerant attitude toward the CP influence issue when it erupted at a May 1946 USWA executive board meeting. But, as the Cold War progressed, the patriotic Murray moved ever closer to support the President's foreign policy. And, when left-dominated CIO industrial union councils denounced Truman's foreign policy for its anti-Soviet thrusts, Murray began to draw lines in the sand.[11]

Even Pressman's great store of resourcefulness could not prevent his personal embroilment when he committed an indiscretion. A letter from USWA District Director Joseph Germano, leading the charge on the anti-CP issue within the Steelworkers, clearly threw down the gauntlet as early as March 1946. Pressman had accepted entreaties to speak at the Abraham Lincoln School in Chicago. Germano and one of his international representatives wrote in protest, calling Pressman's attention to the wide distribution of the speech announcement in local labor circles. "The reason for the coverage in Steel locals is quite obvious to those of us who know the fact—that the Abraham Lincoln School in Chicago, as you probably know, is strictly a Communist school." Germano's international union representatives had spent "many long hours" trying to prevent "an entree [sic] of the agents of the school" into steel local unions. We "feel our job is exacting enough to promote a strict trade union policy" without having to fight off a Soviet-dominated Communist ideology. "We need not say to you that it is somewhat embarrassing to us to find this Communist School using the name of the General Counsel of the United Steeworkers of America" to aid "the cause of Communism indirectly. It must be quite obvious to you that your presence . . . would certainly tend to bring discredit on us, inasmuch as we have consistently told our local unions to lay off the Abraham Lincoln School. . . ." In closing, Germano wrote that we "are hopeful that you can say to us that your name is being used on this circular without your authority and that you shall take steps to remedy this situation." To underscore their point, the two made sure that the letter was copied to Philip Murray.[12]

Never one to stand down from a challenge, Pressman responded in kind. In his answers, he elaborated on how an unnamed acquaintance had pressed him to make a speech on this subject, a subject that he considered very important, and how many prominent speakers had appeared at the school in the past. "I have refrained from answering your letter before this in order to have a cooler judgment than that which I would have exercised upon its receipt," he continued. "I am particularly proud of my record of having meticulously followed the policies of the United Steelworkers of America and of the CIO." He took their letter to mean he had "undertaken a task which is contrary to the policy" of the union and embarrassing to the district director. "That of course is a very serious charge," he wrote, and completely untrue. Had they approached him privately, he would have most likely withdrawn. "But your communication, couched in the terms that it is, casts reflection upon my activities as an agent of the United Steelworkers" and "I must reject any such charge. I shall of course discuss this matter with President Murray since you have taken the initiative of communicating with him," he closed. When brought to Murray's attention, the CIO president did what he believed he had to do at that point to keep internal political squabbles within bounds. He issued instructions to USWA Publicity Director Vince Sweeney to have Germano call Pressman, and while apparently soothing some ruffled feathers, clearly indicated that the district director "thinks it would be better if Mr. Pressman stayed away from this place in Chicago."[13]

The Cold War tensions also renewed the interest of the news media in the struggle for the ideological soul of industrial unionism, and this too put even more public pressure on Philip Murray. Both shortly before the 1946 CIO convention and at a radio interview not long afterward, Murray faced a barrage of questioning about communist influence within industrial unionism. The "heat was on [Murray] publicly," wrote Len De Caux, himself the object of some of it, and "not just in the cabs or off-the-record interviews. I once escorted him to a radio studio for an on-the-air interview by a panel of newsmen," De Caux recalled in his autobiography. Many questions centered on communism in the federation, and Murray, usually "adroit under grilling," was visibly "ill at ease and particularly so when questioned on Pressman." Afterward, one of the panel of reporters, Blair Moody, approached the CIO president and "apologized for" pursuing him "on Pressman." Adopting a jocular tone, Moody said, "'I had to do it, Phil. . . . No offense intended. It's what everyone is saying anyhow. It livens things up. I really think a lot of Lee.'" Moreover, he continued, he could have just as easily made "'about my friend Len here in the same way. . . .'" "Murray's face was like a thundercloud as we walked out," De Caux noted. "I was glad to escape without having to escort him back to his hotel."[14]

In addition, as international tensions increased, policy pressures mounted between Murray and Pressman. Eddie Lahey, the *Chicago Tribune* labor reporter Pressman had cultivated, knew both men independently. Because of this trilateral relationship between Murray, Pressman, and Lahey, the latter sometimes assumed an intermediary position, much as Pressman had done between Lewis and Murray during their times of trouble. "When they would have policy differences or spats, I had my ear going from each of them separately," he asserted. While each of them had an emotional "attraction" for each other in some ways, Lahey thought, "[t]hey [also] had a tension between them." The reporter remembered how Murray had once called him "with his voice throbbing with emotion" after a foreign policy dispute with his general counsel "about the [CIO] convention report." Perhaps the most serious pressure on the presence of Pressman in the CIO, however, came from an outside source.[15]

More and more, J. Edgar Hoover began to appreciate the significance of the information the FBI had garnered on Pressman's CP connections, and had stepped up his warnings to the new Truman administration about the influence of surreptitious radicals in public life. The combination of the bureau's fortuitous surveillance of the substance of the 1943 Hudson–Pressman CIO convention resolutions meetings in Philadelphia and the increasing credence the agency gave to Whittaker Chambers resulted in a series of Hoover memos and a heightening of surveillance on Pressman.

In an April 1946 memo to Attorney General Tom Clark, for example, Hoover informed his superior that Pressman, who had "long been active in important Communist affairs," had been a member of an "underground group of government employees" during the 1930s. Some of the members of that group were "presently under investigation in connection with Soviet espionage activity," Hoover pointed out. "[T]here is little doubt but that Pressman is a member of the Communist Party," he told the nation's chief law enforcement officer. Pressman was also in "frequent contact" with suspected Soviet agents Harry Dexter White, an assistant to Secretary of the Treasury Henry Morgenthau, and Nathan Gregory Silvermaster, another Ware Group alumnus. Both individuals were "subjects of primary importance in the investigation of the Underground Soviet Espionage Organization (NKVD) in agencies of the United States Government," the FBI director wrote. And, at about this time, State Department concerns about Alger Hiss's politics, stemming from congressional criticisms, resulted in Secretary of State James Byrnes calling the former diplomatic aide in for an interview. Hiss denied Communist sympathies. And, in a later discussion with the FBI, done at Byrnes's suggestion, when Pressman's name was brought up, Hiss stated that he had heard many people suggest that his former law school classmate did indeed have radical political sympathies, although he again insisted that he did not.[16]

No doubt, Pressman's own concerns about international developments, and his desire to speak out about it, added to the FBI's desire to focus its investigation on his background and current activities. Speaking before the National Council of Soviet–American Friendship in December 1945, for example, not long after returning from the Soviet Union, an FBI source reported that Pressman "criticized the United States[,] stating that the threat of another world war rested on the United States' policy of furnishing war materials to nations actively engaged . . . in imperialistic rule. He said further the United States could not expect the friendship of the Soviet Union but could expects its distrust if the atomic [bomb] secrets were denied to the Soviet Union."[17]

Though Hoover took an activist stance on informing other government officials about Pressman's politics, to what extent he took this information about Pressman activities Philip Murray is still unclear. For reasons previously noted, Hoover may not have been explicit about Pressman's meeting with Hudson in 1943 in Philadelphia. On the other hand, USWA Research Director Harold Ruttenberg, who left the union in 1946, recalled Murray having been "briefed" about Pressman by Hoover. As to the exact nature of that briefing, nothing is known. Still, "Murray really liked" Pressman, observed Monsignor Charles Owen Rice, for his "splendid" trade union sense and more. Rice remembered one particular incident when Murray recounted how Pressman had had him over to his home for dinner for an evening that he enjoyed immensely, and this from a man who turned down dinner invitations to the White House as being too fancy. But if information like the 1943 convention meeting "came in a way that could be proved," thought Monsignor Rice, "there would have been a showdown."[18]

Despite the internal factionalism, media pressure, increasing policy differences, and problematical government warnings, Murray moved slowly and cautiously toward initiating what was coming to seem inevitable. The election of the first Republican Congress in a generation in 1946 then presented Murray with a host of political and legal challenges. Again, Pressman's skills were once again sorely needed. For that reason, and perhaps for personal reasons as well, the CIO general counsel found it still possible for a time to ride out the storm waters and shifting political tides. While the CIO had always been an amalgam of political forces, for the first eleven years of its existence it had been able to reconcile those contradictions, though certainly not without difficulty. In early Cold War America, however, it began to look more and more that this time reconciliation would not be possible.

SHIFTING POST-WAR LABOR RELATIONS

Any hopes that Lee Pressman had that the bureaucratic corporatism of labor relations would survive into the new era intact soon collapsed as the country entered the turbulent reconversion period. More than anything else, the failure of President Truman's November 1945 Labor-Management conference and the massive strikes that followed signalled that detailed government domination of U.S. labor relations had ended. In the immediate future, clearly the balance of power would rest less on mastering the intricacies of administrative law than on tests of economic strength.

At first, President Truman, as had President Wilson at the end of World War I, believed that both management and organized labor would be able to work out a *modus vivendi* on basic labor relations principles that would ease the transition to a peacetime economy. And, as with the previous initiative, at the war's end, both sides found that fundamental value differences still divided them. The challenge for organized labor would be whether it would be able to survive the anticipated attacks of its opponents better than it had in 1919.

According to Pressman, Murray initiated the idea of a labor-management conference and assigned him the job of lobbying Truman's Secretary of Labor, Lewis Schwellenbach. "He wanted me to push it," recalled Pressman, "and I pushed it, and I probably at that time [I] felt pretty strongly that it was a good idea. It's just in retrospect that I can see its futility," he reminisced years later. Pressman's subsequent reflections were on the mark. The most acute analyst of the conference and the labor relations policies of American business, Howell John Harris, has concluded that the conference ran aground over some very basic ideological differences that seemed especially resistant to government exhortations for cooperation. American managers of the 1940s were no more "accepting" of unionism than managers of U.S. Steel had been in 1919; they opposed it and would have liked to have avoided it wherever possible. However, in the context of a post-New Deal political landscape, which still included the National Labor Relations Acts and a revivified union-ism tied to the controlling Democratic Party, an open shop drive similar to the 1920s did not seem possible.

Instead, the "realists" among U.S. businesses resolved to accept, as it were, the legitimacy of independent representational unionism and collective bargaining on a limited range of issues. Their definition of what was accept-able centered on wages and benefits. In exchange, they wanted policy to push back what business leaders believed were far more profound labor challenges to the role of management in production, such as exclusive control of the labor force on the shop floor level. Management spokesmen regarded this "right to manage" as a central principle of the free enterprise system and not subject to co-determination; moreover, they wanted legislative changes to reflect a "hands-off" policy toward enterprise control subjects in collective bargaining and grievance administration. In order to emphasize how far unions had gone to encroach on management prerogatives, business represen-tatives repeatedly criticized UAW Vice President Walter P. Reuther, then engaged in a strike against General Motors. Reuther's claimed that the corpo-ration, glutted with wartime profits stemming from government largesse, could easily grant a 30 percent wage increase *without* an increase in the price of the company's automobiles. His additional proposal horrified auto execu-tives even more: if his claim was not true, the company should be socially responsible and open its books to prove it could not pay such wage increases out of current levels of swollen wartime profits. Other union leaders, such as Philip Murray, thought Reuther's foray into management territory was ill advised, but did see a role for joint determination of major issues. Thus, Mur-ray continued to favor the trilateralism of the war years as a basis for accord. Neither approach had much chance of success. In later years, Pressman kept a photo of the executive committee of the President's Labor-Management Conference on his office wall, perhaps to remind himself that the gathering "was really a horrible debacle." At the executive committee meetings, "[t]here wasn't a single, solitary thing [that the delegates] could agree on," except "that they were . . . against sin. . . ." "If you talked in generalities, you got everybody's head nodding, but the minute you put your finger on something specific," the sides could not agree. With this collapse of the Truman admin-istration's efforts to negotiate post-war national labor relations treaty, the par-ties turned their attention to the real arena of determination—the picket line.[19]

But, even here, it quickly became apparent how interrelated the issues of state and union-management relations had become as a result of the depres-sion and war experiences. The strikes of 1946 involved virtually every major sector of the U.S. economy, and the parties conducted them in a climate where the government had still not fully disengaged itself from the wage determination process. Therefore, the potential impact of what the Truman administration would do in relation to any given set of collective bargaining negotiations figured prominently into the calculations of each bargainer. And here, as in the past, Pressman's strategic advice on collective bargaining in this type of context proved quite valuable. "And there is no doubt that Lee was the strategist of [most] . . . negotiations, that is, of the overall picture" in the steel industry, asserted Eugene Cotton. He particularly remembered one meeting between Murray, Pressman, and District Director Joe Moloney, where "in the main Lee was the more aggressive . . . one" and he "seemed to be calling the turn on the tactics, which frequently happens with lawyers, with 'take-charge' lawyers, which Lee was."[20]

From the first, the issue of price control surrounded all collective negotiations at the war's end. The National War Labor Board had been vested with what essentially was wage control during the war. After some jawboning by the Truman administration in the hopes of extending the no-strike pledge, which organized labor rejected, the President issued an executive order under which the NWLB would dispose of its final cases and control over national wage policy and would switch to the Wage Stabilization Board. In the new environment, unions and management could bargain freely on economic issues and abandon the Little Steel Formula. Companies could then use any agreement with the union on economics to appeal to the Office of Price Administration (OPA) for price increases under a prescribed set of rules. With strikes starting to sweep the country, on January 21, 1946, the USWA began its work stoppage in the steel industry strike in an effort to achieve a two dollar a day wage increase. The USWA, like most other unions, found that its ability to produce economic gains for its members depended on its ability to shape the government's price stabilization policy in a way that would allow the companies they bargained with to gain price increases to offset wage gains. Then, in the midst of the rapidly escalating national strikes, Truman issued an executive order outlining a new national wage policy, allowing wage increases of up to 18.5 cents an hour. Moreover, under the executive order, the companies could use such wage increases to justify a request for an OPA price increase, but first had to have any negotiated wage increases approved by the Wage Stabilization Board (WSB) before going to the OPA. Wartime profits, business leaders resolved, would not be the coffer out of which collective bargaining would produce gains for workers.

Thus, either agency could derail any negotiated agreement reached between union and management, if it so desired. This mandated lobbying the agencies' administrators, though to a lesser degree than during the war. U.S. Steel executives, in fact, had been so engaged with OPA administrator Chester

Bowles for some time on the issue of exactly what level of price relief would be granted should the corporation effect a collective bargaining agreement with the USWA. Finding Bowles generally unsympathetic, they turned to other more pro-business Truman administration officials. The USWA, for its part, and to its credit, eschewed any initiatives to manipulate prices directly in collaboration with the corporation. It did maneuver, though, with Murray lobbying President Truman and Pressman Secretary of Labor Schwellenbach, to ensure that any price increase granted the steel industry would *not* be announced until the steel corporations had signed on the dotted line with the union. They believed this would keep added pressure on the company to come to an economic agreement.

Direct negotiations between the USWA and U.S. Steel, which had been adjourned since February 6 while each side sought to influence its respective government targets, resumed on February 12 as agreement on the level of allowable price increase neared. During final negotiations, Schwellenbach acted as a conciliator and at one point directly stated to corporation executives that, "Of course you gentlemen recognize that you do not get an announcement of your steel prices until you settle with the Steelworkers' Union," Pressman informed the union's executive board. That statement "was the first time that a member of the Cabinet had told the steel industry that the President of the United States did not intend to let that price order go out until there was a settlement of the wage issue." Using that leverage helped him and Philip Murray obtain a final settlement, whereby any agreement of 18.5 cents per hour or under in steel would have the preapproval of the Wage Stabilization Board for OPA price adjustment. This prevented administrative bureaucrats from engaging in a turf war. In the end, Pressman, at first greatly concerned that steel collective bargaining had spun out of control, was satisfied with the final conclusion. The decision granted a substantial wage increase and, more importantly, in his estimation, a *voluntarily* negotiated union security clause, heretofore unacceptable to the steel industry, except by government fiat during wartime.

In most instances, the other large unions striking during the period 1945–1946 also fared well on economic issues. "The sheer magnitude and solidarity of the strikes was evidence of workers' power," writes the CIO's historian Robert Zieger, and "the rank and file held firm." He concluded, though, that in some ways the 1946 strikes also marked the beginning "of a new order" in industrial relations. Organized labor had demonstrated its ability to shut down the world's largest corporations, but how strongly had capital contested against it? True, it had accepted a limited form of worker democracy by coming to tolerate collective bargaining on economic issues; on its own issues, on the struggle for workplace and enterprise managerial control, business had emerged victorious. But how could business leaders now buttress that victory and protect it from future collective bargaining encroachments? The answer seemed obvious. Corporate executives quickly turned to politics to consolidate their collective bargaining victory on the managerial control issues and write the principles established firmly into national labor law.[21]

The effort to amend the Wagner Act in a more pro-business direction, of course, had begun as nearly as soon as the favorable Supreme Court decision in the *Jones and Laughlin* case had been announced. The most serious pre-war initiative occurred as part of the Smith Committee's investigation of the NLRB in 1940, as previously recounted. But, even during the war, labor's conservative opponents plotted one legislative campaign after another. The NWLB's grant of maintenance of membership and the subsequent expansion of union membership—to 14 million by the war's end—added much political energy to a business leadership determined to recast policy as the federal government's wartime labor relations controls gradually subsided. As those special agencies' powers waned, the NLRA, once and now again the centerpiece of national labor policy, would be the focus of political battle between management and labor. Both the law itself and how it was administered once more became key issues for all unions, especially for CIO affiliates.[22]

And as Pressman soon found out, except for its minor successes in the immediate post-war strike wave, from 1946 on the Truman administration did not strongly resonate to the expressed concerns of the labor movement on either law, policy, or appointments. The Age of Roosevelt, if not over, certainly seemed to be fading fast. During the complex negotiations of the 1946 steel strike, Pressman remarked to Harry Dexter White that "he had never known of an impasse of this description—where everything was going to the dogs[,] and the White House had not even talked with . . . heads of the labor unions[,]" nor had presidential assistants even "been in contact with the unions."

Similarly, Truman appointees to the NLRB were distinctly less amenable to Pressman's persuasions than in the past. In many ways, a creature of the New Deal state, the CIO had always had a symbiotic, if bumpy, relationship with the NLRB. It had saved the federation from near ruin as the war approached, and promised to play a critical role once more. The attitudes of some of Truman's appointees, however, astounded Pressman. New board member James Reynolds, for example, complained to the FBI about "pressure" coming from Pressman and the CIO on labor law issues in the fall of 1946. Philip Murray and Pressman arranged a meeting with Reynolds after his appointment to find out his views on policy. Reynolds offered his view that employer rights should get as much respect as labor's, and that labor law should reflect the need to be able to enforce those rights against union violations. Moreover, the country, Reynolds believed, needed immediate legislation on this point. According to the FBI's report, after listening to too much of this "equality of treatment" rhetoric, "Pressman accused Reynolds of not working for the 'laboring man.'" That remark was enough to make an enemy, apparently, for at an afternoon NLRB conference following their private meeting with Reynolds in the morning, Reynolds issued an implied personal threat. Suspecting that Pressman had gotten wind of a confidential NLRB policy decision as yet unannounced, Reynolds waited to proclaim his concerns about the ethics of the NLRB legal practice until Pressman entered the conference room. "Reynolds stated to the meeting that he believed there was a standard of legal ethics which the board would have to enforce dealing with representatives appearing before it. In that respect," the FBI report summarized, "he would favor disbarment of attorneys who engaged in unethical practice. At that point, Lee Pressman walked out of the meeting," Reynolds told the FBI. Obviously, the days of the Madden board, when Nat Witt, his Ware Group compatriot, sat in an influential policy seat, were no more.[23]

But in what policy direction would the country move, if at all? Though business had become politically ennervated, organized labor too had political resources. From 1946 to 1947, the public debate over fundamental shifts in national labor policy would thus consume much of the CIO general counsel's energies. In fact, even before 1946, Pressman found himself scurrying to derail unfavorable amendment drives. In mid-1945, for example, Pressman convened one of his periodic CIO general counsels conferences to develop detailed analyses of the Ball–Burton–Hatch bill's NLRA amendment proposals. As he reported to the executive boards of both the CIO and the USWA, the presumptions underlying that particular bill signified a profoundly different approach to national labor policy, one that organized labor had not seen for years. It "is not a piece of legislation to be lightly regarded," he warned. "It destroys the fundamental objective of the Wagner Act. . . . It uses very seductive phrases, such as giving equality of treatment to employers and employees, and under the guise of giving equality of treatment the new bill actually tears the heart out of the entire Wagner Act." In effect, Pressman observed presciently, the measure "builds up the fire among the people of the country that labor organizations are something to be denounced, to be feared, and somehow to get control of[,]" instead of reaffirming "the basic purpose of the Wagner Act[,] which is the building and prospering of labor organizations." Union leaders should take the bill seriously. If passed, it would "keep us so busy trying to live that we won't have the time to accomplish the objectives that we and the rest of the people seek" in terms of pursuing social legislation like full employment. Though the measure did not become law, the vigorousness of its advocates sounded a warning bell that labor could expect more of the same in Congress the following year.[24]

Of course, the massive strike wave of 1946 did not help either, in terms of

208 ≈◇≈ *Pursuing Justice*

enhancing labor's public image. As a result, an even stronger movement for "equality of treatment" developed as public hostility toward the strikes mounted during the spring of 1946. Consequently, Pressman found himself working feverishly to defeat the Case bill, another set of allegedly "equalizing" NLRA amendments. Testifying before the Senate in early February, Pressman struggled to shift the focus of the barrage of critical questions he faced from conservative senators. Why is it that corporate behavior in labor relations should be controlled but not that of unions, they asked. "I am not saying that all our labor unions in this country have been, in all of their activities, completely lily-white . . . after all, we are composed of human beings and human beings cannot be perfect," he agreed. Yet, the "issue . . . is the guilt and what should be the punishment."

> So someone tosses in a bill, either in the House or the Senate, and says, "That is the answer." A lot of parties are brought down to testify on the answer. There is never any further investigation as to what is the guilt or what should be the appropriate measure to remedy it. The investigation is addressed to the bills, and the bills, unfortunately all too frequently, are not addressed to the problem but rather to the design that the author of the bill may have, and the design, unfortunately too frequently, is to weaken unions.

> Now when we come here, the representatives of labor, and point out the real motives and design of the bills, we are called to task as if we are trying to give the impression that we have never done any wrong. Now that is not our intent. We are addressing ourselves to this bill, that is the danger which hits us right now, that this may be contemplated as legislation and what it may do, and we are pointing out to you the greater dangers and greater evils which the bill, if enacted, would entail.

The sharp challenges posed by the legislators, and perhaps more importantly, the mild manneredness of the defense by liberals on the committees, convinced Pressman that times had indeed changed. As he informed his colleague Maurice Sugar, who had written him about lukewarm liberal support for a Fair Employment Practices bill at about this same time, "Possibly I didn't make my point clear. It is the liberals who are capitulating and not the others," he informed Sugar. It was becoming increasingly apparent to him that it was "[u]nfortunate but true" that congressional liberals were "not as firm" against antilabor legislation as the "reactionaries are against FEPC." "Their heart is not in the effort," he judged, "either in terms of being against antilabor [legislation] or as being for FEPC." In the end, the Case bill only narrowly failed overturning a presidential veto by Truman—a shift of three votes in the House would have resulted in passage.[25]

Everywhere he turned, it seemed, Pressman faced evidence that the opinion climate had shifted substantially. In an NBC radio debate in Springfield, Illinois, on June 6, 1946, Pressman served as labor representative, debating the question of whether increased restrictions on labor unions were desirable. Along with pro-labor Congressman Andrew J. Biemiller (later legislative director of the AFL-CIO), Pressman argued the labor position against Senator Allen J. Ellender (D-LA) and business leader Henry J. Taylor. Pressman quickly squared off against his main opponent, Taylor. Using class warfare-laden rhetoric, Pressman aggressively charged that the real reason behind the amendment agitation was that the National Labor Relations Act prevented employers from using "every devilish concoction" in their antiunion bag of tricks to prevent union organization. For that reason, the law, the NLRB, and the labor movement they protected all earned the "undying enmity of arrogant industrial barons who still yearn for the archaic era when their word was law and they dictated the working conditions for American workers."

Referring to the bills under current consideration in Congress, the CIO attorney insisted that the restrictive proposals "achieved their present status solely through concocted wild hysteria and the most demagogic appeals to passion and hatred." Henry J. Taylor, however, made the most of the current resentments at the strikes and insisted millions of workers had lost their freedom to the "labor bosses." To counter, Pressman maintained that it was the employers, by their refusal to accept President Truman's wage increase recommendations while still under tight price control restrictions, who had caused the strikes; otherwise, workers would have been "compelled to strike or submit to economic slavery." Taylor seemed to have the sympathies of the audience, though, despite the barbs Pressman repeatedly hurled. At one point, after listening to Taylor's line about the evils of militant unionism one too many times, and perhaps frustrated at the increasingly receptive reaction of the crowd to Taylor's platitudes about workers' freedoms, Pressman gave his opponent (and the audience) an uncomfortable history lesson, pointing out that

> There were approximately fifteen million workers during the Hoover days, eating out of garbage cans, evicted and starving. To them they had no American freedom. And I say to Mr. Taylor, that the only instrument that we have in this country to assist in the establishment of political and economic freedom is the instrument of trade unions though which organized workers attempt to improve their living conditions.

Catcalls and boos descended on Pressman for reminding those in attendance of this discomforting memory of the recent past, when strong and militant unions had not been able to strike successfully for higher wages. Unions were necessary to stimulate the increase in mass purchasing power that would be necessary to soak up the enlarged productive capacity of the post-war economy, Pressman argued. Without unions pressing for higher wages and a higher standard of living, we "will get a return to the economic chaos, about which we smile today, but unfortunately too many . . . American workers remember, with seared souls, what they went through during the period of 1929 to 1932.[26]

Still, despite the increasingly hostile public atmosphere toward union militancy, Pressman carried on, continuing publicly to decry the mind-set that prosperity could be achieved without the government pursuing a high wage, demand-driven economic expansion, in which unions had to play *the* critical role. "It is quite clear that only a policy directed toward maintaining and expanding the purchasing power of the lowest income groups can hope to furnish that huge volume of mass purchasing power which alone can furnish the gigantic market needed for our anticipated output," he told 1946 NLG delegates. "Only from two sources has come, and can come, a social, legal or economic impact in the direction of the needed policy." "One is pending legislation to raise the minimum wage; the other is a strong and vigorous labor movement alert to the need for rising wage levels. Both serve the best interests not merely of the individuals and groups which are direct recipients of higher wages, but of the national economic well-being in our need for an adequate volume of consumer purchasing power in the years ahead." That was why the current political climate was so disconcerting, Pressman noted. The "present temper of Congress" did not indicate that it believed a high wage policy and vigorous union movement were beneficial. "That is not a statement of defeatism," he cautioned his presumably liberal listeners. "It is intended rather as a recognition of a fact and a call to action."[27]

Noting the ambivalent public reaction he was receiving as he pleaded labor's cause, Pressman carried the message back to CIO forums that the prime arena of struggle in the immediate future would be the ballot box. It was clear, given the outcome of the 1946 strikes, he told the USWA executive board, that "The political arena is where the attack will come." Industrialists cannot "meet our organization on an economic front," though they had clearly tried. "They know they are whipped in that fashion . . . so they have shifted, they have gone to an arena where admittedly we are weak." Labor and the common people had to ensure that business leaders and conservatives did not win there, he insisted at a contemporaneous Fur and Leather Workers convention. All sense of complacency regarding politics had to be cast away, because "reaction, deep reaction, will dare to do anything that the people will let them [sic] get away with." Indeed, he added, the next few years would prove to be a historic watershed.

We are now riding on the crest of a tremendous victory on the economic front. If we are to hold those gains, if we are to make certain we will move forward to a new era when democratic rights will prevail and not the privileges of the poll-taxers or the privileges of the monopolies in this country, whether we have one or the other, will depend entirely upon whether the membership . . . will respond to the inspired leadership that we have in the CIO. . . .

And, he warned the CIO convention delegates in the fall of 1946, "if you analyze all these proposals, what they come down to is simply this: how can we so undermine organized labor through legislation that . . . [it] will not have the strength to meet the corporations when they engage in collective bargaining? How can we so undermine and destroy labor unions [so] that management can say 'no' and be safe when they say 'no'?" To the Steel Workers directors, he put it in even starker terms. [I]f we fall down on our [political] jobs between now and November, and there is a reactionary sweep in the Congressional elections," he said, "frankly I am very fearful of what we will face in Congress when it meets in January."[28]

RESPONDING TO TAFT–HARTLEY

Pressman had good reason for those fears. His worst nightmares about what would happen if the November 1946 elections produced a conservative Congress turned, in quick order, into reality. For the first time in a generation, U.S. voters elected a Republican Congress in both chambers. Even worse, many of those candidates had run on the issue of "restoring balance" to U.S. labor relations by amending the National Labor Relations Act to reign in perceived union abuses of power. Among those abuses, they charged, were strikes that affected national security, strikes that affected noninvolved parties, and a number of other union self-help measures that, right or wrong, had become identified with antisocial economic objectives. It thus did not take the new Congress long to have a new set of amendatory proposals ready for the first of the year.[29]

In the Senate, Republican Ohio Senator Robert Taft proposed a bill, and in the House, Republican Congressman Fred Hartley of Indiana did the same. In sum, the changes they proposed for national labor policy were broad scaled, complex, and fundamental. No longer would national labor policy, as expressed in the Wagner Act, seek to encourage the process of unionization; U.S. policy would henceforth be value-neutral on the question by strengthening tenets of individualism regarding the decision to join a union. These principles, Melvyn Dubofsky has argued, had been implicit in the act since its original passage, though largely policy-quiescent in the first decade of NLRA administration. Employers' rights to free speech and to petition for election were made explicit in Taft–Hartley's statutory language, and a number of union unfair labor practice added to "balance" the law and complement the Wagner Act's original employer proscriptions. Union security devices were either made illegal, burdened with complex administrative processes, or turned over to the states for policy determination. And, for the first time since the Norris–LaGuardia Act, passed in 1932, NLRB-initiated injunctions could be sought against union activity under certain conditions. Given the gravity of the legislative proposals, Philip Murray led the CIO witnesses in denouncing the proposed law before labor committee hearings in both chambers. But once more it fell to Lee Pressman to unearth the long-term policy ramifications of what Congress now sought to do.[30]

"As Taft–Hartley ground inexorably toward final passage in May and June" of 1947, writes Robert H. Zieger, "CIO general counsel Lee Pressman extended Murray's critique in a series of penetrating briefs and presentations." As he informed the CIO executive board in the May and June crisis meetings, "[n]othing so serious has hit us before," at least in the memory of industrial unionism's younger apostles. "I say that this legislation will produce a situation that is far more critical and far more serious than anything that the labor movement has seen in our generation." The public perception was that the more "moderate" Taft bill changes that held sway in the final version of the conference committee's report were not at all moderate, he advised. With Truman nominating new board members, instead of FDR, labor could be sure that they "won't be the kind of people we have been accustomed to in the past or the kind of people we have had in the past few years. . . ." Now even the individuals that they had "been criticizing, but who at least have held out a sense of impartiality," looked good.[31]

The Taft–Hartley Act achieved final passage in July 1947, when the Republican 80th Congress overrode President Truman's veto of the measure. And by July, Pressman had extended his analysis regarding how the law's various provisions would affect the USWA in organizing and collective bargaining, and walked the international union's executive board through a detailed, exhausting exposition of known, unknown, and possible ramifications of the new law. Particularly objectionable, he charged, were the prohibitions on labor's political activity, a section that the CIO, the USWA, and other affiliates resolved to test in court, among others. "Obviously, the law was intended to . . . provide an instrument to the employers to be used by them to degrade the living standards of American workers," and in so doing, the politicians who supported the law chose to "incorporate a provision in the same law to deprive those American workers of the . . . right to use the ballot box in an organized fashion, to defeat the very people who have enacted this law." At the conclusion of his presentation, he told the executive board members that his judgment about the significance of the Act was based on "what I saw happening when" the measure "was in the process of being passed—we are not up against an ordinary antilabor bill. You are not up against some people who are just simply a little more conservative in their views than the average American citizen."

> I saw Senator Taft in action, Senator Ball. I had occasion to talk to Senators who are friendly with us, and saw what Taft and his machine did to those Senators to get their vote. This Act reflects a change in American Government policy, . . . toward labor unions, not just in technique, but in the essential content of the policy. You have a situation today that is different in content from anything that we have ever had, because this is the creation of a Government instrument to be used by employers. You are not going to be fighting many employers; it is a Government instrument, and an instrument that is designed and based on a policy which says in so many words, "Weaken, if not destroy, the labor unions themselves."[32]

So, for the next three months, Pressman girded himself to do his utmost to catalyze the political energies of industrial unionism. In August 1947, before the International Union of Mine, Mill, and Smelter Workers (IUMMSW) Convention, he gave his longest, and certainly one of his most aggressive, foot-stomping denunciations of the 80th Congress, sounding a clarion call to political action. Pressman was warmly introduced by IUMMSW President Maurice Travis as embodying the "distinction . . . between a parasitic lawyer and an honest labor lawyer," well serving the organization he represents. With the "shadow of the Taft–Hartley Act hanging over this all and over all of labor today," Travis said, no subject was more important than political action, and CIO General Counsel Lee Pressman was going to inform the delegates exactly why. It was "Lee Pressman, together with some of the other labor attorneys, who sounded the note of alarm, [and] whose analysis of the bill placed" organized labor on notice of how destructively the law could be used. "And then [it was] Brother Pressman and his associates [who] began a crusade to make the working people [of the country] aware of the dangers . . . and helped mobilize the working people to fight against its passage."[33]

"I have been looking forward eagerly to attending a convention of your organization now for many years," Pressman began after sustained applause and a standing ovation, and quickly focused his remarks. Labor leaders should not say to themselves, in looking at the individual provisions of the law, that "'[t]hat isn't so bad. I can get around this one. I can probably live with that one.'" "That, my friends, would be a very, very sad mistake." In effect, he continued, the act had repealed the Wagner Act, if one considered what the underlying purposes of two laws really were. The Wagner Act had been designed to encourage the growth of unions; the Taft–Hartley Act, expressly and as likely to be administered, was designed to weaken, if not destroy, them. Take, for example, President Truman's recent appointee to the new position of NLRB general counsel, Robert Denham, who had just told a newspaper reporter that he was "a Wall Street lawyer" who thought the statute was "long overdue." "What do you expect from a man who says he is a Wall Street lawyer?" Pressman asked rhetorically. Until the Wagner Act had been held constitutional, labor "had the right to engage in collective bargaining but it was a very, very theoretical right." The Mine, Mill, and Smelter Workers, the successor of the militant, hard-rock Western Federation of Miners union, knew this only too well.

> During the days of the Western Federation of Miners you may have had your right to organize but along with that right weren't there the rights of employers to fire you from the plants and the mines when you dared to join a union? Along with your right went the right of the employers to hire his scabs when you were on strike; the right of the employers to hire his thugs and gunmen and shoot down the pickets on the picket line.

"What was your right worth when the employer had those rights as well?" Pressman wondered. It had been the Wagner Act, as first administered, which meaningfully took those antiunion discrimination rights away from the employer. Soon, he predicted, on the basis of supposedly evenhanded treatment of rights under Taft–Hartley's statutory language, labor's enemies would enwrap the movement within the tentacles of bureaucracy. They "want to suck our unions into the depths of red-tape and delay. . . ." To prove his point, Pressman then elaborated a hypothetical representation election process under Taft–Hartley and how employer lawyers could easily drag the process on almost ad infinitum. "Now I'll let you in on a secret," Pressman pursued his point, as to "what the real purpose of all that [election] machinery is. Very simply the real purpose is: You file your petitions and your grandchildren participate in the vote."

The same thing was true of the provisions for restricting union security, for obtaining the checkoff, for allowing unions to be sued for breach of contract, and for sections granting the board the power to seek injunctions against unions. "Today we have a fundamental change, in that we actually have a law that puts the government and the agencies at the disposal of employers to be used as a weapon against labor unions at the request of those employers," he reiterated.

Even though the Taft–Hartley law sought to protect itself by restricting a number of union activities in the realm of politics, Pressman noted, the CIO, at least, was not going to shrink away in fear. "We know what our rights are and no petty Hitler is going to intimidate or scare the CIO or millions of members of the CIO," he thundered to long applause and cheers from the crowd. The federation intended to challenge this section in the courts and pursue its political rights as it always had, only hopefully with more vigor. Despite innuendoes that the CIO would not be able to publish the voting records of the 80th Congress, the CIO executive board intended "to exercise our Constitutional rights and engage in political activity in the Federal campaign" as never before.

Therefore, so too must all the affiliates throw themselves into the campaign. "It is not going to be sufficient merely to pass resolutions or merely sit in meetings and express our indignation at the Tafts and the Hartleys. November 1948 may well be the most decisive political election in the history of our country. If only everyone could have sat in the congressional galleries, as he had, "and watch[ed] those men and women in Congress, watch[ed] their hatred and their contempt for you and the common people of the country," he said, there would be no doubt about producing the requisite progressive political response. "We are in for the struggle of our lives, and by 'we' I do not mean merely the members of organized labor. I refer to the common people, the workers, the farmers, the professional groups—we all have the same problem in common," Pressman insisted. "We are faced with the same enemy."

So, then, the common people could not let complacency win, and in this the Mine, Mill, and Smelter Workers could play an important role in a key geographic area of the Western United States. Political wins in that region would vastly improve the progressive complexion of a new Congress, he counseled. Now it was up to them. "The day of exhortation from your leaders—that's gone," the CIO general counsel told the delegates in his rousing closing. "We have given you our message. We have explained to you what the fight is about, the struggle in which you are engaged. The responsibility, the work, the hard effort, the courage, . . . and the fighting determination to win now rests with the rank and file membership." When Pressman finished, the delegates rose and cheered as he exited the hall. But for all of his bravado, for all of his assertiveness in public, underneath it all, as he strode from the convention hall, Pressman's confidence about the future direction of American politics had to have been deeply shaken, and thus his conviction that the 1948 election would be historic, greatly strengthened.[34]

ASSERTING POLITICAL RIGHTS BEFORE THE SUPREME COURT

The CIO's litigation load had lightened moving into 1947, as the federation anticipated instituting a number of challenges of various provisions of the complex Taft–Hartley Act. Pressman had received a favorable Supreme Court ruling in the *Anderson v. Mt. Clemens* portal-to-portal pay claim case, a decision extending the concept of portal-to-portal pay into factory-type settings, a scheme which eventually led to a hostile legislative reaction stimulated by an outraged business community. Also in 1947, the lawyer lost the long-gestating *United Public Workers v. Mitchell* Supreme Court case. In this suit, Pressman represented the United Federal Workers of America, a CIO national office protectorate, in its challenge against the partisan political prohibitions of the Hatch Act on federal workers. The Hatch Act resulted from a series of Works Progress Administration (WPA) scandals in several states during the 1938 elections, which became a public embarrassment for President Roosevelt and the Democratic Party. Claims of political influence peddling tied to federal employment in the WPA prodded Senator Carl Hatch (D-NM) to propose a law that, among other things, made it illegal for federal workers at all levels, except for the President and his direct appointees, to take an active part in partisan political campaigns.

At the time, a number of liberal Democrats questioned the measure's constitutionality, but President Roosevelt, assured by then Attorney General Frank Murphy that he could find no directly prohibitive case law, signed the act despite inherent ambiguities. In 1940, Congress amended the law so that it would be administered by the U.S. Civil Service Commission's (USCC) long-standing guidelines prohibiting partisan politics within the federal government's classified civil service. Thereafter, the Hatch Act applied to all federal employees, classified and unclassified, no matter what their occupation.[35]

This was fine for most federal employee unions, such as the American Federation of Government Employees (AFGE), an AFL affiliate that eschewed electoral initiatives in favor of lobbying the Washington bureaucracy. But not for the upstart United Federal Workers of America (UFWA), a tiny union of federal employees, founded with the participation of radicals— among others—working in several key New Deal agencies, the WPA among them. Led by an elite, mostly left-wing leadership corps, the UFWA became the first CIO international union to elect a woman president. The union's membership covered all forms of federal employment—custodians, dieticians, laundry workers, food handlers, and so on. Furthermore, it aspired to both collective bargaining and electoral militancy, a prospect that most government administrators, New Deal or otherwise, found abhorrent. The union's militancy irked administration officials all the way up to and including FDR.

At first, the Hatch Act was accepted by the UFWA's leadership. As the country entered the war years, and as the FBI began to use the statute's loyalty provisions to harass a number of militant local union leaders, however, the ramifications of the partisan political restrictions of the law became apparent. To protect the UFWA and advance the concept of meaningful collective bargaining in federal employment lobbying alone would not suffice. They concluded that in order for lobbying to be effective, active partisan politics in federal elections was crucial for the union. Hence, the union's officers retained Lee Pressman to press a constitutional challenge to the political restrictions as administered by the USCC. Expectedly, Pressman lost at the federal district court level in early 1944 and then appealed the case to the Supreme Court.[36]

Pressman's Supreme Court brief argued that the Hatch Act, as amended in 1940, violated the First and Fifth amendments. Moreover, he and his assistant general counsels shrewdly constructed the brief so that the justices on the court who had been administratively involved with the law previously would have legitimate legal rationales for deciding in the union's favor. This was an important point. Once again, Pressman knew that his best chances lay with appealing to the court's "liberal wing," as he had in the *Thomas v. Collins* case, which still consisted of Justices Black, Rutledge, Murphy, and Douglas. In opposition to their judicial activism sat their New Deal brethren—Felix Frankfurter, Stanley Reed, and Robert Jackson. Justice Stone, however, passed away, with the case undecided. President Truman replaced Stone with his friend, former Democratic Kentucky Senator Fred Vinson. Harold Burton, a Republican appointed by Truman, replaced Justice Roberts, who had sat during the *Thomas* arguments. In effect, the voting balance between the liberal judicial activists and the judicial restraint proponents had changed little.

As it was in *Thomas*, the CIO general counsel's strategic problem was to hold the four libertarians as a solid block and convince at least one of the other three Roosevelt appointees. The difficulty here was that Murphy and Jackson had both served as attorney generals at critical times in the Hatch Act's evolution, Murphy during the passage of the bill and Jackson afterward in its administrative implementation. Indeed, Murphy's opinion to FDR maintained that the Act's original implementation (prior to its amendment in 1940) was constitutional. Robert Jackson, as well, rendered official opinions regarding the law's application in the federal service. Thus, if Pressman wished to garner their votes, if they did not recuse themselves, he would have to give these justices an "out" for reversing what had seemed to be their original backing for the law.

It was with this in mind that Pressman's brief attacked the federal district court's decision. Essentially, Pressman conceded that government indeed had a right to stop politically related abuses of authority and to draw reasonable limits on certain types of activity, where the government found coercion, official abuse of authority, or other "substantial" evils. It was this type of activity with which the history of civil service political restrictions had long been involved. But, the brief insisted, where government desired to limit the rights of free expression protected under the First Amendment, and particularly as they pertained to political types of expression, it must mold such restrictions in a way that did not damage constitutionally protected rights. Here was where the Congress failed in its responsibility. It was conceivable that in its original formulation the law could have been administratively interpreted to protect political free speech on the part of federal employees. But, when Congress amended the Act and incorporated the civil service's administrative rules, the law became so sweeping in its prohibitions that it brushed aside constitutionally protected First Amendment rights. And all without adequate justification, for the Hatch Act's legislative history provided no foundation for the necessity of such all-inclusive prohibitions.

The district court had erred in applying the usually acceptable "presumption of validity" standard in this case, the union attorneys claimed. This test meant that if there was an arguably "reasonable" basis for a legislature's action, then the courts should accept the judgment of the legislature. The Hatch Act, however, dealt with fundamental rights of normal political expression, an activity clearly protected by the First Amendment and supported by a string of recent Supreme Court decisions by the Roosevelt court. Pressman sought to avoid alienating Frankfurter and downplayed the "clear and present danger" phrase; nevertheless, he kept its substance by suggesting to the high court that when a legislative body sought to suppress "the exercise of a right upon which the very existence of a democratic government depends," the court should apply more "rigorous" tests. The "statute is operative at precisely that point in this extremely vital area of political expression at which civil rights have their deepest meaning—where others are sought to be persuaded; and their greatest value—where the issues are most controversial," Pressman's brief argued. "For when it is sought to curtail basic rights of expression a substantial showing of the necessity for the limitation must be made."

The UFWA brief then went on to elaborate on how the federal government had made no such showing in this case. Moreover, legislative prohibitions preventing reprisals or coercion already existed or Congress could more narrowly draw such restrictions to avoid eviscerating federal workers' political rights. As it currently stood, the law could be said to protect federal employees "only in the fashion in which 'protective custody' affords protection," the lawyers aptly noted. In applying the law in such a broad fashion— to all categories of federal employees, even those without any hint or hope of wielding administrative or coercive power—the government failed to prove the necessity of the restrictions. It could not seriously maintain that it was necessary to deprive a roller in a U.S. mint of his political rights in order to guarantee public confidence in the impartiality of the federal service.[37]

Ralph Fuchs of Solicitor General J. Howard McGrath's office represented the government. His brief argued that the Hatch Act was constitutional because section 9 was simply the latest in a long line of legislation limiting the political activities of federal civil service employees. Experience had shown, given the 1938 election scandals, that further restrictions were necessary to meet modern administrative needs, and Congress had a reasonable basis for acting. The law worked no terrible deprivation on freedom with regard to public employees. It did not imprison them, for example; at worst, federal employees had to choose between participating in active political management and their jobs. Nor did the law contravene speech, according to the government. It had specifically stated that federal employees could publicly and privately express their opinions on all subjects and candidates. The provisions were therefore reasonable and justified.[38]

Immediately after Pressman's and Fuch's initial oral argument on December 3, 1945, the Supreme Court deadlocked. Since Justice Jackson had gone to Nuremberg, the four activist civil libertarian justices found themselves opposing the four remaining justices, led by Chief Justice Stone, and including Republican Truman appointee Harold Burton, in addition to the other two New Deal appointees, Stanley Reed and Felix Frankfurter. The stalemate continued through the spring of 1946, with the court rescheduling the case for reargument before the full bench. It also asked for elaborations on the point of exactly how the incorporation of U.S. Civil Service prohibitions, via section 15 in the 1940 amendments, affected the constitutional issues.

In the supplementary brief, Pressman attacked the government's claims that no substantive rights had been lost, since federal employees could still participate in nonpartisan campaigns. "It is of no concern to this litigation that Federal employees may engage in campaigns concerning the regulation or suppression of the liquor traffic," his brief charged. It was still beyond question, since Congress did indeed have before it the civil service rules when it passed the amendments, that the Hatch Act prohibited many of the most basic freedoms of a democracy—publishing opinions in a political paper or speaking before a political convention, for example. "In other words, the Act clearly and unequivocally incorporates a direct prohibition of every one of the fundamental exercises of the rights of freedom of speech and of the press which the appellants in this case desire to engage in." The court should declare that "[f]ederal employees are not wards of the State" and "that their constitutional rights . . . must be respected." That latter argument, they maintained, "contains the seeds of a threat to the liberties of the entire population." Clearly, it would not be so big a step as to see such political prohibitions being extended to private employees of companies receiving state monies or contracts.[39]

The deadlock on the court continued into late 1946, and finally resolved itself in 1947. Again, the court's difficulty had much to do with the internal philosophical divisions percolating under the surface of the Roosevelt bench, as well as the transition to what would become the decidedly more conservative Vinson Court of the late 1940s. However, as yet, the problematical divisions lay between the seven Roosevelt appointees.[40]

Thus, though the court was badly split, especially on civil liberties cases, from 1943 to 1947 it had found it possible to reach decisions through internal political coalition building on a case-by-case basis. Pressman's overall strategy for the challenge clearly reflected his perception that he had to laden his briefs with enough alternatives so that he might give one or more nonactivist justices a basis for allying with the court's liberal wing. When both he and Ralph Fuchs reargued the case before the court on October 17, 1946, it was apparent that it would take another such coalition for the union's case to prevail, as the court remained evenly divided about the disposal of the case. By December, however, Pressman's hope evaporated when Justice Murphy, despite being lobbied by Black and Douglas, withdrew. This then left a 4 to 3 split (Vinson, Reed, Frankfurter, and Burton affirming; Black, Rutledge, and Douglas, reversing). The new chief justice assigned Stanley Reed as senior associate to write the majority opinion, and Hugo Black, similarly situated for the minority, to write the dissent.

Speaking for the majority, Justice Stanley Reed declared that the interests of the appellants in "free expression had to be balanced against the need of government for "orderly management of administration." The determination of that need, the court stated, was a question for other branches of government, not the judiciary. The Supreme Court's only duty "in this case ends if the Hatch Act provision under examination is constitutional." And in fulfilling the duty to determine that question, "this Court must balance the extent of the guarantees of freedom against a congressional enactment to protect a democratic society against the supposed evil of political partisanship by classified employees of the government."[41]

Retreading familiar arguments that constitutional rights were not absolute, the opinion relied primarily on the 1882 *Ex Parte Curtis* decision as its major precedent. Reed insisted that this decision, which upheld an indictment of a federal employee under a statute banning the giving or receiving of money for political purposes, was similar to the prohibitions of the Hatch Act. "The decisive principle was the power of Congress, within reasonable limits, to regulate, so far as it might deem necessary, the political conduct of its employees." He contended that this prohibition on financial manipulations had "found acceptance in the subsequent practice of Congress and the growth of the principle of required political neutrality for classified public servants as a sound element for efficiency." The only difference regarding the Hatch Act was that Congress now prohibited the "political contributions of energy by Government employees."

Though Reed accepted Pressman's arguments that political neutrality was not necessary for a merit system, just "because it is not indispensable does not mean that it is not desirable or permissible." Congress could reasonably conclude that such limitations were necessary to guarantee that public workers devoted themselves to the public welfare and "were not over active politically." "Appellants urge that federal employees are protected by the Bill of Rights and that Congress may not 'enact a regulation providing that no Republican, Jew or Negro shall be appointed to federal office . . .'" Reed wrote, citing Pressman's brief. "None would deny such limitations on congressional power but, because there are some limitations, it does not follow that a prohibition against acting as a ward leader or worker at the polls is invalid," he reasoned. Since it was only partisan political activity "that is interdicted" and since political expressions could still be made, publicly or privately, the appellant's claims of unconstitutionality were unwarranted. "There are hundreds of thousands of United States employees with positions no more influential upon policy determination than that" of the claimants in this case. "Evidently what Congress feared was the cumulative effect on employee morale of political activity by all employees who could be induced to participate actively. It does not seem to us an unconstitutional basis for legislation." If the "regulation was within 'reasonable limits,' even though the regulation trenches to some extent on unfettered political action," the court could only interfere "when such regulation passes beyond the general existing conception of governmental power." Given the long history of administrative practice, "court decisions upon similar problems and a large body of informed public opinion. . . . We cannot say with such a background that these restrictions are unconstitutional."

Justice Hugo Black, the First Amendment literalist, spoke in dissent for himself and Rutledge. In contrast to the arid and sterile tone of Reed's writing, Black's opinion burned with passion, even anger. He immediately strode into the constitutional substance of the claims and denounced the contention that in barring federal employees from partisan politics, Congress did not inhibit any fundamental rights, since the law still allowed nonpartisan activity and supposedly public and private expression about candidates. "Since under our common political practices most causes and candidates are espoused by political parties," he noted, "the result is that, because they are paid out of the public treasury, all these citizens who engage in public work can take no really effective part in campaigns that may bring about changes in their lives, their fortunes, and their happiness." This "hopeless contradiction between this privilege of an employee to talk and the prohibition of his talking . . ." could not be reconciled.

According to Justice Black's way of thinking, "whatever opinions employees may dare to express, even secretly, must be at their peril. They cannot know what particular expressions may be reported to the commission and held by it to be a sufficient political activity to cost them their jobs." Even worse, the U.S. Civil Service Commission warned employees against using family members as surrogates in active politics. "Thus are the families of public employees stripped of their freedom of political action," Black wrote. In sum, the Commission rules left to federal workers and their family members the right to attend a rally and to "carefully and quietly express an opinion at their peril." In consequence, as his most angry observation pointed out, federal workers were left with barely more than the right to "vote in silence."

No one would have seriously entertained an idea that "five million farmers or a million businessmen" taking federal subsidies or working on federal contracts would be similarly deprived of their constitutional rights. It could be contended that they too could become a "corrupting influence on politics or government," and where federal employees rights were unprotected, so could other groups find themselves in similar straits. "Popular government, to be effective," wrote Black, "must permit and encourage much wider political activity by all the people. Real popular government," he continued, "means that men may speak as they think on matters vital to them. . . . Legislation which muzzles several million citizens threatens popular government, not only because it injures the individuals muzzled, but also because of its harmful effect on the body politic in depriving it of the political participation and interest of such a large segment of our citizens. . . ." Surely "the Constitution prohibits legislation which prevents millions of citizens from contributing their arguments, complaints, and suggestions to the political debates which are the essence of democracy, prevents them from engaging in organizational activity to urge others to vote and take an interest in political affairs; bars them from performing the interested citizen's duty of insuring that his and his fellow citizens' votes are counted," wrote Black.

Even worse than the legislation was the majority's reliance on a limp precedent only tangentially related to the issue. "No statute of Congress has every before attempted so drastically to stifle the spoken and written political utterances and lawful political activities of federal and state employees as a class," according to the justice. The closest legislation was the Civil Service Act of 1883, which gave general authorization to the "President to promulgate rules" so that "no Government employee" could use official authority to coerce political action. The U.S. Civil Service Commission did later promulgate such rules in 1907. But, Black noted, "this Court has not approved the statutory power of the commission to promulgate such a rule, nor has it ever expressly or by implication approved the constitutional validity of any such sweeping abridgement of the right of freedom of expression." The *Curtis* precedent cited by the majority dealt explicitly with the limitation of "the right of employees to collect money from other employees for political purposes. Indeed, the *Curtis* decision seems implicitly to have rested on the assumption," as Pressman had earlier noted in his briefs, "that many political activities of Government employees [such as active partisan political expression] . . . could not, under the Constitution, be impaired by the legislation there at issue." It was simply wrong to deny millions of "good citizens" the right to enliven their political existence because a "few bad citizens might engage in coercion."

"Our political system, different from many others," closed Black, "rests on the foundation of a belief in rule by the people—not some, but all the people. . . . In a country whose people elect their leaders and decide great public issues, the voice of none should be suppressed—at least such is the assumption of the First Amendment," wrote Black. "The section of the Act here held valid reduces the constitutionally protected liberty of several million citizens to less than a shadow of its substance" relegating millions of public employees "to the role of mere spectators of events. . . ." "It makes honest participation in essential political activities an offense punishable by proscription from public employment. It endows a governmental board with the awesome power to censor the thoughts, expressions, and activities of law-abiding citizens in the field of free expression, from which no person should be barred by a government which boasts that it is a government of, for, and by the people—all the people. Laudable as its purpose may be, it seems to me to hack at the roots of a Government by the people themselves; and consequently I cannot agree to sustain its validity."

Justice Black's ringing words still arouse emotions in those who passionately believe in a democracy of "all the people"—no doubt the reason Pressman kept a photo of the jurist on his office wall for years. However, as he was writing for the minority, the *United Public Workers* case became a landmark constitutional case extending the reach of government control over its employees' political lives and citizenship rights, instead of the beacon for political freedom it could have become. As he had been in the *Thomas* case, Pressman had at least been partially responsible for inspiring rhetoric on the proper place of civil liberties in a democratic society. Unfortunately, the year 1945 apparently had been the high-water mark for Supreme Court constitutional protection of civil liberties as they related to labor. It became increasingly difficult to marshall a majority around central civil liberties tenets thereafter.

That trend became even clearer in mid-1948 with the court's decision in *U.S. v. CIO*—the anticipated CIO challenge to the Taft–Hartley Act's political restrictions. Although he had helped set the case circumstances in motion, by the time the case reached the top court, Pressman had resigned from the CIO to work in Henry A. Wallace's independent campaign for president. To replace him on daily case management he recommended Ohio labor attorney Charles Margiotti. Philip Murray, as a parting sign of affection and confidence, requested that his longtime lieutenant participate in the direction of the case and share in the oral arguments on behalf of the industrial federation, even though he no longer served as general counsel.

From the first, the CIO president and executive board resolved that they would challenge the odious Taft–Hartley's proscriptions against labor union "expenditures" in political campaigns. Pressman advised that a Murray endorsement of a Maryland congressional candidate, printed in the *CIO News* and explicitly stating the industrial union federation intended the endorsement as a challenge, would be the quickest way to move the issue forward *prior* to the critical upcoming presidential election. Thus, the CIO widely and freely distributed copies of the newspaper with the "expenditures" for it coming from regular general union funds. The Department of Justice then moved quickly to secure an indictment against the CIO president, which Pressman sought to have thrown out in U.S. District Court. He succeeded. The district court judge quashed the indictment without letting the case go to trial on the basis of First Amendment violations. The Solicitor General's office subsequently appealed the controversy to the Supreme Court.[42]

The basis of the constitutional arguments articulated by Charles Margiotti, Lee Pressman, and Assistant CIO General Counsel Frank Donner were familiar by now. The new wrinkle was the grand scale upon which Congress had tried to inhibit workers' political freedoms. Now, they argued in their brief, the law aimed to quiet all workers, not just federal or public employees. "The denial of political rights to a labor organization . . . is a denial of political rights to the millions of its members who have . . . joined . . . in order to achieve political goals which as individuals would be beyond their accomplishment," they wrote. "The considerations which inspire men and women to join labor organizations for economic purposes may not be realistically distinguished from those which prompt them to common political action and the inequality of bargaining which besets the employee in the economic sphere is dwarfed by corresponding evils in the political sphere." Election statistics proved that the wealthiest and most powerful families in the country, though few in number, were "prominently identified with employer interests, [and] contributed huge amounts to political campaigns." If democratic unions were not protected in exercising their corresponding rights, "the democratic framework of our entire society will be endangered."

> If an individual is helpless in dealing with his employer, then how can it be said that is he more able to deal with the powerful employer-dominated political interests which, unless restrained, can decisively fix or alter the terms and conditions under which he must live? In sheer self-protection he must associate with others in order to preserve those political values which enforce and promote his economic interests.

"Fundamentally," they continued, "the premise of those who have enacted . . . [the law] is that labor, in order to achieve its goals, is confined to [the direct use of] its economic power. The sponsors . . . apparently believe that the techniques of economic warfare should be encouraged and that labor organizations' time-honored resort to political action should be made a crime." In sum, they closed, "intensification of political activity among our people vitalizes our democracy," promoting broader suffrage, political education, and civic responsibility. And, "because it insures that political policies and platforms will reflect the needs of the people, . . . the outcome of elections will reflect their will, and . . . the efforts of those elected will serve the public interest."[43]

Of course, to convince at least five of the justices of the rationale, it often took the interpersonal persuasiveness that only the forum of oral argument could provide. With his wife and admiring daughters watching him present his oral argument before the Supreme Court, Pressman elaborated on the CIO objections laid out in the brief. As *U.S. Law Week* noted, the issues involved in the case provoked "spirited oral argument," charges, and countercharges, especially from Justice Frankfurter. The latter particularly objected because in his estimation the union and government had conjured up an "agreed upon" case of sorts—one that did not present an actual controversy— in order to determine the validity of the law a priori of any real controversy arising organically. This, he maintained, was in contravention to court principles against deciding constitutional issues that had no factual basis in an actual controversy or a contest between contending parties.

Pressman did not agree with his former professor. Yes, the CIO directly intended this confrontation, he admitted, because on its face the statute "collides with rights in the First Amendment." There was indeed an actual dispute between the government and the CIO here, however. The measure was vague, overly broad, and discriminatory; unincorporated trade associations, for example, equally politically active, did not fall within its net. The real rationale behind the Act's political restrictions was "to prevent laboring people from expressing themselves through their unions. . . ." Labor had participated in politics for many, many years. Why was it just now, shortly after the CIO had expanded its political activities, that it became so critical to deal with alleged "abuses"? The reason was not too hard to find. "What the Government is saying," Pressman pointed out as he had so many times before, "is that as long as political action is not meaningful, 'Go ahead, boys, and have a good time,' but as soon as the activity becomes meaningful . . . 'You can't do anything.'"

The pedantic Frankfurter, irritated at what he charged was almost collusion between the DOJ and the CIO, even went so far as to reprise what must have been a former classroom dialogue with his former administrative law student. Could the Supreme Court hear a case similar to this one, he asked, if the trial judge has simply decided not to waste the jury's time and declared the law unconstitutional without a trail? Pressman admitted that it could not, but that the case before them was not such a situation. "'That's just what I expected you to say,'" Frankfurter criticized, "'and it just confirms my opinion about this case. The difference between the hypothetical case and this one is so slight as to be indistinguishable.'"[44]

In conference, the rancor of the Roosevelt Court in transition played out once more and resulted in a technical disposition of the challenge. The CIO won the case by an 8 to 1 vote (with Burton the sole dissenter); as to the intellectual basis of the decision, however, the court was as divided as ever. With Reed writing for Vinson, Jackson, and Frankfurter, the court held that Philip Murray and the CIO did not violate the political expenditure restrictions of the Taft–Hartley Act in terms of their specific actions in the circumstances of this particular case. Through a none-too-believable analysis of semantics and congressional intent, this wing of the court decided that publishing such political information as had occurred here within *The CIO News* did not violate the law. Expenditure, in other words, was not meant to mean publicizing a political position in a publication by urging its members to vote a certain way, the basis of Murray's indictment.

In essence, "Congress did not intend to include within the coverage of the section as an expenditure the costs of the publication described in the indictment," wrote Reed. "It would require explicit words in an explicit act to convince us that Congress intended to bar a trade union journal, a house organ or a newspaper, published by a corporation, from expressing views on candidates or political proposals in the regular course of its publication." Even more to the point, Reed stated that "[W]e express no opinion as to the scope . . . [of the prohibitions] where different circumstances exist and none upon the constitutionality" of the restrictions.[45]

Wiley Rutledge, writing a separate concurrence for the four liberal activists of himself, Black, Murphy, and Douglas, rightly exposed the legal hairsplitting the other four had done. In an opinion that almost approached the passion of his work in the *Thomas* case, Rutledge dissected the congressional intent behind the political restrictions. The debates had shown that Congress passed this law because it was concerned about the "undue influence" of union political activity, in an attempt to protect the "purity of elections" and secure a "minority protection" for those allegedly opposing their union's political expressions. Rutledge rejected Reed's conclusions; his own examination of the Senate debates, and Senator Taft's explicit legislative expressions, led him and his brethren to decide that "this case is brought squarely within the prohibitions" of the statute. "I doubt that upon any matter of construction the Court has heretofore so far presumed to override the plainly and incontrovertibly stated judgment of all participants in the legislative process with its own tortuously fashioned view," he criticized. "It is invasion of the legislative process by emasculation of the statute. The only justification for this is to avoid deciding the question of validity."

And it was on the question of validity—constitutional validity—that the decision should rest, he and his brethren thought. Incorporating sections of the CIO brief in footnotes, he elaborated just how severely the prohibitions would inhibit—indeed if not prevent—legitimate political expression. He noted how the Act's broad-scale restrictions revealed its true intentions. The Act's representations to protect minority political opinion within union organizations was troubling, he wrote, for in rejecting "the principle of majority rule which has become a bulwark, indeed perhaps the leading characteristic, of collective activities," the law embraced an "atomized individual rule and action in matters of political advocacy." Objectors thereby received all benefits of union political action "without having to pay any part of its costs." Minority protections, if legitimate, could have been handled with much more narrowly drawn language. The fact that they were not, Rutledge believed, indicated that minority protection claims window-dressed a far more troubling legislative goal.

"That object was rather to force unions as such entirely out of political life and activity, including for presently pertinent purposes the expression of organized viewpoint concerning matters affecting their vital interests at the most crucial point where the expression would become effective." Elaborating Pressman's argument, Reed wrote that a "statute which, in the claimed interest of free and honest elections, curtails the very freedoms that make possible the exercise of the franchise by and informed and thinking electorate . . . cannot be squared with the First Amendment." In sum, four justices ruled for the CIO and avoided the constitutional issues involved; four ruled in favor and insisted that the court should have confronted what were clearly important civil liberties questions. And with this ambivalent victory, Pressman concluded his representation of the organization he helped found and had done so much to nurture.[46]

THE MURRAY–PRESSMAN SPLIT

Certainly, by the last half of 1947, Lee Pressman realized that the matters of political ideology that formerly threatened to tear asunder the industrial union federation had returned in full force. Harry Truman mended his political fences with organized labor in anticipation of the upcoming election year by vetoing Taft Hartley and unearthing a broader economic reform agenda. In return, Philip Murray moved toward stronger support of Truman foreign policy abroad, a policy that the remaining CIO leftists considered deeply hostile toward the Soviet Union and their vision of the post-war world. Symbolic of that rapprochement was Murray's 1947 invitation to Secretary of State George Marshall—whose "Marshall Plan" aimed to rebuild war-torn European countries to counterbalance Soviet influence—was anathema to the labor Left—to address the federation's convention. For many years, in his role as secretary of the resolutions committee, observed journalist Murray Kempton, the CIO general counsel "managed there to contrive a rhetoric containing solace for both the Communists and their enemies in the CIO." Now this became even more difficult and distasteful work for Pressman. He "reached the apogee of this peculiar function," Kempton thought, at the 1947 convention, when he constructed a foreign policy resolution that "managed at once to endorse the Marshall Plan and not mention it by name." But even Pressman must have begun to doubt how long he would be able to knit together the factions of the CIO as strong international forces pulled them in opposite directions.[47]

For example, the Taft–Hartley Act's anticommunist affidavit provision began to wreak havoc after an August 1947 NLRB ruling by General Counsel Robert Denham that local union officers who did not sign such affirmations could not be able to use the services of the agency. This made CIO organizations tempting targets for jurisdictional raids by several large AFL unions, whose officers had been only too happy to make such attestations for the board. Slowly, CIO affiliates began to fall in line, in spite of strong arguments by Pressman to the contrary. "The major business before the Executive Board was to decide whether or not the Steelworkers should become" one of the CIO unions willing to sign, wrote anticommunist USWA functionary Meyer Bernstein in November 1947. "It took almost two full days and brought out some of the best debate we have ever had," Bernstein wrote in a letter to his close associate Clinton Golden, who had departed from the union. "[B]est that is by the . . . men opposing our present refusal to sign the non-communist affidavit." "The most demagogic speech was made by Lee Pressman. When the Board first adopted the policy several months ago Lee had made a simple explanation," he recounted, "taking no stand. This time he came all out for reaffirmation." Bernstein went on to denounce how in his opinion Pressman's protestations were vacuous, maybe even politically motivated. "But this is beside the point," the CIO aide asserted. "Everybody agreed the law is a bad one. The question is, what do we do about it?"[48]

Pressman's laying aside his usual practice of trying to shape USWA policy quietly on significant issues marked just how intense and personal the struggle after Taft–Hartley had become. On a personal level, the specter of his Communist attachments haunted the fringes of his public existence, though it is hard to say just to what extent Pressman himself was aware of its expanding subterranean significance. Since the FBI had visited John Abt, telling him it was investigating a case of Communist espionage within the government, and since Abt was afterward called to testify before a secret federal grand jury in New York, it is logical to assume that Pressman knew of these events in short order. During this period, the FBI also maintained its close phone monitoring and physical surveillance of Pressman himself.[49]

Even so, Pressman might have survived had international events such as the Berlin crisis not intervened. As Cold War tensions grew, so did the determination of former Vice President Henry Wallace—bounced from his position as Truman's Secretary of Commerce for speaking against the President's policies—to run for president. With a potential independent presidential candidacy looking more likely, the Communist Party, primarily though Legislative Director Eugene Dennis, insisted trade union CP influentials in the CIO work for an abandonment of Truman and the Democratic Party, despite the vehement protests of many who knew the likely reaction of Philip Murray. Still, many followed the directive. Early in 1948, they made their case at a crucial CIO executive board meeting. "As you know there was a sharp division in the CIO Executive Board on Wallace and the 3rd party," Bernstein informed Golden. "Eleven board members stood up and were counted against Mr. Murray's positions. The eleven, of course, are [sic] Mr. Pressman's bosom pals." They did not succeed. Consequently, "the newspapers these last few days have been carrying reports about Mr. Pressman's impending resignation," and national radio journalist Drew Pearson "flatly asserted that Lee would resign next week." "I for one should be very much astonished if it were to come to pass," he indicated. "Mr. Pressman has not expressed himself publicly on the 3rd party issue and it is obvious he would be a fool to do so. Whatever one might think of Lee, he cannot be accused of acting foolishly." Only the possibility that an order coming from the CP leadership that for the left-wingers within the CIO, a Wallace "campaign is of paramount importance" requiring absolute loyalty, "even at the expense of abandoning a long concealed status," could make them do something like that. "But," he mused, "I think that an exception would be made of Lee."[50]

Bernstein's predictions proved dead wrong, though most likely Pressman had made up his own mind and did not act on direct orders. For whatever reason—whether as an individual he felt compelled by the critical nature of the 1948 election to work for Wallace, or whether his Party commitments propelled him into leaving—Lee Pressman decided to resign as CIO general counsel three days later, after Bernstein wrote his letter. John Abt, who presumably would have known if Pressman had been instructed by the Party to resign and work for Wallace, said that Pressman never discussed his decision to leave the CIO with him at the time, or in the two years afterward while they still maintained a friendship. Enemies, of course, assumed the Party directed Pressman to leave and exulted in the departure. "I was not particularly surprised at Pressman's resignation or departure," Golden wrote back to Bernstein. "I was confident it would come sometime. . . . I only think it was quite overdue. It would seem now that all doubts are removed as to where his loyalties all along have been."[51]

The separation moved both Pressman and Murray emotionally, tied together as they were by the historic advance of industrial unionism in the United States. "When Lee Pressman, the C.I.O's sharply tailored legal eagle, walked out of Phil Murray's Washington office—and out of his job—one day last week," reported *Time* magazine, "he was lugubriously blowing his nose and drying his eyes." "For the first time in his public life," Murray Kempton observed, "he displayed an emotion besides anger or cool confidence; he was crying and it could not have been entirely because he has lost his shield." Such a public exposure of the more sensitive side of the lawyer's passionate feelings was indeed unusual. Philip Murray too felt the wrench of the separation. "Behind him [at the announcement], Phil Murray was so overcome with emotion that he could not even step outside for a news picture."[52]

Despite all of the rumors that swirled through the newspapers after Pressman's announcement, the reasons why each man acted as he did are probably most accurately portrayed by what each said at the time. In his resignation letter, Pressman clearly laid out his rationale. "This decision, as you know," he wrote to Murray, "I have made only after long and very careful deliberation." He expressed his gratitude for the support that Murray had given him over the course of his career with the CIO. That support had "permitted me to direct all of my effort . . . in the interests of organized labor," he noted. Nevertheless, he had "come to the conclusion that in the face of the crucial economic and political developments of today" he desired "to establish an independent status." Pressman wrote that he would reenter a private labor law practice with his old friend Nat Witt in New York, and told reporters from "such a private position it will be possible for me to take part in . . . the Wallace for President political campaign." He appreciated the CIO's offer to assist with the Taft–Hartley litigation challenge, he said, and closed by saying that, "I need hardly tell you what the past 12 years of personal association with you has meant to me. This relationship has provided an experience for which I shall always be grateful."[53]

In response, Philip Murray generously praised the younger man. Accepting the resignation "with a sense of regret," he told Pressman that in "the course of the past 12 years . . . you have rendered an outstanding service to not only the CIO and its members but to me personally." From an independent law practice, he agreed, Pressman could pursue his political desires "without necessarily embroiling yourself or me in difficulties concerning matters of fundamental CIO policy." Moreover, "our personal relationship has provided me considerable pleasure and I feel has been conducive to the advancement of the welfare of the people whom I am privileged to represent."[54]

The CIO president elaborated a bit more in his remarks to the USWA Executive Board shortly following the resignation. "I do not propose to discuss with the members of the Board the more or less intimate details incident to the resignation of Mr. Pressman." However, he wanted to make sure that the board understood the great contributions the lawyer had made on behalf of the federation in both the legal and collective bargaining arenas. When the executive board, "at my personal instigation," took positions opposing the third Party movement and in support of the Marshall Plan, "Mr. Pressman did not take occasion to differ with me before the C.I.O. Executive Board, but he expressed a very sincere difference of opinion in his personal conversation with me about the matters, and then suggested that in view of those facts, perhaps it might be well if he relinquished his positions. . . ." Murray agreed. Since "this disagreement grew out of a very fundamental matter," Murray finished, "I was quite frank in advising Mr. Pressman under the circumstances that he ought to quit, and he promptly agreed that he would."[55]

And so, each man walked away from the announcement both troubled and moved. Pressman had given up the work he loved nearly more than anything else, choosing to leave the movement he helped found to pursue justice by another route. For a time he could look forward to working in a cause that promised a brighter, more honestly progressive America than the one he had found developing under Harry Truman and the renascent Republicans. For his part, Murray returned once again to the politics of refuge, grasping at the available political levers and resultant uneven gains that an alliance with Truman's Democratic Party brought. "Murray held no press conference" on the day of the resignation, wrote reporter Murray Kempton. And "those who saw him during the first few days afterward found him unusually detached and inattentive, as though what he had lost" had been "important to him too."[56]

EIGHT

THE MISCALCULATION

A lthough he did not realize it when he resigned from the CIO, the next two and a half years would put Lee Pressman under the most intense personal pressure he had ever experienced. His decision to work for the Progressive Party came at a critical turning point in the history of modern U.S. politics. The four-way presidential election of 1948 (South Carolina Democrat Strom Thurmond ran on the Dixiecrat ticket in protest of Truman's actions in support of civil rights) accelerated the trend toward the division of American liberalism into two camps, largely based upon judgments about culpability for the rapidly developing Cold War. Unlike the pre-war tensions between pro-and anti-Soviet Progressives that had receded during the hostilities, this time the issue would be joined until its conclusion. Seemingly, as international communism loomed more and more as a "threat" to the country, the public examined the domestic expression of communism and the role it played in American political life, often condemning those to whom at one time it had seemed a political philosophy grounded in justice. For a period of time, communism became a lens through which nearly every public issue refracted.[1]

At first, caught up in the excitement and potential of the upcoming independent presidential campaign of Henry Wallace, and later in his own unsuccessful congressional run, Pressman did not see, or possibly chose to ignore, the gathering storm clouds of a new Red scare. Within six months these roseate possibilities dissipated in a flurry of charges and countercharges. In August 1948, the middle-aged, melancholic *Time* magazine editor and ex-communist, Whittaker Chambers, appeared as a witness before the House Un-

American Activities Committee and dragged an unwilling Pressman into the entrails of what would become one of the most famous trials in the history of American politics, the Hiss–Chambers case. As a result, Pressman discovered his public life was unraveling as the FBI launched a stepped-up investigation into his Ware Group years, his relationship with the American Communist Party, his current law practice, and his Soviet connections. The government also began perjury proceedings against Alger Hiss and started prosecution of top officials of the Communist Party under the Smith Act. Both trials took place in New York's Foley Square Federal Courthouse, providing Pressman with a very visible viewpoint of the changing political atmosphere. He could no longer ignore the growing personal danger to himself and his family, and therefore he began a process of disengagement from his radical political past. The reasons had to be complex, most likely involving fear, anger, resentment, disappointment, and maybe even a sincere ideological change of heart.

What route Pressman would have taken had he actually won a seat in Congress, had the Wallace movement produced a viable new U.S. political force or faction, had the Left not been eviscerated from Progressive American political life by the Cold War, is hard to say. In the spring of 1948, though, he idealistically saw hope for the future and not disaster, characteristically confident that his decision to back Wallace had been made as strategically as he made all decisions. After Pressman lost his congressional bid, his ex-CIO colleague Harold Ruttenberg stopped by to see his former associate. When the discussion turned to a post-mortem on the election, Ruttenberg recalled that his friend shook his head and exclaimed in disbelief, "What a miscalculation!" That Pressman saw his actions in the Wallace campaign as a miscalculation and not as an expression of his romantic idealism says much about his personality, and of the many things he kept hidden, even from himself.[2]

RESIGNATION AFTERMATH

Pressman's resignation, coming as it did on the heels of the CIO Left's thrust to forestall the federation's commitment to Truman's reelection, surprised both friends and enemies. It therefore became easy to attribute it primarily to Party control. Gardner Jackson, for instance, wrote to journalist Ken Crawford to find out the exact circumstances surrounding the decision. "[D]id Lee tell Phil first that he was going to work for the Wallace candidacy and would get out of [the] CIO rather than give up such work," he inquired, "or did Phil tell Lee first that the latter would have to forego the Wallace candidacy or else pull out of [the] CIO? There is a great difference and I think a significant one," Jackson wrote. Pressman's "separation seems to me to be proof positive that Lee is in fact subject to the order of the Communist Party. It is inconceivable to me that he would have relinquished his key CIO post except under orders. The picture of him plugging for Wallace is something to make the gods laugh. I happen to know how he despised Henry during our days together in the Triple A and subsequently." And to their mutual friend Jerome Frank, Jackson wrote, "Some of my newspaper friends who have been covering H.A.]Wallace] on his brainstorming [sic] trips tell me that Lee Pressman goes with him on many of them and seems to be the key strategist of the third party contingent. If proof were needed that Lee is a true disciple of the Kremlin," he again announced, "I would certainly think this is it." "It's highly unlikely that he would have abandoned his potent post in the CIO for this kind of a role if he had not been ordered to."[3]

Perhaps there was not quite as much significance behind Pressman's decision to depart as Jackson believed. For many, even Monsignor Charles O. Rice—certainly no political supporter of Communists—thought that Pressman operated on behalf of the Party with much independence. Even his comrade John Abt was surprised at his colleague's decision to leave the CIO; Pressman, he said, did not discuss the matter with him or relate it to any Party orders. "I was taken aback," Abt recalled. "I knew Lee would never achieve a position of greater influence." True enough, Pressman's commitment to the CIO was deep, and more than one person thought he had been a fool to risk his career to take part in the Wallace campaign.

In all likelihood, the decision arrived not through the specific dictates of Party leaders. Pressman would have been far more valuable to the CP inside of the CIO than outside of it. Rather, the lawyer came to the decision after failing to develop a stratagem of how to campaign for Wallace while still remaining in the CIO. Lee was always scheming," recalled his friend, reporter Ed Lahey. It would not have been out of character, then, for Pressman to have approached Murray for permission to work for Wallace as a private citizen, or even to allow him to take a temporary leave of absence. That did not work with Murray who, after Truman's Taft–Hartley veto and promise to work for repeal, had come to see this particular presidential political endorsement as a hard-nosed trade union issue. When Harold Ruttenberg saw Philip Murray not long after Pressman's resignation, the CIO president "would say that Lee simply did not know him. 'We're supporting Truman, that's our policy,'" Ruttenberg characterized his assessment of the probable exchange between the two men. "'If you want to go support Wallace, you go ahead and do it. But you're not going to do it in the union.'"

Thus, under the circumstances of 1948, Pressman could not back a third Party movement without openly violating the trade union policy. Though this was a tightrope that he had walked for many years with much success, the context had finally changed so significantly that it had become impossible institutionally. Political energies within industrial unionism and the CP, more or less congruent since 1941, had now diverged beyond the point of repair. Ruttenberg reflected that, "Murray was such an honest person in that regard. He wouldn't, you couldn't, carry water on two shoulders. Whereas Lewis, Jack Lewis and Lee Pressman, they would consider it a real achievement to carry water on two shoulders, on both shoulders, if they had to. Not Murray, he'd say, 'Make up your mind.'"[4]

So if it was unlikely that Pressman had been directly ordered to resign from the CIO, why did he? A Pressman speech, given in the heat of his campaign for the national Progressive Party ticket in November 1948, reveals one understandable reason for one schooled at the knee of John L. Lewis: an intense disdain for Truman and Truman Democrats for their retreat from the heritage of the New Deal. Denouncing the "hypocrisy" and "doubletalk" bandied about by both political parties, he tore into the Truman record without hesitation. "For the crumbs of mealy-mouthed promises made solely for the political campaign, the American people are supposed to forget the black record of the Truman Administration and of the Republican Congress," he began. First stood the monument of the Taft–Hartley Act, the law on which only "a few days before Election Day, Mr. Truman has a few harsh words concerning that infamous legislation." But, he asked, are "we to forget that it was Mr. Truman who in his first message to Congress in 1946 called for repressive legislation directed against labor," surely stimulating the move toward Taft–Hartley? He even wanted to draft strikers and/or subject them to court martial, Pressman reminded his listeners. And, "are we to forget," he continued, that it was Truman who broke the coal miners strike before Taft–Hartley, and who "uttered not a word of condemnation . . . against the corporations" who balked against the President's own decision on wage increases during the reconversion period. It was this president who meekly granted the companies unwarranted price increases and relieved them of the excess profits tax? Were the people supposed to forget that Truman "punished" his close friend Senator Carl Hatch of New Mexico, who voted to override the President's Taft–Hartley veto, by appointing him chair of the Democratic National Committee? Hatch was now in the position "with tongue in cheek," Pressman acidly noted, of "advising [Democratic] speakers to urge the repeal of the Taft–Hartley Law—for which he voted." While the Republican Congress bore the prime responsibility for the antilabor law, Pressman admitted, nothing could hide the duplicity of the Truman Democrats. "The Democrats cringe before their handwork [sic] and prefer to use demagogy, [sic] doubletalk and untruths."

Perhaps worst of all, the bipartisan "cold war" now threatened economic future progress. "With a foreign policy which profanes the name of peace, which actually inculcates the doctrine that another war is inevitable, it becomes impossible in practical terms to address the energies and efforts of the American people toward the promotion and improvement of social security, health service, housing or other peaceful projects," Pressman charged. Gone was the foreign policy of Franklin D. Roosevelt, and in its place the two parties "confine themselves primarily in developing a mad war craze [and promoting] red-baiting hysteria." Were the people to forget that it was none other than Mr. Truman's executive orders on government employee loyalty that had authorized "wholesale investigations into the thoughts and political beliefs of those in the federal service," and first fanned the flames of the new Red scare? All in all, the speech succinctly capsulized what Pressman had thought about Truman's presidency all along, but which the constraints of operating within the CIO had held in check. While none of this sentiment was unique—it was common to many left-wingers and liberals during the period 1947–1948—it fairly reflects the line of Pressman's thinking and much of what must have been his motivation to part ways with Murray. He could not stomach organized labor swallowing its pride and endorsing Truman when confronted by such repeated affronts. The diffidence of Roosevelt toward the CIO paled in comparison with the new president's almost activist antilabor actions. By the early months of 1948, Pressman judged, the new president had proved himself unworthy of the votes and allegiance of working people and pursued an unnecessarily militaristic foreign policy.[5]

Of course, personal ambition played a role as well. When Rexford Tugwell, one of his chiefs during his time within the New Deal, signed on with the Wallace campaign in the early months of 1948 to head the platform committee, he did so on the condition that Lee Pressman would serve as its secretary. John Abt, also knee-deep in the Wallace movement, noted that this "was soft work for Lee, who for years had mastered the craft of writing resolutions for CIO conventions." Pressman would obviously serve in the high councils of the Progressive Party campaign. Both Harold Ruttenberg and Abt believed Pressman "pinned his hopes" on the rising future of the Progressive Party, and of the influential role that he might play within it. His name was mentioned more than once as a natural for Secretary of Labor, had Wallace somehow succeeded in gaining the White House, for example. Though a third party victory was certainly an unlikely event, Abt later bemusedly observed that "we all had grandiose ideas of the possibilities of the Wallace campaign." Consistent with a careerist motivation was Pressman's decision in the early summer months of 1948 to run for Congress. CP Legislative Secretary Eugene Dennis suggested a joint American Labor Party-Progressive Party candidacy to Pressman, and his agreement to do so, he later told the FBI, resulted primarily from ego considerations.[6]

Now freed from the policy restraints of the CIO, in the spring of 1948 Pressman readied his family to move back to New York from Washington and began practicing labor law with Nat Witt and Witt's partner, Harold Cammer.

The firm of Witt and Cammer was anything but prosperous prior to Pressman's arrival as "rainmaker," and after the Pressman name attracted new clients from the labor movement's Left, it did not take long for tensions to rise. For a number of years during the early 1940s, after Witt had been rousted out of the Madden NLRB for pro-CIO bias by board member William Leiserson, Pressman had been funneling local legal referrals to Witt's firm. In some ways, recalled Harold Cammer in an interview years later, the firm became Lee Pressman's field operation for labor law in New York City. Even so, it was a distinctly modest field operation. The total capital of Witt and Cammer in 1946 was approximately $7,000. Witt, who hailed from a very poor working-class background, never lost connection with his roots. He regarded serving the labor movement and "helping people that were being persecuted politically" as a "privilege," recollected Cammer. Hence, billing for legal services took on a secondary role in his constellation of things. Pressman, on the other hand, was much more interested in making a comfortable living, and this proclivity of Witt's troubled him greatly. While John Abt singled out Witt as Pressman's closest friend beside himself, or as close a friend as Pressman could have, Cammer characterized the Witt–Pressman relationship as friendly, without observable friction, but not close in terms of intimacy. Both the Pressman and Witt families maintained vacation homes in Randolph Corners, Vermont, and socialized from time to time for years. Even so, as Abt had had competitive experiences with Pressman since the 1930s, he suspected similar things also must have occurred between Witt and Pressman, whose relationship antedated Abt's and Pressman's own. Nat Witt "was a much more sensitive, almost sentimental, character, than I am," Abt observed. "And I think he was constantly being hurt by Pressman." But, for the time being, the requirements of relocating his family, finding a new home, and Progressive Party politics, especially, papered over these differences. Before long, Lee and Sunny Pressman, along with Ann, Marcia, and Susan, had taken up residence in Mt. Vernon, in the first house the family owned, and joined a synagogue to help establish themselves in a largely Jewish suburban community. And for the first time in his life, Lee Pressman would soon have time to undertake the more traditional fatherly duties that his brutal CIO schedule ham made impossible.[7]

Not unexpectedly, left-wing unions found the firm of Pressman, Witt, and Cammer especially attractive. Among the client list were the Communist-led Fur and Leather Workers, the Mine, Mill, and Smelter Workers, the New York City teachers, the Food and Tobacco Workers, the International Woodworkers of America, and the United Public Workers. One of Pressman's first legal challenges after leaving the CIO, in fact, involved his efforts to prevent Irving Potash, an official of the Fur and Leather Workers, from being deported back to the Soviet Union for his Communist membership. Aided by fellow attorney Joseph Forer, the two lawyers contended that the Immigration and Naturalization Service (INS) deportation proceedings violated due process before the U.S. District Court, and then the U.S. Court of Appeals. Pressman and Forer won their points and convinced appellate judges at both levels that the government had misapplied the immigration laws.[8]

Freed from the political constraints of his CIO/USWA general counselship, Lee Pressman could now speak publicly for any cause. He provided a testimonial to the talents of Carol Weiss King at a celebratory dinner held for her by the American Committee for the Protection for the Foreign Born, for example, a Party-related group. In April 1948, Paul Robeson, the most famous African American in the United States, personally invited the Pressmans to a dinner engagement that he and novelist Howard Fast held at Fast's Manhattan apartment in honor of fellow leftist Frederick Field. Pressman's public speeches also took on more strident, antigovernment tones. His law partner Harold Cammer, for instance, read a Pressman speech entitled, "The Truth About J. Edgar Hoover" to the Jefferson School of Social Science, another front organization, in the spring of 1948. As a FBI memo summarizing the speech reported, Pressman attacked the government's loyalty program and the immense power that former Palmer Raid operative J. Edgar Hoover had amassed, claiming the Bureau threatened to become "a police state instrument." Later, Pressman denounced the loyalty bill of Senator Karl Mundt (R-ID) before a special meeting of the Mine, Mill, and Smelter Workers in Salt Lake City, charging that the proposal "was directed against every citizen [and] not against the Communist Party." Who "do you think decides what a Communist organization consists of?" he asked rhetorically. Attorney General Tom Clark and J. Edgar Hoover, he told the delegates, and this posed a great danger to Progressives of all stripes, even those who thought they were in no danger because they were not Communists. "I warn you again that if you meet and bring up the subject of racial discord or[,] if you are in favor of Civil Rights, you will be branded by the FBI as a Communist, and believe me it is not difficult to get the ear of John Edgar Hoover" on that subject.[9]

PRESSMAN AND THE PROGRESSIVE PARTY

As the founding convention of the Progressive Party neared, Pressman's involvement in the Wallace campaign advanced beyond the stage of speech making and behind-the-scenes strategizing. In April 1948, the committee began to put together an outline of the Progressive Party platform. From the first, Pressman, as the director of a group of drafters in New York, became identified by the implacably hostile press and mainstream parties as one of the probable CP sympathizers trying to "dominate" the policy of the new political formulation. Wallace had been "captured" by the Communist Party, so the stories went, even though more than one analysis of the results of the final platform resolutions revealed no overall domination by any particular group of the Wallace coalition. By June, Pressman had forwarded the handiwork of his drafters, the "Outline for Proposed New Party and Platform," to the seventy-four members of the platform committee, according to Curtis Mac-Dougall, who has authored the most exhaustive history of the Wallace campaign. But it proved to be Tugwell who exercised a guiding hand at this stage, notwithstanding charges of Pressman manipulation. "John Abt told me today about your letter regarding the draft of the platform," Pressman wrote to Tugwell on June 8, 1948. "I want you to feel assured that it was only a first" attempt, and that he intended to work diligently to get "a more polished draft" ready for the necessary platform committee discussion. "Somebody has to devote himself to this platform business until it is done," Tugwell cautioned in reply. "The [first] draft was inconsistent, it did not cover the necessary points, [and] it was very badly phrased. . . ." Through the course of the Wallace campaign, and in his own run for a congressional seat, Pressman would repeatedly face a barrage of red-baiting. Thus, his high profile in the Progressive Party ensured that he would develop lightning-rod-like capabilities for drawing the fire of anti-CP forces, even more so than when he was in the CIO.[10]

No doubt, Pressman's antigovernment speeches played a role in stimulating this response, and his stinging criticisms of the Truman administration and J. Edgar Hoover made government officials angry. "Apropos of our conversation this morning concerning Lee Pressman," Hoover wrote to Truman's Attorney General Tom Clark, "I am enclosing herewith a copy of the memorandum which was previously furnished to the White House concerning this individual," a memo that outlined the Hudson–Pressman 1943 CIO convention meeting. Other Pressman critics sought the FBI's help in getting political ammunition as well. "I took a telephone call from . . . the office of Congressman Multer," the Bureau's D. M. Ladd wrote to his supervisor on June 9, 1948. Multer was Pressman's opponent in the upcoming race in New York City's Fourteenth Congressional District. The "Congressman . . . asked . . . if Lee Pressman at this time or any time in the past had held a Communist Party membership card." Ladd put off the inquiry, stating that the riles were confidential by order of the Attorney General and suggested that the congressman make his inquiries via that route. The political advantages of red-baiting in the atmosphere created by the Cold War had obviously become readily apparent to many.[11]

This was a fact of life that Progressive Party adherents, assembling in July after both the Democrats and the Republicans had held their conventions, would soon learn, much to their dismay. But first they had to resolve on what the new

Party stood for by composing a unified platform from the three circulating drafts. It "is doubtful there ever was a national political convention in which more people participated in longer or more acrimonious debates on the fundamental issues of policy," than in the Progressive Party convention of 1948, Curtis MacDougall wrote in *Gideon's Army*. Expectedly, popular press accounts of the convention and platform drafting process alleged that pro-Soviet left-wingers and the Communist Party functionaries had "captured" the Wallace campaign via the platform process. While there was some truth to the observation that many of the tensions within the movement, and particularly within the platform committee, emanated from foreign policy concerns, it was also a gross oversimplification to claim the Wallace candidacy a front for the CP.

Even an analyst generally unfriendly to the CP-influenced Progressive forces as John Cotton Brown admitted as much. Writing a dissertation under the direction of Rexford Tugwell, Brown participated in numerous platform committee meetings to accumulate much of his data. In his study, he characterized Lee Pressman and Martin Popper, and to a lesser extent, John Abt, all activist lawyers, as being among the most influential left-wingers affecting the shape of the platform. Counterposed to them were liberal and non-CP aligned academicians such as Rexford Tugwell, Richard Watt, Paul Sweezy, Leo Huberman, and Frederick Schuman.[12]

Despite the many faults of Brown's study as an intellectual work, he did leave a modestly detailed record of what occurred during the formulation of the platform. The process started with meetings of the small advisory committee that worked to put forward proposals for consideration by the much larger, seventy-four-member, full platform committee. From the first, Pressman and Abt, reflecting their activist bent and their years of experience representing labor, preferred a platform tone that aspired to mobilize a mass movement. As Brown termed it, they wanted language "'appealing to the specific worries, fears, and concerns of the average working man,' short and simple enough for him to read and understand 'when it's passed out at the factory gates.'" The academics, on the other hand, "favored a reasoned rather than a hortatory document," that would "systematically" set out the Party's founding rationale and principles.

Pressman, utilizing observations Brown thought too similar to CP pronouncements and positions, also lobbied for an economic focus. "'Monopoly' was driving toward war to insure Wall Street domination abroad and armaments profits at home, and was attacking the living standards and the civil liberties of the people to silence protest." In sum, Brown concluded that

> the Advisory Committee Draft was still a series of compromises or unreconciled conflicts on *tone*, compromises and conflicts between "militant," agitational left-wing formulations, and calmer, more fully

reasoned, "respectable," non-left-wing formulations. The former flowed logically from various left-wing beliefs concerned with the necessity for militant mass tactics, while the latter flowed logically from various non-left-wing beliefs with the greater faith in the conciliatory processes of "bourgeois-democracy."[13]

The fullest conflict came over differences in how Progressives should interpret the international crises of the early Cold War, and how that interpretation should be reflected in the Party's foreign policy stance. Predictably, Pressman, Abt, and others of similar political beliefs did not impute innate hostility to Soviet intentions; Tugwell, on the other hand, grew increasingly unsure. "We have to decide whether the Russians are playing poker or post office, and I don't think they are playing post office," Brown quoted him as saying. But, as Brown also observed, Tugwell stood mostly alone in his professions about foreign policy as other liberal influentials did not vocally support his arguments, while the "left-wingers firmly opposed Tugwell during these discussions.

Pressman said that he could see no difference between Tugwell's line of reasoning and the Truman Doctrine," Brown noted, which of course most Progressives, and indeed Henry Wallace himself, adamantly opposed. "Either the United States and Russia have good relations and peace, or bad relations and war. And if you want good relations you don't have a draft or a Truman Doctrine," Pressman argued. By the conclusion of the advisory committee process, Pressman's abrasive style rubbed his former New Deal colleague, as well as others, the wrong way. "A marked feature of the Advisory Committee sessions had been considerable personal friction, with frequent heated exchanges, between Tugwell and Pressman, and to a lesser extent between Pressman and several of the others, including one of the left-wingers."[14]

In fact, these verbal fisticuffs symbolized what was soon becoming the media liet-motif on the Progressive Party. The focal point of the Wallace candidacy tacked away from the issue of the liberal inadequacies of President Truman and toward an obsession with communism and its influence, imagined and otherwise, on the Progressive Party and its presidential candidate. Soon Progressives themselves got caught up in it, searching their souls as to how they should respond to this public "perception," fair or not. Pressman, in one of his longest oratorical flourishes paraphrased by Brown at length, did his utmost to caution against letting unfounded media charges determine how they, as Progressives, should respond to critical political issues.

We are not being attacked because our attackers really believe all of us are Communists or that the Party is led by Communists. We are being attacked because of what Wallace says and stands for. If we supported the Marshall Plan we could let in every Communist and find ourselves hailed by those attacking us. The cry "Communist" is never raised against passive unionists but always against militant unionists. Communism is *not* the issue. . . .

Either you are going to remain steadfast to your principles or you are not. I understand the temptation of those of us who come from states where there is not a strong mass movement. But when Jefferson was attacked as a foreign agent he didn't *deny* it. He went to the grass roots and carried the real issues to the people. It's not easy. [But it is] . . . a fight which determines whether we live or die.

In response, an opponent countered, "Such oratory will not go out to the people, but the Platform will . . . and [therefore] it should contain an honest declaration on communism. Many voters . . . are lost in confusion."

Later in the debates, however, Pressman supported compromise language, much to the consternation of some of his ideological brethren. "Throughout all the Platform Committee's deliberations, Pressman seemed much more conciliatory to the non-left-wingers than did Popper," observed Brown, and "also seemed much more conciliatory . . . than he had been in the Advisory Committee." Indeed, Brown at one point speculated about the diversity of left-wing opinion, as supposed CP adherents would frequently not back proposals of one another. Possibly the Party line had not been clarified or miscommunicated, thought Brown. But he also admitted the intriguing possibility that Pressman was "not as responsive to Communist influence as he is generally reported to be." Later, Pressman's role at the full convention became less pronounced than it had been behind the scenes in the platform committee debates, which of course had been his predominant mode of operation all his public life. After a ringing speech in favor of the platform by Rexford Tugwell, Pressman presented the platform section by section, elucidating the thinking and resolves of the committee. The delegates then debated the issues for five of the seven and a half hours that it took to get through the complete document.[15]

Perhaps, as some commentators have noted, the real nub of the arguments in the platform committee was not ideological so much as tactical— what was the most effective *political* wording for the document, given the Progressive Party's objectives? The platform committee debates, Pressman himself later informed MacDougall, were mostly "'a battle between the comma hounds.'" In the judgment of New Deal liberal Tom Emerson, a one-time Madden-board NLRB official and later professor of law at Yale, "'Tugwell never presented his point of view forcefully. He could have dictated but he didn't even fight. He withdrew from the very beginning. As soon as he lost on the preamble . . . he gave up. Pressman, on the other hand, always has been a scrapper.'" While others on the platform committee complained at first of

Pressman's arrogant manner and assertiveness, in the final analysis, the disagreements between Tugwell and Pressman had more to do with the mind-set of the former other than the Machiavellianism of the latter. "Nobody can accuse Pressman of lack of toughness," noted MacDougall. "Pressman has been described to me, by associates of long standing in the CIO," he wrote, "as neither imaginative nor maneuverable, but possessed of a strong intellectual force." Tugwell, on the other hand, was "urbane, academic and timid."[16]

For his part, Tugwell communicated his view of the platform adoption process in an August 1948 open letter to Antonio Borgese, director of Common Cause. In that letter, whatever the nature of his disputes with Pressman, the University of Chicago professor gave a relatively evenhanded assessment. The platform committee, comprised of seventy-four individuals, over which he presided, worked hard. We "argued, we reasoned, we appealed, we sometimes shouted at each other, we compromised when we had to. This went on for most of a sweltering week, night and day. What resulted was something of what each group (for we were soon roughly aligned in groups) wanted, which had been gained by giving other groups something of what they wanted." This should have surprised no one, he wrote. Unlike the established parties, the new Party did not have the long history of dominant, but invisible, interests of sufficient influence who knew how to produce a "smooth, innocuous, calculated to offend no one, but actually favorable to the hidden interests which had dictated it" type of platform. "But we were progressives," he wrote, "long uneasy in the old parties, boiling with ideas," are "voluble and determined. Then, too, we had a certain number of those who appeared to be more interested, when we came to the discussion of the section we labeled "Peace," in furthering the foreign policy of the U.S.S.R. than in anything else. These, from my point of view, were the worst nuisance of all; they were cohesive and persistent; they had some support." While one could guess they were there to protect the interests of the homeland of communism, it could be only a guess. "They, too, were, in any case, argued with, shouted at, and comprised with," through his efforts, among others. Fundamentally, Tugwell concluded, "I was Chairman of a platform committee which produced a fair document, not too good, as I see it, except in a few respects, but not too bad, either, except in a few." But by now, with unrelentingly critical press comment amidst growing international tension, exactly what the public thought of the Progressive Party platform and Henry Wallace was an open question.[17]

PRESSMAN AND THE HISS–CHAMBERS CASE

The actions of the Truman Department of Justice toward domestic communism reinforced the negative perceptions. Though Attorney General Tom

Clark moved cautiously at first, the DOJ sought New York federal grand jury indictments and bench warrants for the arrest of the top officials of the U.S. Communist Party for violating the 1940 Smith Act, and timed them to occur during the convention. It was before this same secret grand jury that John Abt had been subpoenaed to testify in the fall of 1947, after FBI agents visited him and announced a Bureau investigation into an alleged Communist espionage ring active in Washington during the 1930s. Abt kept mum before the agent and later before the grand jury, but he could hardly have doubted that the visit was in some way connected with AAA-era activities.[18]

Whether or not Pressman had been similarly approached is unknown. But most likely, it was not a total surprise to Pressman when Whittaker Chambers began his testimony before the House Un-American Activities Committee on August 3, 1948, shortly after the Progressive Party Convention adjourned. The HUAC's pursuit of Alger Hiss, largely through the efforts of first-term congressman Richard M. Nixon, has been well documented in many works, ultimately resulting in two trials and the diplomat's ultimate conviction for perjury for denying that he knew Chambers. On the morning of Chambers' first appearance, the committee had informed reporters that a "surprise" witness was in the offing, a witness who would support the assertions of its only star witness to this point, Elizabeth Bentley. Bentley, also a self-admitted former courier for a wartime Soviet-controlled espionage group, had come to know some of the Ware Group members through the successor underground cells formed subsequent to its demise in the 1930s. As yet, however, her story remained a curiosity and uncorroborated. Now, an evidently reluctant Chambers provided that support.

That morning Chambers recounted his previous FBI statements regarding the Ware Group and its attendant underground activities, though he did not accuse anyone of espionage. The Ware Group's main purpose had been to exert influence over U.S. government policy. For the first time in public, though, Chambers brought up the name of Alger Hiss as an ex-member of the Ware Group. Hiss, a diplomatic member of the U.S. delegation to the Yalta Conference and an organizer of the founding convention of the United Nations, was certainly the most prominent of the Ware Group alumni who had continued to work within the government for many years. The story hit the news with a greater splash than any HUAC legislator could have hoped, and began what surely remains one of the great political trials in U.S. history.[19]

After Hiss, Pressman assuredly stood second in terms of public name recognition among the former members. Given his recent prominence at the Progressive Party Convention and his own congressional candidacy, it was a foregone conclusion that the HUAC would summon him. In between the seventeen days from Chambers' first day of testimony before the HUAC until the time that it called Pressman, Abt, and Witt on August 20, 1948, several notable confrontations between Hiss—testifying to defend himself at his own request—and Chambers took place. By the time Pressman and the others appeared, the hearings had turned into high public drama and launched the national political career of Richard M. Nixon, even as they dragged down the public lives of Hiss, Pressman, and many others. At one point in Hiss's initial testimony before the HUAC, committee general counsel Robert Stripling sarcastically asked the elegant and aristocratically demeanored Hiss, who had expressed a "high regard" for several individuals alleged by Chambers as being in the CP underground, "Do you [also] have a high regard for Lee Pressman?" Indeed, he did, the New Dealer replied affirmatively. "I knew Pressman first at law school and I have seen very little of him recently. I liked him and admired him as a law student, and knew him and admired him as a fellow lawyer in the Agricultural Adjustment Administration." Whatever personal tension existed between Pressman and Hiss, the latter certainly had no intention of letting the HUAC know of any of his private feelings.[20]

According to Pressman's and Witt's law partner, Harold Cammer, who acted as their private counsel on August 20, there existed little doubt among the three that they would invoke their Fifth Amendment privileges. According to Cammer, Pressman and the others simply worked on the legal technicalities of exactly how to invoke the Fifth Amendment privilege in a fashion sufficient to provide maximum protection of their rights. In other words, the former Ware Group members knew taking the Fifth Amendment was a "given."[21]

As it turned out, Richard M. Nixon, chairing the session that day, "ran it in executive session because he was afraid to take these guys on publicly," Cammer maintained later. As a group, Pressman, Abt, and Witt certainly had reputations for having sharp legal minds, so their "reputations had preceded them," Harold Cammer recounted. Nixon therefore remained wary and decided not to hold public hearings. Other than the odd query by Pressman about accusations of espionage, the former CIO general counsel's testimony was unrevealing, soon devolving into assertions of his Fifth Amendment rights ending with the refrain of "for the same reasons, the same response."[22]

What would Pressman have said at that point if the hearings had been open to the press? Shortly after Chambers' first appearance before the HUAC, the *New York Sun* quoted Pressman as charging an intentional smear. The committee, Pressman said, had an overweening interest in the "stale and lurid mouthings of a Republican exhibitionist who has been bought by Henry Luce [the conservative owner of *Time* magazine] and who claims to have met me twelve years ago." No doubt this was a ploy to take people's minds off the real political issues facing the country, to besmirch the memory of FDR, and to discredit the Wallace candidacy.

In between that time and August 20, Pressman elaborated on his comments in a prepared statement outlining the reasons he decided to invoke the

Fifth Amendment. "I do not believe that it is incumbent upon me to assert my innocence of the charges of crime that have been made against me before this committee," Pressman's undelivered statement began. "Those charges have already received an official and authoritative answer." The FBI had spent three years investigating the claims of Bentley and Chambers and a grand jury thirteen months. The Justice Department's waste of half a million dollars of taxpayer money in a failed attempt "to produce evidence on which a carefully selected grand jury and a zealous prosecutor could find" no basis to secure indictments proved his innocence. The HUAC therefore now resolved to take its turn, ignoring that a constitutionally appropriate body had already "weighed" the charges and "rejected them." "Yet you are [still] subjecting me and the others in my position to conviction—not by a court of law—but to conviction by headline," he charged angrily.[23]

Pressman went on to denounce the committee for usurping the grand jury's secrecy and "re-enacting the grand jury testimony under klieg lights," taking his and others' rights away. "I understand that there has been some talk before this Committee of the need for a wider and more intensive study of American history," Pressman wrote. "Gentlemen, as a first lesson, I commend to you a study of . . . the Bill of Rights." A witch-hunting investigation of this type took away not only a citizen's grand jury rights, but also rights to due process, hearings with evidentiary rules, jury trials, and cross-examination. But it could not and would not be able to divest from him the right of protection from self-incrimination, which he intended to invoke. "I do so with pride—the pride that I share with all true Americans in the heritage of our Bill of Rights." "And I remind you of another lesson of our history," he closed, "the lesson that this provision of the Bill of Rights was not designed by our forefathers to shield the guilty against punishment, but to protect the innocent[, to protect them] against the very kind of Star Chamber proceeding in which this Committee is now engaged."

That statement reveals Pressman's awareness of what the committee actually aimed for in terms of generating press controversy, and also his determination at this point to fight back with a well-designed, publicly acceptable reason for invoking the Fifth Amendment. Touching on Bill of Rights themes that he hoped would resonate with fair-minded Americans, he intended to supply a rationale the proverbial "person in the street" could understand and support, thereby avoiding the overtones of implicit guilt that sometimes attached to witnesses asserting their Fifth Amendment rights. But, in combination with his concern about any alleged espionage charge proffered against him, the prepared statement also seems to suggest that Pressman had become quite concerned about his embroilment in the Hiss case, certainly more so than his colleagues. In contrast, columnist Russell Baker recalled Witt's disdainful demeanor before the HUAC years afterward. "The investigators would read doggedly through their piles of questions, and Witt would work them up to a deep red flush around the cheekbones by pretending to be elsewhere."[24]

THE CONGRESSIONAL CAMPAIGN

Predictably, thereafter red-baiting played a prominent role in Pressman's own congressional campaign. In the late spring of 1948, CP General Secretary Eugene Dennis had come to Pressman's law office to encourage him to run for Congress in Brooklyn on the American Labor Party (ALP)–Progressive Party fusion ticket. The ability to use Pressman's name and his ties with many labor unions as a base for a congressional campaign seemed attractive to the Party, particularly considering incumbent Democratic Congressman Abraham Multer's recent support of Truman's foreign policy and resistance to CP lobbying. Several newspapers reported that Multer—who had a pro-labor voting record—ran CP operatives out of his office and "in revenge," the lawmaker charged, they fielded Pressman to run against him. Although Pressman did not reside in the district, he had been reared there. He announced his candidacy on June 10, 1948, after the Progressive Party Convention, and in August, almost coinciding with the Chambers' revelations, he opened his campaign headquarters on Bay Parkway in Brooklyn. Not unexpectedly, the Pressman candidacy received warm support from the *Daily Worker* and, since there was little difference on domestic policies between Multer and Pressman, the contest soon turned on questions of foreign policy.[25]

Multer also soon received the endorsement of the Republican Party in the district as mainstream political forces closed ranks against the CP-ALP-PP formation. In January 1949, a commentator in Isaac Don Singer's conservative publication, *Plain Talk*, reported in that however much Republicans of the district disagreed with Multer on domestic policy, they believed "that the very basis of the American creed is being challenged by a group of totalitarian apologists and Stalinists, and that our first duty was to smash this foreign invasion in our political life." Quickly, Multer charged that the CP was handsomely financing Pressman's candidacy and amply supplying him with expensive electoral literature. A *New York Post* reporter counted twenty-eight separate and expensive lithographs touting the Pressman candidacy circulating in the district, all "designed to lure and impress unwary minds," the red-baiting rhetoric in *Plain Talk* continued. In addition, it claimed that a mass mailing of nearly 400,000 pro-Pressman items were mailed and 400 canvassers from "outside" the district worked local neighborhoods in house visits. "Many of these were fuzzy-minded 'idealists' who were intoxicated with the propaganda idolizing Lee Pressman," *Plain Talk* reported. The CP-anti-CP fault line extended to the district's labor movement as well. While certainly New York Left-leaning unions strongly backed Pressman, New York State CIO President Louis Hollander opposed the lawyer due to his alleged CP ties and anti-Truman foreign policy positions.[26]

Evidently, Fourteenth Congressional District politics on the eve of the Cold War was no place for the temperate. Pressman's campaign strategy aimed to invoke FDR's persona and the tradition of the New Deal wherever possible, counterposing those warm liberal memories to the Truman administration's anti-Progressive gambits. Thus his campaign literature stressed his early New Deal AAA roots, his work in the WPA and Resettlement Administration—all by now welfare-state icons of Progressive politics—and of course his well-known career as CIO general counsel and labor-civil liberties litigator. His most detailed brochure, "This is Lee Pressman," proudly charted his public career. "Lee Pressman was a member of that small group of men working night and day with Franklin Delano Roosevelt to dig the country out from under the depression," the appeal began. Pressman's attacks on the Milk Trust in the AAA and his WPA and Resettlement Administration work quickly established his New Deal bona fides and connections with the sainted FDR. "The next twelve years are the record of Lee Pressman's service to the country through service to labor," the pitch continued, where he "helped power the CIO from the time CIO stood for a 'committee' to the day it meant 6 million strong." The brochure also highlighted Pressman's participation in the key labor negotiations of the 1930s and 1940s and his acutely valuable litigation work. "He took Tom Girdler into court and made him pay for the Memorial Day Massacre," and he fought for civil rights-labor protections in six state courts. One of Pressman's proudest moments as a lawyer came when he helped secure the expansion of American unionism by winning maintenance-of-membership union security provisions before the National War Labor Board. And, with a bit of campaign hyperbole, Pressman's literature proclaimed that the lawyer had convinced the Supreme Court "*that picketing is an exercise of free speech protected by the Constitution*" and that "the Taft–Hartley [Act's] ban on political expenditures by unions was unconstitutional."

In comparing the records, the Wallace–Taylor–Pressman ticket was the only option for the Progressive-minded voters of the district. "After F.D.R.'s death Lee Pressman saw the people robbed of the fruits of victory by acts of Congress and strokes of the presidential pen. He saw . . . Israel betrayed. He saw the victims of Nazism become displaced persons while Nazis were restored to power in Germany." Therefore, he joined with Henry Wallace to found the Progressive Party and "helped create the platform on which he stands. Such is the stature of the man, that the Republican, Democratic, and

Liberal parties have banded together in an effort to stop him." Even Republican Governor Dewey, the conservative banner-carrier for the presidency, had "singled out Pressman for attack because like [Sidney] Hillman, Pressman is an American of Jewish origin, New Deal figure, and a labor man." Compared to Congressman Multer's foreign policy toadyism of the Truman line, with its several anti-Israel elements, the clear choice for the voters of the district—especially those who were liberal, pro-labor, and pro-Israel—was Lee Pressman.

Indeed, the record of Pressman's public life contained many accomplishments of which to be proud, and personal skills that would have made him a congressman of note, a fact that the national Progressive Party acknowledged. In recognition of this, the national body allowed the lawyer to concentrate on his own campaign time within his own district. The American Labor Party held a fund-raiser at Bensonhurst's HiHo Casino and scheduled Pressman for as many grassroots speaking engagements as possible. One of the few times in which he appeared directly with the national ticket came at a New York area rally as well, at a Yankee stadium where socialist Norman Thomas, Paul Robeson, and myriad other Progressive Party luminaries turned out to build Party support. In his speech at that well-attended rally, Pressman attacked the supposedly progressive New York City-based Liberal Party's alliance with other party machines in the city, and called on voters "to recognize the betrayal of the principles of [Franklin] Roosevelt," who had fought the dirty politics of Tammany Hall. He also pleaded for a return to sanity in foreign policy by supporting Wallace's vision of a restoration of the essence of the Grand Alliance and international cooperation instead of conflict.

In response, Lee Pressman's opponents were only too glad to hoist him on his own petard and remind him of periods in his past when the New Deal seemed like a "bad deal" to the lawyer. "Throughout the length and breadth of the Fourteenth Congressional District," wrote critic Samuel Abrahams in his critical *Plain Talk* campaign resume, "Pressman pretended with more than ordinary sanctimoniousness that he had always striven to uphold the fundamental tenets of Franklin D. Roosevelt's philosophy of government. Mr. Pressman conveniently forgot" that in 1940, during the Nazi–Soviet pact period, he publicly delivered "a scathing attack on the foreign policy then being pursued by President Roosevelt." Worse yet, his opponents quoted alleged Pressman statements from the *Daily Worker*. "The only time that we men and women of labor will have full exercise of our rights [is] when we have the courage to say—we arc not going to war." Those rejoinders, along with repeated attacks by well-known Pressman detractors such as columnist Victor Riesel—ladled on top of the Chambers' revelations, which Abrahams cheerfully "interrogated him on" during his district speeches resulting in evasions—proved he could not sidestep the issue. He was finally forced to tell the *Brooklyn Eagle* that "I have not been and am not now a member of the Communist Party." Furthermore, Pressman also became vulnerable to charges that he was something of a carpetbagger within the district. As his friend Jack Rabkin observed, Pressman had not lived in Bensonhurst for many years, was not particularly active in Jewish neighborhood politics, and was largely a secular, non-Zionist. "I don't know why Lee became hypnotized about his ability to win," he pondered. But truly, "he had deceived himself to the point of absolute belief" that he could unseat an incumbent now uniquely backed by three established parties. Rabkin knew better. "I was confident he didn't stand a chance." He was right about Pressman's surprisingly naive local political sensibilities. Pressman lost by a 4 to 1 margin.[27]

Not that the Progressive Party and Henry Wallace did much better at the national level. As John Abt noted in his memoir, we "hoped for several million votes. When we learned that we only received a million and a half, it was devastating." Even factoring in the various areas where enemies stole or undermined votes, the most favorable outcome Abt could compute was about "three million out of forty-nine million votes cast." Though disappointed, committed Progressive Party activists believed the effort had been worthwhile, however, for if nothing else it pushed Truman to the Left on domestic issues, a clear "co-opting of our domestic program," judged Abt. One by one, New Deal-leaning groups, discomforted by Truman's initial conservative domestic thrusts, returned as the President adopted legislative goals reflecting their concerns. In conclusion, thought both John Abt and Henry Wallace, and presumably Pressman as well, the "Progressive Party lost the election but its issues were the difference between Truman winning and losing."

So for a somewhat rag-tag band of idealists it had been a worthy battle, though Pressman characteristically denied any idealistic or romantic notions on his part and termed it a "miscalculation." Pressman's view of his own persona meant an almost instinctual insistence that all of his actions resulted from carefully "calculated" moves. It was difficult for him to believe he had been so idealistic as to react in any other way than on the basis of a cold-blooded analysis. His Progressive Party involvements and his American Labor Party campaign, however, were in the main refusals to accept the diminishment of the Progressive impulse in American political life. Though deep in denial, somewhere in his subconscious, Pressman must have realized that the Progressive Party would be unlikely to succeed, but judged it worthy of a heroic, perhaps self-sacrificial struggle; he responded out of a strong sense of what the pursuit of justice required at that point in history. As Vivian Gornick so accurately wrote, the radical impulse that moved Pressman and so many others was emotional at its core.[28]

PRESSMAN AND THE FBI

No matter which way he turned after the 1948 election, Pressman could see few ways to avoid a full-scale confrontation between his politics and the rest of his life. True, his resignation from the CIO freed him to speak out unreservedly about what he believed in, but if he continued to do so, he perhaps risked not only himself but the well-being of his family. He had to go no further than open his morning paper to realize just how dangerous American politics had become. First and most obviously, the continuing saga of the Hiss–Chambers case grabbed daily headlines. By November 1948, matters had escalated disturbingly. During a *Meet the Press* interview, unshielded by the shroud of immunity from libel that attached to congressional testimony, Whittaker Chambers had accused Hiss of perjury in responding to his allegations.

In response, Hiss instituted a libel suit, but unbeknownst to the lawyer, Chambers had squirreled away copies of confidential diplomatic information from the late 1930s that he alleged had been given to him by Hiss for transmittal to the Soviet Union via the Communist underground. Some of the information had been typed on the Hiss family's Underwood typewriter, according to Chambers; even worse, four pages of information were in Hiss's own handwriting. This evidence, the *Time* magazine editor said, proved his charges about Hiss's communism and in fact ratcheted up the controversy further. Now Hiss had been accused not only of trying to exercise policy-shaping influence on behalf of the Communist Party—essentially what Chambers had earlier testified to before the HUAC in August and September—but also of engaging in espionage for the Soviet Union.

At first stunned by this evidence, Hiss recovered quickly, admitting the authenticity of the documents for the most part, but claimed that they must have been stolen by others from his desk in the State Department. Soon Richard M. Nixon and the HUAC reentered the fray when committee investigators gained access to an additional cache of microfilm photographs of government documents that Chambers had dramatically secreted in a hollowed-out pumpkin on his Maryland farm. These "pumpkin papers," as they came to be known, consisted of canisters of film the journalist said he had photographed as part of the espionage ring in which Hiss had been the key source. The last of the documents had been reduced to microfilm shortly before Chambers defected from the CP in 1938.

Soon a New York grand jury was once again taking testimony on Chambers' allegations, considering possible indictments against both Hiss and Chambers (the latter for being untruthful in his original testimony regarding acts of espionage). Pressman, Nat Witt, and a procession of others testified before the grand jury through December 1948. Then, in the midst of this grand jury investigation, private Hiss letters dating from 1936 turned up. FBI type-writer experts (as well as Hiss's own expert) then determined that the Hiss Underwood typewriter was the same machine that had retyped the confidential State Department information in the original collection of documents. Once the grand jury became aware of that information, it returned an indictment against the former diplomat for perjury for testifying that he had not spoken to or known Chambers on or about February or March 1938 (the relevant dates of the State Department information contained in the copies). It did not believe Hiss's suggestion that Chambers must have somehow gotten access to the Hiss typewriter to retype the documents himself from what others had given him.[29]

Collaterally, the Justice Department proceeded with its Smith Act case against the top officials of the American Communist Party. After pressing forward the indictments against these twelve individuals in the summer of 1948, legal maneuvering by their attorneys—and Party leader William Z. Foster's serious heart condition—delayed the actual beginning of the trial. While the CP tried to mobilize mass protests against the prosecutions, Judge Harold Medina finally ordered the trial to begin on January 17, 1949, in Room 110 of the Foley Square Courthouse in New York, the same building in which the Hiss grand jury probe had just taken place. Pressman could hardly have been unruffled as Party functionaries such as Gene Dennis—with whom he had had repeated clandestine-like meetings—took their places in the sepulchre-like courtroom filled with over 100 spectators.[30]

Pressman's relevance to both legal defense efforts—and especially to the Hiss situation—was obvious to the FBI as it began preparation to buttress the Department of Justice's case against Hiss with further investigation. Not unexpectedly, Jerome Frank, now a federal Court of Appeals judge in New York, was one of the first avenues pursued. On January 19, 1948, FBI agents talked with Judge Frank in his chambers at the very same Foley Square Courthouse in which the DOJ now tried the leadership of the American Communist Party. Primarily, the interview focused on Frank's perceptions about Hiss, but necessarily encompassed the other alleged Ware Group members of the AAA.

Frank thought Hiss was quite able and bright, but "they never saw eye to eye socially, and, he added, with a grin, 'I believe that Alger looked down on me socially, as he came from a so-called Baltimore aristocracy.'" Frank stated that none of those alleged to have been members of the secret cell had ever given the slightest indication of Communist proclivities, according to Agent John Sullivan's report. Such proclivities, Frank judged, would be "adherence in their work to the Party line in shaping policy," and particularly in attempting "to create confusion and discontent." "He emphasized that he had not observed such tactics permeating Alger's work." In fact, when he heard about the charges of espionage, "he was amazed . . . that Alger was accused of stealing documents. . . ." "He was amazed, he reiterated, because he did not think Alger was a courageous individual—courageous enough to steal." Moreover, Hiss had enough "intelligence" not to turn over stolen documents to third parties and place himself in such a vulnerable position.

As to the others, particularly Pressman, Frank also commented, "Pressman he considered one of the most brilliant and promising young lawyers he had ever met with a gift for executive and organizational work. He considered him shrewd and ruthless, adding that he would do anything to accomplish his ends." When he first knew him at the Chadbourne firm, "he would have classified him as a liberal of the Norman Thomas school of political ideals." Agent Sullivan then asked if the Ware Group had indeed existed as reported, who did he think "would have been the leader in this group. Justice Frank answered immediately and without hesitation, 'Why, of course Pressman!' He stated that Pressman was undoubtedly the strongest willed of the group and because of his drive would have been the most likely to influence the others." In conclusion, though, Frank had to base his observation of his underlings on their work in the AAA, and on that score "he did not believe that they were active in the alleged activities while in his division or that they formed their association while under him." On that last point, as later evidence has shown, Frank concluded wrongly, though it is understandable about how he might be embarrassed that so many of his subordinates came to communism while working under his leadership.[31]

Soon the Bureau cast the net wider and approached former members of the Ware Group. On January 26, 1949, the same FBI agent, John F. Sullivan, along with Agent Donald Adams, interviewed John Abt at the Progressive Party headquarters on Park Avenue in New York. Abt had gone on to become the general counsel for the Progressive Party for a brief period after the 1948 defeats, as it struggled to build a lasting political existence. Abt cooperated to a point, giving information about his own personal employment. He claimed that in all of his public work no government documents had been "classified," as that practice had developed during the war. "He stated that consequently during his period with these organizations he had never handled any classified documents," the investigators reported. "When asked whether he had ever taken out of a Government building any documents, classified or unclassified, and given them to any person not authorized to receive same, he stated that he did not." When asked the same about other individuals, he responded "that he did not care to discuss this matter." The FBI agents informed him "that this was not a reason but an attitude." Abt replied "that was true but that would have to suffice as his reason." "He was asked specifically whether it had ever come to his attention or whether he had knowledge of the fact that Alger Hiss had taken documents out of government offices. de stated that he did not care to discuss this matter." The interview then continued unrevealingly along these lines, as the agents pursued Abt's real or imagined group memberships in various organizations, and his familiarity, if any, with Chambers and Elizabeth Bentley.[32]

The next day it was Lee Pressman's and Nat Witt's turn. Appearing at the law offices of Pressman, Witt, and Cammer on 40th Street, the agents received an essentially guarded response from the former CIO general counsel. Cammer served as Pressman's and Witt's personal counsel during their FBI interviews. After reviewing his education and employment history, Pressman noted that it was at the AAA that he had renewed his acquaintance with Alger Hiss after having worked with him on the *Harvard Law Review* in law school. He admitted that in early New Deal Washington the Pressmans had visited Hiss's home and vice versa, "although he could not classify the association as an intimate one," it being primarily business oriented. "Subject," the agents reported in bureau-speak, "denied that he or his confreres in the AAA had ever held what could be construed as meetings at each other's homes," and that any gatherings at all were for relaxation, at which of course work situations were discussed. Pressman stated that he did not know whether, when he had been in the government, documents had been classified by any scheme, but affirmed that he had not "taken any classified or unclassified documents out of the government buildings and made them available to anyone unauthorized to receive same." Nor had he made the contents of those documents known to anyone or did he know of any other individual who might have done that, including Alger Hiss.

When questioned about Chambers' portrayal of Ware Group meetings at the home of Henry Hill Collins in St. Mark's Court, Pressman admitted that he must have had attended six or so parties at the Collins' home. He did not "recall" Collins living there and he "stated that Matthews Court did not 'ring a bell.'" Pressman claimed these get-togethers could not be characterized as "meetings" in any normal sense of the word. Regarding any questions about organizational associations, Pressman demurred. When asked about CP membership, "subject stated that he desired to point out that he would not discuss these questions because he considered them to be an inquiry into his religious and political beliefs[,] and as such the questions were an invasion of his private affairs, which are protected by the Constitution." Even so, Pressman then went on to deny a number of other Party-related probes, such as whether he had ever been in Party headquarters in New York City. "He was asked if he ever sought guidance and/or policy from the Communist Party with respect to his government work and he stated that he had not. He hastened to add at this point," the FBI agents noted, "that he had always, while in the government service and the CIO, carried out the policies set forth by those agencies."

The FBI operatives then questioned him about associates, and Pressman agreed to note whether he had had work relationships with them in the government or the CIO, but would not discuss issues of political belief. He then refused to discuss his acquaintanceships, if any, with J. Peters, Harold Ware, and even Jerome Frank. "In discussing . . . names . . . it was brought out that the subject would not answer the questions as to whether or not he had knowledge of or had it brought to his attention that these individuals were engaged in espionage acts or any activities inimical to the welfare of the United States." He then went on to deny knowing Chambers, having seen him in news photos. Pressman stated "he did not know him and that he had never heard the name . . . before the recent press disclosures," nor had he heard of any of the aliases that Chambers claimed he used during the period. "When asked about Elizabeth Bentley, he said the name . . . did not ring a bell with him, but qualified this answer by adding, in government work." Finally, when queried about Roy Hudson, whom the Bureau well knew Pressman had been meeting with secretly since at least November 1943, he "flippantly and sarcastically answered, 'Oh, I've heard of him.'" The agents pursued this tack some more but Pressman would not answer. He "placed Roy Hudson in the category that he had no connection with him while in his government work and would not answer questions beyond government associations as it was then in the invasion of private rights' category."

Nat Witt's interview results were largely the same: personal denials about any actions "inimical to the interests of the United States" on his part, refusal to discuss political membership issues, as well as his relationship with Alger Hiss. "He specifically would not discuss if he had known whether or not Alger Hiss had furnished the contents of Government documents or the documents themselves to any unauthorized person in furtherance of such a scheme." "At the conclusion of the interview, Mr. Witt stated that he desired to have placed on the record the fact that he loved his country and the people in it very much." With more than a little sarcasm, the interviewing FBI agents "asked what country he was referring to, and he added, the United States."[33]

Although he later denied having any involvement with the developing Hiss–Chambers case, other than being called before the New York grand jury, in fact, Pressman, at his own initiative, had been in contact with Hiss's investigators and attorneys in the spring of 1949, even before the FBI interview. In the Hiss case, defense records memoranda reflected that Pressman approached Hiss's attorney Edward McLean—like Hiss, a classmate of Pressman's at Harvard Law School—and volunteered to gather relevant defense information about Chambers after having previously passed along rumors circulating about the journalist's homosexuality and mental problems. Pressman told McLean in March that he would "try to find out something specific" about the mental institutionalization rumors and that "Pressman was most cooperative and seemed sincerely anxious to help in every way possible."

Obviously, for good reason, Pressman had taken a deep interest in the peregrinations of the Hiss perjury case. This concern was reinforced by the impact of the law partnership's ties to the controversy. Pressman, Witt, and Cammer assumed that their office was bugged, and before long FBI agents escalated the pressure by sitting purposely in the law firm's waiting room and following the lawyers to lunch, frightening potential clients away. Before long, according to Harold Cammer, the firm "hit on very hard times" financially. Whether the bureau was after Pressman and Witt personally at that point, or whether it hoped that such pressure would help "turn" one or both of them into prosecution witnesses against Hiss, is unknown.[34]

What is known is that these events had an unnerving effect on the usually unflappable Lee Pressman. Within the law firm, Pressman began more and more to discuss with Cammer the necessity of removing his friend Nat Witt from the firm. One reason was Witt's sloppiness about billing practices, a matter on which Cammer agreed with Pressman that there was a problem. However, he also believed that most likely, on a subconscious level, the defiant resistance Witt evidenced to the government inquiries led Pressman to conclude that there was continued danger in maintaining this relationship. Harold Cammer recounted how Pressman initiated these discussions with him many times, much to his dismay, for he had no desire to cast his friend Nat Witt aside. And, when the first Hiss trial concluded with a hung jury in the summer of 1949, with eight to four jurors voting to convict, Pressman even began to act irrationally and "became paranoid. . . ." to a noticeable degree.

In Cammer's judgment, Pressman was looking for a way to shed his past politics, to make a clean breast of it, perhaps to prevent himself from experiencing Hiss's fate. He even explored with Cammer the latter's thoughts about an improbable scheme to convert to Roman Catholicism—as some other ex-Communists like Louis Budenz had done—by approaching the well-known anti-Communist Bishop Fulton J. Sheen. In so doing, he might be able to convince the FBI and the government that he no longer was what he had been. Possibly then he could dissipate the witch-hunt tensions without being accused of becoming a "turncoat." In essence, Cammer believed his law partner "was looking for a decent way to do that" without having to testify against his friends' political loyalties. Despite all of these developments, curiously Witt himself did not seem to sense the internal turmoil that had begun to consume Lee Pressman.[34]

Oddly, even as Pressman struggled to distance himself from his communism, he began an intriguing relationship with the Soviets. Yuri Novikov, Second Secretary of the Soviet Embassy, approached Pressman in the fall of 1949 with a proposal to begin handling estate work for Americans who left property to Russian beneficiaries, work that required a great deal of correspondence with groups of lawyers in Russia. Pressman used the opportunity to sever his relationship with Witt and Cammer—he just came into the office one day, said he was leaving, and left, recalled Cammer. Thereafter, he opened a solitary law practice doing this estate work. Before long, Novikov asked Pressman to refer certain Soviet legal problems to the best New York lawyers capable of handling them. The Russians asked who would be the best defense attorney to represent Valentin Gubitchev, a Soviet United Nations employee, arrested with Judith Coplon, a Department of Justice intelligence clerk in March 1949, for example. Coplon had been passing secret FBI reports of bureau intelligence activities related to its Communist investigations to Gubitchev and the Russians for some time. After being alerted to her unusual interest in such reports by Coplon's supervisor, the FBI set up surveillance and arrested both Coplon and Gubitchev at a rendezvous in New York City. And it was to Lee Pressman that Novikov, on behalf of the Soviet government, came to find out who could best represent Gubitchev. Pressman referred him to fellow left-wing attorney Abraham Pomerantz, a friend from his youth, and aided Pomerantz by writing "several memoranda of law" on possible defenses. In addition, Pressman admitted that he attended several defense conferences where Pomerantz, Novikov, and Gubitchev discussed legal tactics.[36]

Shortly after Pressman became involved in this strange relationship— moving closer to the Soviet Communists even as he distanced himself from his American CP connections—the labor lawyer asserted that he came to the conclusion that "the Russians and their satellites were attempting to retain him openly as their counsel. He felt that if he continued with them," he later told FBI agents, "sooner or later he would be in a position where it would be difficult for him to refuse to accede to any demands they might make of him." Further "disturbing" incidents heightened Pressman's fears. At one point, for example, Novikov instructed him never to use regular mail channels in his estate correspondence and to be sure to always use hand delivery to the consulate or embassy for diplomatic packet transferal. He also was told to assume that his office phones were bugged. On another occasion, the New York Soviet Consulate called him in the middle of the night and notified him to appear at its offices early the next morning. When he did as instructed, expecting some major assignment, he was handed an innocuous letter related to one of the estates he was handling at the time. Finally, during one meeting between Pressman and Novikov, the latter came out of the New York Consulate, got into Pressman's car, and instructed him to drive off, mentioning that they were being followed by the FBI.

During none of their interactions, Pressman claimed, did Novikov ask "him to do anything which to his mind was of an espionage or intelligence nature." But, he noted, "Novikov appeared to exceptionally well informed on current affairs and would invariably query him searchingly" on various topics. When engaged in these conversations, Pressman said he tried to avoid becoming too deeply involved, because they aroused his suspicions about the nature of the Soviets' ultimate designs on his services. Before long, he decided to discontinue the relationship as soon as he could reasonably find a way to replace the lost income. As it turned out, this was fortunate for Pressman, for in January 1953, the U.S. government declared Yuri Novikov, a former Red Army officer, *persona non grata* for conspiring to run an espionage ring with two Americans in Vienna, and returned him to the Union of Soviet Socialist Republics.[37]

Whether this bizarre episode exemplified a Pressman under such intense pressure that he became profoundly disoriented, or a possible flirtation with the idea of a deeper commitment to communism, is difficult to say. It is certain that for an individual intending to move away from his Communist past, sliding into a relationship with the shadowy Novikov worked directly against that objective. Even more puzzling is exactly what reasons the Soviets might have had to engage Pressman in this way. Were they attempting to use Pressman, unwittingly, as an intelligence courier of some sort? If this was the goal, then it had to be one of the most inept espionage efforts on record, for Pressman was hardly the kind of person to be an unwitting dupe and hardly the least likely citizen to be suspected of Communist activity by the U.S. government. Alternatively, perhaps the Soviets wished to strengthen their ties with Pressman in order to extract his legal talents on a higher level. Possibly, and this may be the most likely explanation, the Novikov–Pressman initiative may have reflected an effort by the Soviets to purchase some insurance against Pressman cracking under pressure and turning into a friendly government witness during the second perjury trial of Alger Hiss. By November 1949, the Smith Act prosecutions had concluded with the conviction of the Party's top leaders. In addition, during the raucous trial, their attorneys had been cited for contempt of court for their vigorous defense of their clients. Now, the Department of Justice made ready to pursue Smith Act indictments of second-tier American CP leaders. Thus, even underground "members at large" like Pressman could not think of themselves as being exempt from the danger of imprisonment. So, with the gathering storm of a new Red scare gaining momentum and force, the Soviets may have thought it wise to create some level of dependence on them so that Pressman would continue to remain silent about his Ware Group years.[38]

Quite possibly Pressman himself realized this. By the time the second Hiss case was in full swing in December 1949, journalists who knew Pressman informed FBI sources that the lawyer had been considering a break with the CP. L.B. Nichols wrote to Claude Tolson, J. Edgar Hoover's top aide, that a source had recently called, apparently a male journalist, and "told me Friday and again today that he has information Lee Pressman has broken with the Communists and Left-Wingers." The unnamed journalist indicated that he had been seeking an interview with Pressman for years, and that for all that time "Pressman has refused to talk to him." When he heard about a possible break, the reporter again phoned the lawyer. Pressman "told him he was in sweat moving [his office] and all tied up but as soon as the moving was completed, he would be very happy to have" the unnamed journalist "call upon him . . . and talk to him at length." Nichols asserted that this source would try to plant the idea that Pressman should talk to the FBI willingly. J. Edgar Hoover's handwritten comments on the memo indicated his doubts about these developments. "I doubt Pressman's sincerity even if [he] does recant," he wrote.[39]

Almost contemporaneously, another unnamed journalist, this time a woman, brought information to the FBI regarding a recent luncheon she had had with the labor lawyer. Calling the FBI in February 1950, she told the government agents that "she was acquainted with him and had luncheon with him to keep up her contacts. She thought that her luncheon had been very interesting and she thought she had received information which might be of interest to the FBI. . . ." an agent reported. Before long, bureau operatives contacted her, and by March 1950, she supplied the government with a detailed memorandum of her Pressman conversation. This memorandum does much to illuminate Pressman's mental state in the midst of his looming personal crisis. While the exact date of the meeting is not known, it most likely occurred in January 1950.[40]

"Lee's office is very small," she began, no larger than eight by twelve feet. She noted that his office walls were adorned by family photos, CIO pictorials, and an autographed photo of Supreme Court Justice Hugo Black. "When I went into the office he smiled and said hello, [. . .] sort of half-question." From this and other clues it appeared that this individual may have been close to the CP at some point, and was someone who Pressman may have suspected had separated, at least emotionally. "I said yes . . . and he got up and shook hands." After inconsequential small talk, Pressman put a few minor office matters to rest, and they made their way to the Brass Rail Restaurant in midtown Manhattan.[41]

First the talk turned to John L. Lewis, Philip Murray, and the contemporary labor and collective bargaining scene such as the current controversies over pension bargaining. "Then he looked at me and grinned and said I was undoubtedly interested in more than what he thinks of pensions. I admitted I damn sure was. He said sort of intensely[,] please not to approach him with cliches. 'Don't ask me if I've broken, or if I'm ready to talk,' Pressman said. 'I hate cliches.'" She tried to make light of the issue unsuccessfully. "He said he meant it, that he could not stand the vacuous columns around these days about this one or that breaking or being expelled from the Party." Pressman informed her that the rest of the conversation was "off the record," and she agreed, noting to the FBI that she had no choice. "He laughed, and said that he would answer what he could, and that he would not hedge on anything, but would say no" if he did not want to answer. The talk turned to the disbarment proceedings instituted in New York against one of the defense attorneys in the Smith Act trials, and in his comments Pressman was carefully noncommittal. "He remained his usual impassive self, but this was too much," the reporter wrote. "He knew too little. Every attorney, particularly those engaged in any CP defense . . ." knew more about the case and about that attorney in particular, she thought.

"Talking of trials naturally led to Hiss–Chambers et al. So in my best take it for granted tone," she queried Pressman about the soldier-of-fortune Colonel Dean Ivan Lamb, one of the witnesses in the second Hiss perjury trial. Chambers had named Lamb as being involved with Hiss and Chambers in a military espionage gambit during the mid-1930s, and in private statements to the FBI, Chambers also tied Pressman directly to Lamb. "No perceptible pause, no rapid denial. Just the considered 'Lamb, did you say? I don't recall knowing a lamb.'" He then began to probe her about what she knew about Lamb and she tried another tack. What did he think about the second Hiss decision, which had resulted in a perjury conviction in late January 1950? "Lee said he thought it was to be expected, do you really think in these times that a man like Hiss could get a fair trial," he challenged. Juries, "were scared to turn in any other verdict." As to the defendant himself, Pressman informed her, "Hiss was a very powerful person. You have to know him to understand the charm" he exercised on others. "I can't see Hiss getting mixed up with someone like Chambers." She quickly jumped on the last words: What Chambers was really like. "Lee looked [at me like] na na you little fox you can't trap me. 'I never saw Chambers in my life. Never. I tell you straight.'" As proof, he cited Chat in Chambers' first HUAC testimony, he did not mention Pressman, but after being coached by committee counsel in his second appearance "he said, oh yes, Lee Pressman belongs in that group." He did not know Chambers, Chambers did not know him, and he never saw Hiss much "face to face after 1935." All subsequent contact had been casual. When probing further about the depth of his involvement in the Hiss defense, she asked his opinion about whether he thought Hiss had been shielding someone. Rumors had circulated at one point that Chambers' bisexuality had led to an affair with Hiss's stepson, to which Pressman responded with ignorance, and no comment at all about any conversation he had with the Hiss defense team.[42]

Still, the reporter dug deeper. She understood "CP rank and filers," she said, "but what makes really top notch intellectuals" maintain their commitments "on and on and on after all the fervor has worn off, after all the" allure "of world rebuilding dissolves. I know that no one wakes up one fine morning after being involved for years," and quits, she admitted. "No one likes to open his family to criticism, to the public eye." But, even so, Hiss should have simply "come clean," telling the world that he had joined a political movement that he thought was right at the time, and people would have come to understand that. "'But . . . you're proceeding on the assumption that Hiss was in espionage,'" Pressman observed. "'Yes, I am. Just as I'm proceeding on certain assumptions with you.'" "'Well,'" Pressman shot back, "'HOW do you approach me?'" She told him the same way she would approach Nat Witt and John Abt; that is, she seemed to imply, as intellectuals who became involved in the Party and supported its goals in their life's work, meaning individuals lot involved with the CP at Hiss's level. She then ran down the significance of Pressman's list of current left-wing clients—his work for Pomerantz connected to the Gubitchev case, for example, and his representation of the International Workers Order (IWO), a Jewish insurance beneficiary organization with strong CP ties.

Pressman sidestepped the Pomerantz query completely and argued that his representation of members' constitutional rights—the organization had made the government's subversive organizations list and as a result the innocent were facing persecution—was a just endeavor. He cited the instance of an elderly couple insured under an IWO plan who faced either losing their federal government livelihood (since it had been named by the attorney general as a subversive organization) or their insurance coverage. Moreover, if they dropped membership in the IWO, they would not be able to be buried next to their son, who had died years earlier, in the IWO-only cemetery in which he had been laid to rest. "We then went into a long spiel about [the meaning of] subversive, and the questions of political . . . and thought control, and the questioning of political belief." On this she charged that CP actions in all nations of the world were egregious. "Lee maintained that there was still persecution for belief" in this country. She asked "just stacking up between the two countries, which would he" pick. "Very seriously he said that he loves this country, that he would never want to live elsewhere." Then why continue to justify slave labor camps, concentration camps for political dissenters, and "thought control over art and science. . . ." "He snapped back with that he didn't approve of such things no matter where they took place. That he didn't like the abrogation of civil liberties anywhere." "Lee said, 'Look . . . you have to understand one thing. I always tended to my own knitting. I always followed whatever organization I worked for. And Moscow did not send me in to do a job on the labor unions. That's sure and definite. I think I helped the labor movement in this country.'" Then why did he leave, she asked. To have a normal life with his family, he answered, for "'when your heart is in'" the "'labor movement you just don't get a chance to be with your children. I wanted to be with them, to live a routine life.'"

The conversation then turned to the CIO moves to expel its Communist-dominated unions, which Pressman observed must be breaking Phil Murray's heart. By then, the lunch was almost over. The reporter suggested to Pressman the possibility of speaking to the FBI. "He insisted he wanted to remain out of the limelight for a while, that he needed time to think, that he did not want to be a public figure. Again he said he only wanted to tend to his knitting. I said it depended on what he was knitting. . . ." The reporter's final observations to the FBI were that she "would not be surprised to see Lee testifying for the government on some upcoming case." All in all, she thought that in their conversation he certainly proved to be "one likeable, smart" but untruthful potential anti-Communist convert. On the detailed FBI memorandum that accompanied this intriguing meeting, FBI Director J. Edgar Hoover wrote a snide gloss that in his opinion, at least, there was "no doubt as to these last two qualities."[43]

The portrait rendered by Pressman's journalist acquaintance is essentially one of a man facing his public life's greatest crisis, which by now had become quite personal. If the account is accurately rendered, by early 1950, Pressman was searching for a way to lessen the danger that threatened him and his family, but had not come to a state of ideological transformation. When his luncheon guest became hostile toward the Soviet Union, for example, Pressman quickly pointed out similar injustices in the United States. In his wary sparring with the FBI's source, Pressman seemed to be exploring; exploring not only how potential answers might be received, but also, perhaps, to see just what it might feel like to take the plunge of recantation, to suffer the indignities of throwing himself on his sword publicly, all the while trying to steer clear of the moral wreckage of naming names. Unquestionably, his "miscalculation" had been a miscalculation of the heart, though he did not recognize it as such. Thus he continued to maintain the illusion that if only his plan had been better calculated, better analyzed, better operationalized, and better executed things would have been different. As events over the next eight months continued to fuel public hysteria over international and domestic communism, Lee Pressman was thus well conditioned to fool himself one last time, by concluding once more that only a carefully concocted scheme could rescue him from his predicament.

NINE

PURSUING "COMRADE BIG"

B y the summer of 1950, Lee Pressman concluded that he had to take a dramatic step to avoid entrapment in the new Red scare. In 1949, the Soviet Union's detonation of an atomic bomb and a communist victory in the Chinese civil war had heightened international tensions. More significantly, shortly after the Hiss conviction in January 1950, the British announced that one of their atomic scientists who had worked on the U.S. Manhattan Project, Klaus Fuchs, had been spying for the Soviets. Through Fuchs, the FBI identified a U.S.-based atomic espionage ring allegedly led by Julius and Ethel Rosenberg. The arrests of the Rosenbergs in July 1950 coincided with the invasion of South Korea by Communist forces.

With the nation again at war with the supposed "monolith" of communism, U.S. citizens with left-wing political pasts were even more at risk. Soon shunned by social acquaintances, they had difficulties making a living and became objects of persecution and prosecution for their past or present political beliefs. And at least two, the Rosenbergs, lost their lives in 1953 after their conviction for atomic espionage. No doubt Lee Pressman came to understand the personal ramifications well, and he viewed these unfolding events with growing alarm, as he had previously during the Hiss and the Smith Act trials. How could he extricate himself and his family from these dangers, while at the same time inflicting the least damage possible to his former political comrades? For if he "turned," as he apparently contemplated doing, he faced the prospect of not only describing his own involvement but those of others as well.[1]

This must have been a tortuous personal dilemma, for more than one person who knew Lee Pressman well remarked on his loyalty to others. "If you'd tell me that Pressman would put his arm in the fire for something he believed in, I could understand that," reflected his mentor Jerome Frank. Nevertheless, events had conspired to leave him with precious little room in which to exercise his usually formidable ability to maneuver to his political advantage. He responded, though, in his characteristically dramatic way. He convinced himself he could concoct a scheme that would reverse the flow of political events. Pressman began to believe that he could "ruin" the credibility of the HUAC and its rising political star, Richard Nixon, Hiss's chief persecutor, by admitting membership but stating that Hiss had not been a member. Thus, publicly embarrassed, Nixon and the HUAC would have their credibility undermined, the Hiss appeal might have a new basis, and his personal predicament would lessen.

Despite artfully designed testimony, Pressman's gambit failed. Nixon emerged with an enhanced reputation as a dogged pursuer of domestic Communist subversion. In addition, the lawyer's subsequent attempts to recover from the botched plan so angered the FBI's J. Edgar Hoover that Pressman's legal perils increased, exposing him to an FBI perjury investigation a la Hiss. While the government pursued "Comrade Big"—the name anti-Communist journalists claimed CP rank and filers used for Pressman around Party headquarters—the lawyer could do little afterward but to sit tight and hope for the best. Ultimately, the effort to prosecute Lee Pressman did not bear fruit, though not for lack of trying by the FBI. In later years the lawyer maintained a studied distance from the agency; in spite of repeated contacts, Pressman would go only so far in supplying the government information about the alleged Communist "menace." "Pressman knew that respectability has its rituals," journalist Murray Kempton noted, and "if he must pay its price, the bones he would throw the dogs would be dry as dust." And in the end, as Kempton correctly pointed out, the "bones he threw were his own. . . ."[2]

PRESSMAN AND THE HUAC IN 1950

Ironically, the FBI knew the essentials of Pressman's scheme almost as soon as he publicly resigned as general counsel of the CP-related American Labor Party in early August 1950. The lawyer had not been cooperative in the Bureau's January 1949 interview at Pressman's law offices, an FBI agent noted. "In the last ten months however there have been rumors and reports prevalent that Pressman had broken with the Communist Party," perhaps in an attempt to reconnect with the CIO, the government analyst speculated. One informant alleged that Pressman had written to Philip Murray in January 1950 that he was now "'fed up' with Communist forces and was ready to make a break with them." "The letter asked Mr. Murray to give him, Pressman, one more chance in the CIO." Another FBI informant claimed that Pressman had contacted Philip Murray no less than four times, and that "Murray has told Pressman that he has got to do more to square himself than merely writing a letter of resignation from the American Labor Party. . . ." According to this source, Murray advised Pressman that if he was "sincere and if he has broken with the Communists then Pressman ought to make a full and complete confession[,] publicly declaring himself and try to correct the error" of his ways. "In addition Murray has told Pressman that under no condition will he ever be taken back into the CIO." This information intrigued the Bureau, obviously. Because of Pressman's CP involvements over the years, "if willing to talk, [he] would be able to furnish considerable information on matters of interest to the Bureau. . . . I feel that we have nothing to lose and everything to gain by interviewing Pressman at this time," Agent A. H. Belmont advised. J. Edgar Hoover assented in a penciled notation on the memo to his assistant. "Alright, but I have absolutely no confidence in Pressman. He is sly, dishonest . . . [and] at heart a traitor. I wouldn't trust him irrespective of what he professes," Hoover wrote without any justification. "We must keep in mind that some of these so-called defections from [the] Communist cause may well be phony."[3]

Was Lee Pressman "trying to do a 'Louis Budenz,'" as another FBI memo put it, referring to the ex-Communist editor of the *Daily Worker* who had become a "professional" witness against communism? Perhaps he was, but it should be kept in mind that much of the information supplied by informants to the FBI was given by enemies of Pressman, all of whom usually attributed the worst of motives to their former nemesis. At any rate, the Bureau assigned two agents experienced in Communist issues to contact Pressman for an interview. In the meantime, Pressman had received a new subpoena from the HUAC, as he most likely suspected he would. The "[i]mpression conveyed" at the FBI's contact was that the subject, in FBI speak, was "willing to cooperate and disclose past communist connections but expressed [a] desire to first talk to" the HUAC. Pressman told the agents he would be "willing to be interviewed by [the] bureau after" that appearance, "when he would answer all questions." This position aroused the FBI's suspicions about Pressman's true intentions. Washington officials instructed the New York agents "that in view of Pressman's refusal to be interviewed by the Bureau at this time, no further effort to contact him for this purpose should be made." Moreover, "should Mr. Pressman get in touch with the office and indicate a willingness to be interviewed, that the Bureau should be consulted before any contact is had with Pressman." By now, even the attorney general had developed an interest in what Pressman might have to say.[4]

By August 25, the agency knew the testimony's general outlines. Again, the new source appeared to be newspaper related, twice removed; an individual had apparently learned the essence of the lawyer's anticipated disclosures from a reporter in whom Pressman had confided. "According to this undisclosed informant," an FBI telegram indicated, "Pressman in his testimony will attempt to do as little harm as is possible under the circumstances. He will indicate that he, himself, was a member of the CP and knew that John Abt and Nathan Witt were also members of the CP. According to the informant, he will deny that he knew that Alger Hiss was a member of the CP." "The informant indicated that Pressman is apparently not doing a job for Alger Hiss but that Pressman is so contemptuous of Whittaker Chambers that he is going to take this stand in connection with Hiss." He would deny as well "that he knew anything concerning espionage in connection with his CP affiliation. . . ." but would "admit that he knew Chambers but not under Chambers['] pseudonyms Crosley and Carl. Pressman will also deny he knew Chambers in connection with espionage. . . ."[5]

Pressman had obviously created the stir he intended. But exactly what was he up to? The most reliable source about what was going on in Pressman's mind at the time has to be the account of his friend, Jack Rabkin. Rabkin had known Pressman since their days at City College and in Washington during the early New Deal. He and his wife reconnected with the Pressman family upon the labor lawyer's return to New York in early 1948. One day in August 1950, Rabkin received an unexpected call from his friend, who asked with some urgency that Rabkin meet him at the New York Bar Association. When the latter arrived, he found Lee Pressman in the midst of conducting research on the intricacies of constitutional rights in congressional hearings, a project on which he asked for Rabkin's assistance.[6]

Pressman informed his friend that he had been called to testify before the HUAC, and that he intended to do so. Rabkin, while no radical, was aghast. "'Lee, you're going to be an informer!'" he recalled, exclaiming in shock. "He says, 'Jack, now who am I going to inform on? Abt, Witt,'" and the others? "They know all about" them, Pressman rationalized. "I'm not informing.'" Still, the tax attorney could not believe what he had heard, or fathom the rationale. "'But what's the reason, what's the purpose, what are you going to achieve?'" he recalled asking. "'I'm going to destroy Nixon,'" Pressman informed him. "'I'm going to tell the story of the whole situation in the cell in Washington in the thirties. I'm going to name everybody in that cell. And Hiss is not going to be in that!' He says, 'that's the way I'm going to destroy Nixon.'" Later that afternoon, they shared a train ride to Mt. Vernon. Rabkin pleaded with Pressman that he should not make the ethical lapse of informing; from the point of view of Talmudic law no free society could survive where informing was encouraged or tolerated, he pointed out. Knowing that Pressman was friendly with Rabbi Maccabee at the family synagogue, he convinced his friend to discuss the matter with him from a moral perspective, which Pressman did. Rabkin's efforts failed, for Pressman nevertheless decided to testify. The train ride to Washington must have been one of deep reflection for Lee Pressman. What had his life been about, he must have thought. What were its values, and what values was he pursuing now? What would be the impact of it all on those to whom he was closest in life—his wife Sunny and his three daughters, Ann, Marcia, and Susan; his parents; and his former Ware Group comrades. In particular, he continued to struggle with the consequences for the latter of his "naming names," apparently still unsure of how far he would go. Upon arriving in Washington, he stopped by his brother Irving's office to say good-bye. As adults, the brothers were as emotionally distant as they had been as children, because of their age difference. In essence, Irving had followed his brother's exploits in the newspapers like everyone else. Now, because Lee Pressman thought that this might be the last time he would see his brother for a while, he apparently felt some need for a reaffirmation of family. "He came over to meet me at my office one day," Irving Pressman remembered. "He had a little [shaving] kit with him. He said, well, he's prepared to go to jail. I said, 'what do you mean you're going to go to jail? For what?' He said, 'I'm going up before the committee and I know they're going to ask me, did I know this guy, did I know this guy, did I know this guy'" was a Party member, and so on. He did not think he could do it. "'I'm not going to testify against all my friends.'" This visit stunned his younger brother. "I was horrified," he recalled.[7]

In the end, Pressman did reluctantly "name names," in a way, although Richard Nixon's effort to get Pressman to that point was almost Herculean. A close reading of the emotional undertow in Pressman's 1950 HUAC statement reveals what must have been an absolutely draining experience. "One afternoon, just before he went to run his course before the committee," Murray Kempton wrote in his personality profile of the 1950s, "Pressman sat and talked about the meaning of his life. Who could have believed that it would come to this, he said, and that he of all men would guess so wrong in his decision to leave the CIO? But he preferred to say that he had made the choice because he believed that the Wallace movement was great and powerful and that he was leaving the dying side for the living one." Only forty-four years old, he had walked among the political movers and shakers of New Deal America for seventeen years. Now he faced at best the public humiliation of admitting that he had been moved by the foolish whims of youth in his political attachments, with resulting embarrassment to his family. At worst, he faced wholesale personal betrayal and maybe even a jail sentence.[8]

At the start of the hearings, there "seemed somewhere in the back of his mind the notion that, if he could run it safely, things might be as they were when he was young," wrote journalist Kempton. The labor lawyer had prepared the ground by releasing a brief public statement before he appeared in Washington. "A number of people have written and called me urging me to clarify" why he had resigned from the American Labor Party, his public letter opened. "This, I desire to do," as well as to fight the "many distortions" of "my past activities" to which he had been personally subjected. The immediate stimulus, he claimed, came because of the Korean invasion. "The warfare in Korea threatens to unleash a world conflict which would destroy our civilization. All my life I have opposed aggression. . . . The Communist Party and its forces in the labor movement are the supporters and apologists for an aggressive war. I vigorously oppose this position. I desire to support the United Nations and my country.[9]

"In the early Nineteen Thirties our country was deep in a depression. The future looked black for my generation, just emerging from school. At the same time the growing specter of nazism in Germany presented an equally grave threat. In my desire to see the destruction of Hitlerism and an improvement in economic conditions here at home," Pressman asserted, "I joined a Communist group in Washington, D. C., about 1934." He participated for a year, he said, then left Washington to return to New York. Afterward, he said he "discontinued any further participation in the group." Moreover, "I believe it of interest to comment that I have no knowledge regarding the political beliefs or affiliations of Alger Hiss. I do know that for the period of my participation he was not a member of that group." Pressman went on to proudly cite his service to the labor movement, and closed warning of the "onrushing frightful conflict between the ideological forces [that] today threaten our destruction," resurgent nazism and aggressive communism. "Our survival must be based upon the peoples' understanding of the true meaning and worth of American democracy and their determination to fight for its preservation and full enjoyment," he maintained. "I deeply appreciate that within our democratic way of life, when past beliefs prove false, there is the opportunity for change and to contribute in whatever manner possible toward the dignity and well-being of man and the preservation of peace for all humanity."

Now Pressman prepared to face his inquisitors. When he took his seat in a committee room of the Old House Office Building on August 28, 1950, he knew that the HUAC members savored this new, career-enhancing, anti-Communist opportunity and would press him relentlessly. Nattily dressed in a dark suit, with a lighter tie and kerchief, he arranged his notes neatly in front of him. His demeanor and body language reflected the attack that he expected—his brow furrowed, his jaw jutted forward, and his eyes looked down frequently to consult his notes during his very brief opening statement. Subsequently, his eyes moved furtively from side to side as he shifted his glance from the committee members to the newsreel camera; now and again he placed his hands in front of him, moving them periodically up and down, separating them wider to thrust an index finger toward his questioners in aggressive gesticulation. "Between the abyss of the right and the left," as Murray Kempton described the scene, "he set forth on the course prescribed by the House Committee on Un-American Activities, coolly and carefully and with terrible lacerations of his pride." He "knew that this was a time, like so many other times, requiring economy of emotion" in expression, a skill at which he was quite adept.[10]

Quickly, Pressman confronted the most unpleasant business. "There were three other persons in that [Ware] group in addition to myself. They were all at the time with me in the Department of Agriculture. They have all been named before this committee by others," he said. "I state to you that I am prepared . . . to answer any and all questions regarding my activities in the past up to the present. . . . It would be offensive to me, as it would be to practically all people, to have to name individuals with whom I have associated in the past." He had no information on those individuals, he maintained, that the committee did not already have. He claimed that the committee should consider that, if it should make him divulge those "names," it would chill the desire of other witnesses like himself who were considering abandoning the Party. It might therefore hamper the government from garnering future testimonial evidence, for no one wishes to inform on their past, and perhaps present, friends. "But, . . . that is a decision which the committee will have to make."[11]

In recounting this scene, journalist Walter Goodman noted that while Pressman denied that Hiss had been a member of the Ware Group during the time he had been, he "managed by the fastidious phrasing of his answers to leave the impression that he knew more about Hiss than he was prepared to tell." "I have no knowledge regarding the political beliefs or affiliations of Alger Hiss. And when I say I have no knowledge, I am not endeavoring to quibble with this committee. I appear here, as I necessarily must, as a lawyer. I am a lawyer. When one asks me for knowledge, knowledge to my mind is based on fact, and I have no facts." Furthermore, it would be improper, as a lawyer, for him to comment on a case then under litigation, as the Hiss appeal was moving forward. For "that reason I am trying to be very, very precise. I do know, I can state as a matter of knowledge, that for the period of my participation in that group, which is the only basis on which I can say I have knowledge, Alger Hiss was not a member of the group."[12]

After his opening statement, the formal examination by then-committee counsel Frank Tavenner proceeded. As they began to move through the chronology of Pressman's career in government, Richard Nixon took up the examination. Nixon's questions clearly indicated that he had access to the information contained in the FBI file on Pressman. Noting that upon first arriving in Washington the Pressmans took up residence at the Cathedral

Mansion Apartments on Connecticut Avenue across from the city zoo, Nixon commented, "Weren't you on the second or third floor there?" "That is correct," Pressman answered. "Were you my neighbor, Mr. Congressman?" the labor lawyer asked with mock congeniality. Nixon slyly answered, "I just know Washington."

Thus alerting Pressman to the fact that he had information on him—the extent of which the former CIO general counsel could hardly know in specific detail—Nixon remained quiet for a brief time, as Tavenner continued. As the examination turned toward Pressman's recruitment to the CP by Harold Ware, and his Ware Group co-members, the labor lawyer once again reiterated his tortured posturing as to "naming names." Once again he would not utter the specific names of Abt, Witt, and Kramer, preferring to identify them as the individuals already named by others before the committee, with whom he had worked in the Department of Agriculture. In short order, Tavenner, and of course Nixon, became exasperated, pointing out that six Ware Group government employees had been named before the HUAC. But "not in the Department of Agriculture," Pressman qualified, as if that would be sufficient for these Communist hunters. "What is the question in your mind about the desirability of naming these people?" Nixon inquired. If Pressman truly had left the Party and what it stood for, he "could be of great assistance to the committee by corroborating charges which have been made previously concerning individuals who have been named," whether correctly or falsely. Nixon said he understood the morality and consequences of the issue that Pressman raised. He elaborated by noting that "the experience we have had over the years bears out the fact that the only way we can effectively get at the underground activities of the Communist Party is through individuals who have broken with the Party and who can give us information." "I do not have any knowledge of the affiliation or non-affiliation with the Communist Party of any other Government employee," other than those whom he had indicated directly, Pressman again stated. "You have limited it to Government employees," observed Nixon. "I am waiting for any questions you may ask me with respect to any person who is not a Government employee," the lawyer answered.

And so it went, around and around, now left behind for moments while the committee explored other aspects of Pressman's Communist involvements, then returned to from time to time, with Nixon particularly trying to force Pressman to confirm that Abt, Witt, and Kramer had been CP members; with Pressman all the while reaffirming how difficult that would be for him, yet at the same time inviting the committee to order him to do it. As Walter Goodman remarked, "Pressman explained to Chairman Wood how offensive it was to him to name names and then, in a strange scene, implored the chairman to demand that he do so." At one point Wood stated, "[W]e could have

saved an hour's time if you had answered or announced you declined to
answer, which is your prerogative." Still, Pressman had his own standards
about how the information must come out. "I refuse to decline to answer," he
stated in a double negative. "Suppose you answer it then," the chairman suggested. "Is that a direction from the chairman?" Pressman asked. "It is a suggestion. A person can't decline and acquiesce at the same time," Wood noted.
In the end, the peculiar way in which Pressman "named names" was the following:

Mr. PRESSMAN: If this will satisfy Mr. Nixon, the only three people I have
    knowledge of as members of the Communist Party were the three mem-
    bers with me in the group, who were with me in the Department of Agri-
    culture at the time. The three who have been named along with me in
    that group were the only three in the Department of Agriculture with me
    at the same time I was.
Mr. NIXON: Did you say this morning that John Abt, Nathan Witt, and Charles
    Kramer were the only ones in the Department of Agriculture at the time
    you were who were members of the Communist Party at the time you
    were?
Mr. PRESSMAN: I will put it this way: Do I understand that you are insisting,
    in spite of the point I made this morning, that I answer that question?
Mr. NIXON: I am insisting.
Mr. PRESSMAN: The answer is yes.

Thus somehow, in his own mind at least, he avoided confronting the moral
responsibility of his decision to name his friends as members of the Communist Party—even though he had initiated this odd encounter himself by publicly announcing his break. Certainly, of the moments of his life, this was not
his proudest and the convolutedness of it all signalled just how painful it must
have been. He had not been able to utter the three names himself at any point
in the proceedings, other than to confirm Nixon's question.[13]

As the testimony continued, it expanded to include Pressman's years as
an ideologically motivated, though not formally connected, CP adherent. The
Ware Group essentially had been a Marxist study circle, he claimed, with no
elements of espionage as had been implied by Chambers, for whom he
reserved special bitterness. To "my knowledge Mr. Chambers does not once
state that he attended the meetings and met me at any meeting of the group,"
Pressman asserted, unaware of the specifics Chambers had given in his FBI
statements. "There was always the inference he knew of us as a group, but not
that he met me at the meetings." So the Ware Group, in addition to reading the
Communist literature supplied by Harold Ware and J. Peters, was after all
"[j]ust a mutual admiration society?" scoffed an incredulous committee mem-

ber. "No attempt was made to carry it out in the activities in which you were engaged?" No, the labor lawyer insisted, at least on his part. So, "[y]ou had an iron curtain between your activities in the Department of Agriculture and the things you discussed in group meetings?" came the sarcastic congressional reply. Pressman rightly pointed out, "You are commenting. You are not asking a question." Nor, in recent years did he know the membership status of Abt, Witt, and Kramer, even though the pack of them had been called to testify before the HUAC only two years previously. "And you have not discussed or learned since then as to whether they were still members of the Communist Party?" Richard Nixon probed. "That is right. I have been most careful about not making such inquiries of any human being," his quarry answered.

Pressman's pursuers also wanted to know about CP-inspired activity during his CIO years. While he was CIO general counsel, he admitted, he had had "contacts" with Party officials Roy Hudson and Eugene Dennis. "They would discuss with me their viewpoints, their recommendations, and suggestions, with respect to organizational activities of the CIO while I was counsel for the CIO. I discussed those problems with these people. When they made recommendations or suggestions which I deemed to be of assistance or helpful to the CIO, I accepted them." However, "I state here [and] now, as categorically as I can, that at no time from 1936 until 1948 did I take instructions or directives from anyone, including these leaders of the Communist Party, which were contrary to the established policy of the CIO." Nixon then tried to trap him by implying that he had a key role in "shaping" the CIO resolution opposing foreign military entanglements during the period 1939–1940, a policy which at that time was not "established" as yet within the federation. The congressman from California alleged that Pressman controlled the terms of the debate, and the result was that "in at least two different annual conventions, the CIO did not deviate from the Communist Party line." Without missing a beat, Pressman returned, "Mr. Nixon, if I may say, without being in any way coy about it, I think at the same time substantially the entire leadership of the Republican Party was taking the same position" on foreign policy. Yes, but not for the same reasons, Nixon quickly shot back.

Additional testimony surrounded his relationship with Whittaker Chambers. In a number of FBI interviews, starting in 1945, the *Time* magazine editor made various assertions about Pressman's Party involvements. At various times, the committee's questions attempt to elicit information on a number of Chambers' private assertions. He claimed that he had met Pressman a number of times at the St. Matthew's Court apartment of Henry Collins, also a member of the Ware Group. He also stated that he had told Pressman to take the CIO position on his own responsibility after the Party's central committee advised against it; J. Peters told Chambers the central committee had not been certain that it could "control" Pressman's ambitious nature. Chambers, in addition, alleged how Pressman had initiated an effort to gain some type of military information from an unwitting Gardner Jackson, as well as how he developed a plan to shape Resettlement Administration policy in a pro-CP direction. After Pressman had left the Ware Group and returned to New York, Chambers claimed, the attorney had briefly become something of an assistant to him in his underground work. One assignation involved an approach to the soldier-of-fortune Colonel Dean Ivan Lamb—with whom Alger Hiss had had some contact as well, Chambers charged—in an effort to procure military-related information under direct order from Chambers' underground Soviet principal, Boris Bykov. Chambers informed the FBI about how Pressman had served an an intermediary with Lamb and brought him to a clandestine-like meeting off of Riverside Drive in New York sometime in 1936 or 1937. Nothing came of that meeting, since Chambers said he had become nervous and called it off shortly after seeing Lamb and Pressman arrive. Additionally, he also told the government—amplifying the statements he had made to Undersecretary of State Adolph Berle in 1939, that not long after he had defected from the CP he had introduced Pressman to a Soviet dentist, a Dr. Philip Rosenbliett. The latter was a "quiet, crafty, sorrowful man," Chambers later wrote, who operated an underground communist *yafka*, or "safe-house," in an office building on Broadway near 40th Street in New York. "No sound of drilling ever came from beyond his ground-glass doors," wrote Chambers in *Witness*. "Sometimes for half an hour there might be heard faintly the sound of voices within, rising and falling in Russian cadences." Between 1930 and 1935, the former underground Party emissary asserted, if someone had sat in Rosenbliett's waiting room, "He would have gained a startling and inclusive insight into the activities and personnel of the Soviet Military Intelligence in the United States. . . ." Chambers said that J. Peters later informed him that Rosenbliett had turned Pressman over to a Russian named Mark Moren, and together the two made a trip to Mexico to try to obtain airplanes for leftist forces to utilize in the Spanish Civil War. During the trip, Peters mentioned that some plane trouble had occurred near Brownsville, Texas, which forced an emergency landing. Finally, the HUAC also expressed interest in the nature of Pressman's involvement in the John L. Lewis–William Rhodes Davis Mexican oil deal shortly afterward, though in this Chambers had not had involvement.[14]

By now it was indisputable that most of the information in the FBI files had somehow found its way into the hands of the HUAC's interrogators. Pressman provided various answers to the questions. He denied meeting Chambers in any Washington context. He admitted he had made a trip to Mexico in September 1936 to serve as legal advisor in an attempt to procure planes for the Spanish loyalists. The lawyer noted that the airline manifest would name him as a passenger, but he stated that he made the trip with a client named J. Eckhart, a representative of the Spanish government, who paid him $3,000. He denied any meeting with Dean Ivan Lamb on Roosevelt Drive. But contrary to some of his previous statements, Pressman did not state that he had not met Chambers at all; he now said that he probably had met him sometime in 1936—not in connection with the Ware Group—but when a person he now recognized as being Chambers brought Eckhart to his office in New York City. Chambers, he testified, said that they had mutual friends and that Eckhart was a representative of the Spanish government seeking the services of an attorney for a trip to Mexico. Pressman said that he needed clients and the time and did not ask too many questions, but clearly the whole topic of Chambers angered him deeply. "If I speak heatedly, Mr. Nixon, it is not in connection with responding to your question," but because of the untruths Chambers had spoken regarding him. He sarcastically derided tie veracity of "a man of profound knowledge who could remember in detail occurrences of many years ago. . . ." Even worse, Pressman charged, was what former friends had done to him regarding the intriguing Lewis–Davis Mexican oil deal. A prominent journalist received a story from an individual (perhaps Gardner Jackson) "whose name I do not care to mention at this time [but] who is a drunken paranoiac [sic] who has on his mind Lee Pressman. The story alleged "that the Mexico trip was in relation to Lewis's interest in the Mexico oil deal, an event which had occurred several years after his 1936 trip. He told the committee he called the journalist and laid out the facts for him. The journalist scoffed at Pressman's explanation, claiming that if the lawyer had been there in 1936, at a time earlier than the oil deal, it must have been to lay the groundwork. "Go ahead and meet [the mind of] that kind of individual[,]" Pressman angrily challenged.

Did he recall discussing with Chambers at any other time his decision to go into the CIO, inquired Nixon? "Absolutely not." Did Chambers visit his Washington apartment? "He was never in my apartment in the City of Washington, and he couldn't tell the color of my furniture, either," Pressman asserted, deriding the kind of personal details that made Chambers a believable witness to some in the Hiss case. As to any other activities on behalf of the CP, Pressman remained guarded in his answers, and at times hostile. When Tavenner asked about his involvements with the International Juridical Association, which the committee counsel informed Pressman was cited as a front organization, the lawyer sharply responded, "I must confess, Mr. Counsel, that would not terribly impress me." "I must say you do not particularly impress this committee, either," an offended Chairman Wood shot back. Pressman protested that he was not referring to the membership of the current committee, but the committee as composed in 1944. "I think the last distinction made is typical of so many things you have done today," Congressman

Nixon pointed out, implying that Pressman was trying to have his cake and eat it too.

The HUAC's members consistently expressed many doubts about Pressman's forthrightness, leading the members to question the motivations underlying his break with the CP. Why had he not made his separation immediately known after the Korean hostilities erupted, the committee asked? Pressman explained his decision to part, thusly, "I, during the period of . . . at least a year, and possibly even longer . . . as some of my friends know," had "begun to consider" separating from the Party. The decision that he now took "stems from what I consider to be very profound convictions," not quickly arrived at. "It was not an easy decision to make," he said with chagrin. Korea had been a precipitating factor, in combination "with other problems that had been developing in my mind in connection with my relationship to the Communist Party and its viewpoint. . . ." Pressman believed that the "Soviet Union, after the United Nations had acted, was obligated to take measures, which apparently it had not, to bring about cessation of hostilities." At that point, "I became firmly convinced" that he had to leave the party. "[P]erhaps I was late, later than others; perhaps I made more mistakes than others; if so, that can only be laid at the doorstep of my bad judgment or the fact [that] I am not as acute as I am supposed to be," he explained. But now, he said, "I wanted to make my decision publicly known." "I made it public so that everybody could know exactly where I stand." He hoped, he told his inquirers, that they would be, like he himself was, "more interested in what my viewpoint . . . will be in the future than what it has been in the past." However, without making a full disclosure of all that he knew and of all the individuals he had good reason to believe had been Party adherents, the committee had very little interest in the Lee Pressman of the future. The Lee Pressman of the past was their focus.

As with the committee members, the pundits had not been convinced by the particulars of Pressman's testimony. The stridently anti-Communist socialist publication, *New Leader*, entitled its synopsis of Pressman's testimony: "Lee Pressman Lies," for example. Article author Dick Reynard claimed that Pressman had tried to peddle an "exclusive" on his break to four separate reporters prior to his testimony. The unwarranted conclusion Reynard drew was that Pressman intended that the public would approvingly look upon him as having a "high sense of political morality [that] would prevent his disclosing what he knew about the American and international Communist apparatus. Here, indeed, the public would say, was a man of principle." Reynard went on to skewer Pressman mercilessly. He claimed, without providing proof, that the CIO general counsel had directly lied to both Lewis and Murray about his Party adherence, and that "Mr. Pressman, frequently with tears in his eyes, energetically denied this each time," affirming to his principals that his advice was always "intellectually independent." "This piece has been rough on Mr. Pressman ," Reynard wrote, "but no rougher than he was on thousands of others, when he was riding high in [the] CIO—for Mr. Pressman was a tough, disciplined, Party liner."

Syndicated columnists Victory Lasky and Victor Riesel also expressed deep doubts about Pressman's intentions, the former speculatively claiming that the man known as "Comrade Big" around Party headquarters might be plumping for a return to the newly, Communist-cleansed CIO. Elsewhere, a *Time* magazine writer editorialized similarly. "Last week, Pressman decided to reverse his [political] field. Apparently on the grounds," the author wrote tongue in cheek, "that confession might be good for a goal. . . ." More balanced was Murray Kempton's opinion, written in his regular column shortly after the testimony: "Pressman hoped that his testimony would clear up a lot of myths about him. But how many people are going to believe that his odd story is complete?" "When it is over, most of us will go on thinking that Pressman sits in a kind of half-way house between silence and complete frankness. . . ." Indeed, if anyone received favorable press it was Richard Nixon. At least one paper credited the congressman from California with convincing the committee to subpoena Pressman after his announcement. It was Nixon who, while not prying out incriminating evidence, once again looked the virile, patriotic Communist-hunter that the times seemed to favor. Thus, if Pressman's intent was to destroy Nixon's political career and the HUAC's credibility, his scheme had failed badly.[15]

DEVELOPMENT OF THE FBI PERJURY CASE

Not surprisingly, the FBI had the same general opinion. "It was apparent through the hearing," reported the agent assigned to observe the attorney's testimony, "that when the opportunity afforded itself, Pressman would attack the veracity of Whittaker Chambers." While "Pressman indicated willingness to respond to questions," the bureau observer concluded, in the main "he was not frank and willing to answer questions. His statement was in essence . . . narrow, [and] self-serving . . . and in answer to questions, he was argumentative and his replies susceptible to more than one interpretation. Only in response to penetrating questions, principally by Congressman Nixon, did he make specific replies, although he constantly indicated that he was glad that certain questions were asked and he wished to respond to them."[16]

What the labor attorney did next made matters even worse. The day following his HUAC appearance, the New York FBI office received a call from Pressman, who now "suggested that he would like to get together with the FBI for an interview. He said he had a few questions that he would like to ask also," Agent C. E. Hennrich informed his superiors. At first, the FBI adopted the stance that it would call Pressman back, invite him to come down to its New York office "to furnish any information he desires to furnish." Interviewing agents were not to answer his questions. Moreover, the agents, in their asking questions, "should be careful that such questions do not disclose [investigatory] information to Pressman." Washington's FBI headquarters wished the agents to keep it apprised of any developments.[17]

The potential of Pressman as a rich, mineload of information on domestic communism proved all too attractive, though. Hoover's Washington lieutenants somehow neglected to convey the director's explicit orders that Pressman—since he had seen fit not to talk to the FBI immediately prior to his HUAC appearance—was not to be interviewed unless he himself came to offer information at the offices of the FBI. He did not want it to appear that the FBI was "chasing" Pressman. Thus, unaware of this restriction, local field agents returned the lawyer's call, and when the attorney informed them that he could not come to their offices, "but would like to be interviewed at his office," if possible, they agreed to the location. On the first day of the interview, August 30, 1950, it seemed as though "Pressman appeared to want to cooperate" and did not attempt to be holding back. The attorney told them that he differentiated between a legal forum and a private statement, and thus "where before the legal forum "he had held himself to facts strictly within his personal knowledge . . ." He also "indicated that he would not so restrict himself insofar as his interview with the Agents was concerned." As to Pressman's questions for the FBI, before they began, he queried the agents about why his refusal to speak with the Bureau immediately prior to his 1950 HUAC testimony had become public so quickly, wondering if there had been a leak of information. Implicitly, Pressman seemed to be asking, what did that portend for the information he might provide in this interview and what kind of guarantee would the Bureau make regarding its confidentiality? Further, he said, while in congressional hearings, court, and grand jury proceedings he could not and would not only testify to anything outside of his direct factual knowledge. On the other hand, he "related that he also had information that was based on supposition, innuendo, surmise and hearsay that he would be willing to tell to the agents[,] but that" he would never utter under oath "because of the fact that he had no personal knowledge of these matters." "Pressman [then] asked what answer he should give in the event he was called before the Grand Jury or the House Committee and questioned as to what he had told the FBI, particularly with respect to information that he had obtained through hearsay." The lawyer seemed to be probing as to what level of protection might be available for him to avoid divulging information of this type in a public forum. The agents told him that he would have to exercise his own judgment on that point. This noncommittal answer seemed to trouble Pressman. At the conclusion of the first day of the interview, he again inquired about whether "the agents had received any further instructions as to what answer he might make to the above question . . ." He "was advised that we could, of course, make no suggestions to him in regard to this matter. He then related that by this time his questions had become 'academic.'"[18]

Pressman went over his early biographical chronology and resume. With these vital statistics taken care of, he moved quickly again to distance himself from Alger Hiss. The "subject claimed that they were not on close terms and that Hiss moved on a different social plane than he did, Hiss being close to Felix Frankfurter. . . ." "The subject made the observation that during his college days both at Cornell and Harvard Law School, he was strictly 'apolitical.'" As proof, he claimed that Communist-hunting journalists Ralph De Toledano and Victory Lasky, collaborating on their book *Seeds of Treason*, tried to dig up dirt on him at both Cornell and Harvard and came up empty-handed.[19]

Pressman then moved to his Ware Group years, downplaying his political sophistication, calling himself a "dumb yokel" and "young and impressionable" in trying to explain how he had succumbed to Harold Ware's invitation to join the CP cell in the AAA. He guessed that Nat Witt and/or Charles Kramer might have suggested him as a likely recruit to the CP organizer. At his first group meeting, he knew Witt and Kramer were there, but he was not sure about John Abt. "The subject stated that his group was a very small group. . . ." They would meet at each other's homes and would discuss such "high-falutin" problems as the policies of the AAA as it related to Communist analysis. Ware would sometimes "ask if in connection with their employment with the AAA[,] there was anything of importance that would be of value to the Communist Party," insisting "that there must be something of importance that was not being disclosed to the public. The subject made the observation that he got the impression that his might be the beginning of the utilization of groups by the Communist Party" in a surreptitious manner, and if so, it was "his impression that it was run in a 'fumbling'" fashion, the FBI's summary report recounted.

While Pressman had told the HUAC that he only knew Chambers from the visit to his office with J. Eckhart in 1936, Pressman now qualified his earlier assertion. "He now had a hazy recollection that somebody showed up with" Ware's replacement J. Peters "at one of these meetings, and it might have been Chambers. He characterized him as a 'nondescript' individual and claimed that he never saw this person at any subsequent meetings." The crushing workload of the AAA and Jerome Frank's constant reliance on him for all sorts of tasks, combined with the time demands of the Ware Group, finally "began to physically exhaust" him and he "lost interest" in both the cell and the AAA. He wanted to return to law practice in New York City. "At one of these cell meetings," the lawyer informed the FBI agents, "he told the members of his problems and of his desire to return to New York." Pressman said this discussion concluded "in a bitter fight." The other members tried to persuade him to remain in Washington and to continue his work with the Party, but "the subject was adamant" that he would leave.

Moreover, while he was in the Ware Group, he insisted that Alger Hiss had not been in it, as Chambers had claimed. Pressman did admit, though, "that if Hiss were guilty and was a member of the Ware Group, it could have been that he was pulled out of it before he, the subject, became a member of said group." Pressman also denied that either Victor Perlo or Henry Collins had been original Ware Group members and denied knowing what his other colleagues had done in the Party after he left to practice law in New York. He "has had no discussion concerning the groups with Abt, Witt, or Kramer," the Bureau investigative file summarized, "subsequent to his leaving the group. He claimed that after he left, he made a deliberate point of not talking about it at all."

Pressman repeated his version of his trip to Mexico with Joseph Eckhart, brought to him at the Liebman firm by, he now believed, Whittaker Chambers. Shortly after he arrived, "two men presented themselves at his office, one was Whittaker Chambers," the other Eckhart. He now recognized Chambers after seeing press photos. "At this point he stated that although he is not certain, he is quite sure that the person who came with Eckhart was identical with the individual he characterized as being a 'nondescript' individual who appeared with J. Peters at one of the Harold Ware Group cell meetings." Eckhart stated that he needed the services of an attorney to purchase materials in Mexico for Republican Spain. The labor attorney described the flights and connections to Mexico, noting the airline had their names on file. He denied ever crashing, as in the Chambers' version, or ever going to Mexico with a Mark Moren or a Mark Phillipovitch, as Chambers had originally told Undersecretary of State Berle in 1939. Nor had he, Pressman, ever used the alias "Cole Phillips," as the cryptic notes that Berle had taken during the Chambers meeting seemed to imply. Pressman noted that he paid a courtesy call at the U.S. embassy while awaiting the Mexican government's answer regarding the possible purchase of airplanes. Due to political problems, he and Eckhart were informed that such a sale could not be consummated and they returned, with Eckhart later paying him $3,000 for his services, funds that he deposited in his law firm's general account. He denied any other trips abroad except for his post-war visit to Europe and Russia as part of the official CIO delegation. Pressman also vehemently denied the press reports, fueled by the vituperation of Gardner Jackson, he surmised, that he had been John L. Lewis's emissary on the Mexican oil deal.

Pressman also said that he did not know any Philip Rosenbliett or Dean

Ivan Lamb, as claimed by Chambers, nor had Chambers ever been in his Washington apartment near the zoo[,] or had anything to do with his decision to become general counsel for the CIO. Here, however, he was very careful in his response. The agents asked him what his brother was doing at the time— Chambers had told the FBI that Pressman had complained of the financial strain he had helping his brother Irving through law school during this meeting in the apartment. The lawyer informed them that his younger brother had been attending Yale Law School. An additional question to test Chambers' veracity followed: What kind of furniture did he have at the time? In his statements to the FBI, Chambers had recalled that it had been modernistic. Pressman sidestepped the question. His "answer was that it had slip covers on it and at that time there was not too much furniture."

Pressman then followed with comments about the CP and his career in the CIO. He agreed that Lewis had tacitly accepted CP organizers in the early days because they were the best. Nevertheless, he stated, Lewis, and later, Murray, were reluctant to pry for direct knowledge of his political convictions. It was clear from the first that the Communists "did not dominate them but that the leaders [of the CIO] tolerated them." "While there never was an actual conversation [with Pressman] by Lewis or Murray, it was sort of assumed the subject had contacts either directly or indirectly with Communist Party officials," the agents reported. Therefore, "it was recognized that the subject could talk more freely with the union leaders who were considered 'red' than could Lewis or Murray. The subject's function," according to the former CIO general counsel, "was to tell them to stop disrupting and go along with Lewis and Murray and to continue a united front." This worked, but only until the pact period of 1939 and 1941 and the Lewis–Murray split.

Now, things turned "topsy-turvy." Even then, "with one sweep Murray or Lewis could have driven the Communists out of the CIO." Now, however, the ideological positioning reflected the daily peregrinations of the new industrial federation's top two leaders. In one of the executive board meetings at the November 1939 CIO Convention in San Francisco, Pressman said Lewis informed his brethren that he would not support FDR again. "This was a shock to Murray, who pleaded with Lewis . . . and as a result, Lewis extracted from Murray as a condition of support for Roosevelt that an antiwar resolution be introduced at the convention. In turn, Murray extracted a promise at this meeting . . . that a resolution would be introduced condemning the Communists." Hitler's attack on Russia, of course, changed all that. Pressman insisted that he had always remained independent during that time and throughout his years in the CIO, even though he had met secretly with top Party officials on CIO matters. "He stated that he felt 'beholden' to no one pertaining to his positions with the CIO. This position to his thinking was a break for the Communist Party, and" its officials were only too "glad to talk to him because of the importance of this position."

What he now told the agents, Pressman said, "he was well aware," was "almost perjury to tell the truth" in that it differed materially from what he had told the HUAC. At first, Roy Hudson, Eugene Dennis, and later Jack Stachel "were very solicitous toward him, treated him very graciously and were not too demanding. However, they did tell him of Communist Party policies in connection with the various labor unions that were dominated by the Communists[,] and attempted in a way to have him shape the general policy of the CIO in line with the policies of the Communist Party as they referred to labor unions." This had been no problem, since the policies for much of these years were congruent. Pressman summarized his role as one where

> . . . he actually was the one individual in the CIO to whom the Communist Party brought their [sic] labor . . . problems and policies. In turn, he was the one who attempted to soften up this policy with the Communists, when these policies were in direct conflict with the general policies of Murray and the CIO. He again was the one person who brought these problems to Murray and thrashed them out in an effort to more or less keep the Communists in line, and do whatever they could policy-wise to effect a strong CIO.

During all of these years, from 1938 to 1948, although a Communist philosophically, his contacts were individual because of his importance. "He stated that for this reason he could not furnish the names of other known Communists because he just did not attend closed meetings with such individuals. He also claimed that Hudson, Dennis, and Stachel never indicated to him the names of any Communists, and that they were very careful in this regard."

At the war's end, from 1946 to 1948, Pressman carried on in the CIO, but it became clear to him that the "honeymoon" was over. The CP began to make strident demands on him, demands that he could not find a way to reconcile. The "Communists did make recommendations which were absolutely contrary to the policies of Murray. . . . It was at this time that the subject felt he was making his first break from his ideological ties with the Communist Party[,] because he could clearly see that the policies of the Communist Party were actually to destroy the CIO." Moreover, he became aware of the gossip mill surrounding the alleged testimony of a "Whittaker Chambers[,]" talk about a CP cell in the AAA—an individual's name of which he had no recognition because it certainly had not been used during his Ware days. Nevertheless, he well knew to what the rumor referred. He "stated in retrospection that if the FBI had come to him at that time and asked him to tell them his story, he believes he would have cooperated." Then why did he not come to the agency? Pressman "just passed over this without making any comment."

Because of the irreconcilable internal tensions, he sought a way to get out of the CIO. He did so by his affiliation with the Wallace campaign and by taking up law practice at the invitation of his friend Nat Witt. The Progressive Party campaign consumed most of his subsequent time, first in his capacity as platform secretary and then in his own congressional ALP candidacy. A delegation from the Party's Brooklyn headquarters, "headed by Lester Zirin, came to [the] subject's office and asked him to run . . ." in the 14th District, where he had been raised. He claimed he was reluctant, "but they insisted and indicated that he probably would be successful in being elected and this appealed to his ego." The result was a second step toward ideological separation from the CP; Party functionaries in charge of his ALP campaign repeatedly "wanted him to come out in opposition to Philip Murray" and Murray's policies for labor. As "time went on, it became clear to him that they were just using him" to get to the CIO president. "He stated he refused to criticize the CIO and also refused to criticize Murray."

In the midst of this campaign came the eruption of the Hiss–Chambers case and his naming by the journalist, along with Abt, Witt, and Kramer, as Ware Group members. Immediately, he alleged to the agents, the named parties "had a long conference in connection with their anticipated testimony, and [the] subject related that he himself was in favor of telling his entire story, that is, his connection with the Ware Group in 1934–35. Witt and Abt, however, were strongly opposed to any admissions of his part and pointed out" to him, without specificity, "that because of things that had happened after" Pressman left to return to New York, "Witt and Abt would be unable to tell the entire story. They pointed out that if he told his story, then they might be involved in a great deal of trouble if they refused to answer." Pressman seemed to be indicating that Abt and Witt had knowledge of other CP activities that could put them in considerable personal jeopardy. Because court decisions on the use of the Fifth Amendment mandated that they could not invoke their rights selectively, they could not testify about the Ware Group years. Once again, Pressman claimed, this "discussion ended in a lengthy argument, but in the end Witt and Abt won out and subject agreed to go along with them and stand on their constitutional privilege. . . ." He then continued to follow the same tactics in his New York grand jury appearance and his previous FBI interview. Finally, Pressman recounted his associations with the Soviets and their satellites. He told the FBI about how he came to strike up his brief relationship with Yuri Novikov, his fears concerning his activities in handling estate work in that regard, and his legal work in the Gubitchev–Coplon case. That work consisted mainly of a legal memoranda he wrote for his boyhood friend, Abraham Pomerantz, who defended Gubitchev. Thus, the interview had come to a close.

By the time they concluded the two-day visit with Lee Pressman, the

FBI agents and their supervisor believed that Pressman had withheld much. The New York office readied a synopsis of the interview notes and reviewed the new information they now had in relation to Pressman's earlier FBI statement and his HUAC testimony. Mainly, the Bureau analyst wrote, "for the purpose of setting out inaccuracies and to get a picture of the extent of Pressman's alleged cooperation." Significantly, statements where Pressman could be proved false, or "wherein he has failed to furnish information known to be in his possession," promised to be especially valuable. "Inasmuch as Pressman is now in a position to say he had furnished information to the FBI," the New York office recommended[,] "that upon completion" of the analysis "that we again contact Pressman and subject him to a very vigorous interrogation, covering all phases of his activities with the express purpose of forcing him to cooperate completely or placing him in the position that he would not cooperate." The FBI director had some reservations about the latter tactic. "I doubt the wisdom of this," Hoover wrote on the memorandum. "However we can finally decide after the analysis is completed."[20]

It was soon to become clear exactly why Hoover and the FBI were so concerned about Pressman. Hoover, at least, believed that the lawyer had a Machiavellian purpose beyond self-preservation. The FBI director wrote in one internal memo that he thought "Pressman was a phony, that his conversion was not sincere, and I felt it was largely an act that might be put on in order to help Hiss on the appeal case." The interviewing agents noted Pressman's distinct reluctance to draw in other individuals—Abt, Witt, and Kramer remained the only individuals he named, and even with them he said he knew little about their activities after the Ware years. Pressman's reluctance to be specific about his former comrades' activities seemed to be a "litmus test" of credibility. One Bureau memo reported that "at the time he made his break, after he had received the subpoena to appear before Congress, he had a very serious doubt in his mind as to whether he should 'name names[,]' or refuse to do so." He continued to maintain these doubts even up to the moment the committee swore him in. That he would not speak about what he undoubtedly knew in terms of specific details argued against his recantation being a true ideological break, the FBI analysts surmised.

Possibly, a later report speculated, Pressman may have had multiple motives. He had had trouble finding paying clients; perhaps a clean breast would restore business. Possibly, he may have thought that by testifying he could get back into the labor movement and the CIO. Finally, government analysts speculated that his HUAC foray might be an effort to aid the Hiss appeal, although the interviewing agents believed "the subject did not feel any great sympathy toward" Hiss. But it was when talking about Louis Budenz and Whittaker Chambers that his hostility surfaced most quickly; he "referred" to them "in the most disparaging manner" and located the source of his troubles in their public pronouncements, the FBI interviewers noted. The investigative summary concluded with two observations. If the genesis of Pressman's recent public actions had been self-serving or manipulative, it would be unlikely that more information would be forthcoming from the attorney. It "is possible . . . that he has made a clean ideological break but like some of the other Communists who have defected[,] . . . has not reached the point where he is willing to involve not only himself, but all the other people as deeply as they could be involved." The latter scenario might prove especially fruitful at some point. "If the latter is true, the possibility exists that at some future time Pressman may find himself in the frame of mind to reveal his entire story."[21]

The entire circumstances surrounding Pressman's HUAC testimony and his FBI interview deeply bothered J. Edgar Hoover, who had been closely following developments and issuing what he thought were explicit instructions to his supervising agents. "I am astounded at this," he angrily wrote in one memo. He had given "specific instructions that Pressman *was not* to be interviewed at *his* office," and those instructions had been ignored, he continued. He then called the responsible officials on the carpet, "expressing my extreme displeasure" at the way the investigation had developed, and that "it was absolutely outrageous that his instructions had not been followed. . . ." "I stated I felt Pressman was a phony," wrote the FBI director, "that his conversion was not sincere. . . . He had gone down to HUAC; he could come down to the FBI offices, rather than doing the interview in his office, where "no doubt he had dictaphones and everything else in it. I stated we had prestige to maintain and I did not see any reason we should be chasing the Communists around like that, particularly when they are basically uncooperative."[22]

Hoover, however, was not willing to wait around until Lee Pressman deigned to divulge information to the FBI—on his terms—once more. He at once ordered that Pressman's HUAC testimony be taken to Maryland for review by Whittaker Chambers. There the latter could "point out what he believes to be discrepancies . . . as well as . . . the nature of the information which he feels Pressman withheld." Hoover also launched his agents on a full-scale investigation of "the possibility of developing a perjury case on Pressman." "This matter," Hoover wrote, "should be given thorough and expeditious attention." "This is to remind you that [the] captioned matter is regarded at the Bureau as a very important investigation. . . . Therefore, I must insist that this investigation be given the immediate and full-time attention which it deserves," the director instructed.[23]

The first line of inquiry focused on the observations of Whittaker Chambers and Richard Nixon. Agents first informally interviewed Chambers regarding Pressman's HUAC testimony almost immediately at its conclusion in August 1950. "Chambers is of the opinion that Pressman's [sic] defection is probably insincere and probably part of a plot to, in some way, aid the appeal of Alger Hiss," although he was unclear about how. One thing was certain, "he knows that" the lawyer's revelations regarding "his role in [the] CP and his knowledge of others is far from complete." Since Pressman did not name anyone other that Abt, Witt, and Kramer, "omitting Perlo, Alger Hiss, Donald Hiss, and [Henry] Collins[,]" he aroused the journalist's suspicions. So did his claim that he and Chambers only met once, at his law office, when Pressman asserted that Whittaker Chambers had brought Eckhart to him. Chambers "stated he and Pressman prior to 1938 met many times not only as members of groups but privately" the agents' telex to Hoover recounted. "Chambers is of the opinion Pressman perjured himself . . . since he could select numerous instances if he had an opportunity to review [the] complete testimony." "Chambers appears to feel that" if Pressman had been earnest in his renouncement, he "would have already have contacted Chambers personally as a comrade in defection."

Chambers also informed the FBI emissaries that Tom Murphy, U.S. attorney for the Southern District of New York, believed the confession contrived. Murphy would handle the Hiss appeal for the government and alerted Chambers that he may have to call him to testify sooner than expected because of the recent Pressman public relations flurry. Using the pretext that Pressman had now supplied previously unknown information, Murphy speculated, Hiss lawyers might utilize "Pressman as a witness to lay the foundation for [the] introduction of some possible new evidence fabricated by Hiss and his attorneys." "Chambers represents Murphy as being very concerned over the possible effect of the Pressman defection on the Hiss appeal."

Also, continued Chambers, Representative Richard Nixon "has visited Chambers since [the] Pressman defection. Nixon subpoenaed Pressman . . . on a quote hunch unquote and wanted" Chambers to reappear . . . immediately following Pressman." He hoped to orchestrate "a personal confrontation between Pressman and Chambers" in front of the committee, similar to what had been arranged in the Hiss–Chambers case in August 1948. "Chambers did not desire to do this for many reasons, particularly because the effect of such action by Chambers on the appeal was an unknown quantity, and finally [he] persuaded Nixon that such [an] appearance was inadvisable at this time." Chambers also told his Bureau interviewers that Nixon said he too originally thought Pressman's recantation was phony, "but now is apparently of the contrary opinion."[24]

Further interviews followed. On October 5, 1950, Agents Frank Johnstone and Joseph Trainor brought Pressman's HUAC testimony to Chambers and interviewed him after his review. On October 9, 1950, Chambers then provided a written statement. He reiterated once more for the FBI an itemization of his contacts and experiences with the labor lawyer, wherein he alleged that

Pressman had several deeper CP involvements with him other than those to which the labor attorney admitted. While in the Ware Group, Chambers claimed, Pressman developed several initiatives on his own hook, as previously mentioned. Again, it was Chambers who told Pressman to take the opportunity to become CIO general counsel at one of the Ware Group meetings, during a visit to the latter's apartment. After Pressman's return to New York in 1936, Chambers once again claimed that they renewed their contacts, had their joint meeting with Colonel Dean Ivan Lamb on Riverside Drive[,] and introduced Pressman to Dr. Philip Rosenbliett, which he thought led to the Mexican trip. He also added one new piece of information not heretofore given. "It is my recollection that I saw Pressman [personally] shortly after I introduced him to Rosenbliett. Pressman then told me that Rosenbliett had connected him with a 'Russian' whom Pressman was to assist. J. Peters later told me that Dr. Rosenbliett had turned Lee Pressman over to Mark Moren. . . ." Whittaker Chambers believed this meeting took place in 1937, and most likely that "Moren is the man who went to Mexico with Pressman under the name of J. Eckhart."[25]

Of his "direct knowledge" Chambers affirmed that he knew Pressman had not told his whole story. Pressman knew others had been in the Ware Group and knew that there had been "lower cells." In addition, Pressman had to have at least knowledge of the communism of Alger Hiss. He had to have "direct knowledge, which must be very great" of CP activities within the labor movement. Pressman's apparent desire to continue to shield many other associations that Chambers knew that he had had proved to him that the ideological defection was not complete. He may need clients, Chambers speculated, but Pressman was also "ambitious, self-centered and [an] opportunist. It may have seemed to him the political climate in the United States had changed against Communism to such a degree that is was now expedient for him to break with the Communist Party." Nothing he had yet said, or done, "suggests to me that he is not still a Marxist in his thinking and emotional loyalty." The result of the convergence of Pressman's HUAC testimony, his 1950 FBI interview, and Chambers' October 1950 response, left the FBI with the daunting job of investigation and case development if it wanted to secure a perjury indictment. Over the next three years, before the statute of limitations would run out on Lee Pressman's congressional statements of August 1950, J. Edgar Hoover and his agents set about the task of finding independent corroboration of what Chambers had told them.[26]

THE PRESSMAN FBI PERJURY INVESTIGATION

The first problem the FBI confronted was that the dates and traveling companion of Pressman's Mexican trip differed in the respective accounts.

Pressman said airline records would confirm that he had gone in the fall of 1936 with Joseph Eckhart; Chambers said the trip occurred in 1937, probably with a Mark Moren. In November 1950, agents returned to the Chambers farm at Westminster, Maryland, and tried to reconcile the difference. Recalling contextual events, Chambers still insisted that he had not introduced Pressman to Rosenbliett until 1937. Perhaps, he thought now, the Rosenbliett meeting and the trip with Eckhart had blurred in his mind. He was sure he came to know of Pressman's trip to Mexico after the Rosenbliett–Pressman introduction. Chambers knew that Rosenbliett stayed in the United States until 1937. He recalled J. Peters telling him that Rosenbliett had turned Pressman over to a Soviet agent, Mark Moren, "and at the same time told him a story concerning Moren and Pressman making a trip by plane to Mexico, during which trip they were forced down near the Border." He suggested that they contact the Hotel Albert Chambers, where the journalist said he knew Rosenbliett resided for a period in 1937, after he returned to the United States from a Russian visit.[27]

In an attempt to corroborate Whittaker Chambers' memory, FBI agents checked the 1936 and 1937 editions of the *Brownsville Herald* and found no record or photos of any plane crash or near crash happening near Brownsville, Texas, at least not any that had found its way into the newspaper. They did discover, however, that Pan American traveled that route regularly, the airline that Pressman told the HUAC that he and Eckhart used. The FBI found that Eckhart had been issued permits to reenter the United States at the Brownsville Municipal Airport on September 21, September 28, and October 2, 1936, via Pan American. The manifest showed Pressman's name as a passenger on the September 21 flight. The Civil Aeronautics Board air safety records of the plane inspections for the Pan American flights from Mexico, on which Eckhart had traveled, did not reveal any accident on two of the planes involved in the three flights. One of the planes on which Eckhart had flown, however, indicated "one accident," occurring at Tapachula, Mexico, on October 19, 1936, in which it had been damaged on takeoff, but had been repaired on the field prior to its flight to Brownsville. Passengers had been on board but not named. It is clear that Eckhart himself had flown back and forth to Mexico repeatedly, and that there had been an accident to one of the planes on which *he* had most likely been on. However, only one time, on September 21, 1936, did Pressman's name appear in conjunction with Eckhart's as a passenger. This was exactly what Pressman testified had been his involvement. Also, FBI agents soon concluded that Eckhart and Moren were two different people by tracking Eckhart's and Rosenbliett's Immigration and Naturalization Service (INS) records.[28]

The FBI field investigation, though, did produce a connection between Dr. Philip Rosenbliett and Eckhart, suggesting the possibility that Rosenbliett introduced Pressman to Eckhart and not Whittaker Chambers. On one of his applications for reentry into the United States in December 1935, Eckhart indicated that "the person to whom he was destined at the time of his last entry was [a] 'Philip Rosenblatt'" of 93 West 119th Street in New York City. INS files also reflected medical references related to Eckhart from the 1920s, which "indicated Eckhart had resided at 93 West 119th Street, New York City." Further investigation produced one other tie between Pressman and Eckhart, implying a continuing connection longer than one trip to Mexico. U.S. passport records reflected that on October 5, 1936, Senator Robert Wagner of New York "wrote the State Department requesting that a letter of introduction be prepared for Joseph W. Eckhart of New York to the diplomatic and consulator officers abroad. This letter was to be forwarded to Lee Pressman, counsel for the Resettlement Administration. . . . It was stated that Pressman would see Eckhart before he sailed and would give this letter to Eckhart personally." This meeting, if it was held, occurred after the trip to Mexico. Was this event an example of Pressman once again simply acting as Eckhart's attorney, paralleling the time in which he claimed that Eckhart wanted him to set up a corporation? Or was there a lengthier, more extensive relationship between the two, if there were no other trips to Mexico?[29]

Further investigation indicated two other intriguing facts. Corporate formation records revealed that a certificate of incorporation was filed in New York on December 14, 1936, establishing a company, "which purchased and shipped twenty million dollars worth of material to the Spanish Loyalists." Pressman's name did not appear on any documents as attorney of record but contextually this corroborated that Eckhart was indeed involved in a continuing effort to get war materiel shipped abroad. Furthermore, a new FBI informant, apparently a former CP member, identified Eckhart by photo and claimed he was a Soviet espionage agent with whom he had contact a half-dozen times in 1937. "This informant can further testify that Eckhart told him he was working for the Comintern and was principally engaged in matters of an industrial nature," the investigating FBI agent wrote. "In addition, Eckhart claimed [to this informant] to have established a close personal contact with John L. Lewis, head of the United Mine Workers, and that he had been instrumental in bringing together John L. Lewis and William Rhodes Davis" in the Mexican oil deal. This informant advised that the last time he saw Eckhart he was headed for China, "where he [told the informant he] would adopt a new name and assume a new character."[30]

Finally, the FBI approached the "Red Spy Queen"—Elizabeth Bentley—who added one more tie between Pressman and Eckhart beyond late 1936. In one of her previous statements to the FBI, she told of how CP comrades had introduced her to Eckhart in the late 1930s. Connecticut FBI agents visited her summer home in Clinton, Connecticut, in August 1951 as she was finishing her memoirs. The agents asked her if in the process of completing her book she had unearthed any memories related to Pressman other than what she had already informed the Bureau about previously. Bentley therefore went over the events with them once more. In the fall of 1936, she met Eckhart, who needed a secretary, through a CP friend, and the subtext of her statement alluded to some romantic attraction between them as well as political affinities. After lapses in their contact of some length, they renewed their relationship and Eckhart admitted to her—since he had become convinced that she obviously was a Communist as well—that he was a Soviet agent. In either February or March 1937, he called her again, "at which time they" once again began seeing each other until at least January 1938, meeting at episodic intervals. He told her that he was in the country to purchase U.S. planes for shipment to Spain via Mexico. At one point, when she was living in Greenwich Village, he even tried to enlist her services in furtherance of his mission, and she let him use her apartment for meetings in her absence.

The connection with Pressman was oblique, though. She had never met the lawyer, Bentley told the FBI. But "she remembers specifically one occasion, which occurred somewhere in between early 1937 to January 1938, when "in her presence" Eckhart made a phone call. "At the conclusion of the call, Eckhart informed her that he had just talked to Lee Pressman, who was his attorney." Eckhart said that Pressman was "one of ours" and "that he handled all of 'their' legal business and that he was their right-hand man and very trustworthy." Her "definite impression" was that the fledgling labor lawyer "handled a lot of business for the Communists. . . ." Later, her Soviet principal, Jacob Golos, informed Bentley that Eckhart "was an NKVD agent," a military intelligence specialist assigned to obtain planes for the Spanish Civil War. The agents exhibited to Bentley a photograph of a person whom they believed to be Mark Moren. She stated that the photo was not of the man she knew as Joseph Eckhart, whose photo she had previously identified for the FBI. Thus, by implication, if Bentley were to be believed, there may well have been continuing contacts between Pressman and Eckhart into 1937. As to the other events, however, they were largely as testified to by Pressman. To the best of anyone's knowledge, he had only gone to Mexico with Eckhart once, to do what he had testified he was engaged to do, a legal activity at the time. In the politically charged atmosphere of the early McCarthy Era, though, it seemed unlikely that politicians viewed these interconnections from a detached, or even a rational, perspective, even if Eckhart had not been a likely Soviet agent. That Pressman would downplay this association seems understandable, given the context and the personal danger to him and his family.[31]

Despite the intriguing suggestion by the FBI informant who knew Eckhart in another context, the effort to entangle Pressman in the questionable maneuverings surrounding the alleged Lewis–Davis–Toledano Mexican oil expropriation deal similarly proved barren. Pressman always vehemently denied his personal involvement—before the HUAC and in other forums. It was Lewis's show, for the most part, he claimed, whatever the labor chieftain's reasons, and whatever it was that he did. A number of press reports during the Soviet–Nazi pact years of 1939 to 1941 alleged that Lewis had been instrumental in influencing Mexican labor leaders to prevail upon Mexican President Ernesto Cardenas to sell nationalized U.S. and British oil supplies to Germany in the immediate pre-war period. Lewis, ostensibly after having met international businessman William Rhodes Davis on a cruise, struck up a relationship. He thereafter developed an interest in assisting Davis in efforts to convince the Mexican government to sell the oil to a recently rearmed and war-girding Germany. Pressman enemies Gardner Jackson and Tony Smith believed that the labor counselor had been able to persuade Lewis to undertake the scheme, arguing that it furthered Lewis's interest in maintaining U.S. neutrality. Also, they alleged it was consistent with Pressman's interest in promoting Soviet foreign policy aims, which at this point focused on attempting to head off a conflagration between Hitler and Stalin. As such, to the FBI, it seemed a possible way to prove Pressman's activities on behalf of Communist interests, domestic and foreign. Journalist Ken Crawford had published a number of these allegations in a December 13, 1940, article in the newspaper *PM*. Crawford, reputedly drawing on a number of sources, including Gardner Jackson, wrote that Pressman had made a number of trips to Mexico as Lewis's emissary in the deal. Crawford also supposedly cited "detailed proof" that Pressman had gone to the Mexican border with two Russian military officials to settle claims against . . . the shipping company" the lawyer had helped set up to ship arms to Republican Spain. The claimed source of those reports, and the person who allegedly had a "file" on the deal, the FBI discovered, revealed that many of these stories emanated from a prominent group of newspaper writers active in the anticommunist caucus of the New York chapter of the American Newspaper Guild. This group possibly included none other than Whittaker Chambers. After further investigation, an FBI agent judged that "Pressman may have been the victim of inaccurate or malicious journalism, inasmuch as none of the allegations . . . have been substantiated to any reasonable degree. . . ." and could serve as no basis for a perjury charge.[32]

Nor did Pressman's claim in his HUAC testimony that he had not met the soldier-of-fortune Colonel Dean Ivan Lamb on Riverside Drive in New York during the 1930s produce a potential perjurious statement. The FBI was able to confirm Chambers' story, at least in part. It located Lamb in April 1949. Lamb, recently released from a U.S. military hospital, was "still in a rather delicate condition" and "extremely nervous[,] voluble" and difficult to keep focused. He "identified Whittaker Chambers as an individual he met in a clandestine meeting either in Riverside Park or Columbia [University,] possibly at the direction of Alger Hiss," the Bureau reported. Lamb said that Hiss had asked him to contact munitions companies for information when Hiss was counsel to the Nye Munitions committee during the 1930s, but to keep their contacts secret. When he innocently sent Hiss a Christmas card, the latter abruptly broke off their relationship. The FBI brought Lamb and Chambers together at its New York office. "When Colonel Lamb walked into [the] conference room he walked up to Chambers and identified him as the individual he had the meeting with" on Riverside Drive, around 1936. The two then discussed their recollections, but despite probes from agents, Lamb had no memory of meeting someone named Lee Pressman. He did confirm the location of the meeting that Chambers had recalled as being off of Riverside Drive near 125th Street in Manhattan. At first, Lamb said the meeting occurred in 1934, and he was not sure whether a third individual had accompanied him to this meeting with Chambers. Eventually, after some efforts by the FBI to stimulate his "recollections," Lamb "readily identified Pressman from a news photo" in the *New York Times* "as being the individual he met in Riverside Park sometime about the end of 1936 or 1937. . . ."[33]

Although Chambers could testify that such a meeting had taken place, and Lamb corroborated this as a potential grand jury witness, a legal review of the questions actually asked of Pressman by committee counsel presented difficulties. It "appears that the House Committee's interrogation of Pressman did not go into the details of Pressman's reported clandestine meeting with Lamb sufficiently to incriminate Pressman by his denial," an analysis from the Director's office concluded. "Lamb claims he was not told of the identity of the individual he was to meet, and if such was the case[,] Pressman also may not have been informed as to the identity of the individual he was to meet on Riverside Drive." In fact, Chambers had told the Bureau that, "'I do not think that Pressman used his own name in this matter.'" Thus, Pressman's specific denials about meeting a "Dean Ivan Lamb" may well legally preclude any perjury charge.[34]

Consequently, as the FBI investigation progressed, the eventuality of bringing forth a successful perjury indictment against Pressman narrowed to his statements regarding his Ware Group associations—especially his identification of only four members. Chambers had testified and told the FBI of many more active participants besides Abt, Witt, and Kramer. Therefore, the FBI had one witness. To sustain a charge of perjury legally the government needed corroborating evidence. Clearly, Abt, Witt, and Kramer would not divulge anything; neither would Alger or Donald Hiss. Nor, it seemed, would Henry Collins, Victor Perlo, or Nathan Gregory Silvermaster—the latter two under intensive investigation themselves for possible wartime espionage—or some of the others who had hitherto proved uncooperative.

Nevertheless, there had been several other original members, the FBI eventually learned, some not directly mentioned by Chambers. In November 1950, Nathaniel Weyl, a former employee of the AAA, claimed in a statement to the FBI that he had been an early participant in the establishment of the Ware Group. In a detailed statement, he outlined his youthful conversion first to socialism and then to communism at Columbia University in New York, where he had also known two other alleged Ware Group founders, Victor Perlo and John Donovan. Weyl migrated to Washington in the early 1930s and found employment in the Department of Agriculture. Harold Ware approached him shortly after his arrival in June 1933 and invited him to join the fledgling CP group. At the point when he joined, Weyl informed the FBI, that the group, in addition to Ware, included, "Lee Pressman, Alger Hiss, John Abt, Nathan Witt, Henry Collins, John Donovan, and Victor Perlo." He remembered Charles Kramer joining a bit later.[35]

Over the term of his association, through the middle of the summer of 1934, he attended "fifteen or twenty" meetings in Helen Ware's violin studio off Dupont Circle. Weyl claimed that "his recollection was that Lee Pressman was present at about ninety percent of the meetings he attended, and that he has a fairly clear recollection of Alger Hiss and Lee Pressman being present together at some of these meetings." Everyone knew everyone else, and the rest of Weyl's statement regarding the group's character and activities parallels Hale Hope Davis's memoir, *Great Day Coming*. Any approaches for "special assignments" were made individually. He had never met Chambers at a meeting, nor Donald Hiss or J. Peters, as he left prior to Ware's death in 1935. Weyl went on to give pointed portraits of the personalities of the group's leading members, speculating about their personal motivations for enlisting in the Communist cause and their underlying personality dynamics. He knew Pressman well, because his work at the AAA had placed him in frequent contact with the lawyer. He did not know what Pressman's motivations had been "for shielding Donovan and himself[,] but expressed the opinion that he may have discussed the matter with Abt, Witt, and Kramer and felt certain these men would not talk under any circumstances[,] and for this reason his testimony would not be refuted nor the other individuals exposed."[36]

Initially, Weyl indicated that he did not want his statement to be used, without his permission, as the basis for which he might be called to be a witness in any congressional hearing or legal proceeding. That being the case, the FBI then turned to John Donovan as a potential witness. Donovan, an effective organizer of government employees in his employment with the NRA, despite his noted reputation as a hard drinker, had in later years been critical of the CP. However he was no lover of the FBI either. Donovan eventually ended up in Los Angeles working as a labor organizer. The FBI set about to consider ways in which to "turn" Donovan, thereby helping substantiate either Weyl and/or Chambers. Eventually, the Bureau put both Donovan and Weyl together to share reminiscences. At this "private meeting with me . . . which lasted perhaps two hours," Weyl wrote in a statement he furnished to the FBI, Donovan "gave me his version of his participation in Communist activities while in Washington in the early 1930s. This version was substantially at variance with my own," Weyl informed the Bureau. "Believing that Donovan's statement was his best recollection" and believing it had been an "honest statement, I must weigh the fact that it contradicts mine and consider the possibility that I may have been mistaken. My belief is that the mistake is his, however, and what he had to say did not change my recollection or add any incidents which I remember as having occurred." In a later memo, the FBI Director's office asserted that Donovan "has attempted to base his inability to recall specific incidents, dates and associates in the Communist Party . . . on his alleged excessive drinking habits." The FBI analyst reflected, though, that he "did recall certain facts concerning his activities during the 1930s . . . which indicates that he is possibly withholding pertinent information. . . ." Donovan helped little in the development of the FBI case against Lee Pressman, in the final analysis. Oddly, this left Pressman as the first (and only) witness, up to this point, to give a public credence and corroboration to any aspect of Chambers' story that such a group had indeed existed in the AAA.[37]

THE FAILURE OF THE PERJURY CASE

So finally the potential perjury case against Pressman had, for all practical purposes, narrowed to Chambers' contentions of a wider Ware Group membership, as corroborated by Weyl. By early 1952, the latter had decided to go semipublic with his story and appeared before the Senate Internal Security Committee. In April 1952, the FBI once again appeared at Chambers' doorstep in Maryland. Bureau agents wanted to know whether the former *Time* magazine journalist could think of any other possible witnesses who could or would, under the right conditions, support his story, in addition to Weyl. One possibility might be Alger Hiss's brother, Donald Hiss, Chambers commented. He had heard rumors that Donald Hiss had been under great mental stress "which in time might make him 'approachable.'" Further, Hoover's emissaries also wanted to determine "specifically the minimum number of closed meetings at which Chambers can state definitely that Alger Hiss and/or Victor Perlo or others not named by Pressman as members were present with Pressman." To this query they received what must have been a most disappointing reply. "In this regard, Chambers advised that the only closed meeting at which he can definitely testify that Perlo, Collins and Pressman were present is the meeting which took place shortly after Ware's death in 1935" in Collins' St. Matthews Court apartment. Since Chambers began his connections with the Ware Group *after* Weyl had left, apparently the two could not corroborate each other *directly* as to any specific meeting. And, since Hiss had supposedly been separated from the Ware Group in early 1934 because of his assignment to the Senate Nye Committee investigations, Chambers could not place Hiss and Pressman together at any specific Ware Group get-together. Of course, each of them knew, or must have known, of each other's involvement, he claimed, but he could not testify to that as a fact he knew from his own observation.[38]

Then, in late 1952, the FBI case, certainly not overwhelming by any stretch of the imagination, fell apart. Unfortunately for the government, but fortunately for Pressman, in early November 1952, Whittaker Chambers was stricken with a severe heart attack. The FBI had always realized the desirability of securing additional witnesses against Pressman besides Weyl and Chambers. But Chambers would be the star witness in any proceeding against the former CIO general counsel, thus his availability was crucial. Indeed, the Department of Justice had planned to call Chambers as its first witness before a grand jury on November 14, 1952. Now that opportunity had been lost.

Over the course of many months, the FBI and the Justice Department watched helplessly as Chambers' condition improved at a snail's pace. By December 1952, he still had not recovered enough to give a deposition. "Mrs. Chambers advised that, if necessary her husband would always be available for testimony even though it might cost him his life," FBI agents reported Esther Chambers nobly offering. U.S. attorneys considered arranging a low stress deposition before a petit jury in January 1953, but abandoned it because if an indictment returned, it would necessitate a quick trial and would present too much danger to the journalist, according to his doctors. In the spring of 1953, Esther Chambers informed the FBI that "she is of the strong opinion that agents of the F.B.I. will never again be able to transact any official business with Whittaker Chambers, even in quiet personal interviews." It simply dredged up too many painful past memories, she insisted, as did visits by headline-hunting politicians like the recent one by Senator Joseph McCarthy (R-WI). Finally, the government learned to its chagrin that Chambers would not be available, under any circumstances, before September 1953, and so his usefulness as an incriminating witness against Pressman vanished because the statute of limitations lapsed in August.[39]

Pressman must have been aware of his good luck, for he knew that the FBI must have been trying intensively to put a case together from other sources. In October 1952, he was called before a federal grand jury and invoked the Fifth Amendment. In January 1953, the espionage case against Yuri Novikov—Pressman's former Soviet contact in Russian estate work—erupted in the news. The State Department declared Novikov *persona non grata* and returned him to the Soviet Union. In the wake of this story, FBI agents showed up once more at Pressman's law office to rehash Pressman's contacts with Novikov. Pressman informed them that he had nothing to add to what he previously told the Bureau, but went over his story once more. In closing the interview, Pressman himself "mentioned the recent publicity concerning the allegations of Nathaniel Weyl," the agents wrote to their superiors. He had known Weyl in the AAA, he admitted, but "denied that Weyl was a member of the Ware Group, at least during the time that he, [the] subject, was a member of that group." Pressman called Weyl a "'liar' but was of the opinion that it would be difficult to disprove his assertions as to him. . . ." He also pointed out, though, that "it would be difficult to prove such assertions through Whittaker Chambers since the latter, himself, has never mentioned Weyl as being a member of the Ware Group." Pressman charged that Weyl "was a publicity seeker and that 'it makes for good copy'"—and good money as an aspiring anticommunist memoirist as well.[40]

In the end, the only available Ware Group witness against Pressman was Nathaniel Weyl. Nevertheless, the government continued to maintain its interest in Pressman. In August 1954, U.S. attorneys subpoenaed him to testify before a grand jury sitting in Camden, New Jersey, then considered an espionage indictment against Ware Group member Nathan Gregory Silvermaster. Elizabeth Bentley had named Silvermaster as the leader of one of the espionage rings in which she assisted during the war. Pressman knew Silvermaster and had admitted such; even the FBI admitted that the former CIO general counsel had not been deeply involved in the Silvermaster investigation, though. "Insofar as the Silvermaster case is concerned, Lee Pressman has always been considered one of the fringe subjects," a Bureau memo admitted.

Perhaps he could prove useful in strengthening the case against Silvermaster under the right conditions, the U.S. attorneys thought. The government therefore gave some thought about whether it should attempt to apply the immunity provisions of the Internal Security Act to Pressman. Any further refusal to testify, then, or an effort to invoke the Fifth Amendment, might then result in a contempt charge. For reasons that are unclear, the government did not decide to take that route, and when he appeared, Pressman invoked his Fifth Amendment rights before the grand jury. "In speaking to the Government attorney out of the presence of the Grand Jury," a Bureau report noted, however, "Pressman indicated that he would be willing to furnish additional information but would not serve as a witness or testify publicly." In fact, Pressman "indicated in the alternative that if an attempt were made to apply the Immunity statute to him, he would not talk but would serve a prison sentence on a contempt charge."[41]

Thus Lee Pressman had escaped Alger Hiss's fate. Life had been kinder to Pressman than to his former *Harvard Law Review* classmate, who spent over four years in prison. Ironically, Pressman himself made the FBI's pursuit possible by going public. During these years Lee Pressman must have felt as though the Sword of Damocles hung over his head, as episodic visits from FBI agents and headlines recounting the rampages of Senator Joseph McCarthy constantly reminded him of the tightrope on which he walked. If it were indeed true that Pressman's reason for "turning" was an effort to discredit the HUAC and Richard M. Nixon, his ploy failed miserably. On the other hand, if he had wanted to become a star ex-Communist witness, he certainly could have done so. "For Pressman to have confirmed Chambers on Hiss might have restored his own fortunes if his fortunes were all he cared about," Murray Kempton observed. It is hard to escape the feeling that this entire period in Pressman's life was characteristic of so many other things that he was about and the ironies of his personality, at once coldly analytical, deceptive, self-centered, and ruthless; but at the same time, capable of blatant rationalization to the point of self-delusion, idealism to the point of illogic, and loyalty to the point of personal danger.[42]

One wonders if during these years his thoughts returned frequently, as they must have, to those days in the 1930s when, as the Ware Group assembled, he and his fellow radicals filled the room with the sound of excited voices, with intense discussions about the great political events shaking the world, and the chance they had now been given to be a part of that historic cause. How many times Pressman's mind drifted back to the conspiracies they hatched, the commitments they made, the goals they struggled for in their comraderie is difficult to say. "I can see Victor Perlo now, young and ardent, drawing a map of China on a child's blackboard with a different color of chalk for each province as he traced the route of the Long March being led by Chu Teh, Chou En-lai and Mao Tse-tung," Hope Hale Davis evocatively wrote of the political passions of that time. "We all tried to become as sure of the location of the Huang Ho and the Hang-shui as of the Mississippi and the Hudson." One wonders whether, when he encountered his old comrades on the streets of New York after he had "named names" after a fashion, these memories flooded back.[43]

Indeed, they must have, as a poignant story illustrates. John Abt told of how, not long after Pressman's 1950 HUAC appearance, Nathan Witt ran into his former comrade on a sidewalk in New York. The sensitive Witt, obviously deeply hurt by Pressman's betrayal, turned his eyes quickly away. When Witt told Abt of the encounter, Abt berated Witt for looking away; they had behaved honorably and had nothing to regret, he said to his friend. Shortly afterward, again by chance, Abt found himself facing Pressman in a similar fashion as he walked down lower Broadway. True to his advice, this mild-mannered, soft-spoken, and unpretentious man bore his gaze into Pressman's face—Lee Pressman, disciple of John L. Lewis, student of the ruthless use of power, negotiator with captains of industry and national politicians, underground Communist, and now ex-Communist. For a moment, Pressman held Abt's gaze and then, and strong as he was, turned away from the glare of accountability to which Abt now held him, apparently in shame.[44]

EPILOGUE:
"A QUIET LAW PRACTICE . . ."

I don't think today's generation has nearly as exciting a life as we did when we were in our twenties, but I suppose it's the times. It seems to me that the labor movement with all the strength that it has nowadays should be able to organize several million unorganized workers.

[As for myself] [i]t's hard for me to say whether I am more content now with my quiet law practice, than I was in the New Deal and the labor movement.

—Lee Pressman, 1957[1]

"Just as American Communists came from every sort of life and condition," wrote Vivian Gornick in *The Romance of American Communism*, "they have returned into every sort of life and condition." She continued, "For the most part, they became again Americans who live at a 'reasonable' distance from their politics." Normally, they now considered themselves liberal or mildly socialist, but gone was the compelling drive to activism as they turned to immerse themselves in their professional or family lives. Even so, "none of them are the same *kind* of American they had been before . . . they are all ex-Communists. This piece of identity . . . is *the* vital experience by which nearly every one of them gauges the subsequent course of his or her life . . . the where, who, or what he or she is in the world."[2]

It must have been much the same with Lee Pressman as he turned to recompose his nearly shattered life after August 1950. In the following years he must have turned over in his mind what the two decades of his public career had meant to him, the country, and the world. During the 1960s, he looked with approval on the renewed political activism of the New Left. Though perhaps not enamored of the young radicals' tactics, at least they, along with Civil Rights activists, had continued the pursuit of justice. And in his final years, the fact that this new pursuit of justice in American life seemingly had little to do with the industrial union movement he helped bring into being must have been a great disappointment.

THE RETURN TO PRIVATE LIFE

In the wake of Pressman's failed gamble to undermine the public credibility of Richard Nixon and the House Un-American Activities Committee, for a time, he and his wife Sunny toyed with the idea of fundamentally changing their lives. In late 1950, they embarked on a cruise to Israel, ostensibly for business purposes. However, Pressman also wanted to explore the possibilities of starting his public life over. Sunny, of course, was the family's Hebraist and Zionist, but Lee's recent travails had resulted in his being open to other possibilities to reconstruct his life. According to both his brother Irving and Harold Ruttenberg, Lee's former CIO colleague, Pressman had a number of conversations with Israel's Labor Party officials in the hope of finding a suitable sinecure. When those discussions came to naught, Lee and Sunny returned to New York, where he faced the task of rebuilding a new law practice and settling down, for the first time in his life, to a predictable domestic routine.

On that cruise, the Pressmans began a friendship with a younger couple, Lynne and John Weiner. The Weiners' knew of the recent HUAC press flurry; furthermore, they had been "warned" by friends who noticed Pressmans' name on the ship manifest to "keep their distance." Finding themselves standing next to the older couple during a safety drill, the Weiners ignored the advice and began to engage in small talk with Lee and Sunny. They soon found themselves charmed by both. Lee "was not immediately trusting of us, I felt," remembered Lynne Weiner. "He was raw and his emotions were on edge." That was his way with many people until he got to know and trust them, she also observed; just then, however, it had become a more salient personal characteristic. Even so, upon finding out the Weiners were ardent New Deal admirers, Pressman donned his raconteur hat and regaled the two with a stream of New Deal insider stories and anecdotes. Upon arrival back in New York after the vacation, the two couples began a dinner party, tennis, and social relationship that lasted for many years.[3]

In the 1950s, it fell to Sunny Pressman to help her husband make the difficult transition to being out of the public limelight and also to deal with the pariah aspects of the Communist scare of the early 1950s. While they had rented a series of modest, middle-class homes in the Washington, D.C., area in the 1930s and 1940s, and later in Mt. Vernon, New York, in the late 1940s, Sunny Pressman played the role of the devoted wife. And it seemed as though

Lee Pressman demanded that his wife play such a traditional role in the family's domestic life. It would be a rare occasion when Sunny would challenge her husband publicly. Pressman, typical of many men of his generation, had conflicting ideas about the role of women. In the abstract, and for his daughters, he believed that women could and should pursue any professional goal. "However," remembered Ann Pressman with amusement, "you were also supposed to be a mother and a good hostess. And really entertain well in your home." Within the family, Lee and Sunny were reserved in their interactions. "He and she were very private about their relationship," Ann asserted. During times of stress and trouble, Sunny provided "a tremendous amount of support," and her husband "had a very high regard . . . and a lot of admiration" for his wife. But he also tended to demand center stage and deference from here when at home. As his work for the labor movement escalated, that became less and less frequent, which also added tension to their relationship.[4]

"My mother was . . . two different people" in a way, according to Marcia Pressman. She had one "personality in the company of my father and another personality without my father present." She was always quite "passive . . . to him [when he was on the scene], and when he was not present [in the household, she was] very strong" willed. "My mother was a very strong personality underneath her quiet, passive ways," Marcia concluded. Lee's lengthy family absences left her with the large share of child-rearing duties for years, which troubled her, though she did take vicarious pleasure in her husband's high-profile public career. While Lee did from time to time conduct various fatherly activities with Ann and Marcia, it was not until youngest daughter Susan came along in the 1940s that he had more family time and abandoned his previous role as absentee father.[5]

Thus, Sunny Pressman eschewed the kind of activist orientation toward political life that so intrigued her husband, though she always maintained an intellectual interest in her husband's New Deal comings and goings. Activism would not have worked anyway, thought Marcia. "She didn't like to have people depending on her because she always wanted to be available for" her husband. This was the crux of their relationship. Marcia Pressman believed that underneath her father's frequently aggressive nature lay a good deal of insecurity and dependence. "I think my father was very devoted to his mother . . . and I think he had very strong dependency needs toward a woman." "My mother was the anchor at home while he was the whirling dervish out in the world. But underneath it all, he was emotionally deeply dependent on her and I think his way of protecting himself from his own dependency needs was to manifest a kind of outward blustery . . . bravado. . . ." It was "too bad it had to be that way," she said, years later.[6]

As Irving Pressman observed, after his HUAC experiences, Lee had to have "a recount of his friends," and more than one shunned the family.

According to Ann Pressman, "I think Mom spent a lot of time keeping the social connections, the friendship connections . . . with the people that remained friendly to her and Dad." In addition, she tried to cultivate new friendships, such as the one with the Weiners. That way, "they would have a circle of friends to have as a support group." Marcia Pressman seconded that observation. My "mother was absolutely steadfast in her devotion to him, and it would be times like these where she would rise to the occasion. . . . She absolutely stood by him and really was very much a shoulder for him."[7]

In the family's new domestic life, that also meant patiently trying to smooth out Lee Pressman's rough edges in interpersonal relations. In some ways, leaving the CP had been a relief for the labor lawyer. When Harold Ruttenberg visited him after his 1950 testimony, he thought Pressman looked "like a hod carrier who had a big heavy load lifted off his shoulders." Moreover, internally, Lee Pressman had a tremendous inner strength and capability to overcome adversity; a resiliency that argued he would become a survivor. Nevertheless, his fall from public power must have been a deeply difficult adjustment. His parents, for example, were stunned by his admissions in the press about his Communist Party membership, and not long afterward, in 1953, Pressman's father, Harry, passed away. "It actually broke my father's heart," recalled Lee's brother Irving, "when it was disclosed that Lee became a Communist." Lee Pressman's "defenses in the face of all that uprooting, and whether or not he's in favor with the world or out of favor with the world . . . would be aggression, rather than passivity," observed his daughter Marcia. Since Lee Pressman did not often acknowledge the more vulnerable side of his emotional life, his personality during this period, and for some years after, too often seemed insensitive to others more attuned to their feelings in that regard. As a father, he was a difficult taskmaster; he demanded perfection no matter what the child's age. Every social conversation would be a battle of logic and acumen and every endeavor an insistence on perfection. As Susan Pressman Sragow reflected, "I can remember sitting around the dinner table, and it was really tense. Someone always left the table crying," it seemed. It would be Sunny's role to attenuate these family difficulties. Lynne Weiner more than once watched "with admiration" as Sunny made sure the Pressman daughters got their words in at the dinner table on social occasions, in spite of her husband's proclivity to dominate much of the conversation."[8]

In addition, the immediate concern of earning a living confronted the former CIO general counsel. After he left the CIO left-wing union clients had come to the firm of Pressman, Witt, and Cammer, but after his separation and then his HUAC testimony, he certainly could not expect business from that quarter. Pressman then dabbled with a few corporate clients. From 1951 on, though, he became increasingly visible as a counselor and negotiator for a small maritime union, the Marine Engineers Beneficial Association (MEBA), a relationship that had begun as early as 1948. MEBA President Herbert Daggett put Pressman on a $10,000 a year retainer for the executive committee of the national office based in Washington, despite opposition from the union's powerful anticommunist Local 33 in New York. By now, however, Pressman knew what was required. A well-placed MEBA informant told the FBI that he "has never heard of" Pressman "trying to support or espouse the Communist Party line" in his work with the union after his HUAC appearance. The labor attorney's negotiating acumen and litigation skills had made him "a very capable attorney whose services have been valuable to MEBA," the source reported. The "National Officers . . . have relied heavily upon the subject in their negotiations with the shipping companies," an FBI report recorded. "The informant felt that without the subject . . . the officials . . . would be unable to cope with the companies and it was for this reasons that they have continued to retain" the lawyer, despite his unpopularity with anticommunist elements within the union. "During his association with MEBA subject has never been known to indicate any Communist sympathies and, in fact, he seems to have been particularly careful to avoid any such connections." As an example, the informant pointed out that "on one occasion subject refused to continue at a meeting of various MEBA officials until a pro-Communist member of the union left the meeting." In addition, when advising the union's top officials about whether they should sign the Taft–Hartley anticommunist affidavit provision, Pressman simply "stated what the law was and did not voice an opinion one way or another as to whether they should sign."[9]

THE FBI'S CONTINUING INTEREST

Indeed, the FBI's inability to put together a viable perjury case against Pressman had left top officials at the agency gnashing their teeth, though they still considered him a potential source of information. In late 1954, FBI official L.B. Nichols informed chief Hoover aide Claude Tolson that an informant had called the Bureau saying he had received a call from Lee Pressman. "Pressman told" the informant "that he was now 'clean'; that he was becoming active in the maritime field and that all that he wanted was to make a living and do some good." Pressman wanted the source to make a business introduction for him to a close personal friend of the source, but the informant wondered about Pressman's veracity. Pressman told him to contact the U.S. Attorney General's office at the DOJ who "would vouch for him." During their talk, Pressman "insinuated" that he was again becoming close to John L. Lewis. The informant thought "if Pressman was clean he could probably do a lot of good; if he was not he could be very dangerous in meddling on the waterfront." At any rate, he did not want to introduce Pressman to his friend unless that were true, because his associate had always had "a good anti-Communist background." Nichols' frustration at Pressman's "escape" showed quickly. He told the informant, "on a purely personal and confidential basis[,] that if Pressman was clean, we did not know where he had been laundered; that we have not been satisfied that Pressman had made a clean breast; that if the truth were known Pressman" would still invoke the Fifth Amendment to avoid testifying about his Communist past. He had in fact done so as late as August 1954. Clearly, Nichols felt, the informant should "keep his guard up on any dealings with Pressman."[10]

Such hostility did not stop FBI agents from appearing at Pressman's office from time to time, however, to see if they might encounter him in a more expansive mood than he had heretofore evidenced. The last lengthy FBI interview of Pressman in the FBI files was apparently conducted in May 1955. Pressman once more professed his willingness to cooperate with the government. He continued to caution that "his answers . . . questions would, because of his legal training and thinking, all necessarily have to be divided into two categories . . ." Those categories were facts that he knew firsthand, and those that he surmised via inference, but could not personally affirm as facts. Pressman then reiterated his previous assertions to the Bureau. He explained that after Roy Hudson and Eugene Dennis had reapproached him on behalf of the CP in 1938, they "would question him as to how far they could expect Lewis or Murray to go in the face of CP pressure from left wing unions. He stated further that they would question him on the basic policies the CIO was formulating." Pressman insisted they did not inform him of CP policy on any given issue and that "the CP leaders were apparently using him as a sounding board to get information rather than to have him receive information from them."

Pressman continued that while he surmised certain CIO leaders were CP members, because a few had publicly revealed such or had later renounced Party influence, he did not know that as a fact. He had never attended any of the caucus meetings prior to CIO conventions, which he understood were normally held by the left-wing union officials. Furthermore, Hudson was always most careful not to reveal the identities of any CP CIO leaders, and Pressman maintained he "was never included in any policy or strategy making discussions." Thus, he could not supply "any firsthand information along these lines." Again, in his opinion, CP influence within the CIO had been slight; the presidents of unions identified as Left-controlled were "voluble," he admitted, but "though a concentrated minority" they were never of sufficient strength to really shape CIO policy. Overall, any similarities in the policies of the CIO and the CP were largely "coincidental." Finally, Pressman closed by observing that where CP labor influence continued to exist in the country, such control "is maintained by strong CP leadership on a shop and local level. He stated that as long as CP members are allowed to head shops and locals in negotiations and collective bargaining[,] and as long as they continue to maintain policies of fear and intimidation of the workers in the shops, the election of Communist and pro-Communist leaders will continue to occur in those unions."[11]

Shortly thereafter, the FBI closed its active investigation file on Lee Pressman with little subsequent material appearing after that interview. Ironically, in early 1961, President Kennedy's new Secretary of Labor, Arthur J. Goldberg, Pressman's successor as general counsel of the CIO and USWA, felt compelled to call on the FBI's J. Edgar Hoover shortly after assuming his new duties. Goldberg, a Cold War liberal, had been the architect behind Philip Murray's purge of the left-wing unions from the industrial federation in the late 1940s. He went on to represent the CIO, the USWA and the merged AFL-CIO after 1955 in the many collective bargaining battles and labor legislation struggles of the 1950s. As a result, Goldberg was able to move into government service; first as secretary of labor, then as associate justice of the Supreme Court, and finally as the U.S. ambassador to the United Nations. This was a career path that Pressman, had he chosen another political course, might have traveled. "Mr. Goldberg expressed appreciation for the cooperation which he had received from the Bureau following his appointment" by Philip Murray, the FBI summary memo of the visit recorded, in his efforts "to rid that organization of communists. The Director mentioned as an example the case of Lee Pressman[,] and how he at one time had controlled the passage of resolutions at CIO conventions. The Secretary knew of FBI assistance in this matter," and claimed that Pressman had disavowed Party membership to Murray. Thus did the self-satisfied Cold War liberal and the arch-conservative law enforcer find common ground in national politics among the scattered ashes of domestic anticommunism, as Lee Pressman continued to live his life out of the limelight. As he did, his mind, as did the minds of contemporary historians, turned back to the many historic events of which he had been a part.[12]

PRESSMAN'S ENCOUNTER WITH HISTORY

In the 1950s, historians and political sociologists began to reassess what the New Deal and the rise of the labor movement had signified in American life, and of course Lee Pressman had played a significant role within that history. Hence he became the object of the attention of a number of analysts. The first to approach Pressman was political sociologist Daniel Bell in 1956, who was then beginning a study of the influence of the Communist Party in American life. As noted previously, in that interview the notably precise Pressman seemed unprepared and imprecise in his articulation of the reasons behind his conversion in the 1930s, and this discomfort showed Bell his guardedness in discussing the subject.[13]

Perhaps this was understandable, given the fact that the Pressman's politics had been the subject of two exposes by that point. In 1952, Whittaker Chambers published his memoir, *Witness*. In that work, Chambers recounted his history with the Ware Group and made public a claim that Pressman had played a role as his "special assistant" even in underground CP work after the lawyer left Washington in early 1936. According to Lynne and John Weiner, Pressman was "livid" about the book and for the rest of his life maintained a "contempt" for Chambers that was "unbelievable." They noted that "the only human being that" they "knew Lee Pressman to outwardly and out-and-out hate was Whittaker Chambers." Pressman had regarded Richard Nixon as "loathsome"; but Nixon's endeavors, in Pressman's mind, only reflected poor personal character and were largely issues of political ambition. With Chambers, on the other hand, Pressman maintained what was clearly a burning hostility, though he always remained tight lipped about the specifics of the situation in the 1930s and about Alger Hiss. In addition, in 1955, Murray Kempton published his comparative personality analysis of Gardner Jackson and Lee Pressman in a chapter of *Part of Our Time: Some Ruins and Monuments of the 1930s*. The portrait drew largely on the remembrances of Jackson and of course Kempton's own journalistic observations, which in the end portrayed the labor lawyer in an unflattering light. As Kempton informed Jackson when preparing to write the book, he came to the project with a foreordained vision. "One key chapter . . . would be on you and Lee Pressman. It would be a chapter attempting to show the difference between the radical of the twenties, that ranging free spirit, and the Communist of the thirties, that disciplined careerist. It will be an impersonal chapter, but in a book with few heroes I need hardly tell you what your place would be." It was no surprise, then , that Pressman comes across in so many places as a ruthless Stalinist. As Harold Ruttenberg noted, the personality analysis "is that of Pat Jackson, who knew, worked with, and fought Lee. It is the way Pat saw and remembered Lee." While Kempton's observations are often insightful, overall he did not attempt to render a balanced personality assessment of Pressman. Both Lynne and John Weiner, Irving Pressman, Jack Rabkin, and the Pressman daughters, while admitting their friend's and father's shortcomings, also noted his many admirable qualities. He had a deep sense of loyalty to friends and family, for example, and not infrequently showed a self-deprecating sense of humor. He was always willing to go out of his way to help someone in need, assumed the role of caretaker without complaint, and was inspired by his idealism and his desire to help those less fortunate.[14]

So it is perhaps not surprising that when approached by the Columbia

Oral History Project for an extensive oral history interview, conducted during various dates during 1957 and 1958, Pressman agreed to participate only with the understanding that there would be "[n]o questions about the CP," recalled his interviewer Donald Shaughnessy. Columbia historian Allan Nevins had suggested that his student Shaughnessy contact Pressman. After an initial correspondence, they met at Pressman's tiny law office in the Woolworth Building (he maintained a much larger office in the MEBA Health and Welfare Fund offices). The two agreed that Pressman would come by Shaughnessy's office in the Butler Library at Columbia during the evenings where they would talk for one to two hours a visit. Over the many months these interviews spanned, Pressman had a chance to reflect on the nature of the historic events in which he had participated. To this day, those interviews contain some of the most acute perceptions of the rise of the industrial union movement in the 1930s and 1940s that were available, as well as the personality dynamics between John L. Lewis, Philip Murray, Sidney Hillman, and Franklin D. Roosevelt. They reflect as well, seventeen years after their relationship ended, the tremendous admiration Pressman still maintained for John L. Lewis. In these interviews, however, Pressman analyzed the forces at play dispassionately, as always carefully separated from most of his emotions other than the undisguisable fascination with Lewis. Finally, in 1964, historian Sidney Fine did one more interview with Pressman for his multivolume biography of Frank Murphy. In this conversation, the labor lawyer conducted a similar dissection of the GM and Chrysler Sit-Down Strikes and his other associations with Murphy as attorney general.[15]

Through all this reminiscing, one wonders what Pressman ultimately concluded had been the value of his own public life during the New Deal era. Clearly, he knew he had had a chance to participate in historic events and had seen many of them develop from the inside. Despite the recent resurgence of conservatism and the decline of the significance of the New Deal as the engine driving American political life, its predominance for over nearly fifty years and Lee Pressman's contributions to its evolution meant real accomplishments. Murray Kempton wrote in the mid-1950s that Pressman had always been "a man in between." He meant that phrase in between the CP and the CIO and in between John L. Lewis and Philip Murray. He was that, of course, and much needed. Without Pressman's leftist politics and related intense commitment, the cause would have lacked much of the organizing energy and daring necessary to accomplish its goals. Lewis, Hillman, and even Murray knew this. As Hillman said to Frances Perkins, they could work "through Pressman as they could through no one else." In the final analysis, though, the historic debate about whether the Left subtly "shaped" CIO policy according to Communist desires, or whether the CIO leadership dominated a militant but numerically weak faction should be reformulated. The real significance of the CIO-CP alliance during the New Deal lay in the ability of *both* sides to form a symbiotic structure that advanced the aims of each for over a decade. Considered from this vantage point, Pressman's inordinate aggressiveness and drive, his ability to win the confidence of both Lewis and Murray, was perhaps the crucial element in cementing that mutually beneficial alliance during those years.

But Lee Pressman was also a "man in between" in another, more fundamental way. More critical to the birth and maturation of industrial unionism than the center Left alliance in the CIO, and the reenergization and subsequent expansion of union membership generally, was the symbiotic relationship between organized labor and the New Deal administrative state. Here too a debate centered on whether there was exploitation by one side or the other (usually the state over the labor movement in most recent accounts) is sterile. To understand the rise of organized labor, the focus of the discussion must first be shifted to examining the critical question of how this unique relationship began and evolved. In these endeavors, Pressman's unique combination of personality, ethnicity, class background, education, political development, and AAA experience combined fortuitously to enable him to become the essential liaison between the revived labor movement and the developing New Deal administrative state. Lewis innately understood the crucial role that government power could and did play in the 1930s, but it took Pressman's abilities to make it happen, and his quick-witted intelligence to extend it during the war. As Len De Caux accurately observed, "It was fortunate that Lewis and Pressman came together at this CIO moment in history." Pressman, he noted, was much more than Lewis's "instrument" in accomplishing the industrial union leader's vision. "Without Pressman, Lewis's grand designs might have been less grand, even smeary in spots." In fact, "[w]ithout Pressman to understand" the "detailed implications" of the CIO-New Deal administrative state alliance, "it might have been less effective, even bungled. . . ."[16]

Indeed, one can argue that Lewis did in fact "bungle" that alliance badly from 1940 to 1943. For Philip Murray, too, Lee Pressman was the essential nexus between what would become, partially because of World War II, a different kind of New Deal state than had seemed possible up to the late 1930s. The period from 1939 to 1942 proved particularly voluble, nationally and internationally. True, the CIO preferred a tripartite corporate commonwealth vision of industrial governance, one it never quite achieved. Nevertheless, it was able to exercise considerable, though waning, influence during the course of the war, and made meaningful gains because of Lee Pressman's administrative law capability and political shrewdness. The maintenance of membership provisions in the 1942 Little Steel case was only the most visible of his accomplishments. The considerable union growth that followed that decision consequently left organized labor in a far more advantageous position—in resources and political interconnections—to weather the post-war reassertion of business views on national labor policy that culminated in the Taft–Hartley Act. Had that institutional strength not been available, the results of the massive strike wave of 1946 might have had profoundly different repercussions.

In the end, perhaps Fur and Leather workers president Ben Gold, ironically one of the few open Communists in the labor movement, best summed up Pressman's public career. In his introduction of the CIO general counsel to his union's 1946 convention, he said he was proud to have Pressman speak to them. The lawyer had been "one of the leading figures" in the "great progressive mass movement of the CIO from its very inception."

> His contributions to the struggles of the people, of labor generally, and particularly the CIO, for democratic rights, constitutional privileges and their well-being calls forth for him the respect and recognition of millions of working people who appreciate the value of his . . . assistance, and guidance, particularly when they are faced with the lawmakers and law interpreters. . . . In every storm, in every mass struggle of the CIO, his able advice was a valuable defense of the rights of labor, and the right to organize."[17]

In the 1960s, Lee Pressman continued representing MEBA with his usual efficiency. He also had settled in to enjoy some of the creature comforts that his increasingly moneyed maritime labor law practice brought. In lifestyle and politics, he became the quintessential New York Liberal. In addition, every Friday, the family would make a pilgrimage to his mother's home for dinner, as they had since returning to New York in 1948. After his father's death in 1953, Lee remained "the loyal, faithful, and loving son" to Clara Pressman that he had always been, observed Donald Shaughnessy. His mother eventually learned a bit of English, but until her death in 1964, she continued to have an "almost impenetrable Russian accent." In his mother's home, Pressman found respite, assured of total acceptance. "I would say you would find" my father "most relaxed . . . and being himself, in his mother's house" during these family visits, remarked Marcia. "He could relax and laugh" as perhaps nowhere else.[18]

With the rise of the civil rights and antiwar movements of the 1960s, Pressman once again saw the United States undergoing the throes of internal political anguish and indecision. It must have reminded him of his own political coming of age in the 1930s. He was glad that activists were again speaking out on American life, but on the other hand, the experience he endured from 1948 to 1954 had sobered him about its potential personal consequences. None of his daughters had been particularly active in terms of the political issues of the 1960s. More than one suspected that he may have had mixed feelings about their lack of participation. He was relieved that they had spared themselves the travails he went through, but perhaps, Ann Pressman thought, he may also have been a bit "distressed" that they had not seen fit to become politically engaged. Slightly more distressing was the return of his old nemesis, Richard Nixon, to the national political stage. "Do you really think it's possible that that son-of-a-bitch can get to be president?" he once asked Jack Weiner in amazement. Most troubling of all to Pressman in the late 1960s was what he saw when he looked at organized labor and the AFL-CIO. In the labor movement of the 1960s, he did not see much to admire. Labor organizations and labor leaders had become "fat cats," he once told his daughter Marcia, too complacent and too much part of the establishment, and that was not the way it was supposed to have been. It must have chagrined him to think that the emotional fervor that had built the CIO toward the end of his life had ended up in organizational torpor. The fight for the soul of the labor movement, though, would be a fight for a new generation in a future time. For his part, he continued to pursue justice where he could find it—representing MEBA in negotiations, handling individual members' litigation in health and safety claims, and participating in an occasional labor law conference. He once considered expanding his practice to include corporate law, but informed Marcia that "his stomach just could not take it." Certainly his work in these years was performed on a much smaller stage than the one on which he walked in the 1930s and 1940s. For those maritime workers' lives that he improved in the 1950s and 1960s, though, he still continued to make a difference.[19]

By 1969, the sixty-three-year-old Pressman had crammed much living into one lifetime. In April of that year he discovered he had developed stomach cancer and underwent an operation, determined to beat the disease. He quickly returned to work, often visiting his eldest daughter Ann, now a physician, in Albuquerque, on his way back from West Coast business trips. "We had a chance to visit a lot during that time. I had a young son and he stopped here . . . as he went back and forth," so they saw each other every few weeks. "And we had a chance to do a lot of visiting and talking. We talked about family, we talked about growing up, we talked about feelings. We talked about insecurities," she emotionally recalled.[20]

Still, in the time he had left, Pressman went about his life trying as always to lay low the mighty and elevate the unfairly oppressed. At about the same time, his youngest daughter Susan's husband-to-be was finishing Naval Officer Candidate School. The young man's father had been a career Navy man who thought any association with someone with Pressman's political past would ruin his son's naval career. Family dinners between the future in-laws were, to say the least, difficult. "And my father would be the quintessential Lee and just tweak" him, Susan, a social worker, remembered. On one of these occasions, Susan's father-in-law to be, who had something of a stormy relationship with his son, observed that if reserves were called up for Vietnam, his son would have to salute him. Susan noted the twinkle in her father's eye at this unwarranted slight to his future son-in-law, of whom he was fond. Thereafter, he made a call to Senator Warren Magnuson's (D-WA) office and asked for a favor. Immediately before the graduation, which both families would attend, the commanding officer called the young officer aside and asked, "Who's Lee Pressman? He's going to be sitting on the stage at the graduation and your family will be sitting in the VIP section." When Susan's future father-in-law arrived, they told him where they would be sitting in the VIP section and that Lee, the civilian, was going to be sitting on the stage at the ceremony. "I got to see the look on his face; my father did not," Susan recalled in amusement. When the day's festivities were over, Pressman had still not said anything to her directly except, "Well, how'd you like" the ceremony? And of course, she saw the twinkle in her father's eye. Justice had been done.[21]

Several months later, the cancer returned. "He wanted his doctor to be real honest with him, and his doctor was busy dancing around, pretending," Ann remembered. But by now there was no more pretending. Lee Pressman was dying, and he knew it. And as he faced the other challenges he had faced in his life he now turned to face his last, confronting this last test with the same kind of "stalwartness" he had faced with other pain in his life. Sunny Pressman also was very strong and unemotional during these last days. Pressman's illness shocked everyone because he had always been so physically strong, recalled Jack Rabkin. Lynne and Jack Weiner visited their friend toward the end and Pressman spoke of the tremendous pain he was experiencing, they said, as if "it was [happening] to someone else." Several days later, he was gone. As Ann Pressman said, without in any way trying to be ingenuous, "he lived until he died."[22]

The funeral ceremony in Mt. Vernon was crowded with a procession of black limousines carrying MEBA officialdom and with friends and admirers who had maintained their relationships with the Pressmans over the years. It even drew a few former acquaintances who had deserted the Pressmans in 1950. Senator and former NWLB member Wayne Morse, with whom Pressman had sustained his friendship, eulogized his public accomplishments. From the sit-down strikes to the litigation challenge to Taft–Hartley's political restrictions to the Progressive Party campaign in 1948, Lee Pressman had walked among the movers and shakers of New Deal America, and in the process he had helped make history. It was always Pressman's special strength, Marcia remembered Morse saying, to choose "the very aspect of himself that he was aware was his weakest link" and then try to overcome the limitation.

In the end, for all of his faults, Lee Pressman's strength of will and sense

of purpose had indeed accomplished much. This son of Russian Jewish immigrant parents finished second in his class at Harvard Law School and went on
to play a key role in the Progressive politics of New Deal America. In so
doing, he helped bring into reality and then consolidate the first viable industrial union movement in U.S. labor history. As Marcia Pressman, a psycholo-
gist, reflected, in many ways her "father's passion for helping the working
man was almost redeeming his [own] father's life. . . ." His "own father was,
[at least at one time], a worker, suffering all the indignities and humiliations
and degradations . . . and somehow . . . [as] the first born son in this new country . . . he was not only the Messiah to his family[,] but had this inner need to
redeem them, to redeem his family. [And in so doing in] essence he was creating a new life for people in his father's position." Indeed, for those new
opportunities, the multitudes of common people who benefited from the
revived labor movement and the humane state that Lee Pressman struggled for
in his pursuit of justice still owe him their gratitude.[23]

NOTES

PREFACE

1. Nathan Witt, Oral History Interview, HCLA, PSU.

PROLOGUE

1. Vivian Gornick, *The Romance of American Communism* (New York: Basic Books, 1977), 13.

2. U.S. Congress, House, House Un-American Activities Committee, "Hearings Regarding Communist Infiltration of Federal Departments," August 28, 1950, 81st Congress, 3rd sess., 1950 (hereafter Lee Pressman, HUAC, 1950). A transcript of the testimony is reprinted in Federal Bureau of Investigation, Investigatite Report, Lee Pressman Headquarters File, 100–11820–512, September 29, 1950, Federal Bureau of Investigation, Department of Justice, Washington, D.C. All FBI records, unless otherwise noted, were obtained under a Freedom of Information Act request on Lee Pressman and will hereafter be cited as Lee Pressman, FOIA, FBI.

3. Murray Kempton, "The Dry Bones," in *Part of Our Time: Some Ruins and Monuments of the 1930s* (New York: Simon and Shuster, 1955), 79.

4. Hiss's career and the Hiss–Chambers case are admirably dissected in Allen Weinstein, *Perjury: The Hiss–Chambers Case* (New York: Vintage, 1978, 2d ed. 1997?). Abt's career is chronicled in his posthumous memoir (with Michael Meyerson), John J. Abt, *Advocate and Activist: Memoirs of an American Communist Lawyer* (Urbana, Ill.: University of Illinois Press, 1993) and in John J. Abt, Oral History Interview with Gilbert J. Gall, December 14, 1989 (hereafter Abt, OHI). Witt went on to become Secretary for the National Labor Relations Board (NLRB) and went into pri-

vate labor law practice in 1941. Pressman joined the Witt partnership for a brief period after he left the CIO in 1948.

5. Abt, *Advocate and Activist*, 151

6. Harold Cammer Oral History Interview with Gilbert J. Gall, December 13, 1994 (hereafter Cammer, OHI); U.S. Congress, House, Committee on Un-American Activities, "Hearings, Communist Espionage Activities in Government, Alger Hiss Case," August 20, 1948, 1022–1028, 80th Congress, 3rd sess., 1948 (hereafter Lee Pressman, HUAC, 1948).

7. Lee Pressman, HUAC, 1948.

8. Abt, *Advocate and Activist*, 152; "The Reminiscences of Jerome Frank," Oral History Interview, Columbia Oral History Collection, 1952, Columbia University, New York, N.Y. (hereafter Frank, COHC), 131.

CHAPTER 1

1. Phillip Davis, "Making Americans of Russian Jews," *Outlook* 80 (July 1905): 631–37.

2. Irving Pressman Oral History Interview with Gilbert J. Gall, May 23, 1990 (hereafter Irving Pressman, OHI]; Lee Pressman, FOIA, FBI, 100–1820–433, February 2, 1949. On his immigration application, Harry Pressman listed his birth date as August 15, 1879. He was naturalized as a citizen of the United States on March 13, 1903.

3. Irving Howe, *World of Our Fathers* (New York: Harcourt, Brace, and Co., 1976), 251–52; Irving Pressman, OHI.

4. Pauline V. Young, "The Reorganization of Jewish Family Life in America: A Natural History of the Social Forces Governing the Assimilation of the Jewish Immigrant," *Social Forces* 7 (December 1928): 239.

5. Alfred Kazin, *A Walker in the City* (New York: Harcourt, Brace, and Co., 1951), 17–19.

6. Kazin, *A Walker in the City*, 17–22.

7. Young, "The Reorganization of Jewish Family Life," 239; Kazin, *A Walker in the City*, 22. For the most extensive treatment of how "second generation" Jews experienced the acculturation of themselves and their families, see Deborah Dash Moore, *At Home in America: Second Generation New York Jews* (New York: Columbia University Press, 1981) .

8. Kazin, *A Walker in the City*, 60; Charles S. Liebman, *The Ambivalent American Jew: Politics, Religion, and Family in American Jewish Life* (Philadelphia: Jewish Publication Society of America, 1973), vii.

9. Young, "The Reorganization of Jewish Family Life," 240; Irving Pressman, OHI.

10. Irving Pressman, OHI.

11. Ann Pressman Oral History Interview with Gilbert J. Gall, December 18, 1990 (hereafter Ann Pressman, OHI); Marcia L. Pressman Oral History Interview with Gilbert J. Gall, December 21, 1990 (hereafter Marcia Pressman, OHI).

12 "The Reminiscences of Lee Pressman," Oral History Interview, Columbia Oral History Collection, Columbia University, New York, N.Y., various dates, 1958

(hereafter Lee Pressman, COHC), 3–4, 33–35. Revealingly, in his extensive oral history interview for Columbia University, Pressman did not once mention his childhood polio. Also Marcia Pressman, OHI; Irving Pressman, OHI.

13. Lee Pressman, COHC, 4, 33–34; Irving Pressman, OHI.

14. Irving Pressman, OHI.

15. Lee Pressman, COHC, 35; Jacob Rabkin Oral History Interview with Gilbert J. Gall, March 12, 1992 (hereafter Rabkin, OHI); Irving Pressman, OHI.

16. Irving Pressman, OHI; Lee Pressman, FOIA, FBI, 100–11820–25, February 20, 1943.

17. Ann Pressman, OHI; Marcia Pressman, OHI.

18. Lee Pressman, COHC, 35–36, 4.

19. Irving Pressman, OHI.

20. Lee Pressman, FOIA, FBI, 100–11820–668, November 5, 1952; Young, "The Reorganization of Jewish Family Life," 243.

21. Lee Pressman, FOIA, FBI, 100–11820–668, November 5, 1952; Young, "The Reorganization of Jewish Family Life," 242.

22. Harold Ruttenberg Oral History Interview with Gilbert J. Gall, July 16, 1989, copy housed at the Historical Collections and Labor Archives, Patee Library, Penn State University (hereafter Ruttenberg, OHI/GJG), 2, 12, 25.

23. Lee Pressman, FOIA, FBI, 100–11820–30, November 24, 1943; Lee Pressman, COHC, 7–8.

24. Weinstein, *Perjury*, 72–77. Pressman's brief for the prestigious Ames Moot Court Competition epitomized the social divergence and self-identifications among Harvard Law School's student clubs. The student clubs sponsored participants in the moot court competitions. Pressman and his partner Ben Heller wrote a brief for the [Benjamin] Cardozo Club. Their opponents were members of the Jeremiah Smith club. The contrast between the Jewish and Anglo–Saxon jurists' namesakes for the clubs could hardly be more apparent. See Lee Pressman and Ben Heller, "Brief for Respondents," *Colonial Trust v. Oklahoma Sugar Refinery and Sales*, Ames Moot Court Competition Brief, Harvard Law School Archives, Harvard University, Cambridge, Mass. (hereafter HLS). Students who present in the "latter rounds of the Ames Competition" achieve one of the "higher honors obtainable in the School" by arguing before eminent jurists and sometimes even U.S. Supreme Court justices, according to Arthur E. Sutherland. See Sutherland, *The Law at Harvard: A History of Ideas and Men, 1817–1967* (Cambridge, Mass.: Harvard University Press, 1967), 344.

25. Alger Hiss, *Recollections of a Life* (New York: Seaver Books, 1988), 10; Lee Pressman, COHC, 4–5.

26. Hiss, *Recollections of a Life*, 10, 13. The Pressman quote about Hiss is reprinted in Weinstein, *Perjury*, 76. Cammer, OHI.

27. Lee Pressman, COHC, 6–7.

28. Lee Pressman, COHC, 7–8.

29. Lee Pressman, COHC, 8.

30. Frank, COHC, 131.

31. Robert J. Glennon, *The Iconoclast as Reformer: Jerome Frank's Impact on American Law* (Ithaca, N.Y.: Cornell University Press, 1985), 15–21; Abt, OHI; Frank, COHC, 131; Irving Pressman, OHI.

32. Irving Pressman, OHI; Frank, COHC, 132.

33. Rabkin, OHI; Glennon, *The Iconoclast as Reformer*, 21–22; Kazin, *A Walker in the City*, 78.

34. International Juridical Association, *The International Juridical Association Bulletin, 1932–1942*, Ann Fagan Ginger, ed., 3 vols. (New York: Da Capo Press, 1982), vol. 1, "Introduction"; Ann Fagan Ginger, *Carol Weiss King: Human Rights Lawyer, 1895–1952* (Niwot, Colo.: University Press of Colorado, 1993), 117–23, 146–69.

35. Lee Pressman Interview with Daniel Bell and William Goldsmith, March 20, 1956, Daniel Bell Collection, Box 2–64, Robert F. Wagner Labor Archives, New York University, New York, N.Y. (hereafter Lee Pressman, Bell, OHI, and RWLA, NYU), 1–2; Ginger, *Carol Weiss King*, 123–24; Lee Pressman, FOIA, FBI, 100–11820–512, September 29, 1950.

36. Hellerstein quoted in Weinstein, *Perjury*, 98; Rabkin, OHI; Lee Pressman, FOIA, FBI, 100–11820–512, September 29, 1950.

37. Glennon, *The Iconoclast as Reformer*, 25–26; Lee Pressman, COHC, 9–10.

38. Jerome Frank to Lee Pressman, April 10, 1933; Lee Pressman to Jerome Frank, April 12, 1933, Box 6–148, Jerome Frank Papers, Yale University Library, Yale University, New Haven, Conn. (hereafter Jerome Frank Papers, YUL).

39. Lee Pressman to Jerome Frank, June 13, 1933, Box 6–148, Jerome Frank Papers, YUL; Lee Pressman, COHC, 10.

CHAPTER 2

1. Lee Pressman, FOIA, FBI, 100–11820–661, September 11, 1952; "The Reminiscences of Gardner 'Pat' Jackson," 1952, Columbia Oral History Collection, Columbia University, New York, N.Y. (hereafter Jackson, COHC), 561–62; Abt, OHI; Frank, COHC, 132, 146. John Abt, who also joined the AAA staff, indicated that he and Alger Hiss were also both highly regarded by Frank. Other AAA alumni who went on to further fame included Adlai Stevenson and Abe Fortas. While Pressman's projections of "certainty in human form" attracted some personality types to him, what made him particularly valuable as a counselor in addition to his self-assuredness was his ability to strategize and execute. In many instances over the next two decades, Pressman translated his confident strategic and tactical analyses of situations and people into productive results for his mentors. Many willingly echoed Jerome's Frank's assessment: "He was incredibly able and made life possible for me by his organizational skill. It was amazing." Frank later recollected how "at least twice" future presidential candidate and then AAA lawyer Adlai Stevenson "sat in a room with his mouth agape in wonder at the brilliance of Lee Pressman."

2. Abt, OHI. Many of the quotes from my oral history interview with Abt also appear in John J. Abt, *Advocate and Activist*, 30–35.

3. Lee Pressman to Jerome Frank, August 11, 1933, Box 875, AAA Central Correspondence, Series 1 (hereafter AAA Correspondence), Record Group 145 (hereafter RG), National Archives (hereafter NA). The history and controversies surrounding the Agricultural Adjustment Administration are many. One of the first interpretations was

that of Arthur Schlesinger Jr., *The Coming of the New Deal* (Boston: Houghton Mifflin, 1959), 28–50. More recent treatments are given in Glennon, *The Iconoclast as Reformer*, chapter 3, which concentrates on Jerome Frank's legal conceptions of New Deal lawyering and Peter H. Irons, *The New Deal Lawyers* (Princeton, N.J.: Princeton University Press, 1982), chapters 6, 7, 8, and 9, which examines the effectiveness of the use of litigation as a means of social reform in New Deal agencies. John Abt's recent memoir also has interesting material on the AAA. Irons, *The New Deal Lawyers*, 150; Lee Pressman to Jerome Frank, August 15, 1934, Box 875, AAA Correspondence, RG 145, NA.

4. Lee Pressman, COHC, 11; Lee Pressman to Mr. Frank, August 2, 1933, Box 875, AAA Correspondence, RG 145, NA.

5. Lee Pressman, COHC, 44–46; Glennon, *The Iconoclast as Reformer*, 78–80, 94–101. The Peek quote is in Schlesinger, *The Coming of the New Deal*, 50–51.

6. Jerome N. Frank to Mr. Brand, August 1, 1933, Box 373; Wayne C. Taylor to Mr. Lee Pressman, August 24, 1933, Box 875,both AAA Correspondence, RG 145, NA.

7. Abt, OHI.

8. Jackson, COHC, 411–12, 426; Abt, *Advocate and Activist*, 30; Abt, OHI. In his Columbia oral history, Jackson said his wife Dode immediately disliked Pressman for his all-too-obvious effort to ingratiateiand claimed she had never seen him at the Sacco–Vanzetti hearings. Pressman maintained in two separate oral history interviews during the 1950s that he was basically apolitical as a college student at Cornell and Harvard. In his Columbia University oral history, he even expressed wonder et how he could have been totally uninvolved in the Sacco–Vanzetti case at the time. "That's one of the amazing things which in retrospect I don't understand, really. I was so steeped in law work there, adjusting myself to the problems, that I had no contact whatsoever with the Sacco–Vanzetti case," he told his interviewer Donald Shaughnessy. See Lee Pressman, Bell, OHI, 1–2 and Lee Pressman, COHC, 8, 36.

9. Abt, *Advocate and Activist*, 30; Irons, *The New Deal Lawyers*, 148–52; Lee Pressman, COHC, 12; Thomas Reed Powell to Felix Frankfurter, December 6, 1993, Box A, Thomas Reed Powell Papers, Harvard Law School, Harvard University, Cambridge, Mass. (hereafter Thomas Reed Powell Papers, HLS).

10. Lee Pressman, COHC, 13, 14, 24.

11. Powell to Frankfurter, December 6, 1933, Box A, Thomas Reed Powell Papers, HLS.

12. Abt, *Advocate and Activist*, 35; Hiss, *Recollections of a Life*, 67; Jackson, COHC, 467, 473. The city slicker story was popularized by Arthur Schlesinger Jr., who repeated the famous, and likely, apocryphal story of Lee Pressman rising in anger at one hearing on the macaroni code, demanding to know what the "macaroni growers" were going to think about the industry proposal. As of course macaroni was never "grown" by anyone, as he well knew; Pressman later wrote to Frank's widow "Schlesinger's references to the so-called macaroni code . . , are made out of whole cloth." Lee Pressman to Florence Frank, March 9, 1959, Box 65, Jerome Frank Papers, YUL. On the interagency wrangling, see Irons, *The New Deal Lawyers*, 150; Lee Pressman to Jerome Frank, August 15, 1934, Box 875, AAA Correspondence, RG 145, NA.

13. Lee Pressman to Rexford Tugwell, Memorandum-Pressman (made in 1937), Box 40, Rexford Tugwell Papers, Franklin D. Roosevelt Library, Hyde Park, N.Y. (hereafter FDRL).

14. The purge has been repeatedly chronicled and dissected in Schlesinger, *The Coming of the New Deal*, Irons, *The New Deal Lawyers*, and Glennon, *The Iconoclast as Reformer*. Also see Abt, *Advocate and Activist*, 35–37.

15. Jackson, COHC, 616–20.

16. Lee Pressman, COHC, 25; "The Reminiscences of Frances Perkins," Columbia Oral History Collection, 1951–1955, Columbia University, New York, N.Y. (hereafter Perkins, COHC), 230–37.

17. Lee Pressman, FOIA, FBI, 100–11820–661, September 11, 1952; Lee Pressman, COHC, 20.

18. Lee Pressman, COHC, 21–22.

19. Lee Pressman to Mr. Hopkins, March 9, 1935, with attached memorandum, "Various Provisions to be Reinstated in Joint Resolution in Conference and Reasons Therefore," March 8, 1935, Box 79, Harry Hopkins Collection, FDRL; Abt OHI; Abt, *Advocate and Activist*, 46–47.

20. Lee Pressman, COHC, 23–25.

21. Lee Pressman to Rexford Tugwell, "Memorandum-Pressman (made in 1937)," Box 40, Rexford G. Tugwell Papers, FDRL.

22. John Strachey, *The Coming Struggle for Power* (New York: Modern Library, 1935, orig. ed. 1932), 398, 402.

23. Pressman told the FBI during August 1950 that he had joined the Ware Group "sometime in 1934." In his most revealing admissions on this subject, spoken to political sociologist Daniel Bell in 1956, Pressman stated that he had been a member of the CP from about "the latter part of 33 til [sic] about 34. The latter part of 34 possibly." See Lee Pressman, FOIA, FBI, 100–11820–661, September 11, 1952; Lee Pressman, Bell, OHI, 27. Pressman was speaking of his formal, dues-paying affiliation; Pressman's "informal" ideological association continued, as even he admitted, until 1950.

24. Whittaker Chambers, *Witness* (New York: Random House, 1952), 8–12. Also see the new biography of Whittaker Chambers by Sam Tanenhaus, *Whittaker Chambers* (New York: Random House, 1997).

25. Chambers, *Witness*, 191.

26. Chambers, *Witness*, 192–93, 196.

27. Gornick, *The Romance of American Communism*, 14, 91, 116.

28. Gornick, *The Romance of American Communism*, 8, 14.

29. Gornick, *The Romance of American Communism*, 29, 94; Lee Pressman, FOIA, FBI, 100–11820–661, September 11, 1952.

30. Lee Pressman, FOIA, FBI, 100–11820–661, September 11, 1952; Abt, *Advocate and Activist*, 39–40; Chambers, *Witness*, 332.

31. Lee Pressman, FOIA, FBI, 100–11820–661, September 11, 1952. Abt, *Advocate and Activist*, 41; Lee Pressman, Bell, OHI, 36.

32. Chambers, *Witness*, 338–39.

33. Chambers, *Witness*, 340–41.

34. Chambers, *Witness*, 335, 343–45.

35. Hiss–Chambers, FOIA, FBI Files, Guy Hottel to Director, FBI, "Alger Hiss Internal Security—R," FBI Headquarters, Washington, D.C., 74–1333–4670, November 27, 1950.

36. Hope Hale Davis, "Looking Back at My Years in the Party," *New Leader*, February 11, 1980, 11, 13. Also see Hope Hale Davis, *Great Day Coming: A Memoir of the 1930s* (South Royalton, Vt.: Steerforth Press, 1994) for an evocative portrait of the Ware Group and the motivations that moved intellectuals to communism. In her *New Leader* article, Davis mistakenly identifies the Pressman home as having been in Virginia. Until Pressman returned to law practice in New York in early 1936, he lived in an apartment on Connecticut Avenue across from the Washington Zoo, Cathedral Mansions. Pressman may have been using an acquaintances home for hosting this 1935 meeting, however. He told the FBI that "they held cell meetings at apartments other than those which belonged to the cell members. He explained that if for some reason a meeting was to be held at the apartment of one of the cell members and something came up which would not make this feasible, the individual might obtain the key to someone's apartment who was not using the apartment on that evening." Lee Pressman, FOIA, FBI, 100–11820–661, September 11, 1952. In personal conversations with Davis she has stated that she never met Chambers in her association with the group, nor was Alger Hiss, of her direct knowledge, affiliated with the Ware group.

37. Hope Hale Davis, "Looking Back at My Years in the Party," *New Leader*, February 11, 1980,12.

38. Lee Pressman, Bell, OHI, 36–37; Gornick, 13.

39. Lee Pressman to Gardner Jackson, n.d. [fall 1935?], Box 63, Gardner "Pat" Jackson Collection, FDRL. Pressman also must have approached Nat Witt for assistance as well. NLRB member Edwin Smith wrote to his co-board members that, "I understand from Nat Witt that Lee Pressman is now practicing law in New York. Lee was one of the first assistants to Jerome Frank in the old AAA. My own contacts with him have led me to consider him a very intelligent person. He is much interested in the field of labor relations. I think he would be a good person to keep in mind to use as a Trial Examiner in New York." Smith quoted in James A. Gross, *The Reshaping of the National Labor Relations Board: National Labor Policy in Transition, 1937–1947* (Albany: State University of New York Press, 1981), 143. Also see Lee Pressman to Gardner Jackson, Box 63, n.d., Gardner "Pat" Jackson Collection, FDRL. Jackson, COHC, 562–63. Lee Pressman, COHC, 38–39.

40. Melvyn Dubofsky and Warren Van Tine, *John L. Lewis: A Biography* (New York: Quadrangle Books, 1977), 220–21; Lee Pressman, Bell, OHI, 39.

CHAPTER 3

1. Irving Pressman, OHI; Kempton, *Part of Our Time*, 62.

2. Lee Pressman, Bell, OHI, 3–4; Lee Pressman, COHC, 25–26.

3. Lee Pressman, Bell, OHI, 4–5; Lee Pressman, COHC, 26.

4. Ruttenberg, OHI/GJG, 2–3; Sragow, OHI; Lee Pressman, Bell, OHI; Marcia Pressman, OHI. This stood in sharp contrast to the only comment Marcia Pressman ever heard her father mention about his relationship with his own father, the signifi-

cance of which will be discussed later. Commenting on some forgotten incident wherein her grandfather must have suffered some affront, Lee Pressman remarked, with a shake of his head, that Harry Pressman "would never hurt a flea."

5. Lee Pressman, Bell, OHI, 39; Lee Pressman to John L. Lewis, March 3, 1936, Reel 11:0176, Part I, *The CIO Files of John L. Lewis*, Microform, Robert H. Zieger, series editor, (Frederick, Md.: University Publications of America, 1988), (hereafter *The CIO Files of John L. Lewis*). Also Lee Pressman to Jett Lauck, March 3, 1936, Box A7A-13, CIO Central Office Files, 1937–1941, Catholic University, Washington, D.C. (hereafter CIO Central Office, CU); John Brophy Oral History Transcript, Box A5–38, John Brophy Papers, Catholic University (hereafter Brophy, OHI, CU), 664. On Brophy's past history with Lewis (he had been his political opponent within the UMWA) and his role in the CIO, see Dubofsky and Van Tine, *John L. Lewis*, 121–60, 222–47. The best institutional history of the CIO is Robert H. Zieger's masterful study *The CIO, 1935–1955* (Chapel Hill, N.C.: University of North Carolina Press, 1995).

6. Brophy, OHI, CU, 665–66.

7. Brophy, OHI, CU, 667–68. Heywood Broun was a famous journalist and cofounder of the American Newspaper Guild. Brophy's account is taken directly from his oral history transcript for the Columbia Oral History Project, a copy of which is in his papers. The oral history itself, in an edited version, is available in Brophy's published memoir, *A Miner's Life* (Madison, Wis.: University of Wisconsin Press, 1964), 260. See also John L. Lewis to James Carey, May 23, 1936, Lee Pressman Personal Papers, in possession of his daughter Susan (Pressman) Sragow, copy in possession of the author.

8. Lee Pressman, Bell, OHI, 5; Lee Pressman, COHC, 26–28, 138. By most accounts, the Pressman–Lewis connection came through his own efforts via Roche, although Gardner Jackson also claimed that he had a hand in bringing Pressman into the CIO, perhaps through some contact with Lewis, unknown to Pressman. "I like to think I've had something to do with his [Lewis's] appointing Lee Pressman as counsel for the new C.I.O. steel committee," Jackson wrote Felix Frankfurter, apparently several days prior to when Pressman stated he received the call to go to Pittsburgh from Lewis. "Lee will be a big factor in this whole industrial labor movement before it gets far, unless I miss my guess." See Gardner Jackson to Felix Frankfurter, June 11, 1936, Box 28, Jackson Papers, FDRL. Pressman always denied any such connection, perhaps because he was unaware of it.

9. Biographical portraits of each of these individuals can be found in Gary M Fink, *Biographical Dictionary* of American Labor, rev. ed. (Westport, Conn.: Greenwood Press, 1984; orig. ed., 1974); Harold Ruttenberg, OHI/GG, 1.

10. See David Brody, *Steelworkers in America: The Nonunion Era* (Cambridge: Harvard University Press, 1960), and *Labor in Crisis: The Steel Strike of 1919* (Philadelphia: J.B. Lippincott, 1965) for the best analyses of these events.

11. Philip Murray, *THE PROBLEM BEFORE THE SWOC ON JUNE 17, 1936*, November 8, 1936, and CIO Executive Board Minutes, July 2, 1936, July 21, 1936, August 10, 1936, Box 14, Katharine Pollock Ellickson Collection, I, (hereafter Ellickson Collection), Archives of Labor History and Urban Affairs, Walter P. Reuther Library, Wayne State University, Detroit, Michigan (hereafter WPRL, WSU); Ruttenberg,

OHI/GG, 1–3, 9; Lee Pressman, Bell, OHI, 10; "The Reminiscences of James B. Carey," 1958, Columbia Oral History Collection, Columbia University, New York, N.Y., 195–96 (hereafter Carey, COHC).

12. Brophy, OHI, CU, 670–71, 677–78.

13. Sanford D. Horwitt, *Let Them Call Me Rebel: Saul Alinsky—His Life and Legacy* (New York: Alfred A. Knopf, 1989), 99–101, 215–22; Sragow, OHI. Horwitt's work, of course, solely analyzes the Alinksy–Lewis relationship; the quite similar response of Pressman is based on my own analysis of the lawyer's personal reactions to the union president, which seem to me to be of a piece with Alinksy's.

14. Letter, Douald Shaughnessy to Gilbert J. Gall, September 15, 1994; Lee Pressman, COHC, 126.

15. Lee Pressman, COHC, 31–32; Lee Pressman, Bell, OHI, 19–21.

16. Gardner Jackson to Lee Pressman, September 17, 1936, Box 63, Gardner Jackson Papers, FDRL.

17. Lee Pressman to John L. Lewis, October 6, 1936, Reel 12:0352, Part I, *The CIO Files of John L. Lewis*. Lewis uncharacteristically wrote back that he had talked to a number of people about Pressman's recommendation, and "it seems to be the consensus that I should not run the risk of embarrassing the President by making statements that could be construed as being definite public demands by labor." See John L Lewis to Lee Pressman, October 19, 1936, Box 98175, United Mine Workers of America Archival Collection, HCLA, PSU. For details on the LNPL and Lewis's 1936 campaign speeches, see Dubofsky and Van Tine, *John L. Lewis*, 249–52; Robert H. Zieger, *The CIO*, 39–40.

18. Lee Pressman to Sidney Hillman, December 4, 1936, Sidney Hillman to Lee Pressman, December 16, 1936, January 13, 1937, all Box 82, Amalgamated Clothing Workers of America Records, Labor-Management Documentation Center, Cornell University, Ithaca, N.Y. (hereafter ACWA Records, LMDC). For Hillman's role in politics and legislation in the CIO, and his interactions with Pressman in this regard, see Steven Fraser, *Labor Will Rule: Sidney Hillman and the Rise of American Labor* (New York: Free Press, 1991).

19. The history of the LaFollette Committee is ably chronicled in Jerold Auerbach, *Labor and Liberty: The LaFollette Committee and the New Deal* (Indianapolis, Ind.: 1966). For additional insight into the origins of the committee, see Gilbert J. Gall, "Heber Blankenhorn, the LaFollete Committee, and the Irony of Industrial Repression," *Labor History* 23: 2 (Spring 1982): 246–53. For Abt's recollections see Abt OHI and Abt, *Advocate and Activist*, 58–60.

20. Lee Pressman, HUAC, 1950; testimony reprinted in Lee Pressman, FOIA, FBI Files, 100–11820–661, September 11, 1952. Unless otherwise noted, quotes are from the FBI source. In his FBI statement following his HUAC testimony (100–11820–661), Pressman claimed that "subsequent to his eeparture from the Ware Group sometime in 1935, until about 1938, he had no connections whatsoever with the Communist movement, although he admitted that ideologically he could be considered a Communist during those days. . . . It was his best recollection that Eugene Dennis and Roy Hudson came into his office in the CIO in Washington, D.C., approximately in 1938. . . ." See Gilbert J. Gall, "A Note on Lee Pressman and the FBI," *Labor History* 32: 4 (Fall 1991): 551–61.

21. On the Berle, see Weinstein, *Perjury*, 62–66, 157n; Lee Pressman, FOIA, FBI Files, 100–11820–661, September 11, 1952; Chambers, *Witness*, 340, 435–37.

22. Chambers' 1949 statement summary is in Lee Pressman FOIA, FBI Files, 100–11820–439, September 20, 1949. In both his 1950 HUAC and FBI statements, Pressman denied meeting with Chambers other than possibly two times. Once he thought Chambers brought a Joseph Eckhart, a representative of the Spanish Republican government, to his law office in New York, and once possibly when Chambers appeared as a "nondescript" individual at one of the Ware Group meetings in the company of J. Peters. In his 1950 FBI statement, Pressman, in speaking on how he obtained his CIO position through his contacts with Josephine Roche, denied that the Party had anything to do with his CIO appointment. But when asked where he resided at the time, he said 3000 Connecticut Avenue [the Cathedral Mansions Apartment Complex], wherein the "interviewing agents commented that this was near the Washington Zoo and the subject nodded in agreement. In addition, at this point he was asked what his brother was doing at this time, and he stated that his brother, who was younger than he, was attending Yale Law School. He was further asked if the furniture in his apartment at that time was antique or modernistic, and his answer was that it had slip covers on it and at that time there was not too much furniture." Thus the FBI report noted Pressman's evasive response. See Lee Pressman, FOIA, FBI Files, 100–11820–661, September 11, 1952.

Also, Murray Kempton's dual portrait of Pressman and Gardner Jackson, published in the mid-1950s, noted, "Much later, Gardner Jackson searched his memory for one moment in their years together when he could recall an act indicative of soft emotion in Lee Pressman. He could remember only that Pressman had sacrificed to send a younger brother to Yale Law School. . . ." See Murray Kempton, *Part of Our Time*, 53. Jackson, of course, was a close friend of Pressman's during the mid-1930s and perhaps would have knowledge of a personal fact such as this. It is harder to imagine how Chambers, in 1949, would have knowledge of these kinds of personal facts without having personal interaction with Pressman more involved than the lawyer admitted.

23. The CP policy toward the CIO is ably set out in Harvey Levenstein, *Communism, Anti-Communism, and the CIO* (Westport, Conn.: Greenwood Press, 1981), and Harvey Klehr, *The Heyday of American Communism: The Depression Decade* (New York: Basic Books, 1984).

24. Christopher H. Johnson, *Maurice Sugar: Law, Labor and the Left in Detroit, 1912–1950* (Detroit, Mich.: Wayne State University Press, 1988). The standard account of the GM Sit-Down is Sidney Fine's detailed study, *Sit-Down: The General Motors Strike of 1936–1937* (Ann Arbor, Mich.: University of Michigan Press, 1969). A recent participant portrait is given by Henry Kraus, UAW publicity director, in *Heroes of Unwritten Story: The UAW, 1934–1939* (Urbana, Ill.: University of Illinois Press, 1993). Also see Kraus's earlier memoir, *The Many and the Few: A Chronicle of the Dynamic Auto Workers*, 2d ed., (Urbana, Ill.: University of Illinois Press, 1985; orig. ed., 1947).

25. Fine, *Sit-Down*, 193–95, 231–65; Lee Pressman Oral History Interview with Sidney Fine and Robert Warner, Michigan Historical Collections, Bentley Library, University of Michigan, Ann Arbor, Mich. (hereafter Lee Pressman, Fine, OHI), 1–16; Lee Pressman, Bell, OHI, 21–26, Lee Pressman, COHC, 54, 63. Fine, relying on a con-

temporaneous diary entry by CIO organizer Adolph Germer, credits Germer with originally suggesting the stock ownership angle. Pressman, in his oral histories, implies,
though unclearly, as the incident had become shrouded with the passage of time, that
it may have originated with him. Kraus, whoowas also there, credits it to Pressman in
both of his books, and points out that Germer incorrectly claimed credit for originating other actions in other incidents. It would be a tactical idea that characteristically
would have occurred to someone such as Pressman quite quickly, given his Wall Street
legal background and work on corporate reorganizations. Pressman simultaneously
leaked the discovery to news reporter Ed Lahey, who was in Michigan covering the
GM strike for the *Chicago Tribune*. The Lahey–Pressman relationship developed
thereafter into both a mutually advantageous media connection and a personal friendship.

26. Lee Pressman to Larry Davidow, January 30, 1937, Part I, Reel 1: 0342, *The
CIO Files of John L. Lewis*.

27. Johnson, *Maurice Sugar*, 200–01. Pressman quoted in Kraus, *The Many and
the Few*, 204–05. Lee Pressman, Bell, OHI, 24; Lee Pressman, Fine, OHI, 12–13.

28. Lee Pressman, Bell, OHI, 25–26; Lee Pressman, Fine, OHI, 16; Kraus, *The
Many and the Few*, 232–33.

29. Lee Pressman, Fine, OHI, 20–27. See the works of Sidney Fine and Henry
Kraus cited earlier for the detailed accounts from differing perspectives. Lewis's role
in the GM strike is highlighted in Dubofsky's and Van Tine's *John L. Lewis*, 248–72.

30. Lee Pressman, Fine, OHI, 19; Fine, *Sit-Down*, 304–07.

31. Lee Pressman, COHC, 69–70.

32. A good summary of the probable Lewis-Taylor motivations is found in
Dubofsky's and Van Tine's *John L. Lewis*, 272–77; Lee Pressman, COHC, 78–82. For
Murphy in the Flint and Chrysler strikes, see also Sidney Fine's *Frank Murphy: The
New Deal Years*, vol. 2, (Chicago: University of Chicago Press, 1979).

33. Alinsky, quoting Pressman, is reprinted in Murray Kempton's *Part of Our
Time*, 61–62. Given the identification Alinsky himself had with Lewis, it possibly may
well reflect, in part, how he *interpreted* his Pressman interview. Pressman repeats the
Keller confrontation in both Bell's and Fine's oral histories, given after Kempton's
book was published, but these accounts drop the semimillenial tone of the Alinsky
quote. See Lee Pressman, Bell, OHI, 15–19; Lee Pressman, Fine, OHI, 31–40.

CHAPTER 4

1. Irving Bernstein, *Turbulent Years: A History of the American Worker,
1933–1941* (Boston: Houghton Mifflin, 1970), 474; James A. Gross, *The Making of
the National Labor Relations Board* (Albany, N.Y.: State UniverNity of New York
Press, 1974), 5–24.

2. Robert Zieger makes this important point by calling the industrial union
movement a "fragile juggernaut," in *The CIO*, 1.

3. Ruttenberg, OHI/GJG, 21.

4. Joseph Kovner to Lee Pressman, February 25, 1937, Part II, Reel 2: 0720,
The CIO Files of John L. Lewis; Joseph Kovner, Oral History Interview with Gilbert

J. Gall, February 26, 1990 (hereafter Kovner OHI); Memorandum in Support of Application of Anthony Wayne Smith for Admission to the Bar of the United States District Court for the District of Columbia," October 3, 1940, Robert Jackson Papers, Box 68, FDRL; Anthony Wayne Smith, Oral History Interview with Gilbert J. Gall, February 28, 1990 (hereafter Smith, OHI).

5. Joseph Kovner, OHI; Abt, *Advocate and Activist*, 174.

6. John L. Lewis, *Memorandum for Mr. John Brophy*, April 26, 1937, Box A7A–2, CIO Central Office Files, CU. Pressman's initial salary was $10,000 a year.

7. Robert H. Zieger, *The CIO*, 1.

8. For a good synopsis of the course of the Little Steel Strike, as well as Girdler's quote, see Peter Gottlieb, "Steel Strike of 1937," in Ronald L. Filippelli, ed., *Labor Conflict in the United States: An Encyclopedia* (New York: Garland Press, 1990), 502–08. Unless otherwise noted, my chronology of the strike events is taken from this source.

9. J.K. [Joseph Kovner], "Summary Analysis of NLRB Decisions," April 15, 1937, Box 18, Katharine Pollack Ellickson Papers, I, Archives of Labor History and Urban Affairs, Walter P. Reuther Library, Wayne State University, Detroit, Michigan (hereafter WPRL, WSU). Strictly speaking, the Supreme Court's ruling on constitutionality came in a set of decisions issued at the same time, which has collectively come to be known as the *Jones and Laughlin* decision. Kovner's references to majority and minority rights refer to whether a group of unionized emphoyees that was in a minority had a right to some claim of union representation, or whether employees had to constitute a majority of an employer's workforce in order to obtain recognition.

10. Lee Pressman, Memo, Re: Conference between officials of Youngstown Sheet & Tube and officials of Steel Workers Organizing Commettee, held on April 28, 1937," Box 12, USWA Collection, Legal Department (hereafter USWA Legal Department), Historical Collections and Labor Archives, Pattee Library, Penn State University, University Park, Penn. (hereafter HCLA, PSU).

11. Lee Pressman, COHC, 192–94.

12. Charles P. Taft, Lloyd K. Garrison, E. F. McGrady, "Report of Federal Steel Mediation Board to Secretary of Labor Frances Perkins," Box 12, USWA Legal Department, HCLA, PSU.

13. Gross, *The Reshaping of the National Labor Relations Board*, 176–79.

14. Lee Pressman to J. Warren Madden, June 18, 1937, Case C–184: 1946 Republic Steel Co., Informal File, Box 355, Records of the National Labor Relations Board, Record Group 25 (hereafter NLRB RG 25), NA.

15. Smith, OHI. Kovner and Smith, while working closely with Pressman for four years, nevertheless became identified with the anticommunist wing of the CIO national office. In our oral history interview, Smith did not find persuasive Pressman's speculation about the motivation of Murray's decision to call the Little Steel strike without consulting Lewis (as Pressman implied in his Columbia Oral History Interview). "Doesn't make sense at all," Smith stated. "Nobody was going to draw Phil Murray into a strike to prove his manhood. The decisiwns all were being made by John L. Lewis at that time." Moreover, Smith insisted that he was quite aware of Pressman's communist sympathies at an early date. He asserted that one of the earliest indications

to him of Pressman's politics was his ill-considered legal advice at the key SWOC strategy meetings on Little Steel. Smith claimed Pressman shaded his legal advice in a way consistent with CP policy at the time. As a result, according to the assistant general counsel, the leadership called the strike "on the basis of Lee Pressman's legal advice to them that although they had not been certified as representatives of the workers and the union they were, nonetheless, entitled to minority representation rights. That was the communist position" on the NLRA at that point, he claimed. While the attorney admitted that majority versus minority representation rights was not entirely clear at that time, he said that what law there was indicated this alleged advice was most likely incorrect. Smith claimed that documentation showing Pressman's advice in the pre-strike SWOC strategy meetings existed in meeting minutes in Secretary David McDonald's handwriting, the original copies of which he had had in his possession for some time afterward due to a countersuit brought by Republic Steel against the SWOC. To date, however, I have not been able to locate any corroborating documentation in the USWA archival collection supporting Smith's contentions about Pressman's recommendations on the Little Steel strike.

16. Smith, OHI. For a general overview of the SWOC legal department's Little Steel activities, see the various memos and correspondence in the USWA Legal Department, Boxes 12 and 27, HCLA, PSU. Also see Gross, *The Reshaping of the National Labor Relations Board*, 26–34.

17. Kovner, OHI; Gilbert J. Gall, "CIO Leaders and the Democratic Alliance: The Smith Committee and the NLRB," *Labor Studies Journal* 14: 2 (Summer 1989): 3–27.

18. Lee Pressman, COHC, 215.

19. Lee Pressman to B.J. Damich, John L. Mayo, Frank A. Hardesty, William Lavelle, Aaron A. Cohen, "Re: Republic Steel Decision," November 4, 1938, Box 27, USWA Legal Department Files, HCLA, PSU.

20. Meyer Bernstein to Nathan Cowan, "Re: Republic Steel Przystal Case," February, 9, 1939; Meyer Bernstein to Lee Pressman, "Re: Youngstown Sheet & Tube Co.," February 14, 1939; both Box 20, USWA Legal Department, HCLA, PSU.

21. Nathan E. Cowan to Anthony Wayne Smith, October 27, 1938; Ignatius Maryanski to Philip Murray, July 21, 1939; both Box 27, USWA Legal Department, HCLA, PSU.

22. *Republic v. NLRB*, 107 F2nd 472 (November 8, 1939); Lee Pressman to Philip Murray, September 25, 1939; Lee Pressman to Mr. Philip Murray, "Re: Status of Labor Board cases," January 9, 1940, Box 20, USWA Legal Department, HCLA, PSU.

23. Robert H. Zieger, *The CIO*, 105–07.

24. Lee Pressman, "MEMORANDUM FOR: Mr. Philip Murray Re: Republic Steel cases and Youngstown Sheet & Tube," May 3, 1940; Lee Pressman to Philip Murray, June 11, 1940; Box 20, USWA Legal Department, HCLA, PSU.

25. [Meyer Bernstein], Conference Minutes, Youngstown Sheet and Tube, October 30, 1940, Box 20, USWA Legal Department, HCLA, PSU.

26. Lee Pressman to the National Labor Relations Board, "Re: Youngstown Sheet & Tube Company and Steel Workers' Organizing Committee: Proposed Settlement," December 6, 1940, Box 20, USWA Legal Department, HCLA, PSU.

27. Memo, February 25, 1941, Box 20; [Meyer Bernstein], Conference Minutes, Youngstown Sheet and Tube, March 17, 1941, Box 6; Lee Pressman to Philip Murray, July 10, 1941, Box 20; Lee Pressman, "MEMORANDUM ANALYZING RIGHTS OF EMPLOYEES ENTITLED TO REINSTATEMENT AND PARTICIPATON IN MONEY AWARDED UNDER THE STIPULATION ENTERED INTO BETWEEEN THE STEEL WORKERS ORGANIZING COMMITTEE, YOUNGSTOWN SHEET AND TUBE COMPANY, AND NATIONAL LABOR RELATIONS BOARD," n.d. [1941], Box 20; all USWA Legal Department, HCLA, PSU.

28. [Meyer Bernstein], Conference Minutes, Republic Steel, October 21, October 29, and November 4, 1940; all Box 12, USWA Legal Department, HCLA, PSU.

29. Lee Pressman to Meyer Bernstein, February 11, 1941; Anthony Wayne Smith to Lee Pressman, "SUBJECT: Prelminary memorandum on Republic Steel Settlement," March 15, 1941; Lee Pressman, "MEMORANDUM ANALYZING STIPULATIONS BETWEEN THE STEEL WORKERS ORGANIZING COMMITTEE AND REPUBLIC STOEL CORPORATION COVERING THE OHIO PLANTS," July 24, 1941; Lee Pressman to Philip Murray, July 11, July 21, 1941; all Box 12, USWA Legal Department, HCLA, PSU. Getting recognition proved not the same as being able to secure a contract, however, especially in the case of Bethlehem Steel, which continued to back its company union. It took a massive strike by SWOC supporters to finally bring the company to the table. See Mark McColloch, "Consolidating Industrial Citizenship: The USWA at War and Peace, 1939–46," in *Forging a Union of Steel: Philip Murray, SWOC, and the United Steelworkers*, Paul F. Clark, Peter Gottlieb, and Donald Kennedy, eds., (New York: ILR Press, NYSSILR, Cornell University, 1987), 46–55.

30. Transport Workers Union, Proceedings of the Third Biennial Convention, September 26, 1941, 143, American Labor Union Conventions and Proceedings, microform, Part I (Frederick, Md.: University Publications of America, 1980), (hereafter ALUCP).

31. Lee Pressman, COHC, 236–38, 247–50; CIOPROC, 1938, 60; CIOPROC, 1941, 96.

32. Lee Pressman, COHC, 251; CIOPROC, 1938, 69; 1940, 237.

33. Lee Pressman, Fine, OHI, 44; Lee Pressman, COHC, 252–53.

34. See Pressman's testimony in U.S. Congress, House, Subcommittee No. 1 of the Committee on the Judiciary, "Hearings on H.R. 9745," April 20, 1938, 75th Cong., 3rd sess., pp. 7–21.

35. Lee Pressman, COHC, 254–56; U.S. Congress, House, Subcommittee No. 1 of the Committee on the Judiciary, "Hearings on H.R. 9745," April 20, 1938, 75th Cong., 3rd sess., p. 20; Lee Pressman, Fine, OHI, 44–45.

36. Lee Pressman, COHC, 220.

37. Lee Pressman, COHC, 215–18.

38. Many AFL unions who benefited from board protections in organizing, however, opposed the stance of the national leadership on amending the NLRA. For a detailed chronicling of the NLRB's policy developments and political difficulties during this period, see Gross, *The Reshaping of the NLRB*, 5–85; Lee Pressman, COHC, 216–17.

39. Lee Pressman, COHC, 222, 228–29.

40. Anthony Wayne Smith to Meyer Bernstein, March 31, 1939, April 15, 1939; Lee Pressman to National and International Unions and Organizing Committees, Selected State Industrial Union Councils, "Re: *Amendments to the Wagner Act*," April 18, 1939, all Box 6, USWA Legal Department, HCLA, PSU.

41. See Pressman's Senate testimony in U.S. Congress, Senate, Committee on Education and Labor, "Hearings, National Labor Relations Act and Proposed Amendments," 76th Cong., 1st sess., Part 22, August 3 and 4, 1939, pp. 4189–4346. Unless otherwise noted, citations about Pressman's testimony are from these hearings.

42. For Pressman's travails in the House, see U.S. Congress, House, Committee on Labor, "Hearings, Proposed Amendments to the National Labor Relations Act," 76h Cong, 2nd sess., Feburary 21, 1940, and February 26, 1940, pp. 2649–2662 and 2695–2713, respectively; Lee Pressman, COHC, 223. On the nature and significance of the Smith Committee investigation of the NLRB, see Gross, *The Reshaping of the NLRB*, 86–225, and Gall, "CIO Leaders and the Democratic Alliance," 3–27. See Pressman's comment on the Smith Committee amendments in Pennsylvania Industrial Union Council, *Proceedings of the Third Annual Convention*, April 30, May 1, May 2, 1940, Reading, Penn. (Harrisburg, Penn., 1940), 34–36. Leiserson had been a frustration of Pressman's for some time, although Leiserson did have CIO support among needle trade unionists. See Lee Pressman to John L. Leis, May 6, 1940, Gustave A. Strebel to John L. Lewis, April 30, 1940, Lee Pressman to Gustave A. Strebel, May 4, 1940, Part II, Reel 12: 0133, *The CIO Files of John L. Lewis*.

43. Pressman had some early court activity in the GM case, as noted, and in 1938 in a criminal case related to the NLRB's *Fansteel* case, the latter ultimately deciding on the illegality of the sit-down strike tactic. See Lee Pressman, COHC, 265–72. Also see Lee Pressman to Philip Murray, November 3, 1938, "Subject: Fansteel Corporation," Box 36, Jerome F. Frank Papers, YUL.

44. Thomas Reed Powell to Lee Pressman, May 14, 1937, Box C, Folder 20, Thomas Reed Powell Papers, Box C, Folder 20, HLS.

45. Gardner Jackson to Lee Pressman, September 17, 1936, Box 63, Gardner Jackson Papers, FDRL.

46. Lee Pressman to Felix Frankfurter, May 20, 1937, Felix Frankfurter Papers, Box 88, Library of Congress, Washington, DC (hereafter LC).

47. CIOEB, June 13–15, 1939, pp. 39–58, WPRL, WSU; CIOPROC, 1939, 38–39. Also see E. B. McNatt, "Labor Again Menaced by the Sherman Act," *The Southern Economic Journal* 6: 2 (October 1939): 208.

48. CIOPROC, 1940, 78–80; Lee Pressman, COHC, 274–87; Lee Pressman to John L. Lewis, March 25, 1940, Part I, Reel 19: 0256, *The CIO Files* of John L. Lewis; Lee Pressman, Joseph Kovner, Anthony Wayne Smith, "Brief on Behalf of Congress of Industrial Organizations *Amicus Curaie*," *Apex Hosiery v. Leader*, No. 638, October Term, 1939, *Records and Briefs of the U.S. Supreme Court* (hereafter USSCRB), Microform; *Apex Hosiery v. Leader*, 310 U.S. 409 (1940). For a very acute analysis of the significance of the *Apex* case, see International Juridical Association, *IJA Monthly Bulletin* 8: 12 (June 1940): 125, 131–36 in International Juridical Association, *Monthly Bulletin 1932–1942* (hereafter *IJAB*, 1932–1942), Book II, compiled and indexed by Ann F. Ginger (New York: DaCapo Press, 1982).

49. For the relationship between labor organizing, civil libeties and the LaFollette Committee, see Auerbach, *Labor and Liberty*.

50. Abraham J. Isserman, "CIO v. Hague: The Battle of Jersey City," *The Guild Practitioner* 36 (1979):1432; Lee Pressman, Joseph Kovner, Anthony Wayne Smith, "C.I.O. Legal Bulletin: *The Hague Case*, 2: 2 (August 15, 1939), Part II, Reel 4: 0751, *The CIO Files of John L. Lewis*; *Hague v. CIO*, 307 U.S. 496; CIOPROC, 1939, 40. Again, for an excellent analysis of the Hague case, see IJA, *IJAB*, 8:1 (July 1939):1, 48 in *IJAB* 1932–1942.

51. Lee Pressman, "The Norris–LaGuardia Act and the National Labor Relations Act," *National Lawyers' Guild Quarterly* 2 (1940): 236–43. Unless otherwise noted, all of Pressman's remarks are taken from this source.

52. CIOPROC, 1938, 6768.

53. Lee Pressman, Fine, OHI, 41–44; Sidney Fine, *Frank Murphy: The Washington Years*, volume 3 (Ann Arbor, Mich.: University of Michigan Press, 1984), 76–96; Henry A. Schweinhaut, "The Civil Liberties Section of the Department of Justice," *Bill of Rights Review* 1 (spring 1941): 209–15.

54. Lee Pressman to Frank Murphy, February 10, 1939, Box 24–32, Frank Murphy Papers, Michigan Historical Collections, Bentley Library, University of Michigan, Ann Arbor, Michigan (hereafter MHC, UM).

55. CIOPROC, 1940, 76–77. Admittedly, the image of J. Edgar Hoover's FBI agents working strenuously to guarantee labor's civil liberties seems, at the very least, incongruous.

56. See Sidney Fine, "Frank Murphy, the *Thornhill* Decision, and Picketing as Free Speech," *Labor History* 6: 2 (1965): 99–120 for a detailed examination of the evolution of Murphy's opinion, and also Fine, *Frank Murphy: The Washington Years*, 169–77, on Pressman's role. For *Carlson's* significance, see Margaret R. Broadwater, "Labor and the First Amendment: Thornhill to Logan Valley Plaza," (Ph.D. diss.: Rutgers University, 1976), 97–101.

57. Broadwater, "Labor and the First Amendment," 99–100.

58. *Carlson v. California*, 310 U.S. 106; Lee Pressman, Joseph Kovner, Anthony Wayne Smith, Richard Gladstein, Aubrey Grossman, Benjamin Margolis, "Brief for Appellant, Case No. 667, October 1939 Term," (herafter Carlson Brief), USSCRB.

59. *Carlson v. California*, 310 U.S. 106; Carlson Brief.

60. Lee Pressman, "CIO Legal Bulletin," 3: 2 (February 1941): 1–9, Part II, Reel 7: 0092, *The CIO Files of John L. Lewis*.

Chapter 5

1. Robert H. Jackson, "The Call for a Liberal Bar," in Ann Fagan Ginger and Eugene M. Tobin, eds., *The National Lawyers Guild: From Roosevelt Through Reagan* (Philadelphia: Temple University Press, 1988), 23–24. Longtime labor attorney and UAW counsel Maurice Sugar had been instrumental in setting the forces in motion that founded the NLG, the liberal lawyer's alternative to the conservative, corporate-law dominated American Bar Association, in 1936. See ibid., 7–9.

2. Frank P. Graham, "The Union Maintenance Policy of the War Labor Board," in Colston E. Warne, et. al., *Yearbook of American Labor: War Labor Policies*, vol. 1, (New York: Philosophical Society, 1945), 151. Graham actually wrote the decision of the full NWLB in the Little Steel cases, which was based on the hearings and findings of a three-member panel decision.

3. On the internal controversies within the National Lawyers Guild see Jerold S. Auerbach, *Unequal Justice: Lawyers and Social Reform in America* (New York: Oxford University Press, 1976), and Ginger and Tobin, 31–36.

4. Edward (Ted) Lamb and Robert H. Jackson, "Defending Unpopular Causes: The Danger of Contempt and Disbarment," in Ginger and Tobin, *The National Lawyers Guild*, 26–27.

5. Lee Pressman to Morris Ernst, March 22, 1938, Box 366, Jerome Frank Papers, YUL.

6. Lee Pressman to Jerome Frank, May 18, 1938, Box 36, Jerome Frank Papers, YUL.

7. Draft Letter, [Lee Pressman] to Charles Evans Hughes, May 16, 1938, Box 36, Jerome Frank Papers, YUL.

8. Lee Pressman to John L. Lewis, May 3, 1938, *The CIO Files of John L. Lewis*, Part I, Reel 16: 0550; Interdepartmental Committee to Coordinate Health and Welfare Activities, *Proceedings of the National Health Conference*, July 18–20, 1938, Washington, D.C. (Washington, D.C.: U.S. Government Printing Office, 1938), 105–07; Lee Pressman to John L. Lewis, December 5, 1939, Box A7A-17, CIO Central Office Files, 1937–1941, CIO Papers, CU; Lee Pressman, to John L. Lewis, January 7, 1941, *The CIO Files of John L. Lewis*, Part II, Reel 7: 0092; U.S. House, Subcommittee No. 1 of the Committee on the Judiciary, *Hearings on H.J. Res. 553*, June 12, 1940, 76th Cong., 3rd sess., 7–19.

9. Jackson, COHC, 749; Rexford Tugwell Diary, December 4, 1939, Box 32, Rexford Tugwell Papers, FDRL.

10. *"Notes on interview with John Brophy* (Bill Goldsmith), March 20, 1956, Box 2–64, Daniel Bell Collection, Tamiment Institute, RWLA, NYU; Lee Pressman, COHC, 160–71, 180–81; Jackson, COHC, 714.

11. Jackson, COHC, 769.

12. Jackson, COHC, 672–73, 714; Gardner Jackson to Jerome Frank, February 14, 1941, Box 28, Gardner Jackson Papers, FDRL.

13. Gall, "A Note on Lee Pressman and the FBI"; Lee Pressman, COHC, 152–80; Lee Pressman, Bell, OHI, 39–45; Brophy, OHI, CU, 670–78. The most exhaustive study of the impact of the Communist Party on the CIO is Levenstein, *Communism, Anti-Communism, and the CIO*. Also see Bert Cochran, *Labor and Communism: The Conflict That Shaped American Unions* (Princeton, N.J.: Princeton University Press, 1977); Steve Rosswurm, ed., *The CIO's Left-Led Unions* (New Brunswick, N.J.: Rutgers University Press, 1992); and Zieger, *The CIO*, 253–93.

14. John J. Abt to Sidney Hillman, July 5, 1938, Box 66–2, Amalgamated Clothing and Textile Workers of American Records, Labor-Management Documentation Center (hereafter LMDC), Cornell University; Abt, *Advocate and Activist*, 84–85; Abt, OHI.

15. Abt, *Advocate and Activist*, 87; Perkins, COHC, 237–44, 431–32, 474–78, 563.

16. Jackson, COHC, 750.

17. Smith, OHI.

18. Smith, OHI; Lee Pressman, COHC, 128–31; 359–64. For an overview of Dubofsky's and Van Tine's reading of Lewis's involvement, see *John L. Lewis*, 331–32, 345–46. Interestingly, Pressman's position regarding Lewis being the driving force in the Mexican oil deal finds some support in a memo from J. Edgar Hoover about the FBI's telephone surveillance of Davis and Mexican officials. In April 1938, the FBI monitored daily phone calls from "a person giving the name of Davis," in New York to Mexico City, giving information received from German cablegrams on the movements of the German steamships *SS Kitty Braenig* and *SS Leiften*. Then, according to a confidential FBI report to President Roosevelt, on April 18, 1938,

> between five and six PM, a man using the name of John Lewis at Washington D.C., telephoned Elizando Carrillo at Mexico City and told him that Davis would leave New York on the 3 PM plane that day en route to Mexico City. Lewis told Carrillo to tell President Cardenas of Mexico . . . that Davis was all right and could be depended upon. . . . Lewis told Carrillo to tell Cardenas that Italy and Germany were the only countries which it would be safe for Mexico to deal with and instructed Carrillo to see Cardenas that night . . . and furnish this information to him without fail. . . . This telephone call emanated from Long Distance Loop 59 in Washington, D.C., which is listed to the United Mine Workers of America.

Elizando Carrillo was the son of the Mexican Consul General in San Antonio and head of the Workers University of Mexico. An additional document translated from Spanish, a speech by labor leader Vincente Lombard de Toledano, to the Communist-led Mexican labor federation Confederacion del Trabajadores de Mexico, also conveyed to FDR with the surveillance information, contained additional references to a close alliance with Lewis, claiming his assistance in aiding communist causes. This document, in all likelihood, was either a fake or speechifying hyperbole by Toledano. Nevertheless, the phone surveillance was intriguing as to Lewis's behind-the-scenes maneuvering in foreign affairs. President Roosevelt's only response to Hoover was that "In regard to that Mexican C.T.M., I think we should seek to run down the money source that keeps it going." Whether he suspected the money was coming from John L. Lewis or Josef Stalin is unclear from the surviving documents. See J. Edgar Hoover to Marvin H. McIntrye, *Strictly Personal and Confidential*, June 17, 1938, and September 14, 1938, with attachments dated May 3, 1938, and September 14, 1938, President's Secretaries Files, Box 55, FDRL.

19. Abt, *Advocate and Activist*, 85–86; Abt, OHI; Lee Pressman, COHC, 116–17. For an excellent recounting of the decline of the Lewis–Murray relationship, see Dubofsky and Van Tine, *John L. Lewis*, passim; Zieger, *The CIO*, 135–39.

20. Lee Pressman to John L. Lewis, November 10, 1939, Reel 4: 0751; Lee Pressman to John L. Lewis, November 30, 1939, Part II, Reel 4: 0001, *The CIO Files of John L. Lewis*.

21. "Speech of Lee Pressman, General Counsel of the Congress of Industrial Organizations on National Network of Columbia Broadcasting System, Wednesday, January 3, 1940, 10:15 to 10:30 P.M., Eastern Standard Time," Box 63, Gardner Jackson Papers, FDRL.

22. Lee Pressman, "Protection of Labor Under National Defense," A National Conference on Labor's Rights and the Defense Program," Labor Law Committee of the National Lawyer's Guild, December 13 and 14, 1940, National Lawyer's Guild, Records of the National Committees, Alexander Meicklejohn Institute, University of California, Berkeley, California (hereafter NLG Records).

23. Lee Pressman, "The Right to Strike and Compulsory Arbitration," *Lawyer's Guild Review* 1: 4 (1941): 40–45, copy in NLG Records.

24. Dubofsky and Van Tine, *John L. Lewis*, 339–64; Lee Pressman, COHC, 108–15, 382.

25. Lee Pressman, COHC, 389. Murray had taken moves to purge the SWOC of suspected CP staffers in 1939, and rumors often circulated that Hillman and Murray were ready to go even further trying to persuade Lewis to purge the national office of Party influence as well. See Louis Stark, "Swift Red 'Purge' Planned by Lewis," *New York Times*, October 17, 1939, p. x, col. 1–3.

26. Smith, OHI; Lee Pressman to John [L. Lewis], October 26, 1940, Part II, Reel 5: 0247, *The CIO Files of John L. Lewis*.

27. Lee Pressman, COHC, 389–95,

28. Kempton, *Part of Our Time*, 29; Levenstein, *Communism, Anti-Communism, and the CIO*, 93–95; Len De Caux, *Labor Radical: From the Wobblies to the CIO, A Personal History* (Boston: Beacon Press, 1970), 380; Abt, *Advocate and Activist*, 87–88.

29. Lee Pressman to John L. Lewis, "Re: Dr. Leiserson's proposal for legislative measures affecting the existing rights of labor," n.d. [January 1941]; "Re: Various pending proposals in Congress aimed to curtail or eliminate basic rights of labor," July 7, 1941; "Mr. John L. Lewis, Chairman, Labor's Non-Partisan League," July 29, 1941, all Part II, Reel 7: 0092, *The CIO Files of John L. Lewis*.

30. Lee Pressman, COHC, 117, 194–95, 325, 420.

31. Lee Pressman, COHC, 116–17, 332, 420.

32. Lee Pressman, COHC, 330–34.

33. Smith, OHI.

34. Kovner, OHI; Levenstein, *Communism, Anti-Communism, and the CIO*, 144.

35. Lee Pressman Statement, *Proceedings of the 3rd Biennial Convention of the Transport Workers Union of America*, September 26, 1941, 144–45, (hereafter TWUPROC, 1941), ALUCP.

36. Alinsky, *John L. Lewis: An Unauthorized Biography*, 231.

37. Melvyn Dubofsky, "Labor's Odd Couple: Philip Murray and John L. Lewis," in Clark, Gottlieb, and Kennedy, *Forging a Union of Steel*, 30–44; Charles O. Rice Oral History Interview (hereafter Rice, OHI, HCLA, PSU); Ruttenberg, OHI, HCLA, PSU.

38. Howell John Harris, *The Right to Manage: The Industrial Relations Policies of American Business in the 1940s* (Madison, Wis.: University of Wisconsin Press,

1982), 41. For an excellent overview and synthesis of this period, see Melvyn Dubofsky, *The State and Labor in Modern America*, (Chapel Hill, N.C.: University of North Carolina Press, 1994), chapters 6 and 7. Akin to Dubofsky's interpretation of the pros and cons of the state–labor alliance of the 1930s and 1940s are Zieger, *The CIO, 1935–1955*; Gilbert J. Gall, "The CIO and the Democratic Alliance"; Joshua Freeman, "Delivering the Goods: Industrial Unionism in World War II," *Labor History* 19:4 (Fall 1978): 570–93.

The role of the state in labor movement development has been a highly controversial one. See, for instance, Nelson Lichtenstein, *Labor's War at Home: The CIO in World War II* (New York: Cambridge University Press, 1982), and Christopher Tomlins, *The State and the Unions: Labor Relations, Law, and the Organized Labor Movement in America, 1880–1960* (New York: Cambridge University Press, 1986), both of whom view the outcome as exploitive. Murray's capabilities as a labor leader are analyzed, too critically, I believe, in Ronald Schatz, "Philip Murray and the Subordination of the Industrial Unions to the United States Government," in Melvyn Dubofsky and Warren Van Tine, eds., *Labor Leaders in America* (Urbana: University of Illinois Press, 1987), 234–57.

39. Eugene Cotton Oral History Interview with Gilbert J. Gall, December 7, 1989 (hereafter Cotton, OHI); Rice, OHI, HCLA, PSU; Len De Caux Oral History Interview, 29–31, March 11 and 18, 1961, WPRL, WSU (hereafter De Caux, OHI).

40. For an excellent discussion of these controversies, see Lichtenstein, *Labor's War at Home*, 52–72. For the crisis mentality of the top CIO leadership in mid-December 1941, see Lee Pressman's legislative report to the executive board, "Minutes of CIO Executive Board Meeting Sat., December 13, 1941—Morning session," Box 11, CIO Secretary-Treasurer's Office: James B. Carey Papers, WPRL, WSU.

41. TWUPROC, 1941; Lee Pressman, "New Problems Facing the Labor Lawyer," March 7–8, 1942, *Lawyers Guild Review* 2: 8 (1942): 8–10.

42. Lee Pressman, "New Problems Facing the Labor Lawyer," 8–10.

43. The perambulations of the NWLB wage and union security policies are chronicled in Pressman's Legal Department Report to the 1942 CIO convention proceedings. See CIOPROC, 1942, 67–73. The evolutionary development of the union security policy eventually adopted by the NWLB, the maintenance of membership provision, is set out in Frank Graham's, "The Union Maintenance Policy of the War Labor Board," in Warne, et. al., 145–61. Graham's review is notable for the length it goes to try to prove that the NWLB's maintenance-of-membership device had never forced any individual worker to join a union against his or her will, an indicator of how sensitive the board had become to employer criticism on this issue.

44. Lee Pressman, COHC, 306–08; Harold Ruttenberg, OHI/GJG.

45. See Steel Workers Organizing Committee Brief and Reply Brief, National War Labor Board, Cases Nos. 30, 31, 34, 35, February 1942, and May 7, 1942, Box 11, Harold Ruttenberg Papers, HCLA, PSU. Also see the presentation of the brief found in Records of the National War Labor Board (Part II), Box 269, RG 2, NA.

46. Philip Murray to William H. Davis, February 19, 1942, Box 269, NWLB Records, RG 2, NA; Cotton OHI; Ruttenberg, OHI/GJG.

47. See the Little Steel Decision in *War Labor Reports* 1: 324 (1942), especially 397–98 for Pressman's statement. On the problems that the SWOC was having attract-

ing many new industrial recruits who replaced its members of the late 1930s now in the service, see Lichtenstein, *Labor's War At Home*, 67–81, and "Ambiguous Legacy: The Union Security Problem During World War II," *Labor History* 18: 2 (spring 1977): 214–38.

48. For more on the evolution and consequences of the NWLB's union security dilemmas, see Harris, *The Right to Manage*, 48–49, 107–09.

49. Verbatim Transcript, National War Labor Board, Hearing Before the Board, U.S. Steel Corporation (Case 364), August 18, 1942, Box A–13, CIO Papers, Legal Department Files, CU.

50. Ibid.

51. *War Labor Reports* 2: 453 (1943).

52. CIOPROC, 1942, 73, 283–89; USWA, *Proceedings of the United Steel Workers of America Executive Board* (hereafter USWAEB), November 17, 1942, 104–31, Box 41, HCLA, PSU; CIO, *Proceedings of the Executive Board Meeting* (hereafter CIOEB), November 5–8, 14, 1942, 104–25, WPRL, WSU; Zieger, *The CIO*, 144–47, 163–69. On the challenges facing labor during the period 1941–1942, see Lichtenstein, *Labor's War at Home*, 21–25, 72–78.

53. Lichtenstein, *Labor's War at Home*, 80–81.

CHAPTER 6

1. Cotton, OHI.

2. Lee Pressman, Joseph Kovner, Anthony Wayne Smith, and Max Geline, "Appellants' Brief," *Allen-Bradley v. Wisconsin Employment Relations Board*, Case No. 252, October Term, 1941, USSCRB, and *Allen-Bradley v. Wisconsin Employment Relations Board*, 315 U.S. 740 (1941). Pressman thought the decision of the court was much too kind to the Wisconsin board, but the union did get decision language indicating that state labor relations legislation in direct conflict with federal statues would be preempted. See CIOPROC, 1942, 79.

3. The South's critical importance to the CIO was evident in its decision to implement its post-war organizing drive, Operation Dixie. See Barbara S. Griffith, *The Crisis of American Labor: Operation Dixie and the Defeat of the CIO* (Philadelphia: Temple University Press, 1988), and Michael Goldfield, "The Failure of Operation Dixie: A Critical Turning Point in American Political Development?" in *Race, Class, and Community in Southern Labor History*, Gary M Fink and Merl E. Reed, eds. (Tuscaloosa, Ala.: University of Alabama Press, 1994), 166–89.

4. Ernest Goodman, OHI; Eugene Cotton, OHI. The list of CIO general counsels around this time included John Abt, Nathan Witt, Maurice Sugar, Ernest Goodman, Abraham Isserman, Victor Rabinowitz, David Scribner, and Richard Gladstein, among others. Indeed, the study of the contributions of labor lawyers to industrial unionism deserves a collective biography. Also see Victor Rabinowitz's recently published memoir, *Unrepentant Leftist* (Urbana, Ill.: University of Illinois Press, 1997).

5. Ernest Goodman Oral History Interview with Gilbert J. Gall, December 27, 1989 (hereafter Goodman, OHI).

6. Goodman, OHI; Lee Pressman, "The Norris–LaGuardia Act and the National Labor Relations Act," *National Lawyers' Guild Quarterly* 2 (1940): 236–43; *Hague v. CIO*, 307 U. S. 496 (1939); *Carlson v. California*, 310 U.S. 106 (1940); *Thornhill v. Alabama*, 310 U.S. 88 (1940).

7. Goodman, OHI.

8. Goodman, OHI; *Collins v. Thomas*, 141 Texas 591, 174 SW (2nd) 958 (1943); *Thomas v. Collins*, 323 U.S. 516 (1945); Lee Pressman, Eugene Cotton, Ernest Goodman, Arthur Mandell, and Herman Wright, "Brief for the Appellant," No. 569, October 1943 Term, USSCRB, (hereafter Lee Pressman et al., "Brief for the Appellant").

9. Cotton, OHI; Goodman, OHI.

10. The history of the "Roosevelt" Court of the 1940s with attendant controversies is detailed in Fine, *Frank Murphy: The Washington Years*, 145–466. For an additional analysis, see C. Herman Pritchett, *The Roosevelt Court: A Study in Judicial Politics and Values 1937–1947* (New York: Octagon Books, 1948).

11 *Schenck v. U.S.*, 249 U.S. 47 (1919). In addition to the citations in the previous footnote, also see Arthur A. Schlesinger Jr., "The Supreme Court: 1947," *Fortune* 35 (January 1947): 73–79, and Wallace Mendelson, "Clear and Present Danger—From Schenck to Dennis," *Columbia Law Review* 52 (March 1952): 313–33. For a later example of how this debate continued to play out during the Truman years, see Gilbert J. Gall, "The CIO & the Hatch Act: The Roosevelt Court and the Divided New Deal Legacy of the 1940s," *Labor's Heritage* 7:1 (summer 1995): 4–21.

12. *Thomas v. Collins*, 323 U.S. 516 (1945).

13. Lee Pressman et al., "Brief for the Appellant." More modern examples of the relationship of social movement activation and the litigation process can be found in Richard Kluger, *Simple Justice: The History of Brown v. Board of Education and Black America's Struggle for Equality* (New York: Alfred A. Knopf, 1976), and Alvin Tushnet, *The NAACP's Legal Strategy Against Segregation, 1925–1950* (Chapel Hill: University of North Carolina Press, 1987). Also see Paul Burstein, "Legal Mobilization as a Social Movement Tactic: The Struggle for Equal Employment Opportunity," *American Journal of Sociology* 96: 5 (March 1991): 1201–1225.

14. Lee Pressman et al., "Brief for the Appellant." Unless otherwise noted, all further references to the CIO brief are from this source.

15 Goodman, OHI; Fine, *Frank Murphy: The Washington Years*, 308–09.

16. Goodman, OHI; Fine, *Frank Murphy: The Washington Years*, 308–09; Fowler V. Harper, *Justice Rutledge and the Bright Constellation* (Indianapolis, Ind.: Bobbs-Merrill, 1965), 344.

17 Wiley Rutledge, First Draft, *Thomas v. Collins*, No. 569, October, 1943 Term, May 24, 1944, Box 105, Wiley Rutledge Papers, Manuscripts Division, Library of Congress, Washington, D.C. (hereafter Wiley Rutledge Papers, LC). Five early drafts, dated May 24, May 25, May 31, June 1, June 2, and June 12, 1944, are found in this file. Overall, seventeen opinions circulated on this hotly argued case, a total of twelve by Rutledge, two by Roberts, two by Jackson, and one by Douglas. Also see Harper, *Justice Rutledge*, 344–45.

18. Goodman, OHI. Quotations regarding the oral reargument are taken from *U.S. Law Week*, "Legality of State Labor Act Questioned," 13:14 (October 17, 1944):

3149+. Unless otherwise noted, all citations about the oral reargument are taken from this source.

19. *Thomas v. Collins*, 323 U.S. 516 (1945).

20. Goodman, OHI; Harper, *Justice Rutledge*, 307.

21. *Thomas v. Collins*, 323 U.S. 516 (1945). All quotations to opinions in *Thomas* cited later are taken from the official published decision, unless otherwise noted.

22. W. Howard Mann to Wiley Rutledge, January 19, 1945, Rutledge to Mann, February 8, 1945, both in Box 118, Wiley Rutledge Papers, LC. For two excellent historical surveys of the constitutional problems as related to questions of labor liberty, see Leon Fink, "Labor, Liberty, and the Law: Trade Unionism and the Problem of the American Constitutional Order," *Journal of American History* 74 (1984): 904–25, and James Gray Pope, "Labor and the Constitution: From Abolition to Deindustrialization," *Texas Law Review* 65: 6 (May 1987): 1071–1136.

23. Stuart Scheingold, *The Politics of Rights: Lawyers, Public Policy, and Political Change* (New Haven: Yale University Press, 1974), 135–36.

24. *CIO v. McAdory*, 325 U.S. 472 (1945); Lee Pressman, Crampton Harris, "Brief of Appellants," *CIO v. McAdory*, Case No. 855, October 1944 Term, USSCRB; *U.S. Law Week*, "Arguments Before the Court: Labor Organizations: State Regulation," 13: 38 (April 10, 1945): 3388–3394. Pressman and Goodman also successfully took a similar state law challenge to the Colorado Supreme Court at the same time, where they also won. See Lee Pressman to Mr. Murray, January 5, 1945, Box A–12, Legal Department Files, CIO Papers, CU; Goodman, OHI. For an interesting work chronicling the intellectual history of New Deal reform ideology, see Alan Brinkely, *The End of Reform: New Deal Liberalism in Recession and War* (New York: Alfred A. Knopf, 1995).

25. There are many works that deal with the Bridges cases. One of the most detailed from the legal perspective is Stanley I. Kutler, "If At First . . . : The Trials of Harry Bridges," in Stanley I. Kutler, *The American Inquisition: Justice and Injustice in the Cold War* (New York: Hill and Wang, 1982), 152–82. Ann Fagan Ginger also exhaustively examines the *Bridges v. Wixon* case in her biography of Carol Weiss King.

26. Ginger, *Carol Weiss King*, 239–40; Philip Murray to the President, February 17, 1945, Box A–12, Philip Murray Files, CIO Papers, CU.

27. Ginger, *Carol Weiss King*, 412.

28. Ginger, *Carol Weiss King*, 413–14; Lee Pressman, FOIA, FBI, 100–11820–439x, May 12, 1950.

29. *Bridges v. Wixon*, 326 U.S. 120 (1945); Stanley I. Kutler, "If At First," 141–42; Ginger, *Carol Weiss King*, 414–18; Fine, *Frank Murphy: The Washington Years*, 427–28.

30. Lee Pressman, FOIA, FBI, 100–11820–439x, May 12, 1950; Lee Pressman to Frank Murphy, June 19, 1945, Box 43–27, Frank Murphy Papers, MHC, UM. Pressman also wrote to Murphy on his opinions one other time regarding a case in which he was not involved, the *Steele v. L&N Railroad* decision. This case struck down racial discrimination in the railroad brotherhood unions. Murphy's concurrence, he thought, would prove to be historic, and "will hearten beyond description those who insist that

out of this war must emerge the complete destruction of Nazism and all its phases, particularly the abominable discrimination based upon race, creed or color." Lee Pressman to Frank Murphy, December 19, 1944, Box 43–22, Frank Murphy Papers, MHC, UM.

31. Goodman, OHI. See Pressman's convention statement on the state antilabor law tests in CIOPROC, 1943, 321–23.

32. The background to the War Labor Disputes Act, Lewis's 1943 strikes, and the CIO leadership's conundrum is well analyzed in both Dubofsky and Van Tine, *John L. Lewis*, 415–44 and Lichtenstein, *Labor's War at Home*, 157–77. Also see Pressman's testimony against Smith–Connally in U.S. Congress, House, Committee on Military Affairs, "Hearings, Full Utilization of Manpower," April 7, 1943, 78th Congress, 1st sess., 299–326, and his comments to the USWA executive board in USWAEB, 11–19, June 22, 1943, Box 41, USWAEB Collection, HCLA, PSU.

33. USWAEB, 112, November 17, 1942, Box 41, USWAEB Collection, HCLA, PSU; CIOEB, 116–17, November 5, 8, 14, 1942, Box 22, CIOEB Collection, WPRL, WSU; CIOPROC, 1944, 74–75.

34. Harris, *The Right to Manage*, 41; Lichtenstein, *Labor's War at Home*, 82–108.

35. Lee Pressman to Philip Murray, August 27, 1943, "Re: Stoppages at Cleveland Plant of American Steel and Wire," Box A–2, CIO Papers, CU.

36. USWAPROC, 1944, 38–40, 102–04.

37. USWAPROC, 1944, 170–75.

38. USWAEB, 17, 21, June 14, 1944, 17, Box 41, USWAEB, Collection, HCLA, PSU; National Maritime Union, *Proceedings of the International Union Convention* (hereafter NMUPROC), July 6, 1945, 202–03, Reel 126, Part I, ALUCP.

39. NMUPROC, July 6, 1945, 202–03, Reel 126, Part I, ALUCP.

40. USWAEB, 10–100, November 26, 1944, and December 1, 1944, 21–118, both Box 41, USWAEB, HCLA, PSU.

41. CIOEB, 296–308, November 16–19, 25, 1944, Box 13, CIOEB Collection, WRPL.

42. USWAEB, 27–52, July 30, 1945, Box 42, USWAEB Collection, HCLA, PSU; NMUPROC, July 6, 1945, 206, Reel 126, Part I, ALUCP.

43. NMUPROC, July 6, 1945, 208–10, Reel 126, Part I, ALUCP. For one of Pressman's last NWLB arguments, see NWLB, Verbatim Transcript, "U.S. Steel Corporation of Delaware and United Steelworkers of America," February 23, 1945, Washington, D.C., Box A–13, CIO Papers, CU. The most complete history of the CIO-PAC is James C. Foster, *The Union Politic: The CIO's Political Action Committee* (Columbia, Mo.: University of Missouri Press, 1975). Interestingly, John Abt claims in his memoir that the original inspiration for developing a political action committee came to him and Pressman from Eugene Dennis, the CP's legislative director. Abt and Pressman then approached Hillman and Murray with the idea. The top offices then set the internal CIO bureaucracy into motion to work toward its creation. Though Hillman was to head the committee and Abt was to be his counsel, Abt said that Pressman, once again showing his competitive "imperialist" streak, insisted he be named co-counsel along with his Ware Group comrade. Pressman, in his brief comments about the CIO-PAC in his Columbia Oral History interview, made no such claim (understandably)

about the PAC's origins. See Abt, *Advocate and Activist*, 99–101, and Lee Pressman, COHC, 433–36.

44. See, for example, Mgsr. Rice's mea culpa, "Confessions of an Anti-Communist," *Labor History* 30: 3 (Summer 1989): 449–62. Carey's career as an anti-communist FBI collaborator is sketched in Sigmund Diamond, "Labor History vs. Labor Historiography: The FBI, James B. Carey, and the Association of Catholic Trade Unionists," in *Religion, Ideology and Nationalism in Europe and America: Essays Presented in Honor of Yehoshua Arieli* (Jerusalem, Israel: Historical Society of Israel and the Alman Shazar Center for Jewish History, 1986), 299–328. The left-right CIO struggles in the national office are of course also detailed in Levenstein, *Communism, Anti-Communism, and the CIO*, and in Zieger, *The CIO*, 253–93, both of which contain citations about the bountiful labor-communism historical literature.

45. Telegram, Gardner Jackson to Philip M. Murray, n.d. [1941?]; Gardner Jackson to Philip Murray, October 1, 1943, both Box 51, Gardner Jackson Papers, FDRL.

46. A Ruttenberg relation, a Party member, had informed him that common Party meeting talk was that the CP had centrally placed Pressman within the CIO. Ruttenberg claimed he told this to Pressman, "who with a pleading smile asked if I would tell Murray," which of course he did. Ruttenberg, OHI/GJG, and Ruttenberg, OHI, 23–24, HCLA, PSU; Letter, Harold Ruttenberg to Gilbert J. Gall, January 1, 1991, copy in possession of author. Interview Notes, "Steel Workers and the Communists" (Phil Murray and Lee Pressman), Interview with Clint Golden, October 26, 1955, (Daniel Bell), Box 3, Bell Collection, RWLA, NYU.

47. Len De Caux, *Labor Radical*, 263–65.

48. The history of Pressman's relationship to the FBI over a number of years is found in Gall, "A Note on Lee Pressman and the FBI," 551–61. Also see J. Edgar Hoover to Major General Edwin M. Watson, Personal and Confidential, October 22, 1943, Franklin D. Roosevelt Papers, Official Files, Box 16, OF 10B (Department of Justice), FDRL.

49. Gilbert J. Gall, "A Note on Lee Pressman and the FBI," 554.

50. See the summary log in Lee Pressman FOIA FBI Files, 100–11820–439x, 279, May 12, 1950, cross-referenced from Roy Hudson's FBI HQ file 100–7602–468, October 31, 1944.

51. D.M. Ladd to the Director, March 25, 1947, Lee Pressman, FOIA, FBI Files, March 25, 1947, 11820–313.

52. J. Edgar Hoover to Bridgadier General Harry Hawkins Vaughn, December 5, 1945, Box 169/P, President's Secretary's File, Papers of Harry S. Truman, President's Secretary's File, Harry S. Truman Library (hereafter HSTL). A more detailed, though edited, version of this FBI memorandum summarizing the surveillance is reproduced in Gall, "A Note on Lee Pressman and the FBI."

53. Interview Notes, "Murray, Pressman and the Communists," Oct. 27, 1955, Conversation with Jim Carey, (Hotel Roosevelt, Pittsburgh) (hereafter Carey Bell Notes, Box 4; RWLA, NYU (hereafter James B. Carey Bell OHI), RWLA, NYU; Interview Notes, Clinton Golden (hereafter Golden Bell Notes), Box 3, Daniel Bell Collection, RWLA, NYU. On Ernst and Hoover see Harrison E. Salisbury, "The

Strange Correspondence of Morris Ernst and John Edgar Hoover, 1939–1964," *The Nation*, December 1, 1984, 575–88.

54. Carey Bell Notes; Golden Bell Notes, RWLA, NYU.

55. Memorandum, *"COMMUNIST ACTIVITIES IN ORGANIZED LABOR,"* [n.d. mid-1944?] Box 18, General Intelligence Survey of the United States, Franklin D. Roosevelt Papers, Official Files, OF 10B (Department of Justice), FDRL; Lee Pressman, FOIA, FBI Files, 100–11820–439x, May 12, 1950.

56. J. Edgar Hoover to Bridgadier General Harry Hawkins Vaughn, December 5, 1945, Box 169/P. Papers of Harry S Truman, President's Secretary's File.

CHAPTER 7

1. De Caux, *Labor Radical*, 446; Rice, OHI, HCLA, PSU; Kempton, *Part of Our Time*, 74. The characterization of Wallace's Progressive Party Campaign as "Gideon's Army" is from participant-observer Curtis D. MacDougall's multivolume history, *Gideon's Army*, 3 vols. (New York: Marzani and Munsell, 1965).

2. Lee Pressman, COHC, 427–51; Abt, *Advocate and Activist*, 113.

3. See, for example, Pressman's remarks in Lee Pressman, "A Basis for Inter-American Cooperation," Address before the Committee on Industrial, Economic, and Social Legislation of the Third Conference of the Inter-American Bar Association, Mexico City, July 31–August 8, 1944, reprinted in *Lawyer's Guild Review* 4:10 (1940):10–13; Abt, *Advocate and Activist*, 113–14.

The WFTU conferences coincided with the issuance of the "Duclos" letter by French Communist theoretician Jacques Duclos, which implicitly criticized American CP leader Earl Browder's decision to reform the U.S. domestic Party as an "interest" group. Within the American party, the Duclos letter launched an internal power struggle between Browder and William Z. Foster. Foster ultimately won and returned the U.S. CP back to its original formulation. To some observers, the Duclos letter signalled a return to a more aggressive or expansionistic form of international Marxism. Under either version of U.S. communism, though, the participation of Communist trade unionists in the WFTU would be important, for it was hoped that the organization could play a potentially significant role in the coming international peace conferences. For a fascinating "inside" look at the issuance of the Duclos letter and its subsequent impact on the internal political life of the Party, see Joseph R. Starobin, *American Communism in Crisis, 1943–1957* (Cambridge, Mass.: Harvard University Press, 1972), 71–120. On Browderism, see Maurice Isserman, *Which Side Were You On?: The American Communist Party During the Second World War* (Middletown, Conn.: Wesleyan University Press, 1982), 187–243.

4. Fraser, *Labor Will Rule*, 543–47; Abt, *Advocate and Activist*, 111–12. For a new look at Foster's career, see Edward P. Johanningsmeier's excellent study, *Forging American Communism: The Life of William Z. Foster* (Princeton, N.J.: Princeton University Press, 1994).

5. Lee Pressman, COHC, 427–52; Abt, *Advocate and Activist*, 113–16.

6. Lee Pressman, COHC, 453–64; Abt, OHI.

7. Len De Caux Travelogue Memorandums, n.d. [1945], Box 7, Len De Caux

Papers, WPRL, WSU [later reprinted as the official CIO report]. Unless otherwise noted, all references to the CIO delegates experience in Paris, Berlin, and the Soviet Union come from these documents.

8. Carey, COHC, 339; Lee Pressman, COHC, 459; Abt, *Advocate and Activist*, 122.

9. Abt OHI. Years later Pressman realized that they had been shown servile labor organizations. "[N]o Russian official need fear that Kuznetsov, as head of the Russian trade union movement, would ever utter a statement contrary to the official government position of Russia on any national or international policy," he remarked in an interview. If an Anglo-American trade union leader was "servile to the government, it's not because of compulsion. He's servile because of his own personal servility." See Lee Pressman, COHC, 461.

10. Carey, COHC, 350.

11. Levenstein, *Communism, Anticommunism, and the CIO*, 189–93.

12. John Doherty and Joe Germano to Lee Pressman, March 11, 1946, Box A4–25, 1945–1946, Murray Files, CIO Papers, CU.

13. Lee Pressman to Joseph Germano, March 14, 1946; Philip Murray to Mr. Vin Sweeney, March 22, 1946, both Box A4–25, 1945–1946, Murray Files, CIO Papers, CU.

14. De Caux, *Labor Radical*, 480–81; Levenstein, *Communism, Anti-Communism, and the CIO*, 219.

15. Edwin Lahey, COHC, 78, 98, 107. Even Lahey was subjected to anticommunist lobbying. Father Haas of Catholic University, another member in the pantheon of anticommunist labor priests, "came to my house one night." He wanted "to talk to me about my association with Lee Pressman. I didn't know what the hell to think. You'd think I was keeping company with a whore or something."

16. Lee Pressman, FOIA, FBI Files, 100–11820–62, J. Edgar Hoover, *MEMORANDUM FOR THE ATTORNEY GENERAL*, Re: LEON PRESSMAN, aka, Lee Pressman, *PERSONAL AND CONFIDENTIAL*, April 3, 1946. Apparently, tension existed on both sides of the Hiss–Pressman relationship in the 1940s. Carey noted their coolness toward each other when they met at the United Nations founding convention in San Francisco. "He [Hiss] referred to Pressman as being—well, you can clean it up a bit—he wouldn't give the sweat off his balls to that Commie bastard," was the way Carey characterized the diplomat's interpersonal reaction to Pressman. The CIO secretary–treasurer detected something more than ideology, "there was something personal involved," he thought. Given Hiss's breeding, it is quite unlikely that he expressed his discomfort with Pressman in that fashion, though Carey's observations of the interpersonal interaction between the two may well have been accurate. Carey, COHC, 325.

Pressman's connection with Harry Dexter White, which the FBI followed closely through 1946 and 1947 through physical surveillance and phone taps, also stemmed from the latter's access to economic foreign policy information. The information contained in the FBI files appears only to reveal that Pressman and White shared a ride to work, that they socialized to an extent, and that Pressman utilized White to help the USWA shape policy within the Truman administration during the 1946 steel strikes. Chambers claimed White had supplied him with important Treasury

Department information during the period 1937–1938, which he later released to corroborate his claims about internal government espionage groups. White died from a heart attack shortly after testifying before HUAC when the Hiss–Chambers case hit the headlines in 1948.

Furthermore, the information about the Silvermaster connection released to date also reveals little more than a number of Pressman–Silvermaster social contacts. The Silvermasters were named by Elizabeth Bentley as being one of the two government espionage groups active in Washington during the war that passed her information to Soviet contacts (she stated Victor Perlo, also an alleged Ware Group alumnus, led the other group).

Whether or not White or Silvermaster were spies is inconclusive, but it can be said that FBI documents, at least those released, reveal nothing about the Pressman, White, and Silvermaster relationships, other than they were casual business professional associations in the 1940s. Lee Pressman, FOIA, FBI Files, 100–11820–439x, 522–39, 542–48, 679, May 12, 1950. Interestingly, Harvey Klehr, John Earl Haynes, and Fridrikh Igorevich Firsov have published a recent collection of translated Soviet documents related to the American Communist Party and Soviet intelligence operations in the United States. They conclude that, taken together, those documents provide important corroborating evidence suggesting the truth of the testimony of Elizabeth Bentley and Whittaker Chambers. See *The Secret World of American Communism* (New Haven, Conn.: Yale University Press, 1995), 309–21. On this general topic, also see Weinstein, *Perjury*, 22–24, 237–40 and David Rees, *Harry Dexter White: A Study in Paradox* (New York: Cowhard, McCann, and Geoghagen, 1973).

17. Lee Pressman, FOIA, FBI Files, 100–11820–439x, 522–39, 542–48, 679, May 12, 1950.

18. "I shall always remember Murray telling me about Edgar Hoover briefing him on Pressman," wrote Ruttenberg. See Harold Ruttenberg to Gilbert J. Gall, April 8, 1992, copy in possession of the author. Lee Pressman, MEMORANDUM FOR: Mr. Philip Murray, November 26, 1946, Box A–32, Murray Files, CIO Papers, CU; Monsignor Charles Owen Rice Oral History Interview with Gilbert J. Gall, June 25, 1992, (hereafter Rice/GJG OHI).

19. Lee Pressman, COHC, 466–70; Harris, *The Right to Manage*, 58–90, 111–17; Lee Pressman, "Re: Status of War Labor Disputes Act and Price Control Law," August 8, 1945, Box 11, James B. Carey Files, CIO Secretary-Treasurer's Collection, WPRL, WSU. Also see Arthur F. McClure, *The Truman Administration and the Problems of Post-War Labor, 1945–1948* (Rutherford, N.J.: Farleigh Dickinson University Press, 1969).

20. On the ambiguous nature of the impact of wartime controls on post-war collective bargaining in the steel industry, see Lee Pressman to Philip Murray, December 11, 1945, Box A–25, Murray Papers, CIO Papers, CU, and Ernest Green to Maurice Sugar, April 17, 1946, Box 71–18, Maurice Sugar Papers, WPRL, WSU; Cotton, OHI.

21. See Pressman reports, USWAPROC, 1946, 36–37; USWAEB, 4–41, Box 42, February 21, 1946, USWAEB Collection, HCLA, PSU; Zieger, *The CIO*, 225–27.

22. Harris, *The Right to Manage*, 109–39; Gall, "CIO Leaders and the Democratic Alliance," 4–27.

23. Lee Pressman, FOIA, FBI Files, 11820–439x, 563, May 12, 1950.

24. USWAEB, 205–41, July 31, 1945, Box 42, USWAEB Collection, HCLA, PSU; CIOEB, 129–58, July 14–15, 1945, Box 2, CIO Executive Board Collection, WPRL, WSU.

25. Pressman's testimony can be found in U.S. Congress, Senate, Committee on Education and Labor, "Labor Fact-Finding Boards Act," February 11, 1946, 711–43, and "Labor Disputes Act of 1946," February 27, 1946, 235–61, quote on 252–53, 79th Congress, 2nd sess., 1946; Lee Pressman to Maurice Sugar, February 8, 1946, Box 71–18, Maurice Sugar Papers, WPRL, WSU.

26. "Town Hall Meeting of the Air Broadcast: Should There Be Stricter Regulation of Labor Unions?", NBC, Springfield, Illinois, June 6, 1946, Sound Recording 200ATMA322, Motion Picture, Sound, and Video Branch, NA.

27. Lee Pressman, "Post-War Wages, Prices and Fiscal Policy," *Lawyer's Guild Review* 6 (1946): 466–68.

28. USWAEB, 351–55, June 29, 1946, Box 42, USWAEB Collection, HCLA, PSU; USWAPROC, 1946, 85–90; CIOPROC, 1946, 291; International Union of Fur and Leather Workers, *Proceedings of the Constitutional Convention* (hereafter IUFLWPROC), 152–53, May 20, 1946, ALUCP.

29. On labor's political ineffectiveness in the 1946 elections, see Foster, *The Union Politic*, 49–76.

30. On the passage of Taft–Hartley, see R. Alton Lee, *Truman and Taft–Hartley: A Question of Mandate* (Lexington: University of Kentucky Press, 1966). On the significance of the union security restrictions, see Gilbert J. Gall, *The Politics of Right-to-Work: The Labor Federations as Special Interests, 1943–1978* (Westport, Conn.: Greenwood Press, 1988). An interesting recent study on the long-term significance of Taft–Hartley is James A. Gross's, *Broken Promise: The Subversion of U.S. Labor Relations Policy, 1947–1994* (Phildelphia, Penn.: Temple University Press, 1995). On the implicit individualism hidden within the original law, see Melvyn Dubofsky, "A Fatal Flaw: Individual Rights and the Wagner Act, " *Proceedings of the Forty-Eighth Annual Meeting, Industrial Relations Research Association*, Paula Voos, ed., January 5–7, 1996, (Madison, Wis.: Industrial Relations Research Association, 1996), 373–80.

31. CIOEB, 270–91, May 16–17, 1947; CIOEB, 7–18, 84+, June 27, 1947; both Box 3, CIOEB Collection, WPRL, WSU.

32. USWAEB, 13–126, July 2, 1947, Box 42, USWAEB Collection, HCLA, PSU. Senator Taft charged that Pressman was the real author of the rationales underlying President Truman's veto message. Eugene Cotton confirmed that Pressman had a close working relationship with Truman aide Clark Clifford, and laid out the CIO's point-by-point brief against Taft–Hartley when he and Murray appeared at the White House to request that the President veto the law. Many of those points did find their way into the veto message. Cotton, OHI.

33. International Union of Mine, Mill, and Smelter Workers, *Proceedings of the Constitutional Convention* (hereafter IUMMSWPROC), August 26, 1947, 123–36, Part II, ALUCP. Unless otherwise noted, all further Pressman remarks are taken from this speech.

34. CIOPROC, 1947, 190–94.

35. Lee Pressman to Philip Murray, "Re: Litigation in which National CIO Office is involved," September 12, 1947, CIO Secretary-Treasurers Collection, James

B. Carey Papers, Box 11, WPRL, WSU; *Anderson v. Mt. Clemens Pottery*, 90 L.Ed. 416; Lee Pressman and Edward Lamb, "Brief of Appellants," *Anderson, et al. v. Mt. Clemens Pottery*, Case No. 342, October Term 1945, USSCRB; USWAEB, 202–61, May 19, 1947, USWA Executive Board Collection, Box 11, HCLA, PSU. The UFWA case was first argued before the Supreme Court in December 1945. A deeply divided Roosevelt Court restored it for reargument in mid-1946 after Chief Justice Harlan Fiske Stone died. Pressman took the reargument forward in October 1946 and finally received the court's decision in February 1947, *United Public Workers v. Mitchell*, 330 US 75 (1947). The name of the union changed to the United Public Workers after a merger in 1946; Gall, "The CIO and the Hatch Act," 4–7.

36. Gall, "The CIO and the Hatch Act," 8–12.

37 Lee Pressman and Frank Donner, "Brief for the Appellants," in Philip B. Kurland and Gerhard Casper, eds., *Landmark Briefs and Arguments of the Supreme Court: Constitutional Cases*, vol. 45 (Arlington, Va.: University Publications of America, 1975), 45–115.

38. J. Howard McGrath and Ralph F. Fuchs, et al., "Brief for the Appellees," in Kurland and Casper, *Landmark Briefs*, 117–73.

39. Lee Pressman, Frank Donner, Milton V. Freedman, Of. Counsel, "Supplemental Brief for Appellants," in Kurland and Casper, *Landmark Briefs*, 193–202.

40. For an analysis of the Roosevelt court as it was being transformed into the Vinson court in the late 1940s and early 1950s, see C. Herman Pritchett, *Civil Liberties and the Vinson Court* (Chicago: University of Chicago Press, 1953).

41. Stanley Reed, Draft of Majority Opinion, *United Public Workers of America (C.I.O.) et al. v. Mitchell*, Case No. 20, October, 1946 Terms; Stanely Reed, Memoranda to the Conference, December 28, December 31, 1946, January 10, January 16, 1947; Felix Frankfurter to Reed, December 20, 1946, January 13, 1947; all Box 98, Stanley Reed Papers, Manuscripts Collections, University of Kentucky at Lexington, Lexington, Kentucky (hereafter Stanley Reed Papers, UK). Unless otherwise noted, all quotes from the majority and minority decisions are taken from the official published text at *United Public Workers of America (C.I.O.) et al. v. Mitchell*, 330 U.S. 75 (1947).

42. *U.S. v. CIO*, 335 U.S. 106 (1947). Margiotti and Pressman argued the case in April 1948 and received the decision in June.

43. Charles Margiotti, Lee Pressman, and Frank Donner, "Brief for Appellees," *U.S. v. CIO*, Case No. 695, October Term 1947, USSCRB.

44. "Arguments Before the Court: Ban on Union Political Expenditures," *U.S. Law Week*, 16: 43 (May 4, 1948), 3327–3329; Marcia Pressman, OHI.

45. Wiley Rutledge, "Bench Memo" and Conference Notes (Conference of May 1, 1948), "*United States v. C.I.O.*, Philip Murray, Officer Thereof," No. 695, O.T. 1947, Box 161, Wiley Rutledge Papers, LC; Fred Vinson, "*Memorandum for the Conference, No. 695—United States v. CIO*, May 5, 1948, Box 250, Fred Vinson Papers, Manuscripts Collections, UK; Stanley Reed, "CIO, NOTES IN INDICTMENT," and attachments, n.d., [May 1948], Box 112, Stanley Reed Papers, UK; quotes from *U.S. v. CIO*, 335 U.S. 106 (1947).

46. *U.S. v. CIO*, 335 U.S. 106 (1947).

47. Kempton, *Part of Our Time*, 75.

Notes ❖ 343

48. Meyer Bernstein to Clinton Golden, November 21, 1947, Box 3–23, Clinton Golden Papers, HCLA, PSU.

49. Lee Pressman, FOIA, FBI Files, 100–11820–439x, May 12, 1950; Lee Pressman, FOIA, FBI Files, 100–11820–402, Memo, SAC, Pittsburgh to Director, FBI, December 8, 1947; Lee Pressman, FOIA, FBI Files, 100–11820–403, Memo, Director, FBI to SAC, Pittsburgh, December 19, 1947.

50. Meyer Bernstein to Clinton Golden, February 3, 1948, Box 3–23, Clinton Golden Papers, HCLA, PSU.

51. Clinton Golden to Meyer Bernstein, February 21, 1948, Box 1–19, Clinton Golden Papers, HCLA, PSU; Abt, OHI.

52. "End of the Line?" *Time*, February 16, 1948, vol. 51, p. 25; Kempton, *Part of Our Time*, 76.

53. A copy of Pressman's resignation letter and Murray's response is in USWAEB, 21–29, February 16, 1948, Box 43, USWAEB Collection, HCLA, PSU.

54. USWAEB, 21–29, February 16, 1948, Box 43, USWAEB Collection, HCLA, PSU.

55. USWAEB, 21–29, February 16, 1948, Box 43, USWA Executive Board Collection, HCLA, PSU.

56. Kempton, *Part of Our Time*, 76.

CHAPTER 8

1. An interesting background review of the ideological divisions in American legal liberalism over communism is in Jerold Simmons' "Morris Ernst and Disclosure: One Liberal's Quest for a Solution to the Problem of Domestic Communism, 1939–1949," *Mid-America* 71:1 (January 1989):15–30.

2. Harold Ruttenberg, OHI/GJG. For the continuing interest that the Hiss–Chambers case evokes, see Alger Hiss's recent obituary in the *New York Times*, November 22, 1996, p. 1.

3. Gardner Jackson to Ken Crawford, April 5, 1948, Box 18; Gardner Jackson to Jerome Frank, April 21, 1948, Box 28, Gardner Jackson Papers, FDRL.

4. Ruttenberg, OHI/GJG, 31; Abt, *Advocate and Activist*, 148.

5. Lee Pressman Speech, November 1948, Lee Pressman Personal Collection [hereafter LPPC]. A small set of Lee Pressman's personal papers exists in the possession of his youngest daughter, Susan Pressman Sragow. Ms. Sragow kindly allowed me copies of these documents. The originals remain in her possession.

6. Ruttenberg, OHI/GJG, 31; Abt, *Advocate and Activist*, 148; Abt, OHI; Lee Pressman, FOIA, FBI, 100–11820–661, September 11, 1952.

7. Cammer, OHI; Abt, OHI; Financial Statements: Witt and Cammer, July 31, 1946, LPPC; Ann Pressman, OHI; Marcia Pressman, OHI; Sragow, OHI; Rabkin, OHI.

8. Lee Pressman, FOIA, FBI Files, 100–11820–439x, date, 860, 868, 888, 986. Interestingly, Potash's codependents were Gerhart Eisler, a Comintern representative to the United States, who later jumped bail, and CP members John Williamson and Ferdinand Smith.

9. Ginger, *Carol Weiss King*, 460–70; Lee Pressman, FOIA, FBI Files, 100–11820–439x, May 12, 1950, 917, 977; Paul Robeson to Lee Pressman, April 23, 1948, LPPC.

10. MacDougall, *Gideon's Army*, vol. 2, 534–35; Lee Pressman to Rexford Tugwell, June 9, 1948, Rexford Tugwell to Lee Pressman, June 11, 1948, both Box 18, Rexford Tugwell Papers, FDRL. The primary authors of the New York outline were David Ramsey and Tabitha Petran, according to MacDougall. Also arguing against Pressman's role as a Machiavellian manipulator was the fact that the steering committee worked from three separate drafts to produce a final outcome, and that Pressman solicited and gave serious consideration to the thoughts of platform committee members who were not able to participate in person. See Frederick Schuman to Lee Pressman, July 10, 1948, Box 36, Rexford Tugwell Papers, FDRL.

11. Lee Pressman, FOIA, FBI Files, 100–11820–412, March 4, 1948, Memo, Director, FBI to the Attorney General, 100–11820–426, June 9, 1948, D.M. Ladd to Mr. Tamm.

12. John Cotton Brown, "The 1948 Progressive Campaign: A Scientific Approach," Ph.D. diss., University of Chicago, 1949, 139–41. Brown attended almost all platform advisory and full platform committee meetings as a participant–observer. His analysis was drawn from his field notes.

13. Brown, "The 1948 Progressive Campaign," 149–52.

14. Brown, "The 1948 Progressive Campaign," 154–56.

15. Brown, "The 1948 Progressive Campaign," 166–67; MacDougall, *Gideon's Army*, vol. 2, 569–86.

16. MacDougall, *Gideon's Army*, vol. 2, 534–45.

17. Rexford Tugwell to Antonio Borgese, with open letter, August 20, 1948, Box 36, Rexford Tugwell Papers, FDRL.

18. The best history of the Smith Act trials is Michael Belknap's, *Cold War Political Justice: The Smith Act, the Communist Party, and American Civil Liberties* (Westport, Conn.: 1977); Abt, *Advocate and Activist*, 133, 150.

19. Weinstein, *Perjury*, 1–11. Klehr, Haynes, and Firsov, *The Secret World of American Communism*, 312–17, cite Comintern and CPUSA documents in Soviet archives that provide some ancillary corroboration for Bentley's story.

20. Hiss quoted in Weinstein's, *Perjury*, 14.

21. Cammer, OHI.

22. Cammer, OHI; Lee Pressman, HUAC 1948, 1022–1028.

23. Lee Pressman, FOIA, FBI Files, 100–11820–433, February 2, 1949, 12; Lee Pressman, HUAC Statement, Undelivered, [1948], LPPC. Unless otherwise noted, all further quotations about Pressman's undelivered HUAC remarks are from this document.

24. Baker's portrait of Witt before the HUAC is quoted in Abt, *Advocate and Activist*, 175. Also see Kenneth Reilly, *Hoover and the Un-Americans: The FBI, HUAC, and the Red Menace* (Philadelphia: Temple University Press, 1983).

25. Lee Pressman, FOIA, FBI Files, 100–11820–661, September 11, 1952, 100–11820–433, February 2, 1949, 10, 100–11820–439x, May 12, 1950, 1076.

26. Samuel Abrahams, "$250,000 for Lee Pressman's Lost Campaign," *Plain Talk* (January 1949): 41–42; Lee Pressman, FOIA, FBI Files, 100–11820–433, February 2, 1949.

27. Abrahams, "$250,000 for Lee Pressman's Lost Campaign,"; Lee Pressman, FBI, FOIA Files, 100–11820–433, February 2, 1949, 13; "This is Lee Pressman," Campaign Document [n.d. 1948?], LPPC, italics in the original; Rabkin, OHI.

28. Ruttenberg, GJG/OHI; Abt, *Advocate and Activist*, 163–64; Gornick, *The Romance of American Communism*, 13–15.

29. The interagency rivalry between the Truman Justice Department, the Republican-dominated HUAC, and the FBI as to the investigation is a fascinating dimension of the *Hiss* case. See Weinstein, *Perjury*, 175–95, 270–305. An indictment for espionage did not issue because of statute-of-limitations problems. Chambers, though, escaped the wrath of the grand jury.

30. Belknap, *Cold War Political Justice*, 35–65.

31. Hiss–Chambers, FOIA, FBI Files, File #59, 74–1113, 59–64, February 8, 1949.

32. Hiss–Chambers, FOIA, FBI Files, File #59, 74–1113, 65–69, February 8, 1949.

33. Lee Pressman, FOIA, FBI Files, 100–11820–661, September 11, 1952, 100–11820–439, September 20, 1949; Hiss–Chambers, FOIA Files, File #72, 74–1333, 45–48, February 21, 1949.

34. Weinstein, *Perjury*, 381, see footnotes 11 and 12 on 631 (memos dated January 17, February 7, and March 7, 1949); Cammer, OHI.

35. Cammer, OHI. As an interesting aside, New York Congresswoman Bella Abzug, then a young lawyer, worked for a brief time at the firm of Pressman, Witt, and Cammer. She apparently rubbed Pressman the wrong way, and he convinced Cammer that she had to be fired.

36. Lee Pressman, FOIA, FBI Files, 100–11820–688, March 13, 1953. The information on Pressman's relationship with Novikov comes from two interviews he gave to the FBI, one on August 30–31, 1950 and another on January 26, 1953.

37. Lee Pressman, FOIA, FBI Files, 100–11820–688, March 13, 1953. Pressman's concerns escalated even further when FBI-surveilled Novikov visited him unannounced at his house in Mt. Vernon, bringing two bottles of a highly prized brand of vodka. On the Novikov–Verber–Ponger case, see George Carpozi, *Red Spies in Washington* (New York: Trident Press, 1968), 31–32, 41–43.

38. Stanley I. Kutler, "'Kill the Lawyers': Guilt by Representation," in Kutler, *The American Inquisition*, 152–82; SAC [Special Agent in Charge], Baltimore, to Director, FBI, Lee Pressman, FOIA, FBI Files, 100–11820–443, November 30, 1949.

39. Lee Pressman, FOIA, FBI Files, 100–11820–444, December 5, 1949, L. B. Nichols to Mr. Tolson.

40. Lee Pressman, FOIA, FBI Files, 100–11820–447, February 2, 1950, H. B. Fletcher to Mr. Ladd; 100–11820–446, February 4, 1950; L. B. Nichols to Mr. Tolson, with attachment, summarizing the source's lunch with Pressman; 100–11820–448, March 6, 1950. Unless otherwise noted, all information regarding this luncheon with Pressman is taken from this document.

41. The FBI's FOIA process expunged a word in that sentence that contextually could have been a salutation such as "comrade." The reporter's answer, "I said yes," seemed to be meant to imply to Pressman that while she may have been critical of the CP currently, olds bonds still existed at the personal level.

42. Obviously, this journalist had a perverse sense of what "off the record" meant, for although this interview did not appear in print, it quickly made its way into the files of the FBI.

43. Lee Pressman, FOIA, FBI Files, 100–11820–449, March 6, 1950, M.A. Jones to Mr. Nichols.

CHAPTER 9

1. Weinstein, *Perjury*, 470; David Caute, *The Great Fear: The Anti-Communist Purge Under Truman and Eisenhower* (New York: Simon & Schuster, 1978), 62–69; Gary May, *Un-American Activities: The Trials of William Remington* (New York: Oxford University Press, 1994); Robert Chadwell Williams, *Klaus Fuchs, Atom Spy* (Cambridge, Mass.: Harvard University Press, 1987).

2. Kempton, *Part of Our Time*, 74, 79.

3. Lee Pressman, FOIA, FBI Files, A. H. Belmont to D. M. Ladd, 100–11820–459, August 11, 1950.

4. Lee Pressman, FOIA, FBI Files, 100–11820–480, August 21, 1950, Mr. Nichols to Mr. Tolson; 100–11820–462, August 25, 1950, Mr. L. B. Nichols to Mr. C. A. Tolson; 100–11820–459, August 21, 1950, Telex, Hoover to SAC [Special Agent in Charge], New York; Telex, 100–11820–479, August 22, 1950, [Earl] Scheidt to Director, Urgent; 100–11820–487, August 24, 1950, Mr. L. L. Laughlin to Mr. A. H. Belmont; 100–11820–486, August 24, 1950, E. H. Winterrow to Mr. D. M. Ladd, with Memo, Director, FBI to the Attorney General.

5. Telex, [Earl] Scheidt to Director, Urgent, August 25, 1950, Alger Hiss Papers, FBI Records, #4629, HLS.

6. Rabkin, OHI. Unless otherwise noted, all information regarding Pressman's decision to testify before the HUAC is taken from the Rabkin interview.

7. Ann Pressman, OHI; Marcia Pressman, OHI; Irving Pressman, OHI.

8. Kempton, *Part of Our Time*, 78.

9. "Text of Pressman Statement," *New York Times*, August 28, 1950, p. 1, col. 1. Unless otherwise noted, all following quotes from his public statement are taken from this source.

10. Silent newsreel outtakes of Pressman's 1950 HUAC testimony exist in the National Archives Sound and Motion Picture Division, NA; Kempton, *Part of Our Time*, 79.

11. Lee Pressman, 1950, HUAC, reprinted verbatim in Lee Pressman, FOIA, FBI Files, 100–1820–661, September 11, 1952 . Unless otherwise noted, all quotes and summations from the testimony are from this source.

12. Walter Goodman, *The Committee: The Extraordinary Career of the House Committee on Un-American Activities* (New York: Farrar, Straus, and Giroux), 288.

13. Goodman, *The Un-Americans*, 288–89.

14. Lee Pressman, FOIA, FBI Files, 100–11820–439, September 20, 1949; 100–11820–661, September 11, 1952; Chambers, *Witness*, 340, 435–37; Weinstein, *Perjury*, 62–66, 157n.

15. Selections of press commentary by Lasky, Riesel, and Kempton appear in

Lee Pressman, FOIA, FBI Files, 100–11820–661, September 11, 1952. Also see Dick Reynard, "Lee Pressman Lies," *The New Leader*, September 9, 1950, pp. 6–8; *Time*, September 4, 1950, p. 12; C.P. Trussel, "Pressman Names Three in New Deal as Reds with Him," *New York Times*, August 29, 1950, p. 1, col. 1.

16. Lee Pressman, FOIA, FBI Files, 100–11820–481, August 28, 1950, SAC to the Director.

17. Lee Pressman, FOIA, FBI Files, 100–11820–470, August 29, 1950, Mr. C. E. Hennrich to Mr. A. H. Belmont; 100–11820–469, August 29, 1950, Mr. A. H. Belmont to Mr. D. M. Ladd.

18. Lee Pressman, FOIA, FBI Files, 100–11820–493, August 31, 1950, A. H. Belmont to Mr. Ladd; 100–11820–494, August 30, 1950, A. H. Belmont to Director, FBI; 100–11820–475, August 31, 1950, A. H. Belmont to D..M. Ladd.

19. Lee Pressman, FOIA, FBI Files, 100–11820–661, September 11, 1952. Unless otherwise noted, all of the following data is taken from Pressman's 1950 interview with the FBI, mostly completely summarized in this document.

20. Lee Pressman, FOIA, FBI Files, Mr. A. H. Belmont to Mr. D. M. Ladd, August 31, 1950, 100–11820–475, August 31, 1950.

21. Lee Pressman, FOIA, FBI Files, 100–11820–463, September 1, 1950, Memorandum for Mr. Tolson, Mr. Ladd, Mr. Belmont, Mr. Nichols, and 100–11820–512, September 29, 1950.

22. Lee Pressman, FOIA, FBI Files, 100–11820–493, August 31, 1950, A. H. Belmont to Mr. Ladd; 100–11820–463–464, September 1, 1950, John Edgar Hoover, Memorandum for Mr. Ladd, Mr. Belmont, Mr. Tolson; Memorandum for Mr. Tolson, Mr. Ladd, Mr. Belmont, Mr. Nichols.

23. Lee Pressman, FOIA, FBI Files, 100–11820–473, September 5, 1950, Director, FBI to SAC, New York; 100–11820–475, September 7, 1950; 100–11820–533, November 16, 1950, Director, FBI to SAC, New York.

24. Lee Pressman, FOIA, FBI Files, 100–11820–483, August 31, 1950, Telex, Carson to Director and SAC New York.

25. Lee Pressman, FOIA, FBI Files, 100–11820–503, October 11, 1950.

26. Lee Pressman, FOIA, FBI Files, 100–11820–503, October 11, 1950.

27. Lee Pressman, FOIA, FBI Files, 100–11820–509, September 12, 1950, Mr. D. M. Ladd to the Director; 100–11820–520, N9vember 9, 1950, SAC, Baltimore to Director, FBI. Moren, alias Mark Phillipovich, alias Mark Zilberg, may have been military attache at the Russian embassy in the 1930s. Chambers' 1945 statements were generally consistent with what he had allegedly told Berle in 1939. In 1945, Chambers told the FBI that "Mark Moren was [a] somewhat mythical underground character who was heard about in Communist circles during the Spanish civil war[,] but that he, Chambers had never met him nor seem him nor did he know of any information that would identify him." At that time, he also said that Pressman accompanied Moren to Mexico to buy arms for Spain in late 1937, "and that a small Texas newspaper had reported both of their names in connection with an airplane accident in Brownsville, Texas." Moren was later identified by Walter Krivitsky, a defecting Soviet espionage agent, as Mark Zilberg. This material is contained in the unreleased FBI files (65–57803–10, 65–57803–22–24), brief summaries of which are cross-referenced in the Pressman, FOIA, FBI Files.

28. Lee Pressman, FOIA, FBI Files, 100–11820–509, September 12, 1950, Mr. D. M. Ladd to the Director. A review of other Texas regional newspapers for a span of months in 1936 produced similar results.

29. Lee Pressman, FOIA, FBI Files, 100–11820–549, November 28, 1950; 100–11820–509, September 12, 1950.

30. Lee Pressman, FOIA, FBI Files, 100–11820, March 5, 1951, Mr. F. M. Baumgardner to Mr. A. H. Belmont; 100–11820–661, September 11, 1952.

31. Lee Pressman, FOIA, FBI Files, 100–11820–661, September 11, 1952; 100–11820–618, August 3, 1951, SAC, New York to the Director, FBI.

32. Lee Pressman, FOIA, FBI Files, 100–11820–528, November 13, 1950, SAC, New York, to Director, FBI; 100–11820–579, December 8, 1950, Mr. F. J. Baumgardner to Mr. A. H. Belmont; 100–11820–595, April 23, 1951, F. J. Baumgardner to A. H. Belmont, 100–11820–595.

33. See the elaborate series of Lamb-related telegrams in the FOIA Hiss–Chambers FBI Files at FBI Headquarters, Washington, D.C., especially serials 74–1333–2919, 2920, 2921, 3001, Files #73, 77, April 2, April 6, 1949. One should keep in mind two offsetting factors: 1) It seems that the FBI inordinately "coached" Lamb's memory at various points and might have tainted his credibility; and 2) At the time of its initial contact with Lamb, the Bureau wanted his help in order to develop the Hiss case, not to prosecute Pressman.

34. Lee Pressman, FOIA, FBI Files, Director, FBI to SAC, New York, 100–11820–530, November 9, 1950.

35. Hiss–Chamber FBI Files, 74–1333–4670, November 27, 1950, Guy HAttel, SAC, Washington Field, to Director, FBI.

36. Hiss–Chamber FBI Files, 74–1333–4670, November 27, 1950, Guy Hottel, SAC, Washington Field, to Director, FBI; Davis, *Great Day Coming*, 65–86.

37. Lee Pressman, FOIA, FBI Files, 100–11820–576, March 19, 1951, Director, FBI to SAC, Baltimore; 100–11820–710, June 24, 1953, SAC, WFO [Washington Field Office] to Director, FBI; 100–11820–710, July 2, 1953, Director, FBI to SAC, Los Angeles.

38. Lee Pressman, FOIA, FBI Files, 100–11820–639, February 21, 1952, James M. McInerney, Assistant Attorney General, Criminal Division, to the Director, Federal Bureau of Investigation; 100–11820–644, April 22, 1952, SAC, Baltimore to Director, FBI.

39. Lee Pressman, FOIA, FBI Files, Telex, 100–11820–670, November 6, 1952; Telex, R. B. Hood, 100–11820–667, November 5, 1952; A. H. Belmont to D. M. Ladd, 100–11820–691, March 27, 1953; SAC, Baltimore to Director, FBI, 100–11820–679, December 22, 1952; SAC, Baltimore to Director, FBI, 100–11820–693, April 8, 1953; SAC, WFO to Director, FBI, 100–11820–680–681, January 2, 1953.

40. Lee Pressman, FOIA, FBI Files, 100–11820–691, March 27, 1953, Telex, A. H. Belmont to D. M. Ladd; 100–11820–683, January 26, 1953.

41. Lee Pressman, FOIA, FBI Files, 100–11820–769, September 15, 1954, W.A. Branigan to A. H. Belmont; 100–11820–768, September 16, 1954, Director, FBI to SAC, NY; Nathan Gregory Silvermaster FBI HQ Files, 75–1121, August 20, 1954; 75–1121, August 20, 1954, A.H. Belmont to L. V. Boardman.

42. Kempton, *Part of Our Time*, 80.

43. Hope Hale Davis, "Looking Back at My Years in the Party," *New Leader*, February 11, 1980, 11–13.

44. Abt, OHI.

EPILOGUE

1. Quoted in "Lee Pressman, Labor Lawyer and Ex-C.I.O. Counsel, 63, Dies," *New York Times*, November 22, 1969, p. 47, col 1.

2. Gornick, *The Romance of American Communism*, 190–91.

3. Irving Pressman, OHI; Ruttenberg, OHI/GJG; Oral History Interview, Lynne and John Weiner with Gilbert J. Gall, October 31, 1991 (hereafter Weiner, OHI).

4. Ann Pressman, OHI.

5. Marcia Pressman, OHI.

6. Marcia Pressman, OHI.

7. Irving Pressman, OHI; Ann Pressman, OHI; Marcia Pressman, OHI.

8. Irving Pressman, OHI; Ann Pressman, OHI; Marcia Pressman, OHI; Susan Pressman Sragow, OHI; Weiner, OHI; Harold Ruttenberg to Gilbert J. Gall, January 1, 1991, copy in possession of the author.

9. Lee Pressman, FOIA, FBI Files, 100–11820–604, June 9, 1951; 100–11820–634, November 6, 1951.

10. Lee Pressman, FOIA, FBI Files, 100–11820–773, October 28, 1954.

11. Lee Pressman, FOIA, FBI Files, 100–11820–787, June 13, 1955.

12. Lee Pressman, FOIA, FBI Files, 100–11820–797, April 24, 1964, Supplemental Correlation Summary. For Goldberg's career as successor to Pressman, see Stebenne, *Arthur J. Goldberg*.

13. See generally, Lee Pressman, Bell, OHI; Daniel Bell to Gilbert J. Gall, November 13, 1992.

14. Weiner, OHI; Harold Ruttenberg to Gilbert J. Gall, January 1, 1991; Murray Kempton to Pat [Gardner Jackson], n.d. [1953–1954?], Box 41, Gardner Jackson Papers, FDRL; Ann Pressman, OHI; Marcia Pressman, OHI; Susan Pressman Sragow, OHI. For a nontraditional attempt to assess Pressman's personality, see Gilbert J. Gall and Walter M. Weintraub, M.D.,"Verbal Behavior and Personality Analysis in Historical Biography: Lee Pressman as a Test Case," *The Psychohistory Review* 24: 3 (Spring 1996): 293–324.

15. Lee Pressman, COHC; D. F. Shaughnessy to Gilbert J. Gall, September 15, 1994, copy in possession of the author; Lee Pressman, Fine, OHI. The subject of communism was also a forbidden topic within the family. Susan Pressman Sragow, OHI. Also, Pressman was quite critical of Cold War liberal Arthur Schlesinger's histories of the New Deal. See Lee Pressman to Florence Frank, March 9, 1959, Box 65, Jerome Frank Papers, YUL.

16. De Caux, *Labor Radical*, 262.

17. FLWIUPROC, 1946, ALUCP.

18. D. F. Shaughnessy to Gilbert J. Gall, September 15, 1994; Marcia Pressman, OHI.

19. Marcia Pressman, OHI; Lee Pressman, "The LMRDA and Franchise in the Union," *Proceedings of New York University 17th Annual Conference on Labor*," May 25–27, 1964, Thomas G. S. Christensen, ed., (Washington, D.C.: BNA Books, 1964), 383–98.

20. Ann Pressman, OHI.

21. Susan Pressman Sragow, OHI.

22. Rabkin, OHI; Weiner, OHI.

23. Marcia Pressman, OHI.

BIBLIOGRAPHICAL NOTE

The items cited in the endnotes form the basis for this work's bibliography. However, there are three fine bibliographical compilations on the history of the CIO and labor and the state. See Robert H. Zieger, "Toward a History of the CIO: A Bibliographical Report," *Labor History* 26: 4 (Fall 1985): 487–516 and "The CIO: A Bibliographical Report and Archival Guide," *Labor History* 31: 4 (Fall 1990): 413–40 on the CIO. For an extensive bibliography of labor and the state, see Melvyn Dubofsky, *The State and Labor in Modern America* (Chapel Hill: University of North Carolina Press, 1994).

INDEX

A

Abraham Lincoln School, 198–199
Abrahams, Samuel, 249
Abt, John, 1–4, 17, 23, 25–26, 30, 33,
    37–40, 59,77, 114, 121, 123–124,
    192, 194–195, 197, 228–229, 234,
    236–237, 239–241, 250, 253–254,
    261, 266, 270–271, 278–279,
    282–283, 285, 291–292, 296–297
Adams, Donald, 253
Agribusiness, 25
Agriculture Department, U.S., 1, 20, 30,
    37, 269–271, 292
Agricultural Adjustment
    Administration, 1–3, 21, 23–31, 34,
    38, 40, 44, 59, 118–119, 164, 187,
    233, 244–245, 248, 252–254,
    278–281
Alinsky, Saul, 54–55, 73–74, 133
*Allen-Bradley v. Wisconsin Employment
    Relations Board*, 161
Amalgamted Association of Iron, Steel,
    and Tin Workers, 50, 56, 83
Amalgamated Clothing Workers of
    America, 15, 52, 58, 121

American Committee for the Protection
    of the Foreign-Born, 238
American Federation of Government
    Employees, 216
American Federation of Labor, 21, 44,
    49, 50–51, 62, 69, 71, 76, 97–99,
    101–102, 105, 109, 124, 135–136,
    174. 193, 216, 228
American Federation of Labor-Congress
    of Industrial Organizations, 305, 310
American Labor Party, 4, 23, 59, 236,
    247–250, 264–265, 267, 282
American Law Institute, 116
Anderson v. Mt. Clemens, 216
Anti-Semitism, 11–16, 124
Apex v. Leader, 104–105

B

Bachrach, Arthur, 27
Baker, Russel, 246
Ball-Burton-Hatch Bill, 207
Ballard, Charles, 90
Ballard, Ernest, 88
Bell, Daniel, 39, 42, 185, 189, 305–306

Bellevue-Stratford Hotel, 189
Belmont Hotel, 265
Bensonhurst (Brooklyn), 10, 250
Bentley, Elizabeth, 244, 246, 254–255, 288–289, 295
Bergdorf Detective Agency, 56
Berle, Adolph, 60, 273, 279
Bernstein, Meyer, 83, 85, 90–91, 98, 228–229
Bethlehem Steel, 78, 92, 94–96
Biddle, Francis, 175, 177
Biemiller, Andrew J., 209
Bittner, Van, 51, 80
Black, Edward, 64–65
Black, Hugo, 116–117, 164, 167, 171, 176, 217, 219, 220–223, 259
Bloor, Ella Reeve (Mother), 38
Borgese, Antonio, 243
Bowers, Ralph, 88
Bowles, Charels, 205
Brand, Charles, 25
Brandeis, Louis, 27–28
Brass Rail Restaurant, 259
Bridges, Harry, 175–176, 188
Bridges v. Wixon, 158, 175–178
Broadwater, Margaret, 110
Brooklyn Eagle, 250
Brookwood Labor School, 51
Brophy, John, 48–50, 52–53, 64, 77, 120, 122, 131, 144, 186
Broun, Heywood, 49
Brown v. Board of Education, 117
Brown, Donaldson, 69, 71
Brown, John Cotton, 240–242
Brownsville Herald, 287
Budenz, Louis, 256
Burton, Harold, 217
Butler Library, 307
Bykov, Boris, 273
Byrnes, James, 201

C

Cammer, Harold, 3–4, 16, 236–237, 245, 254, 256–257, 302

Captive Coal Mine Crisis, 1941, 137
Carey, James B., 49–50, 184, 189, 194, 196–197
Cardenas, Ernesto, 290
Carlson v. California, 109–110, 160
Carnegie, Andrew, 51
Carnegie Building, 71
Carnegie-Mellon, 195
Caroline Products case, 164
Case Bill, 208
Chadbourne, Stanchfield, and Levy, 16–17, 21–22, 253
Chamber of Commerce, 105
Chambers, Esther, 294
Chambers, Whittaker, 3–4, 34–35, 39–40, 42, 60–61, 187, 200, 232, 244–247, 249, 251–252, 254–255, 260, 266, 271–274, 276, 279–281, 283–284, 286–287, 290–295, 306
Chicago Tribune, 200
China, 43, 111, 263, 288
Ching, Cyrus, 139
Chou-En-Lai, 111, 296
Chrysler Sit-Down Strike, 72–74, 103, 164, 307
Chrysler, Walter, 71
Chu-Teh, 296
CIO News, 224, 226
CIO v. McAdory, 174
Citrine, Sir Walter, 194
Civil Aeronautics Board, 287
Civil Liberties Unit (Department of Justice), 95–96
Clark, Tom, 200, 238–239, 244
Clayton Act, 104
Clear and Present Danger, 164, 171
Colbert, Tex, 72
Cold War, 159, 198–202, 229, 233, 235, 241, 248, 305; and labor, 193–198
Collins, Henry, 39–40, 254, 272, 279, 285, 291, 293
Columbia Broadcasting System (CBS), 125, 130
Commonwealth of Steel, 113–114, 133, 143

Communist Party, American, 1–4, 18,
    34–38, 59–62, 113–114, 120–124,
    127–129, 159, 175, 193, 195,
    200–201, 229, 258–259, 265,
    267–281, 284–286, 288–290,
    292–293, 296–297, 299–300,
    302–309; in CIO, 184–191, 228, 261;
    Hiss-Chambers case, 243–247, 254;
    in Progressive Party, 240–243,
    247–251; in Smith Act prosecutions,
    251–252, 260–261, 263
Congress (Committee) of Industrial
    Organizatons, 3, 45, 47–59, 60–78,
    81–85, 89, 92–99, 101–104, 106,
    108–110, 112, 116–117, 192–194,
    205–206, 210, 232–233, 236–239,
    245, 248, 251, 254, 259, 267, 270,
    272, 274–276, 279–283, 286,
    294–295, 300, 302, 204–305,
    307–311 ; CIO attorneys, 158,
    160–162, 207; CIO litigation,
    163–178, 215–227; CIO-PAC, 159,
    184, 287; Cold War, 198–202; and
    communism, 114, 122, 124, 127,
    184–191, 228, 261; conventions,
    (1939) 280, (1940) 127–129, (1943)
    187–191, (1946) 211, 200; and inter-
    national labor, 193–198; in Labor's
    Non-Partisan League, 118; in NWLB
    Cases, 1941–1942, 138–144;
    Pressman resignation, 230–231; and
    Taft-Hartley, 212–215
Coplon, Judith, 257, 282
Cornell University, 11–13, 278
Cowan, Nathan, 85–86
Cotton, Eugene, 134–135, 140,
    159–161, 165, 204
Crawford, Ken, 233, 290

D

Dagget, Herbert, 303
Daily Worker, 38, 247, 249, 265
Das Kapital, 46
Davidow, Larry, 64, 66–67

Davis, Chester, 23, 30
Davis, Hope Hale, 40–42, 292, 296
Davis, Phillip, 5
Davis, Walter Rhodes, 123, 273,
    288–290
Davis, William H., 138–139, 181, 182
De Caux, Len, 62, 122, 129, 135,
    185–186, 192, 196–197, 200, 308
Democratic National Committee, 235
Denham, Robert, 214, 228
Dennis, Eugene, 60, 229, 272, 281,
    304
DeToldeano, Ralph, 278
Dewey, Thomas, 248
Dickinson, Fagan, 165
Dixiecrat, 232
Dollar-a-Year Men, 134, 136
Donner, Frank, 224
Donovan, John, 40, 292–293
Donovan, William, 74
Douglas, William O., 164, 167, 169,
    171, 176, 217, 220, 226
Dubinsky, David, 50
Dubofsky, Melvyn (and Van Tine,
    Warren), 45, 69–70, 211

E

Eckhart, Joseph, 274, 278–279, 285,
    287–289
Ellender, Allen, 209
Emerson, Thomas, 20, 242
Employee Representation Plans, 52, 78
Ernst, Morris, 105, 115–116, 189
Ex Parte Curtis, 220, 222

F

Fascism, 128–129, 158
Fahy, Charles, 87–88, 176
Fair Employment Practices Committee
    (FEPC), 208
Fair Labor Standards Act, 95
Fairless, Benjamin, 71

Federal Bureau of Investigation (FBI), 38, 40, 61, 109, 118, 120, 186–191, 200–201, 206–207, 216, 228–229, 263–266, 269, 271–273, 233, 236, 238–239; in Hiss-Chambers case, 244–247; and Lee Pressman, 251–262

Federal Emergency Relief Agency (FERA), 32–37

Field, Frederick, 238

Fifth Amendment, 217, 245–246, 282, 294–295, 304

Fine, Sidney, 307

First Amendment, 164–178, 217–218, 221, 223–225, 227

Foley Square Federal Courthouse, 233, 252

Food and Tobacco Workers Union, 237

Ford, Henry, 75, 96

Forer, Joseph, 238

Fortas, Abe, 20

Fortune magazine, 165

Foster, William Z., 252

Franco, Francisco, 187

Frank, Jerome, 4, 17–18, 20–21, 23–28, 30–31, 33–34, 56, 105, 116, 234, 252–253, 255, 264

Frankenstein, Richard, 139

Frankfurter, Felix, 14–16, 23, 44, 19–20, 102–103, 111, 217–219, 220, 225–226, 278

Frick, Henry Clay, 51

Fuchs, Klaus, 218–220

Fuchs, Ralph, 218–220

Fur and Leather Workers Union (International), 237, 309

G

Gaddola, Paul, 67–68

Garment industry, 5–6

General Motors, 45, 62–72, 75, 80, 92, 102–103, 121, 164; Flint Sit-Down Strike, 56, 62–71, 307

Germano, Joseph, 198–199

Germer, Adolph, 64

Ginger, Ann Fagan, 19–20

Girdler, Tom, 75, 78, 80, 83, 86, 90–91, 93, 133, 248

Gladstein, Grossman, and Margolis, 110

Galdstein, Richard, 110, 175–176

Glennon, Robert J., 17

Globe Doctrine (NLRB), 97

Gold, Ben, 309

Goldberg, Arthur, 305

Golden, Clinton, 51, 71, 83, 122, 185–186, 189, 228–229; industrial council plans, 131

Goldsmith, William, 189

Golos, Jacob, 289

Goodman, Ernest, 161, 178; in *Thomas v. Collins* case, 161–175

Goodman, Walter, 269–270

Goodyear Strike, 48

Gornick, Vivian, 34, 37, 42, 47, 250, 299

Grand Alliance, 158–159, 249

Grand Jury, 277

Great Depression, 18–19, 51

Gross, James A., 89

Greene, Nathan, 19, 67, 176

Grossman, Aubrey, 110, 175

Gubitchev, Valentin, 257, 261, 282

H

Hague v. CIO, 105, 110, 115, 160, 166

Hapgood, Powers, 64

Hartley, Fred, 211

Harris, Howell John, 134, 179, 202

Harvard Law School and *Harvard Law Review*, 12, 14–16, 20, 26, 28, 102, 164, 170, 175, 218, 254–255, 295, 312

Hatch Act, 177, 216–220

Hatch, Carl, 216, 235

Haywood, Allen, 131, 198

Heinz case, 91

Heinrich, C.E., 277

Hellerstein, Jerome, 20

Henderson, Leon, 140
Hetzel, Ralph, 139
Hillman, Sidney, 58, 71–72, 86–87, 121–122, 124, 126, 128, 184, 186, 194–196, 307; in NDMB, 134–135
Hiss, Alger, 1–3, 14–16, 19, 21, 25, 28–30, 39, 40, 233, 244–247, 251–256, 260–261, 263–264, 266, 268–269, 273–274, 278–279, 283, 285–286, 291–296, 306
Hiss-Chambers case, 1–3, 187, 233, 243–247, 251, 255, 258, 260, 282
Hiss, Donald, 3, 285, 291–293
Hitler, Adolph, 123–124, 129, 132–133, 184, 268, 280, 290
Hollander, Louis, 248
Holmes, Oliver Wendell, 164–165
Hoover, J. Edgar, 186–191, 200, 201, 238–239, 258–259, 262, 264, 265, 277, 283–286, 293, 303, 305
Hoover, Herbert, 133
Hopkins, Harry, 32–34
Horwitt, Sanford, 54–55
Hotel Albert Chambers, 287
Hotel Commodore, 125
Hotel Roosevelt, 187
House Un-American Activities Committee (HUAC), 1–4, 59–60, 233, 244–246, 251, 260, 264–270, 272–273, 275, 277–278, 281, 283–284, 286–287, 290–291, 296, 300–303
Howe, Irving, 6
Hudson, Roy, 60, 187–190, 200, 239, 255, 272, 281, 304
Huberman, Leo, 240
Hughes, Charles Evans, 116–117
Hutcheson, William, 45

I

Immigration and Naturalization Service, 74, 177, 238, 287–288
Industrial Council Plans, 131, 135
Industrial Union Councils, CIO, 131

Inter-American Bar Association, 194
Internal Security Act, 293
International Juridical Association, 18–20, 159, 175, 274
International Longshoreman and Warehouseman's Union, 275
International Woodworkers of America, 237
International Workers Order, 261
Israel, 248, 300

J

Jackson, Gardner, 23, 26–29, 30–31, 44, 57, 59, 102, 103, 118–119, 185, 233–234, 273–274, 279, 290, 306; and Lee Pressman break, 119–120, 122
Jackson, Robert, 113, 164, 169, 174–175, 177, 217, 219, 226
Jefferson School of Social Sciences, 238
Jews and Judiaism, 5–15, 36–37, 248, 250, 261
Johnson, Christopher, 64
Johnstone, Frank, 85
Joint Anti-Fascist Refugee Committee, 187
Jones and Laughlin, 75, 78–79, 83, 103, 110, 206–207
Justice Department, U.S., 21, 95–96, 108–109, 174, 177, 186, 190, 224–225, 243, 246, 252, 257–258, 294, 303

K

Katz, Isadore, 104
Kaiser, Henry, 196
Kazin, Alfred, 6–8, 18
Kelly, Nicholas, 72
Kempton, Murray, 2, 15, 47, 73–74, 128, 193, 227, 230, 254, 267, 269, 276, 296, 306–307
Kennan, George, 194

Kennedy, John F., 305
Kennedy, Thomas, 185
King, Carol Weiss, 19, 76, 176, 238
Knudsen, William, 69–71
Kovner, Joseph, 19, 77–79, 82–83, 98, 122–123, 159, 185; and Lee Pressman break, 130–133
Kramer, Charles, 1–4, 38–40, 119, 270–271, 278–279, 282–283, 285, 291–292
Kraus, Henry, 67
Kutznetsov, Vasselli, 195

L

Labor's Non-Partisan League (LNPL), 57, 65, 118–120, 129
Labor Department, U.S., 21, 32, 142, 174
Ladd, D.M., 239
LaFollette Civil Liberties Committee, 59, 63, 105, 139
Lahey, Eddie, 234, 260
Lamb, Dean Ivan, 260, 273–274, 279, 286, 290–291
Lamb, Edward (Ted), 56, 115–116
Landis, James, 67, 175, 177
Lasky, Victor, 276, 278
Latin America, 123, 194
Lauck, W. Jett, 48–49
Lenin, Nicholai, 46
Leibman, Charles, 8
Leibman, Blumenthal, and Levy, 21, 279
Leibman, Robbins, and Pressman, 77
Leiserson, William, 101, 237
Lend-Lease Legislation, 131–132
Levenstein, Harvey, 129
Levinson, Edward, 45
Lewis, John L., 3, 17, 45–50, 52–53, 57–58, 62, 77–78, 80–81, 87, 93–96, 98, 103–104, 108, 117, 119–121, 125–126, 133, 178–179, 184, 186, 188, 235, 259, 273–275, 279–280, 288–289, 290, 297, 303–304, 307–308; and FDR break, 127; in

Captive Coal Mine Crisis, 135–136; in Chrysler Sit-Down Strike, 71–74; and foreign policy, 119, 124; in GM Sit-Down Strike, 62–71; hiring of Pressman, 50; impact on Lee Pressman, 51–59; and Mexican Oil Deal, 123; and Philip Murray relationship, 126–133; U.S. Steel Agreement, 71–72, 142
Lewis, Kathryn, 55, 123
Little Steel Formula (NWLB Case), 76, 138–144, 161, 178, 180, 182–183, 188, 204, 308
Little Steel Strike, 78–93, 98, 101, 109, 178
Luce, Henry, 245

M

MacDougall, Curtis, 239–240, 242–243
Madden, J. Warren, 82, 84, 97–98, 101, 207, 237, 242
Magnuson, Warren, 311
Mann, Howard, 174
Mao-Tse-Tung, 41
Marbury, William, 15
Margiotti, Charles, 223–224
Margolis, Benjamin, 110
Marine Engineers Benefit Association (MEBA), 302–303, 307, 309–311
Marshall, George, 228
Marshall Plan, 227, 231, 241
Martin, Homer, 69, 72
Marx, Karl and Marxism, 38, 42, 46, 271, 286
Mayflower Hotel, 71
McCarthy Era, 289
McCarthy, Joseph, 294, 296
McDonald, David, 80
McGrady, Edward, 65–66
McGrath, J. Howard, 218
McLean, Edward, 255
Medina, Harold, 252
Meet the Press, 251
Memorial Day Massacre, 78–81, 248

Mexican Oil Deal, 123, 273–274, 288–289
Meyer, Arthur, 138–141
Millis, Harry, 101
Mine, Mill, and Smelter Workers Union
 (International), 213–215, 237–238
Mitch, William, 51
Morgenthau, Henry, 201
Moloney, Joseph, 204
Moody, Blair, 200
Moren, Mark, 273, 279, 287, 289
Morse, Wayne, 311
Mortimer, Wyndham, 63, 69
Mount Vernon, New York, 237, 266, 311
Multer, Abraham, 239, 247–248
Murphy, Frank, 81, 95, 108, 110,
 216–217, 220, 226, 307; in GM Sit-
 Down Strike, 62–71; in Chrysler Sit-
 Down Strike, 1937, 72–74; in
 Supreme Court, 164, 167, 171,
 176–177
Murphy, Tom, 285
Murray, Phillip, 17, 50–52, 56, 58,
 71–73, 76, 78–80, 82, 85–93, 104,
 119, 121, 124, 162–163, 175–177,
 179, 184, 188–191, 193–195,
 203–207, 212, 223–224, 226–227,
 233, 236, 259, 262, 275, 280–281,
 304–305, 307–308; as CIO president,
 128–129; and communism, 184–191,
 198–202; John L. Lewis relationship,
 126–133; and Lee Pressman resignation, 229–231; in NWLB cases,
 133–144; support for FDR, 128–130

N

National Association for the
 Advancement of Colored People
 (NAACP), 117–118
National Association of Manufacturers,
 97, 124
National Broadcasting Corporation
 (NBC), 209
National Council for Soviet-American
 Friendship, 201

National Defense Advisory Commission,
 87
National Defense Mediation Board,
 135–138
National Industrial Recovery Act and
 NRA, 23, 25–27, 51, 57, 292
National Labor Relations Act, 39, 58,
 66, 75, 84, 93–94, 106, 111–112,
 203, 206, 208–209, 211–212, 214 ;
 amendment campaign, 95–102
National Labor-Management
 Conference, 190–191, 202–203
National Labor Relations Board, 20, 44,
 59, 64, 76, 94–97, 99, 101–102, 109,
 112, 119, 126, 134, 138–139, 142,
 160, 176, 206–207, 209, 212, 214,
 228, 237, 242; Globe Doctrine, 97; in
 Little Steel Strike, 78–93; in Little
 Steel case 83–93
National Lawyers Guild, 106, 113–115,
 117, 136–137, 210; and Labor Law
 Committee, 125–126
National Maritime Union, 182–184
National War Labor Board, 76, 114, 136,
 160, 178–184, 204, 206, 248, 311;
 Little Steel Formula, 138–144, 161,
 179, 188; no strike pledge, 136
Nazi-Soviet Non-Aggression Pact, 1939,
 123–124, 126–127, 249, 290
Nazism, 128–129, 248; Invasion of the
 Soviet Union, 132
Nevins, Allen, 307
New Deal, 20–21, 46, 57, 80, 93, 102,
 111, 113–114, 174, 198, 203,
 235–236, 241–242, 248, 250, 254,
 266, 300–301, 305, 307–308,
 311–312; communist infiltration of,
 1–4; liberalism of, 28, 33–34,
 114–119, 144, 159, 192, 232; realities of reform, 24
New Deal Administrative State, 75–76,
 82, 94–96, 98, 138–144, 178–191,
 206, 216
New York Bar Association, 266
New York City Teachers Union, 237
New York Post, 247

New York Sun, 245
New York Times, 291
New York University, 10–11, 20
Nichols, L.B., 258, 303–304
Nixon, Richard M., 1–4, 60, 209,
    244–245, 251, 264, 266–267, 270,
    272, 274–276, 284–285, 296, 300,
    306, 310
NKVD, 201, 289
No Strike Pledge, 136
Norris-LaGuardia Act, 19, 50, 100, 104,
    212
North American Aviation Strike, 1941,
    136
Novikov, Yuri, 256–258, 282, 294–295
Nowak, Stanley, 184
Nye Munitions Committee, 39, 291, 294

O

O'Connor, John J., 90
Office of Price Administration, 182,
    204–205
Office of Production Management, 135
Oil and Chemical Workers Union, 163

P

Padway, Joseph, 109
Palmer Raids, 238
Pan-American Airlines, 287
Pearl Harbor, 136–138, 144
Pearson, Drew, 229
Peek, George, 25
Perkins, Frances, 31–32, 44–45, 65–66,
    80, 121, 307
Perlo, Victor, 3, 39–41, 279, 285,
    291–293, 296
Peters, J., 60–61, 255, 371–273,
    278–279, 286–287, 292
Phillips, Cole, 279
Phillipovitch, Mark, 279
Pinchot, Gifford, 77
Pittsburgh Press, 51

Plain Talk, 247–249
PM Magazine, 290
Polier, Isadore, 19, 38, 40
Pomerantz, Abraham, 257, 261, 282
Popper, Martin, 240, 242
Portal-to-Portal Pay, 216
Portsmouth Steel Strike, 56
Potash, Irving, 237
Powell, Thomas R., 27–28, 102–103
Pressman, Ann, 9, 43, 77, 267, 301–302,
    310–311
Pressman, Clara, 6, 8, 9, 51–55, 309
Pressman, Harry, 5–6, 8, 18, 54, 302
Pressman, Irving, 8, 10, 12, 14, 17–18,
    207, 280, 300–302, 306
Pressman, Lee, 1–4, 10, 23, 26, 35, 57,
    125–126, 137–138, 184, 186, 186,
    198–202, 208–210, 213–215, 238,
    241–242; Anthony Wayne Smith and
    Joseph Kovner break, 130–133; CIO
    Convention, 1943, 187–191, 239; CIO
    resignation, 227–234; communism and
    break from, 1–4, 20, 23, 29–34, 43,
    59–62, 121, 198, 256–262, 266–286;
    ethnicity and class, 7–8, 13–16, 56;
    death, 310–312; in early CIO, 47–50,
    52–54; education, 10–17; and family,
    10–12, 14, 18; historical significance,
    305–312; impact of John L. Lewis,
    51–59, 307; and international labor,
    193–198; as lawyer-strategist, 4, 13,
    16–23, 25, 27–29, 30–31, 48–49, 58,
    62–74, 76–93, 99–101, 104–111,
    161–191, 210–227; in Little Steel
    Formula NWLB cases, 133–144; and
    New Deal, 31–33, 57, 75–76, 95–96,
    117–118; parents and youth, 5–11;
    personality, 9, 12–14, 16, 23, 27, 31,
    33, 43, 49–59, 113–114, 242–244;
    Progressive Party and Congressional
    Campaign, 3, 235–236, 239–243,
    247–251, 282, 311; and Truman,
    198–202; Ware Group, 34–43,
    270–275, 278–281, 292–293, 296
Pressman, Marcia L., 9, 11–12, 34, 77,
    267, 302, 309–312

Pressman, Sunny (Sophia), 11–12, 14, 18, 44, 267, 300
Pressman, Susan. *See* Sragow, Susan Pressman
Pressman, Witt, and Cammer, 236–238
Progressive Party, 232, 235–236, 238–244, 247, 249–250, 253

Q

Quill, Mike, 92

R

Rabkin, Jacob (Jack), 10, 18, 20, 250, 266–267, 311, 306
Randolph Corners, Vermont, 237
Red Spy Queen, 288
Reed, Stanley, 171, 217, 219–221, 226–227
Republic Steel, 75, 78–80, 82, 84–93, 104; NWLB cases, 1941–1942, 133–144
Resettlement Administration, 33, 44, 248, 273, 288
Riesel, Victor, 249, 276
Reuther, Roy, 66
Reuther, Walter, 190, 203
Reynard, Dick, 275–276
Reynolds, James, 206–207
Rice, Charles Owen (Mgsr.), 133–135, 185, 201, 234
Roberts, Owen, 102, 164, 169, 171–172, 177, 217
Robeson, Paul, 238, 249
Roche, Josephine, 31, 45, 47
Roosevelt, Franklin D., 3, 20, 23, 34, 51, 55, 57–58, 63, 65–66, 75, 81, 84, 86, 92, 95–96, 98, 101, 118–119, 126, 178–180, 184, 187, 190–191, 194, 198, 206, 216, 236, 245, 248–249, 280, 307; foreign policy, 124, 128–131, 135–137, 156, 162–163; Supreme Court, 164–178

Rosenberg, Julius and Ethel, 263
Rosenbliett, Philip, 273, 279, 286–288
Rutledge, Wiley, 164, 167–176, 217, 220, 226
Ruttenberg, Harold, 13, 47, 51–52, 76, 185, 201, 233–236, 300, 302, 306; industrial council plans, 131; in NWLB cases, 133, 138–140
Ruttenberg, Stanley, 139

S

Sacco-Vanzetti case, 15, 20, 23, 28, 102
San Francisco General Strike, 175
Schenck v. U.S., 164
Scheingold, Stuart, 174
Schlesinger, Arthur Jr., 23, 165
Schumann, Frederick, 242
Schwellenbach, Lewis, 202, 205
Shasta County, California, 110
Shaughnessy, Donald, 307, 309
Sheen, Fulton J., Bishop, 256
Sherman Anti-Trust Act, 104
Silvermaster, Nathan Gregory, 201, 291, 295
Singer, Isaac Don, 247
Slichter, Sumner, 12
Smith, Anthony Wayne, 77, 83, 90, 96, 98, 122–123, 127–128, 159–160, 185, 290; break with Pressman, 130–133
Smith-Connally War Labor Disputes Act, 178, 233, 244, 252, 258, 260, 263
Smith, Edwin, 97, 119
Smith, Howard Worth, 82, 84, 97, 101, 206
Smith, John Thomas, 69–71
Smith, Oscar, 88–90
Socialist Party, 64
Southern Poll Tax, 118
Southern Conference on Human Welfare, 117
Soviet Union and Soviets, 123, 129, 158, 174–175, 184, 190, 192–194,

Soviet Union and Soviets *(continued)*
198–199, 201, 237, 241, 243, 251,
256–258, 261–262, 275, 282,
288–289, 294–295
Spanish Civil War, 273, 274, 288, 290
Sragow, Susan Pressman, 55, 267,
301–302, 310–311
Stachel, Jack, 281
St. James Hotel, 187–189
Stalin and Stalinists, 247, 290, 306
State Department, U.S., 187, 194, 201,
251–252, 288, 294
Steel Labor, 51
Steel Workers Organizing Committee,
50–53, 56, 71–72, 75, 78–79, 81–93,
95, 103–105, 112, 122, 124, 131,
133; in NWLB cases, 138–144
Stephens, John, 142, 179
Stone, Harlan Fiske, 164, 169–171, 177,
217, 219
Strachey, John, 33–34
Stripling, Robert, 3–4, 245
Stuyvesant High School, 9
Sugar, Maurice, 64, 66–68
Sullivan, John, 252–253
Sugar, Maurice, 64, 66–68, 161–163,
187, 208
Supreme Court, U.S., 27, 67, 75, 78–79,
83, 85–88, 91, 102–104, 107–108,
110–111, 116–118, 142, 158–159,
193, 248, 305; CIO litigation,
163–178, 215–227; Roosevelt
Supreme Court, 164–178, 218–219;
Vinson Court, 217–227
Sweeney, Vincent, 51, 80, 122, 139,
199
Sweezy, Paul, 240

T

Taft-Hartley Act, 178, 193, 211–216,
223–227, 228, 230, 234–235, 248,
303, 309, 311
Taft, Robert, 211, 226
Tavenner, Frank, 269–270, 274

Taylor, Glenn, 248
Taylor, George, 183
Taylor, Henry J., 209
Taylor, Myron, 71, 142
Taylor, Wayne, 25
Texas Supreme Court, 163
Thomas, Norman, 248, 253
Thomas, R.J., 163, 165–169, 171
Thomas v. Collins, 158–176, 217, 226,
223
Thornhill v. Alabama, 109–111, 166
Thurmond, Strom, 232
Time magazine, 230, 232, 245, 251, 272,
276, 293
Tolson, Claude, 258, 303
Trades Union Congress, 193–194
Trainor, Joseph, 285
Transport Workers Union (TWU), 92,
132, 136
Travis, Robert, 63, 66
Travis, Maurice, 213
Treasury Department, U.S., 180
Tugwell, Rexford, 20, 25, 29–30, 32–33,
118, 236, 238–243
Truman Doctrine, 241
Truman, Harry S., 192, 198, 200,
202–206, 208, 212, 227, 229,
231–235, 239, 241, 243, 247–248,
250

U

Union Security, 114, 137–144
United Auto Workers (UAW), 63–71,
136, 139, 186, 190, 203; *Thomas v.
Collins* case, 162–175
United Electrical, Radio, and Machine
Workers (UE), 49–50
United Federal Workers of America,
216, 218
United Mine Workers of America
(UMWA), 45, 47–48, 50–51, 53, 57,
71, 77, 95, 123, 130, 133, 288
United Nations, 3, 195–196, 268, 275,
305

United Public Workers of America, 216, 223, 237

U.S. Civil Service Act and Commission, 216–217, 222

U.S. Court of Appeals, 252

U.S. District Court, 224, 238

U.S. Gold Policy, 124

U.S. Law Week, 225

U.S. Rubber, 137

U.S. Steel, 71–72, 75, 79, 92, 94–95, 141–144, 179–180, 203–205

U.S. v. CIO, 223–227

United Steel Workers of America (USWA), 121, 143–144, 180–181, 198–202, 203–207, 210–212, 228, 231, 305; National Wage and Policy Conference, 180; post-Little Steel Formula NWLB cases, 178–183, 238

V

Vaughn, Harry, Brigadier General, 191

W

Wage-Price Controls, World War II, 137

Wage Stabilization Board, 204–205

Wagner Act. *See* National Labor Relations Act

Wagner, Robert, 288

Wallace, Henry, 4, 232, 26, 28–31, 118, 120, 192–193, 223, 229, 233–234, 236, 238–243, 245, 248–250, 267, 282

Walsh-Healey Act, 94

War Department, U.S., 124

War Labor Disputes Act. *See* Smith-Connally Act

War Production Board, 179

Ware Group, 34, 38–43, 46, 59, 61, 119, 187, 194, 207, 233, 244–245, 252–254, 258, 267, 269–270, 272–274, 278–282, 283, 286, 291–292, 294–296, 306

Ware, Harold, 34, 37–38, 40, 61, 255, 270

Watson, Edwin, Major General, 187

Watt, Richard, 241

Watts, Robert, 90

Weiner, Lynne and Jack, 300, 302, 306, 310–311

Western Federation of Miners (WFM), 214

Weyl, Nathaniel, 40–41, 292–295

White, Harry Dexter, 201, 206

Williamson, John, 187

Willard Hotel, 65

Wilkie, Wendell, 127

Witt, Nathan, 1–4, 19–21, 26, 38–40, 59, 77, 81, 84, 114, 230, 236–237, 244, 246–247, 251, 254–257, 261, 266, 270, 272, 278–279, 282–283, 285, 291–292, 302

Wood, John S., 1–2, 270, 274

Works Progress Administration, 32–33, 248

World Federation of Trade Unions (WFTU), 192, 194–196

World War I, 124, 137, 202

World War II, 113–114, 124–125, 132, 137

Y

Yale Law School, 17, 76, 280

Yalta Conference, 3, 244

Yankee Stadium, 249

Young, Pauline, 6–8, 12–13

Youngstown Sheet and Tube, 78–80, 85, 87–88, 92

Z

Zieger, Robert H., 78, 205

Zionism, 300

Zirin, Lester, 282